Tourism and Welfare

Ethics, Responsibility and Sustained Well-being

Tourism and Welfare

Ethics, Responsibility and Sustained Well-being

_____

Derek Hall and Frances Brown

www.cabi.org

CABI is a trading name of CAB International

CABI Head Office
Nosworthy Way
Wallingford
Oxfordshire OX10 8DE
UK

Tel: +44 (0)1491 832111
Fax: +44 (0)1491 833508
E-mail: cabi@cabi.org
Website: www.cabi.org

CABI North American Office
875 Massachusetts Avenue
7th Floor
Cambridge, MA 02139
USA

Tel: +1 617 395 4056
Fax: +1 617 354 6875
E-mail: cabi-nao@cabi.org

A catalogue record for this book is available from the British Library,
London, UK.

Library of Congress Cataloging-in-Publication Data

Hall, Derek R.
Tourism and welfare: ethics, responsibility, and sustained well-being /
Derek Hall and Frances Brown.
        p. cm.
Includes bibliographical references and index.
ISBN-10: 1-84593-066-5 (alk. paper)
ISBN-13: 978-1-84593-066-0 (alk. paper)
1. Tourism. 2. Tourism—Social aspects. I. Brown, Frances, 1956- II. Title.

G155.A1H35 2006
338.4'791--dc22

2005030184

Typeset by AMA DataSet Ltd, UK.
Printed and bound in the UK by Biddles Ltd, King's Lynn.

Contents

_____

Figures

All photographs are by the authors.

Tables

_____

Boxes

The Authors

_____

Derek Hall is Visiting Professor at HAMK: University of Applied Sciences, Mustiala and Forssa, Finland. He recently retired as Professor of Regional Development and Head of the Leisure and Tourism Management Department at the Scottish Agricultural College, Auchincruive. He has published widely on tourism, the environment, transport and development in socialist and post-socialist societies. He edited the recently published *Tourism and Transition: Governance, Transformation and Development* and jointly authored with Lesley Roberts *Rural Tourism and Recreation: Principles to Practice*, both published by CABI. He was Assistant Editor of *Environmental Scientist*, the house journal of the Institution of Environmental Scientists, 1997–2003.

Frances Brown is the former editor of *Tourism Management* and author of *Tourism Reassessed: Blight or Blessing?* (Butterworth-Heinemann). She has lectured on tourism at the Universities of Strathclyde, Glasgow and Paisley, and has undertaken tourism research for the University of Surrey. She is currently Editor of the journal *Space Policy*, and has written on space tourism.

Preface

_____

The concepts of welfare and well-being represent a diffuse and relatively neglected area within tourism studies. This is despite the increasing importance of such issues as ethics, wellness, human rights, ethnocentrism, corporate social responsibility, industry practice and behaviour codes, green consumerism and the perceptions and management of 'sustainable' development.

Our welfare emphasis – a holistic approach to the characteristics and external impacts of tourism development that does not invoke the absolutist ideals of sustainability – seeks to offer an appraisal of tourism that can both illuminate the major interrelationships of the sector and assist in raising awareness and the better management of some of its implications. In promoting a welfare perspective, therefore, this introductory volume aims to offer both conceptual direction and practical reflection.

The book elaborates ideas the authors first presented in the paper, 'Towards a welfare focus for tourism research', published in _Progress in Tourism and Hospitality Research_ in 1996 (Hall and Brown, 1996). Some of the material in Chapter 6 is derived from research part-funded by the Scottish Executive Environment and Rural Affairs Department (SEERAD) and undertaken at the Scottish Agricultural College (SAC).

We have greatly appreciated the continued support and encouragement we have received from Rebecca Stubbs, Claire Parfitt and the rest of the commissioning, editorial and production staff of CABI.

Frances Brown and Derek Hall
by the Seabank ponds
Maidens, Ayrshire
September 2005

Abbreviations and Acronyms

ABTA   Association of British Travel Agents
ACCV   Anti-Cancer Council of Victoria (Australia)
ADA   Americans with Disabilities Act
AGE   acute gastroenteritis
AHLA   American Hotel and Lodging Association
AIDS   acquired immune deficiency syndrome
AIEST   Association Internationale d'Experts Scientifiques du Tourisme
APPA   appreciative participatory planning and action
ATIA   Australian Tourism Industry Association

BA   British Airways
B&B   bed and breakfast
BBC   British Broadcasting Corporation
BITS   Bureau International du Tourisme Social
bn   billion (thousand million)
BSA   British Surfing Association
BTA   British Tourism Authority

CAA   Civil Aviation Authority
CBNRM   community-based natural resource management
CD   compact disc
CRT   Centre for Responsible Tourism
CSD   (United Nations) Commission on Sustainable Development
CSR   corporate social responsibility
CV   curriculum vitae

DBV   Deutscher Bäderverband e.V.
DDA   Disability Discrimination Act
DfID   Department for International Development
DfNS   debt-for-nature swap
DG   Directorate General (European Commission)
DRAB   assess for danger, check response, airway and breathing
DVD   digital video disc
DVT   deep vein thrombosis

EAP	Environment Action Programme (OECD)
EC	European Commission; European Community
ECTWT	Ecumenical Coalition on Third World Tourism
E. coli	*Escherichia coli*
EEC	European Economic Community
EFA	ecological footprint analysis
ENAV	Italian air navigation services agency
ENSO	El Niño Southern Oscillation
ESPA	European Spa Association
ETB	English Tourist Board
ETC	English Tourism Council
ETS	emission trading scheme
EU	European Union
FAACE	Fight Against Animal Cruelty in Europe
FCO	Foreign and Commonwealth Office
FDI	foreign direct investment
FITSA	Fair Trade in Tourism South Africa
FMD	foot-and-mouth disease
FOC	flag of convenience
GATT	General Agreement on Tariffs and Trade
GDP	gross domestic product
h	hour(s)
HDI	Human Development Index
HIV	human immunodeficiency virus
HRA	Himalayan Rescue Association
HSE	Health and Safety Executive
ICCL	International Council of Cruise Lines
ICT	information and computing technology
IDG	International Development Goal
IIED	International Institute for Environment and Development (London)
IiP	*Investors in People*
ILAM	Institute of Leisure and Amenity Management
ILO	International Labour Office of the United Nations
IMF	International Monetary Fund
IMO	International Maritime Organization
IPE	International Petroleum Exchange
IPP	Inka Porter Project
IPPG	International Porters' Protection Group
ITF	International Transport Workers Federation
IUCN	World Conservation Union (International Union for the Conservation of Nature)
IUDZG	World Zoo Organization
LA21	Local Agenda 21
LDC	less developed country
LEA	local education authority
LED	local economic development
LPG	liquefied petroleum gas

MASTA	Medical Advisory Services for Travellers Abroad
MDG	Millennium Development Goal
min	minute(s)
mn	million
MNC	multinational company
NCSD	National Commission for Sustainable Development (Barbados)
NCWOR	non-consumptive wildlife-oriented recreation
nd	no date; no data
NGO	non-governmental organization
NGPG	non-governmental pressure group
NHS	National Health Service
NTIC	National Tourist Information Centre (Bulgaria)
ODI	Overseas Development Institute (London)
OECD	Organisation for Economic Cooperation and Development
PCFFF	Policy Commission on the Future of Food and Farming (Curry Commission)
PFO	patent foramen ovale
PHT	post-holiday tension
PPT	pro-poor tourism
PRA	participatory rural appraisal
PRSP	*Poverty Reduction Strategy Paper*
QoL	quality of life
REKA	Swiss Travel Fund
RICE	rest, ice, compression and elevation
RSPB	Royal Society for the Protection of Birds
RSPCA	Royal Society for the Prevention of Cruelty to Animals
SAC	Scottish Agricultural College
SARS	severe acute respiratory syndrome
SBO	stating the blindingly obvious
SCIEH	Scottish Centre for Infection and Environmental Health
SDIs	sustainable development indicators
SEERAD	Scottish Executive Environment and Rural Affairs Department
SFR	staying with friends and/or relatives
SL	sustainable livelihoods
SME	small and/or medium-size enterprise
SNV	Dutch development NGO
SOEID	Scottish Office Education and Industry Department
SPCA	Society for the Prevention of Cruelty to Animals
SPCK	Society for the Propagation of Christian Knowledge
STD	sexually transmitted disease
ST-EP	Sustainable Tourism – Eliminating Poverty
TANA	Tour Agencies of Nepal Association
TEN	Trans European Network
TIAA	Travel Industry Association of America
TIES	The International Ecotourism Society
TNC	transnational corporation/company
TUC	Trade Union Congress

UAE	United Arab Emirates
UCLH	University College London Hospital
UN	United Nations
UNCED	United Nations Conference on Environment and Development
UNCTAD	United Nations Conference on Trade and Development
UNDP	United Nations Development Programme
UNEP	United Nations Environment Programme
UNESCO	United Nations Educational, Scientific and Cultural Organization
UN-FCCC	United Nations Framework Convention on Climate Change
UV	ultraviolet
Varda	Victims of Air Related DVT Association
VAT	value-added tax
VFR	visiting friends and/or relatives
VRTT	virtual-reality travel and tourism
VSO	Voluntary Service Overseas
VT	volunteer tourism/tourist
WCED	World Commission on Environment and Development
WCS	*World Conservation Strategy*
WHO	World Health Organization
WHS	World Heritage Site
WSSD	World Summit on Sustainable Development
WTO	World Tourism Organization
WTTC	World Travel and Tourism Council
WWF	Worldwide Fund for Nature (formerly World Wildlife Fund)

1

Introduction and Context

If something is sustainable, it means that you can go on doing it indefinitely. If it isn't, you can't.

(Jonathon Porritt, 1996: 27)

Box 1.1. Chapter aims and summary.

This chapter seeks to: provide an introduction and context for the chapters that follow.
It does this by: reviewing the key terms and concepts employed in the book and establishing an analytical framework for them.
Its key concepts are: welfare, ethics, stakeholder, responsibility, sustainability, well-being, quality of life.
It concludes that: a welfare-centred approach highlights the trade-offs, compromises and inequalities that characterize tourism processes. Tourism's contribution to enhanced welfare can be assisted by a pursuit of ethical principles and the location of responsibilities amongst stakeholders.

This introductory text aims both to emphasize the welfare dimensions of tourism processes and to suggest ways in which the conceptual debate surrounding the nature and role of tourism development can be advanced by employing a welfare lens for analysis. We suggest that such an analytical approach can help us to:

- illuminate the distribution of benefits and disbenefits resulting from tourism activity;
- identify the locus of ethical and practical responsibilities – and implicitly power relationships – that accompany it;
- obviate the dichotomy of production and consumption studies in tourism (Ateljevic, 2000); and
- appreciate the wider, often chaotic, context within which tourism development processes are set.

In doing this, we argue that our approach – a welfare paradigm – can usefully augment and inform the sustainability debate in tourism. A number of critiques of tourism and sustainable development and of 'sustainable tourism' as an ideology and liberal palliative (e.g. Butler, 1990; Wheeller, 1991, 1993, 2005; Sharpley, 2000, 2001) have argued that the sustainability syndrome is at best a diversion. It is particularly a diversion from acknowledging that mass tourism, far from fading, is growing, and that focusing on enhancing its benefits and ameliorating its negative impacts would be time and effort better spent. This does, however, assume acceptance of the principle that the continued growth of global tourism is welfare-positive, a contested issue that is addressed particularly in the con-cluding chapter.

'Welfare', as a concept and concern, is applicable to both mass and 'alternative' forms of tourism and their implications. In this sense it is 'mode-blind' and as such helps to draw us away from the divisive debates on the nature, applicability and value of 'sus-tainable' forms of tourism. Indeed, we would argue that there is a need to (re)focus the debate on the impacts, (dis)benefits and implications of tourism development more firmly upon:

- the ethical dilemmas behind individual and collective actions and behaviour;
- the nature and location of responsibi-lity within (and having an impact upon) the tourism sector; and
- the welfare trade-offs and outcomes of these.

This needs to be undertaken while recogniz-ing, as a fundamental analytical position, that tourism is embedded in wider social, economic, political, ecological and cultural processes, with the result that it may be diffi-cult and sometimes unrealistic to try to iden-tify and isolate the specific influences and consequences of tourism development and activity from the outcomes of a wide range of other societal and environmental change processes.

We employ stakeholder perspectives as a vehicle for our welfare-centred analysis and in part as an organizing framework for the structure of the book. By focusing on the need to recognize, accommodate and address the various trade-offs that tourism development processes incur, we exemplify how attempts to increase the welfare of one set of participants may negatively affect the welfare of another. At the same time we acknowledge that major trade-offs may often relate to and be derived from basic inequalities that transcend the tour-ism industry as a result of the international system of political and economic depend-ency relationships.

Further, we argue that employing the notion of 'welfare' as a focus for an examina-tion of the phenomenon of tourism enables us to extend our frame of reference beyond that of human participants and to draw into our conceptual debate the welfare of and ethical considerations concerning non-human animals involved in providing tour-ism experiences for humans, and ecological relationships with and of the natural envi-ronment that provides the setting for those experiences.

In this way, a welfare-centred approach can provide a conceptual and organizing framework that allows us to address:

- issues of access to tourism (Chapter 2);
- the nature, motivations and behaviour of tourists and the outcomes of their tourism experiences (Chapter 3);
- the experience of living and working in tourism destinations (Chapter 4);
- the pursuit of pro-poor tourism as an ethically based, tourism-employment-led development strategy (Chapter 5);
- animal welfare rights and the role of the environment in tourism (Chapter 6); and
- the location, balance and discharge of power and responsibility in relation to the above (Chapter 7).

What do we Mean by Welfare?

'Welfare' is defined by *Chambers Twentieth Century Dictionary* as a 'state of faring or doing well: freedom from calamity, etc.: enjoyment of health, etc.: prosperity'. It can be regarded as a quality of well-being that can be maintained, enhanced or threatened by interaction with external agencies. In the case of tourism, such external agencies may embrace the mutual relationships of tourists, tourism employees and employers, resident populations and environments, and include a wide range of private, public, voluntary and partnership organizations and structures that directly and indirectly, wittingly and unwittingly, interact with tourism processes.

Some cultural interpretations of 'wel-fare' may carry ideological baggage with pejorative connotations, particularly notions of dependency, such as 'being on welfare'. It is also a relative term, rather like poverty or wealth, strongly related to the societal and environmental context within which it is being addressed.

Notions of welfare owe much to utilitarianism (Weale, 1978; Pinker, 1979; Goodin, 1988; Barry, 1990; Plant, 1991; Smith and Duffy, 2003), which, in its classical form (Bentham, 1982), argues that individual welfare is tied to human happiness and that public policies should aim to achieve the greatest happiness of the greatest number. Thus an act is considered morally right if its outcome yields more pleasure than pain in comparison with alternatives available to the agent (Honderich, 1995). But utilitarianism has been criticized for its inability to consider social justice. If happiness is maximized for the greatest good, there is a likelihood that it must be achieved to the exclusion of a minority in order to secure greatest benefits (Smart and Williams, 1973; Sprigge, 1987; Kagan, 1989; L'Etang, 1992).

Adopting utilitarian assumptions, however, welfare economists (Culyer, 1973; Clarke and Ng, 1993) contend that an optimization of (social) welfare can be reached when one person's well-being can be improved while rendering others' no worse off, or if the total welfare of society is sufficiently increased to compensate fully those members adversely affected (a 'Pareto optimum') (Drover and Kerans, 1993: 3–4).

But international tourism, as an articulation of relative development and wealth, as a component of globalization, global inequalities and resource consumption, sometimes appears to turn utilitarianism on its head by trying to maximize happiness for minority (developed world) tourists at the relative expense of the majority (less developed world) 'hosts'. Or, rather, it is an ethnocentric interpretation of utilitarianism. As a consequence, the nature and implications of tourism development processes are such that rarely can an optimum (sustainability?) be achieved. Trade-offs between sectoral dimensions – economic, cultural, political, ecological – and between and within groups of actors – tourists, tourism workers, host populations and environments – render the achievement of such optima largely chimerical.

The well-being of contemporary (Western) society can be conceptualized in terms of three (competing?) visions:

- consumerism: where 'well-being' is derived from the quantity and variety of material goods to which consumers have access;
- welfare-statism: 'well-being' is secured from the quantity (if not variety) of public goods and services citizens receive as a right; and
- eco-welfarism: where 'well-being' results, organically, from the quality of the relations between people and between people and nature.

In relation to the conceptual and policy relationships between welfare, well-being and sustainability, evidence suggests that when individuals are more secure financially – but not necessarily wealthier – they are more likely to care about the well-being of future generations and of the environment. Gowdy (2005) therefore argues that focusing social and developmental policy on well-being rather than on per capita consumption might have crucially positive implications for sustainability. This is an important consideration in our welfare focus.

The philosophical approach we take to 'welfare' – a quality underpinned by ethical considerations, the acknowledgement of responsibility and directly applicable at a number of different levels from the individual to the global – while consonant with eco-welfarism, owes much to the vision of (global) society posited by Richard Titmuss (Titmuss, 1968; Abel-Smith and Titmuss, 1987; Field, 2002). This is a conception of social altruism and responsibility where the world's richer countries, acting from an ethical concern, take measures to prevent the poorer countries being denuded of skilled manpower. Titmuss's (1976: 127) notion of 'a welfare world' recognized 'the injustices and waste in the unrestricted free international movement of goods, material and capital', and argued that only when richer countries assumed principles of 'community responsibility' on a global scale, through policies designed to reverse the exploitation of poorer countries, could any of those countries with any justification regard themselves as 'welfare societies'. Ironically, of course, the transfer of some degree of power and responsibility from the nation state to supranational organizations has actually accelerated the very processes of labour mobility that Titmuss abhorred. Tourism has no small role in this (see Chapters 4, 7 and 8).

There are three further caveats to Titmuss's position. First, as indicated above, he saw dangers in the use of the term 'welfare state', particularly when applied solely within the limited framework of the nation state. Thus the debate that has been raging in the social welfare literature for several years concerning the nature and relevance of Espin-Andersen's (1990, 1999) typology of welfare regimes might be viewed as something of an unnecessary diversion (Kasza, 2002; Bambra, 2005), except that it has generated interesting critiques on the position of gender in welfare (Sainsbury, 1994, 1999; Bambra, 2004). Secondly, as Rodger (2003) argues in the UK context, Titmuss's vision of society and welfare as being characterized by social altruism has been displaced by support for welfare based on self-interest and the principle of mutual insurance. Rodger contends that social and economic changes that have resulted in social polarization have weakened 'functional democracy'. By this he means the reciprocal dependence of one social group or class on another. He views this as leading to possible 'decivilising tendencies' and a decline in mutual empathy. A possible outcome of this is what Rodger (2003: 403) refers to as 'post-emotionalism', a quality that he characterizes through four indicators: a breakdown in mutual knowledge across the class divide, the intellectualization of feelings, interaction based on false 'niceness', and the manipulation of emotions. This has some resonance with Hendry's (2004) concept of the 'bimoral' society, whereby traditional ethical and moral principles have become overshadowed by values of entrepreneurial self-interest (see Chapter 7).

Thirdly, Kasza (2002) suggests that, although the notion of 'welfare regimes' has become a centrepiece of comparative welfare research, most countries exhibit a disjointed set of welfare policies as a result of five features of welfare policymaking. These are: the cumulative nature of welfare policies, the diverse histories of policies in different welfare fields, the involvement of different sets of policy actors, variations in the policymaking process, and the influence of foreign models (Kasza, 2002: 271). As a result, Kasza suggests that few national welfare systems are likely to exhibit an internal consistency necessary to justify the concept of a welfare 'regime' and that policy-specific comparisons may offer a more rewarding focus for comparative research.

Notwithstanding these caveats and the fact that 'welfare' can have pejorative connotations, we suggest that it is the least inadequate single-word term to express the qualities under discussion. 'Welfare' can encompass social, behavioural, medical, psychological, cultural, economic, political, environmental and moral dimensions, and is implicitly underscored by important analytical questions of resources, relationships and identity (Drover and Kerans, 1993: 5). The key components of welfare relevant to tourism analysis can include:

- health/freedom from disease and ill health (e.g. Clift and Page, 1994, 1996; Clift and Grabowski, 1997; Wilks and Page, 2003);
- physical safety and security/freedom from physical harm (e.g. Pizam and Mansfeld, 1996; C.M. Hall et al., 2004);
- emotional and spiritual well-being/ freedom from stress and anxiety (e.g. Nahrstedt, 2004);
- financial security/freedom from poverty (see Chapter 5);
- appropriate accommodation/housing provision (see Chapter 4);
- access to necessary services.

The relative nature of 'welfare' poses a problem as well as offering several strengths. While we may say that welfare values can be applied differently to humans compared with animals, and perhaps again differently between different non-human animal species (although, of course, such contentions are contested: see Chapter 6), we may be in danger of presenting a too flexible and adaptive model for an industry in which benchmarking and equivalence of experience are perceived as important tools for the raising and/or assurance of 'quality'.

The positive aspects of this relativism are, however, first, that a welfare focus can highlight the culturally and environmentally rooted ethical dilemmas that arise from differential culture contact, and the behaviour resulting from the social constructions of cultural and environmental images encouraged by the tourism industry and acted out by tourists in destination areas. Second, and somewhat paradoxically, it can offer a framework for comparing social and ethological outcomes of tourism processes with the ideals of global welfare agencies. Thus, for example, according to its 1948 constitution, the World Health Organization's (WHO) objective is the attainment by all peoples of the highest possible level of health, emphasizing that 'health is a state of complete physical, mental and social well-being and not merely the absence of disease or infirmity' (Anderson, 1987: 5; Nahrstedt, 2004: 183). Does tourism development assist such ideals and, if so, how and with what (differential) consequences (see Chapters 3 and 4)?

As suggested earlier in this chapter, our concept of welfare also embraces 'well-being', a term that has been applied occasionally in the context of tourism development (e.g. Jafari, 1987: 158; Urry, 1995; Gilbert and Abdullah, 2002). Welfare theory has positioned the notion of well-being as encompassing qualities of enjoyment, achievement, personal relations, liberty, health, security and meaningful work (Griffin, 1986; Hahnel and Albert, 1990; Sumner, 1992), and most of these are applicable within a welfare paradigm for tourism. We also draw on the similar terms 'life chances' and 'sustainable livelihoods' (see Chapter 5), which have been popular in the development literature and have been employed in relation to tourism largely by development sociologists such as de Kadt (1979: 34–49).

'Wellness' – 'a combination of well-being and fitness . . . physical activity combined with relaxation of the mind and intellectual stimulus, basically a kind of fitness of body, mind, and spirit, including the holistic aspect' (Schobersberger et al., 2004: 199–200) – has come to represent a fashionable tourism 'niche'. It also articulates a greater individual and social awareness of physical and psychological health (see later in this chapter).

In developed countries, more attention is being paid to the concept of quality of life (QoL), of which notions of welfare are a central part. In their turn, leisure and tourism are important contributors to this concept, both in their own right and through their relationships with welfare issues. At an individual level, quality of life may be influenced by both specific and general aspects of (the perception of) education, changes in family life, crime, religion, the role of the media in society and globalization (Swarbrooke, 2003). According to C.M. Hall (2003a: 29), ideally QoL issues should be part of the central component of any tourism policy.

Max-Neef (1992) related quality of life to the degree and way in which fundamental human needs are satisfied. Such needs can be grouped into nine categories – subsistence, protection, affection, understanding, participation, leisure, creation, identity and freedom. Society changes, not in its fundamental needs, but in the way it wants to satisfy those needs (Postma, 2003), and in doing so has embraced tourism.

Traditional economic indicators are poor measures of welfare (Gowdy, 2005), and as a consequence a number of attempts have been made to develop composite quality of life measures. The Human Development Index (HDI) employed by the United Nations Development Programme (UNDP, 2005) is one of the most widely applied examples. Such measures have assisted the process of shifting conceptions of development from a purely economic perspective to embrace centrally social and cultural dimensions of capital and capacity.

Our use of the term 'welfare' is less comprehensive than QoL or HDI, but, as an exploratory means of bringing focus to a range of aspects of tourism development that require the identification of responsibility, we hope to tilt the weight of emphasis on the impacts and implications of tourism development a little more towards the need explicitly to recognize and locate the ethical dimensions and dilemmas that underlie decision-making processes.

In summary, what we refer to in this book as 'a welfare-centred approach' and 'a welfare paradigm' incorporates the following strands:

- a 'welfare' framework concept: to augment and inform 'sustainability' approaches to tourism processes at local and global levels;
- policy-relevant welfare dimensions of tourism processes: such as the health of tourists, the employment conditions of tourism workers or the condition of captive animals in tourist attractions;
- tourism as welfare: tourism's contribution to improved welfare, e.g. through 'social tourism' and 'wellness tourism' or through pro-poor tourism and contributions to maintaining viable rural communities and the conservation of wildlife; and
- tourism impacts on welfare: for example, diverting resources away from social provision for residents within destination areas.

Despite much attention paid by academics, not least in a multiplicity of case-study examples from less developed countries, the tourism-impacts literature has been relatively slow to evolve conceptually since the early seminal texts of Young (1973) and Mathieson and Wall (1982). Even with modifications, revisions and critiques of these frameworks (e.g. Dogan, 1989; Archer and Cooper, 1994; Rátz and Púczko, 2002; Mason, 2003), from a welfare perspective, a number of shortcomings continue to exist. Despite the work of a few advocates for a strong political dimension to tourism analysis (e.g. Richter, 1992; C.M. Hall, 1994b; F. Brown, 1998), such analyses and their importance in locating and evaluating power dimensions and relationships are relatively few, and this area is still significantly under-researched. In particular, the impacts literature, while often critical of tourism's effects, has, until recently (Smith and Duffy, 2003), given little consideration to the field of ethics and the lessons it can provide when evaluating or planning tourism developments. It is this area that we turn to next.

Ethics

Ethics is 'the science of morals, that branch of philosophy which is concerned with human character and conduct; a system of morals or rules of behaviour' (*Chambers Dictionary*). It is concerned with offering a 'moral' set of reference points underpinning behaviour, particularly in the context of relationships and identity, and emphasizing social responsibility in perceptions and decision making (Carroll, 1989: 30; Wheeler, 1994: 4–7). Ethics has only been drawn into a relationship with tourism over the past decade and a half. But there is a growing literature suggesting that it should be a central, critical concern of the industry and of those evaluating tourism and its implications (e.g. Przeclawski, 1994; Fennell and Malloy, 1995; Hultsman, 1995; Karwacki and Boyd, 1995; Payne and Dimanche, 1996; Malloy and Fennell, 1998b; Fennell, 1999, 2000; Fennell and Przeclawski, 2003; Smith and Duffy, 2003). This is a compelling argument: several characteristics of tourism render it an appropriate object for ethical scrutiny and the application of ethical ideals (Fennell and Przeclawski, 2003: 140). For example, tourism:

- is centrally concerned with human behaviour;
- involves several different types of actors representing a range of perspectives and objectives;
- has an applied context;
- has social, cultural, economic, ecological, political and other dimensions; and
- partly reflecting all of the above, can create a range of different combinations of impacts in a wide variety of contexts across the globe.

Smith and Duffy (2003) identify at least eight ethical approaches that can be taken to tourism development issues: moral relativism, utilitarianism, rights, distributive justice, communicative ethics, the ethics of care, the ethics of difference and the ethics of authenticity. They consider a key issue of ethics in tourism to be that of understanding the 'Other' (Smith and Duffy, 2003: 166): the implications of culture contact through tourism and the unequal (power) relationships both between tourists and destination residents and between (usually) 'Northern' tourism and travel companies and (often) 'Southern' destination environments. These are dimensions that run through much of this book.

In our welfare-centred approach, the 'Other' can be characterized as individuals and groups from different cultures, non-human animal species and unfamiliar environments. It is both an objective phenomenon or (unconnected?) series of phenomena and, more importantly for the framing of tourism, socially (and mutually) constructed and reconstructed. It is subject to tourist and 'host' reflection and reinterpretation (Chapters 2–6) and to industry re-imaging and reconfiguration (Chapters 4–7).

But Smith and Duffy (2003: 163) touch upon a fundamental paradox that has perhaps inhibited ethical research in tourism:

> ethical values are usually strongest where the relationship between self and other is maintained and developed over time and where self and other can be (emotionally and geographically) *close* to each other. Yet from the tourist's point of view, holidays entail only fleeting visits to distant places where personal or close contact with others is usually extremely limited.

Yet the corollary may be less true: destination residents may experience their 'Other' – tourists from different cultures from their own – for prolonged periods or even continuously. In other words, and this is hardly an original thought, issues that may be fleeting for or hidden from tourists visiting a destination may be ever pervasive for the residents of that area.

What Garber *et al.* (2000) have referred to as a 'turn to ethics' has been reflected in tourism only relatively recently through studies that have begun to draw together the work of development theorists and ecologists on the effect of tourist behaviour on other humans and on ethical considerations arising from the environmental consequences of tourism processes (Lea, 1993; Ahmed *et al.*, 1994; Fennell, 2000; Franklin, 2003). The Association Internationale d'Experts Scientifiques du Tourisme (AIEST) Congress held in Paris in 1992 (Przeclawski, 1996) proposed the establishment of a special commission to deal with ethics and tourism (Fennell, 2000: 61–62). And in 1995, the Cairo meeting of the International Academy for the Study of Tourism proposed a *Declaration of Ethics in Tourism* (Fennell and Przeclawski, 2003).

Subsequently, the World Tourism Organization (WTO) moved to adopt a global code of ethics. Smith and Duffy (2003: 3) argued that 'it is impossible to separate ethics from the question of development in general and tourism development in particular'. Indeed, 'development' has long been equated with modernization and westernization and has tended to be dominated by 'Chicago' school economics and latterly by the 'Washington Consensus', adopted by international financial agencies and development decision makers. The Consensus holds that the three keys to prosperity are to be found in macro-stability, liberalization (lowering tariff barriers and market deregulation) and privatization:

> Largely through the means of 'conditionality' – policy reforms in exchange for the money that the IMF and World Bank lend – this development philosophy is transmitted to debtor countries in Latin America, Asia and Africa . . . In the absence of an inter-state consensus, the USA has flexed its powerful muscles to pursue unilaterally, *inter alia*, a development agenda for the Third World that has been to promote its own interests.
>
> (Soederberg, 2002: 608)

Such policy prescription has been widely criticized as ethnocentric and economically reductionist (e.g. Goulet, 1997; Simpson and Roberts, 2000; Remenyi, 2004). As one response to this, a new paradigm of development has emerged, and development ethics has come to be recognized as a distinctive sub-discipline. This has been derived from two converging trends: on the one hand, the way development agencies have embraced ethical theory and, on the other, the move from a critique of mainstream ethical theory to the creation of strategies to guide particular development practice (Goulet, 1997).

Clark (2002) argues that the cultivation of development ethics has the potential to produce a coherent understanding of human well-being for guiding development policy and thinking. But, while since at least classical times philosophers have reflected on the nature and character of a good life, they have not tested their theories of well-being in the public domain or related their understanding of the 'good' to the values of ordinary people. Clark suggests that this is partly because philosophers (in contrast to social scientists) have lacked the necessary tools and expertise for such tasks. Yet it is only through the synthesis of scientific enquiry and philosophical reflection that we can uncover the central human values behind a more realistic and reliable development ethic (Clark, 2002).

A wide range of issues appears to have stimulated and encouraged an ethical awareness within the tourism industry. In the tourism academic literature the focus of ethical consideration within tourism, limited though it has been, has tended to shift over time, embracing such issues as:

- the commodification of culture (Mac-Cannell, 1973; Cohen, 1988);
- training, education and human resource management (Whitney, 1989; Upchurch and Ruhland, 1995; Chen *et al.*, 2000; Yeung *et al.*, 2002; Ross, 2003; Yaman, 2003; Costa, 2004; Jamal, 2004);
- the role of indigenous peoples (Laxson, 1991; Hollinshead, 1992; Sizer, 1999);
- cultural relativism and tourism (Ahmed *et al.*, 1994);
- degradation of the natural environment (Romeril, 1989; Stark, 2002; Holden, 2003; Carter *et al.*, 2004);
- sexual exploitation (Thanh-Dam, 1990; C.M. Hall, 1992, 1994a);

- business ethics and tourism (Walle, 1995);
- marketing (Wheeler, 1992, 1993, 1995);
- codes of practice and behaviour (Payne and Dimanche, 1996; Malloy and Fennell, 1998b; Fleckenstein and Huebsch, 1999); and
- stakeholder management (Robson and Robson, 1996; Ryan, 2002).

Some time ago, Hultsman (1995: 556) defined a tourism ethic as a foundational and articulated notion of what tourism professionals collectively accept and tacitly understand as being 'principled' behaviour. But such an expression appears to sidestep the ethic 'problematic' of relativism: ethics are not discernible per se, but are subjective and, as a basis for behaviour, are continually evolving at a personal level. Further, it does not indicate who these consensual tourism professionals are, nor does it interrogate how their understanding of 'principled behaviour' stands up to external comparison and scrutiny.

And it raises further questions. How is the tourism ethic actually articulated? Is the tourism industry's self-perceived role and ethical position in the world the same as it was more than a decade ago when Hultsman offered the above observation? How have subsequent events, such as '9/11' and increasing awareness of the urgent need to combat both climate change and global poverty, influenced the tourism ethic alongside the apparent recalibration of other ethical assumptions within the (Western) world such as governments' re-evaluation of the limits to 'human rights'?

Ethical issues have gained their more recent relative prominence in tourism for a number of reasons. First, as noted previously, tourism is not easily separated from other social, economic and political processes, and, indeed, it is often not desirable to try to do so. Thus there have been implications for and influences upon the tourism industry from such (Western consumer) trends as ethical consumerism (Shaw and Clarke, 1999) and fair trade policies, with the result that ethical/responsible/'fair trade' tourism initiatives have aimed to assist destination countries in reaping more of the benefits and bearing fewer of the costs of tourism activity (see Chapter 5).

Second, 'global' crises such as the severe acute respiratory syndrome (SARS) outbreak, terrorism and subsequent economic downturns in a number of countries have exposed the vulnerability of many of those working in and dependent upon the tourism industry for a livelihood. This highlights some of the ethical dilemmas accompanying the promotion of tourism as a means of economic growth and employment.

Third, an apparently increasing ethical concern among travellers has been articulated by non-governmental organizations (NGOs) such as Tearfund, which has sponsored research (Gordon and Townsend, 2001) suggesting that over half of those tourists interviewed would prefer to take a holiday with a company that has a written code concerning tourism employees' working conditions, tourism's relationship with 'the environment', and companies' support of destination area charities. Other notable pressure groups such as Tourism Concern (2002) have launched programmes to highlight important ethical issues for the tourism industry, such as conditions for porters on mountain trekking expeditions (see Chapter 5). War on Want, in conjunction with a major labour union, has published a damning criticism of the employment conditions for many cruise line employees (War on Want and ITF, 2002; see also Chapter 4).

Similarly, ethical issues appear to be increasingly influencing decisions of intending tourists regarding travel motivations (e.g. de Botton, 2002, 2005), choice of destinations and behaviour at and on the journey to these (Clark, 2004: 344). Observers such as Fennell (2000) thus contend that all areas of the travel sector are increasingly being asked to consider their social and environmental impact. Yet evidence of tourists acting responsibly is limited (Boulstridge and Carrigan, 2000). Although market research suggests that ethical considerations are brought into tourist purchasing behaviour (Curtin and Busby, 1999; Cleverdon and Kalisch, 2000; Tearfund, 2000), the market

for ethical holidays remains small (Weeden, 2005: 236). As emphasized in Chapter 3, it seems that, for most tourists, holidays are times for not wanting to think about or be troubled by problematic issues.

Carrigan and Attalla (2001) suggest a number of reasons why consumers of a wide range of goods and services express a low level of ethical activity:

• lack of information: although this may simply reflect a lack of effort to gain access to it;
• lack of pressure for companies to become 'actively ethical': while consumers often punish unethical companies, they do not necessarily reward ethical organizations. According to Carrigan and Attalla (2001) many people believe that businesses have a responsibility not to cause harm but that they do not automatically have an obligation to help others (for example, sponsoring a local community project);
• the gap between expressed attitude and actual behaviour: a range of studies has suggested that, although consumers for a wide range of goods and services express socially responsible attitudes, often no more than 20% actually act upon these views (see later in this chapter and Table 1.1); and
• lack of personal impact: if an organization's behaviour has no direct impact on an individual, they are unlikely to take any action. 'Ethics' tends to be viewed in generalist terms and relatively few consumers are aware of specific company cases.

Notably, there is little published evidence to suggest that any significant numbers of travellers are consciously turning to greener forms of leisure transport. Indeed, as noted elsewhere (e.g. D. Hall, 1999, 2004d), the wider debates, both academic and popular, on the sustainability of tourism and concerning the sustainability of transport seem to have remained largely separate. Does such relative lack of engagement reflect what Fennell (2000: 60) refers to as a lack of an 'ethically based tension' between the media and the public regarding tourism?

Unlike medicine, the environment or business, and perhaps partly because it embraces all of these, he argues that tourism is often seen as an 'untouchable' golden goose.

Given the range of academic and NGO critiques, particularly in relation to tourism's impacts, at first glance it might appear that something is being missed here. However, in the real world, tourism's lure and perceived economic seductiveness – its symbolic power (Pugh, 2003; see also Chapter 7) – is sometimes, perhaps more often than we would care to admit, impossible to resist. This may be partly because we are all compromised and subverted by it, drawn into the game in different guises, covertly or overtly – as tourists, perhaps as hosts, as actual or aspiring workers in the industry, as researchers, as consultants, as teachers and trainers – as both consumers and sustainers of the tourism juggernaut.

This complicity applies not least to:

- those in the popular media, who, with a few honourable exceptions, benefit from a wide range of personal perks afforded to them by the tourism and travel industries; and
- the media corporations, who own large chunks of the tourism and leisure industries and who will only focus on an issue for the short time that it is attention-catching (and implicitly media-product selling): a reality highlighted in the 'issue-attention cycle' concept (C.M. Hall, 2002, 2003b).

Fennell (2000) argues that there may be two reasons why the public and the media only recognize a few truly significant negative tourism dilemmas:

- tourism issues are not considered sufficiently newsworthy by editors and other filtering 'opinion formers', except, ironically, when their negativity is related to tourists from the media's own constituency – i.e. readers/viewers or staff – as was the case with the December 2004 Indian Ocean tsunami and the 2002 Bali bombing; or, more flippantly, rare occurrences of 'air rage' (Bor, 2003), particularly if they involve 'celebrities'

behaving badly (see Husband, 2005); and
- people do not want to hear about negative aspects of tourism, given that most of us are part of the problem and that, as noted earlier, holidays are when we want to relax, have fun and forget about 'ordinary' life.

So we have our attention diverted from the real issues of cultural and environmental change and economic impoverishment deriving from global inequalities of power and responsibility by 'reality' television series based in airports, involving repeated examples of intending passengers missing flights and harassed staff fending them off; or in package resorts, with 'undercover' reporters exposing the entertaining horrors of 'holidays from hell'; or in overseas timeshares and second homes, where seekers of Shangri-La manage to appear impossibly hapless when trying to organize essential building work or vainly attempting to balance mismanaged finances. 'Reality' television/vicarious tourism has become the bread and circuses for many contemporary Western societies.

Ethics and Responsibility

Although almost a decade and a half ago Lea (1993) could refer to a new climate of corporate responsibility within tourism, the industry's sense of responsibility in a number of cases needed to be kick-started by external agencies. Non-governmental pressure groups (NGPGs) and NGOs were in the forefront of ethical debates relating to responsibility and conduct (Botterill, 1991; Gonsalves, 1991). The late 1970s and 1980s saw the demand for and codification of new industry guidelines, as such codes were developed for both tourism companies and the tourists for whom they should be responsible (e.g. ATIA, 1990; BITS, 1992; D'Amore, 1992, 1993). The 12-point *Code of Ethics for Tourists* developed by the Christian Conference of Asia in the early 1980s was notable, and was followed by literature inspired or produced by the

Bangkok-based Ecumenical Coalition on Third World Tourism (ECTWT) (e.g. O'Grady, 1981; Holden, 1984; Amoa, 1985; O'Grady, 1990).

In arguing that 'sustainability' is insufficient as an objective for the tourism industry, Ryan (2002) has suggested that theories of 'sustained value creation' may be borrowed from the management literature. Managers within tourism should be looking to add value for environments, communities, entrepreneurs and tourists, albeit within the ethical objectives outlined by the WTO's (2001) *Global Code of Ethics for Tourism* charter. However, while all might agree with the intentions of such charters, the pragmatic issues of management responsibility that are raised are complex and, in turn, raise serious issues concerning patterns of power and how such power to implement policies is to be both determined and practised responsibly.

To take a simple example, Malloy and Fennell (1998b) analysed 414 individual ethical statements from 40 tourism codes of ethics. They found that 77% of these merely provided injunctions and did not inform stakeholders of the reasons why they should abide by certain guidelines. Such codes thus failed to adequately locate and explain the nature of stakeholder responsibility towards the environmental context of the tourism experience. While Farrell *et al.* (2002b) draw a distinction in this respect between 'inspirational' and 'prescriptive' code types, Malloy and Fennell (1998b) advocate that policymakers should develop codes that are 'teleological' – emphasizing purpose – in order to enable tourists and other stakeholders to understand the consequences of their actions and thus the reasons why certain guidelines are deemed necessary. Such an approach is more likely to result in compliance through reasoning, they argue, while also acting to better inform and educate visitors. A national park notice stating 'Do not touch wildlife: the bond between parent and young can be disrupted, and the survival of the young jeopardized' would be more effective than one simply stating 'Do not touch wildlife' (see Fennell, 2000: 62).

Thus, although such codes relate explicitly to visitor behaviour, at least some of the responsibility for that behaviour should rest with both the visit organizers and the environment managers. Negative outcomes may result from 'inappropriately' articulated codes, interpretation and other experiential cues provided by managers and planners who are placed in a pivotal position. Resulting ignorant behaviour on the part of visitors is referred to by Fennell as 'ethical transgressions', although this infers a knowledge and awareness of the inappropriateness and irresponsibility of their behaviour on the part of tourists, which may not necessarily be the case. Such behaviour might include not wearing proper attire when entering a sacred temple or inadvertently scaring wildlife, and may stem from a lack of preparation or knowledge on the part of the tourist, from the tourist operator's ignoring local customs in order to cater for perceived tourist needs, or simply from poor and inappropriate information and interpretation provision and code presentation.

The responsibility for the 'ethical transgression' may therefore be shared or may not rest essentially with the visitor at all, although the locus and division of responsibility may not be readily apparent from the empirical context. What is clear from this and from Fennell's advocacy of 'teleological' codes of ethics is that the achievement of ethical objectives requires an assumption of responsibility.

In 1989 the World Tourism Organization adopted the term 'responsible tourism' in preference to 'alternative tourism' as a means of promoting an escape from the pejorative connotations of mass tourism. This was partly because the image projected – of 'responsibility' – was clearly a more positive one, suggesting an element of proactivity, prior contemplation and finely judged ('sustainable'?) behaviour on the part of both tourists and tour operators. It also avoided uncomfortable clarifications concerning exactly what 'alternative tourism' might be an alternative to. Further, while the concept of 'alternative tourism' was not new – there having been 'mass' and 'alternative' forms of tourism since at least Roman times – the academic literature has been characterized by the industry-unfriendly fact that it appears to have been easier to understand and articulate the negative results of mass tourism than to formulate a realistic and coherent positive view of 'alternative' tourism. Indeed, Weaver (2003) complains that there has been a relative lack of new thinking and writing in the area of alternative tourism since the early 1990s.

But 'responsible tourism' is a tautology. As a strapline, alongside 'sustainable', 'soft', 'low-impact' and the rest of the wish-list prefixes employed by tourism and associated consumer product promoters, it is clearly another marketing cliché, and yet one that ought to have some practical advocacy value. However, the empirical research on the tourism industry in this respect is not encouraging.

Masterton (1992: 18) found that almost all tour operators interviewed agreed that abuse of the planet was a bad thing, in theory. In practice, however, most operators did not want to discuss their environmental responsibilities. The simple fact is that most are not practising sound ethical tourism (Malloy and Fennell, 1998a). Indeed, Miller (2001) interviewed 35 senior representatives from the UK tourism industry to discern what factors influenced the degree of responsibility shown by their organization, and found that the potential for market advantage and fear of negative public relations were key factors determining company actions (see also Chapter 7).

Yet responsibility is a vital element in any debate on tourism development and its attendant welfare issues. Just as the achievement of ethical objectives requires an assumption of responsibility, so, almost as the corollary, responsible attitudes require an ethical underpinning if they are to result in ethical outcomes. It is within this context that Fennell and Przeclawski (2003: 140) offer an interactional model of tourism ethics, arguing that it is based on the assumption 'that tourism will emerge and remain an agent of good will if actors are capable of making ethically sound decisions' (see also Fennell, 2000).

Book Structure and Justification

This book is organized into eight chapters.

This first chapter, having established the book's aims and objectives and outlining its contents, has examined, defined and interpreted the key terms and concepts adopted and applied in subsequent chapters. It establishes the volume's context by setting out its philosophical and ideological underpinnings and framework.

A consideration of holidays as an element of the quality of life precedes a brief examination of how the tourism industry has embraced welfare values, in the promotion and content of health and wellness tourism activities. Although such a trend may simply reflect good business and the adoption of fashionable terms to promote further niche products, it does reflect a conscious attempt to relate tourism, in this case if only for tourists, to explicit notions of enhanced welfare. This final section thus acts as a prelude to the chapters that follow, in terms of access to tourism (Chapter 2) and the welfare of the tourist (Chapter 3).

If tourism participation is hypothesized as enhancing the quality of life, then such a welfare component should be accessible to all who require it. Chapter 2 examines issues of access to and participation in tourism opportunities, and the barriers that may inhibit or prevent certain groups in society – or, rather, in certain (tourist-generating) societies – from so participating. It highlights the structural, social and international differentiation exemplified by such constraints.

Chapter 3 employs the concept of the 'tourist welfare cycle' as a vehicle to articulate a welfare-centred focus on tourists. The 'cycle' represents a simple modification to the characterization of the stages tourists pass through from the contemplating of and preparation for a holiday to the return home and the socially critical context of post-holiday welfare. The chapter highlights perceived shortcomings in information that reduce the potential welfare of travellers, particularly in terms of impacts on preventive measures to protect health. But the chapter also emphasizes the personal responsibility all tourists have – and express through their behaviour – both for their own welfare and for those with whom they come into contact, an ethical dimension taken up in subsequent chapters. A perpetual theme of the book raised in the chapter is the question of blurred or overlapping responsibilities and the fact that the relative weight of responsibilities falling on the shoulders of stakeholders varies according to the nature of the issue, the time and the place. In articulating this, the chapter highlights the difficult question of skin cancer resulting from sun exposure: the latter an activity which is the *raison d'être* for much of the tourism industry, and the former a condition that may not be detected for up to 30 years and is thus almost impossible to relate back to likely causal factors. Thus we are faced with ethical dilemmas that result from trying to locate responsibility for a causal relationship that, while being obvious, is none the less difficult to prove.

Our welfare-centred approach in Chapter 4 focuses on those living and working in the tourism destination. One of the much-touted mantras of sustainable tourism, that it needs to be predicated on the participation of the local 'community', fails to acknowledge the inadequacy of the latter term. In any destination, the role and significance of tourism will vary greatly, and such a role will interact differently with other aspects of the destination's development sectors in different ways. Notions of 'community' tied to 'tourism sustainability' may not reflect such a situation adequately. A focus is placed upon the ethical nature of interactions between the major tourism actors within the destination, with trade-offs, competitive and complementary roles being examined. The welfare of destinations is discussed with reference to disease and crime within the context of a heightened awareness of the apparent need for security, safety and 'surety'. The welfare of tourism employees is examined, at the destination workplace, as labour migrants and at sea within the context of cruise tourism. This acts as a context for the following chapter.

Chapter 5 focuses on the nature and efficacy of pro-poor tourism (PPT) as an ethically based, tourism-employment-led development policy. Is tourism employment an appropriate mechanism for levering citizens of some of the most impoverished countries in the world out of poverty? It is certainly emphasized that tourism can only be one of a range of mechanisms involved in 'poverty reduction'. Yet, by arguing that poverty can be relieved through greater participation in tourism employment, there is an implicit understanding that tourism should therefore be expanding in the poorest countries and regions. This is a contested notion and confronts the ethical trade-off between (essential?) employment provision and (scarce?) resource consumption. Further, being promoted by Western development NGOs and government departments, does PPT simply offer another route by which economic imperialism, through tourism, may extend its tentacles, or is it an appropriately liberating and remunerative option?

Chapter 6 turns attention to a welfare-centred approach to the non-human animals involved in tourism and their wider captive and 'natural' environments. Viewing the roles and relationships of animals in tourism through a welfare perspective helps to focus on the human–animal relationship, the management of that relationship and its ethical context. In relation to the 'wildlife' environment, perceptions of animals, their relative merit and value, not least as 'edutainment', appear strongly culturally determined, and this has important implications for their welfare and for the quality of human interactions with them in recreational environments. Expressions of responsibility through codes of conduct and behaviour are related to the ever-broadening scope of the concept of 'ecotourism'.

In the penultimate chapter, 7, we explore the nature of tourism industry responses to welfare dilemmas and the growth of ethical concern through an explicit embrace of notions of corporate social responsibility (CSR). We ask whether this trajectory within the tourism industry will actually enhance the welfare of stakeholders through such dimensions as those reflected in the book's previous chapters.

By attempting to draw together the threads of the book, Chapter 8 offers a summary and conclusions, setting our welfare approach to tourism firmly within a global context.

We recognize that the chapter structure may not be wholly satisfactory. In any book, the interlinkages between elements and chapters often means that the dividing line between and order of material within chapters and sections becomes a little arbitrary. In this case, in a book attempting to pursue a holistic perspective, the problem becomes more acute. But we have tried to avoid substantial and repeated cross-referencing.

Stakeholders

The focus on stakeholders and the recognition of their mutual responsibilities is critical to our welfare-centred approach to tourism. 'Stakeholders' may be viewed as any individual or group influencing or affected by collective objectives. This presupposes a moral obligation, based on recognized ethical principles, incumbent on those setting the objectives to involve 'stakeholders' in meaningful participation within decision-making processes. Resulting mutual obligations and responsibilities should help to cohere such processes into socially responsible action (Ryan, 2002: 20), which may be derived from positions of power, mutual benefit, enlightened self-interest, enterprise self-preservation and ethical awareness.

One crucial objective element of stakeholding is power, both in terms of mutual responsibilities and in the ability to translate proposals into concrete action. The power to deliver action implies that those in a subordinate role accept the primacy of those who are dominant. For this to be realistic, however, mutual advantage needs to exist (Ap, 1992; Ryan, 2002: 20). Of course this is complicated in practice by the fact that stakeholder groups are rarely homogeneous or consensual, and it fails to sit easily with the notion of non-human

animals and inanimate environments as stakeholders.

None the less, within a framework of an unequal distribution of power and authority, the World Tourism Organization's *Global Code of Ethics for Tourism* (WTO, 2001) promotes a framework code of behaviour and action for tourism's stakeholders (as defined in Box 1.2) to pursue and as a moral context within which to set it.

A logical conclusion for those who argue that in our postmodern times tourism is all-embracing and all-consuming is the obvious, if not necessarily helpful, contention that we are all stakeholders. This can be most forcefully argued from an environmental perspective: the impact that tourism and travel are having on the planet, most notably through climate change, affects us all, and those of us in the 'developed' world each carry a heavy individual and collective responsibility to modify drastically our resource-intensive consumptive behaviour, of which tourism and travel are a major component (see Chapter 8).

This is, indeed, a logical response to the WTO's call for 'stakeholders' to implement the Global Code's principles, which declare 'sustainability' to be at their heart. But, like it or not, the WTO's approach – even its recent conversion to notions of pro-poor tourism (WTO, 2005; see also Chapter 5) – remains locked within an ethos predicated on profit-generating, industry-expanding intentions.

Box 1.2. WTO description of tourism stakeholders.

- National, regional and local administrations
- Enterprises and business associations
- Workers in the sector
- Non-governmental organizations
- Bodies of all kinds belonging to the tourism industry
- Host communities
- The media
- Tourists themselves

'All have different albeit interdependent responsibilities in the individual and societal development of tourism.'

Source: WTO, 2001.

For some (e.g. D'Sa, 1998) a global ethics code represents little more than tinkering around the edges of a juggernaut in need of radical reappraisal (see Chapters 5, 7 and 8). To appreciate this a little more, we need to go back to the eight 'fundamental truths' that McKercher (1993a) articulated nearly a decade and a half ago (Box 1.3). These were enumerated in response to the apparent lack of research on the underlying reasons why tourism's adverse impacts appear to be inevitable, regardless of the type of tourism activity.

McKercher (1993a: 7) argued that the recognition and understanding of these 'fundamental truths' could play a key role in developing future sustainable tourism policies. Appearing in the very first issue of *Journal of Sustainable Tourism*, this objective was perhaps not unexpected. More importantly, he suggested that, by accepting the inevitability of these truths as a (pre?) condition of tourism development, planners, policymakers and industry leaders could begin to develop effective policies and programmes to minimize impacts. He claimed that 'it may be possible to harden host communities and environments to make them more resistant to adverse impacts'

Box 1.3. Summary of McKercher's 'fundamental truths about tourism'.

1. As an industrial activity, tourism consumes resources, creates waste and has specific infrastructure needs.
2. As a consumer of resources, it has the ability to over-consume resources.
3. Tourism, as a resource-dependent industry, must compete for scarce resources to ensure its survival.
4. Tourism is a private-sector-dominated industry, with investment decisions being based predominantly on profit maximization.
5. Tourism is a multifaceted industry and, as such, it is almost impossible to control.
6. Tourists are consumers, not anthropologists.
7. Tourism is entertainment.
8. Unlike other industrial activities, tourism generates income by importing clients rather than exporting its product.

Source: McKercher, 1993a: 7.

(McKercher, 1993a: 7), although some might argue that this is looking at the 'problem' from the wrong end.

Fennell (2000: 67) has elaborated McKercher's emphasis by offering some five paradoxes of tourism (Table 1.1).

While to many of us with the benefit of hindsight, McKercher's and Fennell's offerings may be stating the blindingly obvious (SBO), they do emphasize prime contextual realities that are still often overlooked, forgotten or ignored in the literature, namely that tourism is:

- a grossly imperfect vehicle for human and environmental welfare within a grotesquely imperfect world;
- far from being a democratic activity, even though it is often viewed in tourist-generating societies as representing liberal values of freedom and democracy (Box 1.4); and
- a heavily politicized and political activity.

While highlighting the fact that the political arena is a dangerously contentious theatre, Brian Wheeller (2005: 267) points out that:

> the actual development of tourism – the necessary wheeling and dealing – takes place in the real world, warts and all. Whereas elaborate academic tourism planning discussions, and discourse on sustainability, still remain essentially confined to, and cocooned in, the protected dream world of textbook theory . . . immune to the pressures and vicissitudes of actuality. The question of corruption and the levels of intensity to which it is practised are conveniently ignored in the supposedly 'holistic', yet somewhat arbitrary, sustainable tourism vacuum.

He quotes the assertion of William Rees-Mogg (1999: 18), a former editor of *The Times*, that 'the world has the worry that corruption is now spreading throughout politics. One can almost say that corruption has now become the global norm.' And this applies not only to politics:

> There is also a growing debate about the relationship between businesses in the

tourism industry and . . . their staff, customers and investors. This debate ranges far and wide including everything from salary levels to food safety to honest financial reporting. This interest . . . is, of course, not just limited to tourism; it is a general concern fuelled by the numerous business scandals seen around the world in recent years. It clearly underpins the rise in interest in the concept of corporate social responsibility.

(Swarbrooke, 2003: 5–6)

While government has a role as interest protector (C.M. Hall, 2000, 2003a), a 'hollowing out' of the state and the dispersal of power to a multiplicity of unelected and semi-governmental agencies and business interests involved in the often fragmented 'governance' of regions, societies and environments has resulted in a democratic deficit (Blowers, 1997): in practice, a weakened ability of government to protect its citizens from exploitation. This

Table 1.1. Fennell's 'five paradoxes of tourism' (from Fennell, 2000: 67, augmented).

The paradoxes	Our comments
1. Many tourists want to relax, act differently from at home, and thus do not want to be bothered to consider their impacts, which they may not be able to see, or are not aware of, anyway.	Certainly much of the tourism industry will conspire with that. Despite McKercher's 'fundamental truth' 6, we are constantly told that consumers, including those of tourism and leisure, are becoming both more ethically aware and motivated. Is this wishful thinking? Does this represent the gap between what people say, to reinforce their preferred ideal self-image, and what they actually do? (e.g. Carrigan and Attalla, 2001; see earlier in this chapter).
2. People holidaying away from home are likely to have an overall greater negative impact than if they stayed at home, yet tourism has been enshrined as a human right.	Rights need to be balanced by responsibilities (see Chapter 7).
3. Local people want the economic benefits of tourism, and even some of the benefits of cultural exchange . . . but could manage much better without the actual tourists.	Not all 'local people', not in all places. Such benefits, although ultimately financial, are often cloaked in terms of 'cultural' or 'social enrichment'. And of course crude economic tools such as cost–benefit analysis cannot easily accommodate the (ultimately subjective) value of 'social enrichment' or 'cultural erosion' (see Chapter 4).
4. Tourists, not being their usual workaday selves, are not in a mode to be appropriate role models, yet may offer, in this inappropriate, atypical mode, the only opportunity for particular culture contact for local peoples.	The 'responsibility of travelling' needs to be taken seriously by both those who travel and those who facilitate such travel: this should include global environmental as well as cultural considerations. Similarly, the tourism industry, in both source and destination regions, needs to take a greater responsibility for the welfare of destination residents in the face of (possibly unwanted and uninvited) tourist activity. How far have codes of behaviour/conduct penetrated 'mainstream' tourism? (see Chapters 3 and 4).
5. The economic rewards from tourism are likely to be divisive and their benefits polarized within certain social, employment and spatially located groups within wider society.	Tourism is no different from any other economic sector in this respect. No pure egalitarian society has ever been achieved outside a few small communes and perhaps kibbutzim: and what impact have they had on their surrounding social environments?

raises important questions concerning the ethical underpinnings of tourism processes and location of responsibilities for stakeholders' welfare. Under these circumstances, how valid or realistic is the continuing discussion, seeking and promotion of 'sustainable tourism'?

Revisiting Tourism and Sustainable Development

As a much-debated global policy issue, the essence of sustainable development, drawing upon holistic ecological concepts, is that economic development is dependent upon the sustained well-being of the physical and social environment upon which it is based (Redclift, 1987; Butler, 1991). This philosophy was promoted in four key and oft-cited sustainable development publications of the 1980s and 1990s:

- the *World Conservation Strategy* (WCS) (IUCN, 1980), which promoted the adoption of sustainability measures in the face of a wide range of pressing global environmental problems;
- the report of the World Commission on Environment and Development (WCED) (1987), which established the concept of sustainable development in the policy arena with the aim to 'make development sustainable to ensure that it meets the needs of the present without compromising the ability of future generations to meet their own needs' (WCED, 1987: 43) (Box 1.5);
- the World Conservation Union's *Caring for the Earth*, which carried the sustainability debate forward while emphasizing sustainable development's role in 'improving the quality of life while living within the carrying capacity of supporting ecosystems' (IUCN, 1991: 10); and
- Agenda 21: as a substantive outcome of the United Nations Conference on Environment and Development (UNCED) – the Rio 'Earth Summit' (1992) – this was promulgated as an action plan towards sustainable development for the 21st

century, emphasizing the participation of ordinary people, including the poorest, in decision making (Postma, 2003). It was recognized and adopted by the European Commission (2003) and by signatory national governments (e.g. House of Lords, 1994). The majority of Agenda 21 initiatives and actions are required to take place at the local level. The Agenda's Chapter 28 calls for each

---

Box 1.4.   Travel as a symbol of freedom.

Two days after the 7 July 2005 suicide bombings in London, Simon Calder could write:

> Even though the attack was targeted haphazardly against humanity, rather than specifically at tourists, it is a natural reaction to want to stay safe at home.
> Yet the best response to those who seek to diminish our lives is to expand our horizons: to travel more, not less; to celebrate our freedom to meet people across the world; to understand their lives, hopes and fears.

This was published the day after a much watered-down final communiqué on combating climate change was issued by the G8 summit leaders in Gleneagles, Scotland.

Source: Calder, 2005.

Box 1.5.   Brundtland's five key principles of sustainability.

The World Commission on Environment and Development (WCED) (1987), chaired by the Norwegian prime minister Gro Harlem Brundtland and usually referred to as the Brundtland Report, identified five key principles of sustainability:

- holistic planning and strategy-making;
- preservation of essential ecological processes;
- protection of both human heritage and biodiversity;
- development embracing productivity that can be sustained over the long term for future generations;
- achievement of a better balance of fairness and opportunity between nations.

Sources: WCED, 1987; Bramwell and Lane, 1993; Butler and Hall, 1998.

local authority to develop (originally by 1996) a 'Local Agenda 21' (LA21) plan. The presence of such a plan became a performance indicator for UK local government leisure and cultural services (ILAM, 2000), and the importance of this in encompassing tourism planning and development became widely recognized (ETC, 2001; European Commission, 2003; UNEP, 2003). A key factor of LA21 planning is the promotion of awareness to all sectors of the community and the seeking of their participation in the formulation of such plans (Leslie and Hughes, 1997). *Agenda 21 for the Travel and Tourism Industry* (WTTC *et al.*, 1996) was the first sector-based response, emphasizing the view that tourism has a role to play in enhancing the sustainability of local communities (WTTC *et al.*, 1996; Leslie, 2005).

An inordinate number of interpretations and (re-)evaluations of these formulations have followed.

In the 1980s and 1990s the tourism industry took 'sustainability' to its heart, or at least its sleeve, invoking ideals and practices of 'sustainable tourism' at every opportunity, and publishing sustainable tourism development plans, sets of principles and indicators. Subsquently, a range of critiques (e.g. Tourism Concern and WWF, 1992; Wheeller, 1993; Bramwell, 1994; Cater and Lowman, 1994; Lane, 1994; Coccossis and Nijkamp, 1995; Hunter, 1995, 1997; Bramwell *et al.*, 1996; Coccossis, 1996; Mowforth and Munt, 1998, 2003; Swarbrooke, 1999; McCool and Moisey, 2001; Sharpley, 2001) have appeared, acknowledging and often pursuing notably different interpretations of and perceiving contrasting desired outcomes for 'sustainable tourism'. Hunter (1997), for example, drawing conceptually on the work of Jafari (1989), summarized four positions taken in the literature towards tourism and sustainability, before going on to suggest four possible alternative approaches.

But by the new millennium, at the 2002 World Summit on Sustainable Development (WSSD) in Johannesburg, representatives from many less developed countries argued that environmental sustainability was a luxury they could not afford because it represented an obstacle to economic development. Tourism was often perceived as one – often a key – element of that economic development and, thus, by definition, not consistent with holistic sustainability ideals.

Policy implementation gaps

Let us therefore briefly restate some of the reasons why sustainable tourism development has remained a contested concept. First, as noted above, it has been interpreted in different ways, although this can be said of almost any widely adopted or pursued ideal. Indeed, while Hunter (1997) recognizes different approaches and interpretations, he argues that notions of 'sustainable tourism' require flexibility in order to meet realistically the needs of differing circumstances.

More particularly, second, sustainable development as a holistic concept embraces certain principles and requirements that cannot be fulfilled through tourism (Sharpley, 2001):

- the fragmented, multi-sectoral, private-sector-dominated and profit-motivated tourism production system is incapable of providing a holistic approach that integrates tourism's developmental and environmental consequences within a global socio-economic and ecological context;
- sustainable development focuses upon long-term fair and equal access to resources and opportunities based upon self-reliance, but this is unlikely to be achieved through tourism, given the structure, ownership and control of the industry, which more closely resembles the dependency model of development theory; and
- the emergence of the 'green' tourist, frequently cited as the justification for promoting sustainable forms of tourism, cannot be taken for granted: for example, pioneering 'travellers' may open up pristine areas for exploitation (Gordon and Townsend, 2001), while large

numbers of tourists remain ignorant of or indifferent to exhortations to behave 'sustainably'.

Third, the prime objective of sustainable tourism development appears to have become the sustaining of tourism itself: to preserve the natural, built and socio-cultural resource base upon which tourism depends in order to perpetuate tourism rather than aspiring to wider, holistic and altruistic ideals (Sharpley, 2001). As a consequence, such an inward, product-centred focus has largely removed the 'development' element of the process.

Fourth, and reinforcing this, is the fact that tourism is essentially a business, and the stated objectives of 'sustainable' tourism limit the potential for development by attempting to adapt the market to a relatively specific product. As a consequence, the creative side of development is overlooked (Butcher, 2003).

Fifth, much of the industry focus on and declaration of sustainable tourism relates to activity at the destination. Rarely is attention drawn to the usually unsustainable transport and travel modes – aircraft, motor vehicles – that many tourists necessarily employ in order to be able to visit destination areas.

Sixth, near obsession with 'sustainable tourism' development has diverted attention away from the fact that other forms of tourism may make a significant contribution to socio-economic development in destination areas through income and employment opportunities, with subsequent linkages to other sectors of the economy, such as construction, transport services and food production (Chapter 5).

Seventh, although one of its fundamental principles is local community involvement and control, the nature of sustainable tourism development has tended to be highly prescribed: yet there is a need to recognize the appropriateness to local needs of different forms of tourism and thus the welfare needs of the different stakeholders of diverse tourism environments (Chapter 4).

Eighth, the reality of winners and losers from tourism development and the need for trade-offs (Chapters 2–6) severely reduces the value of the holistic ethos of sustainability in relation to tourism's consequences. Compromises need to be identified and managed; they are unlikely to meet the sustainability ideal of consensus.

Ninth, policies aimed at 'sustainability' need to be underpinned by three fundamental principles (Sharpley, 2000):

• holism: development needs to be considered in an integrated way within a global political, socio-economic and ecological context. Yet, while notions of sustainable development have come to influence a range of policy actions, this holistic ethos is often lost sight of as applications have tended to focus upon either individual components of development, such as the sustainability of agriculture, or considerations of the 'natural' environment in relative isolation, without taking an integrated approach to the interdependence of sociocultural, economic, political and ecological elements of development;

• futurity: there is a need for due regard to be given to the long-term appropriate use of natural and human resources. How can promoters prefix the label 'sustainable' to a product whose implications and impacts may not be apparent for several years or even decades?

• equity: development should be fair and equitable – providing opportunities for access to and use of resources for all members of societies. As an ideal for equity in development, policy issues for tourism and recreation should embrace ethical and welfare considerations. Continually, such questions should be posed as: should tourism be encouraged if it leads to increased social and economic inequality in one region or country? How appropriate is it to propagate rural tourism initiatives if the majority of the benefit is received in another region or country? How much adverse landscape and environmental change as a result of tourism is acceptable? (After Unwin, 1998; Roberts and Hall, 2001.)

Tourism as it is currently structured cannot easily meet – and be seen to meet – these requirements. Some of these shortcomings at least partly reflect apparently simplistic assumptions made by promoters and policymakers that:

- the often contradictory aims of economic, social and ecological development can be easily reconciled (Curry, 1992); or that
- tourism development can be considered in isolation from the other components providing the social, economic and ecological contexts for development processes; and
- tourism can be compatible with sustainable development principles – an assumption tending to underscore the way in which many policymakers have encouraged tourism development for rural, 'natural', 'peripheral' and 'developing' areas, with 'sustainability' often being adopted as a mantra, almost assuming that simply declaring a sustainable policy approach will assure sustainable outcomes.

Hunter (1997: 850) argues that the emergence of such 'an overly simplistic and inflexible paradigm of sustainable tourism' results particularly from the fact that sustainable tourism as an objective appears to have evolved largely in isolation from wider debates on the meaning of sustainable development.

Partly as a consequence, for some time commentators have identified a significant 'implementation gap' (e.g. Wheeller, 1993; Butler and Hall, 1998) between the policy ideal of sustainability and its application in tourism. Why is this significant for a welfare perspective? Partly because the term 'sustainable tourism' implies, amongst many other things, that the welfare of tourists, hosts, workers and environments embraced by tourism can be maintained and perhaps enhanced: (i) for the foreseeable future; and (ii) in balance and harmony both with tourism and its wider context and with each other's competing welfare needs and aspirations.

However, much of the tourism industry is comprised of small, often one-person enterprises, which may lack the necessary resources and knowledge to pursue sustainability ideals. In Finland, for example, arguably the most ethically oriented and aware society in Europe, Björk (2001) found that, while a major element in the interpretation of 'sustainable tourism' by small tourism companies was focused on the natural environment, most actions undertaken towards sustainability were seen to be at a specific, business-oriented tactical level rather than being strategic. A significant majority of companies saw the need for external support in directing them towards a more sustainable phase. This reflects the clearly observable fact that a significant sector of tourism is unable on its own to contribute to any strategic development of sustainability goals, pointing to the need to share the responsibility for helping enterprises to act sustainably.

Björk (2001) advocated the need for a partnership model to permit the effective pursuit of 'sustainable tourism', and the academic literature repeats the argument that it is necessary for tourism to be appropriately embedded within the particular set of linkages and relationships that make up the components of local and regional development. But it often fails to pinpoint the ethical requirements and location of responsibility for the attainment of or the consequences of seeking to attain such ideals. Yet the need for cooperation and partnerships emphasizes, at least for stakeholders comprising the supply side of tourism development, the importance of mutual welfare and the requirement for the sustained well-being of other actors in the tourism development process.

That tourists have sought, through the act of tourism, to enhance their own welfare, if only temporarily, is perhaps too self-evident to merit comment. Yet that process is central to the concept of tourism and to the *raison d'être* of the tourism industry. It therefore provides a critical starting point for a welfare-centred evaluation of tourism processes. In the following section, therefore, we anticipate the tourist-focused Chapters 2 and 3 by addressing some of the more explicit welfare-enhancing aspects of tourism.

Tourism as Welfare?

Much comment on leisure and tourism adopts a productivist approach, whereby work is viewed as the prime need in human existence (Rojek, 1995). As part of leisure, tourism is seen as supporting the organization of work by providing opportunities for rest and relaxation. This conceptual perspective positions tourism as making only a relatively marginal contribution to the quality of life.

Yet, even from such a perspective, studies of the relationship between leisure and work indicate a growing willingness to exchange money for more (and better-quality) leisure time (e.g. Schor, 1991; Gratton, 1995). The apparent desire for increased leisure and tourism consumption represents a shift in the focus of consumption away from physical goods towards services and experiences. This in its turn suggests that welfare is increasingly viewed in terms of access to such services and experiences. Leisure time in general, and holiday time in particular, is recognized as offering a central set of experiences that people value in terms of their quality of life (Cushman et al., 1996; Jansen-Verbeke and van Renkom, 1996; Richards, 1999).

But, while tourism participation has increased markedly, a growing literature has highlighted a number of structural constraints on this (see Chapter 2). Access to travel opportunities is manifestly not equally distributed, both within and between different societies, but is structured and constrained by variations in disposable income, discretionary time availability, gender, (dis)ability, nationality and a range of societal and personal factors.

In the literature on tourism and travel motivations, a range of seeking and escaping behaviours have been explored (e.g. Boorstin, 1964; MacCannell, 1976; Cohen, 1979; Krippendorf, 1989; Dunn Ross and Iso-Ahola, 1991). Iso-Ahola (1980) argued that individuals seek an optimal level of stimulation, or optimal arousal, between too little stimulation (boredom) and too much stimulation (stress). Richards (1999) suggests that, rather than being clearly separated, seeking and escaping motives are in fact being incorporated into the same tourism experiences. 'Old' tourism motivations, such as rest and relaxation, are being overlain with (not so) 'new' motivations, such as skill acquisition, culture and nature (Poon, 1993).

Although beach tourism has remained dominant in Europe, holidays do appear to be taking on an increasing number of functions, with tourists shoehorning ever more activities into their vacation time. In the past, holidays may have been havens of rest, but today they are increasingly an extension of the busy consumption patterns that characterize many people's lifestyles (Richards, 1996). This suggests a displacement of everyday social and personal development functions into the 'quality' time provided by holidays. In terms of welfare enhancement, therefore, holidays can play a triple role (Richards, 1999):

- providing physical and mental rest and relaxation;
- providing the space for personal development and the pursuit of personal and social interests; and
- being used as a form of symbolic consumption, enhancing status.

The last two of these are embraced by the rapidly growing phenomenon of 'volunteer tourism' (McGehee and Norman, 2001; Wearing, 2001; Callanan and Thomas, 2005), which is promoted (somewhat paradoxically) as an altruistic and self-developmental experience. As such, the interaction of 'self' with the 'other' in a variety of contexts may fall short of idealized expectations, particularly as much 'volunteer tourism' is undertaken by relatively inexperienced idealistic young adults from Western societies during their gap year between school and university (Griffith, 2003; Hindle et al., 2003). Callanan and Thomas (2005: 183) suggest that the 'volunteer tourism rush' is fuelled by 'an ever increasing "guilt-conscious" society', which appears consonant with Butcher's (2003: 3) argument that the recent moralization of tourism is a product of disillusionment with modern (Western) society. But, while Butcher sees this reflected in the new moral tourist's external search for community and spirituality in the cultural and environmental 'other', an equally important trend is tourists' search within themselves.

Thus the sybaritic phenomena of spa and health holidays (e.g. Duckett, 2002; Swiac, 2003) and the more recent popularity of 'wellness' and holistic tourism represent one end, and perhaps the most explicit element, of a spectrum of welfare-conscious tourism activities that focus on the self (and which are amenable to cultural analysis through, for example, concepts of embodiment: e.g. see Moore, 1994: 15; Veijola and Jokinen, 1994; Morgan, 2005).

Wellness, well-being and holism

Establishment of the WHO in 1948 acknowledged a global approach to health and well-being (Anderson, 1987). Of course, the concept of travelling for health improvement goes back at least to classical times. More recently, increasing popularity of the wellness concept has acted to stimulate both a more leisure-based health concept and a revival and (re)development of the long-recognized health-oriented leisure sector (e.g. Goodrich and Goodrich, 1987). The physician Halbert Dunn is claimed to have developed the concept of 'wellness' – a lexical conjoining of 'well-being' and 'fitness' (Dunn, 1961) – in 1959 (Müller and Lanz, 1998; Lanz Kaufmann, 1999). At the heart of the wellness concept lies the WHO definition of health noted earlier in the chapter (Anderson, 1987: 5): 'a state of complete physical, mental and social well-being and not merely the absence of disease or infirmity'.

The concept of wellness hotels and notions of health tourism have been in the forefront of this process, with the development of gyms, saunas, fun pools and wellness centres following. But, in the European context at least, contradictory trends have been highlighted. On the one hand a growing global leisure-based health orientation has become incorporated into a self-conscious fitness lifestyle. But at the same time in a

number of countries there has been a reduction of social financial support for collective wellness, as a result of which traditional European health resorts such as spas and sanitariums faced a crisis in the later 1990s (Nahrstedt, 2004). By the mid-1990s 13.5 million people were visiting 1500 spas in Europe (ESPA, 1995), but, in the face of economic problems following reunification, in 1996 the German government drastically reduced the support it provided for 'treatment holidays'. The number of overnight stays at many Central European spas fell in the following year by 30% or more (DBV, 1998), and this forced spas and other health tourism destinations to reinvent themselves and to develop health and wellness provision for self-paying guests. The European Union (EU) accession of a number of Central and Eastern European states with Habsburg heritage spa and health centres, such as Slovenia and Slovakia, has also assisted a resurgence in this sector and a regeneration of the facilities in these countries (e.g. Letic and Rumbak, 2004; NTIC, 2004; Spa Golf Club, 2004). This in turn has contributed to national (re-)imaging and branding (D. Hall, 2004a).

The origins of health tourism destinations often relate to a combination of natural attributes, such as the presence of thermal and/or mineralized waters, and cultural recognition of the attributes of such resources. Some destination countries, such as Australia (Bennett et al., 2004), are disadvantaged in the contemporary competition for health-related niche markets in lacking such attributes. But in a number of cases there has been a notable broadening of (albeit domestic) markets, such as in the Åre Valley of Sweden (Nilsson, 2001), growing from a narrow aristocratic elite to a much wider cross-section of society.

Health education and raising awareness levels of the welfare implications of lifestyle have become an essential basis for health tourism, not least because in Western societies individual lifestyle is a dominant underlying factor in premature death (Hertel, 2001). This has stimulated interest in, and some degree of fusing of, different approaches to health from different world cultures. These have included Asian approaches such as traditional Chinese medicine, yoga, Ayurveda, t'ai chi, qigong, reiki and shiatsu interacting with Western physical therapy.

Yet the legitimacy and efficacy of 'health holidays' remain contested. Although there is a substantial scientific literature in relation to the products of the spa industry (Hillebrand and Weintögl, 2001), some commentators argue that, in ethical terms, the promotion of health holidays should be accompanied by scientific proof of their medical value (e.g. Schobersberger *et al.*, 2004).

Tourism has clearly always been seen as a process of self-regeneration as well as relaxation, education or indulgence (Ryan, 1997), and the growth of holistic holidays as one dimension of wellness has been notable (Smith, 2003; Smith and Kelly, 2004). Holistic retreats tend to offer combinations of therapies and counselling, pathways to spiritual development, creative enhancement and many other routes to the reconciliation of body, mind and spirit. The Findhorn Foundation (<http://www.findhorn.org>) is such a retreat in north-east Scotland, attracting 14,000 participants annually and reckoned to support 300 jobs locally.

The growth of the holistic tourism sector suggests that there is an increasing desire to focus on the self rather than on the 'other' and on 'existential' rather than 'objective' authenticity (Wang, 1999). The irony of this holism is that, of course, being wholly focused on the self, its egocentricity contrasts sharply with the spatial and temporal holism of sustainable development ideals. In this context, 'tourism is at least as much a quest to be as a quest to see' (Seaton, 2002: 162), although one might cynically suggest that it is also, as a lifestyle phenomenon, as much about being seen, and particularly being seen to be undertaking fashionable, status-enhancing activities. As such, holistic tourism is an extension of home life and 'a means of improving . . . [it] . . . rather than escaping from it' (Smith and Kelly, 2004: 3).

In relation to Cohen's (1996) typology of tourists based on their motivations and experiences – recreational, diversionary, experiential, experimental and existential – holistic tourists are arguably both 'experimental' and 'existential'. The first three categories of tourists are largely escaping routine, boredom or alienation, but are not necessarily expecting to find meaning elsewhere. In contrast, 'experimental' tourists

Fig. 1.1. Tai Ji Retreat, Holy Isle, Firth of Forth, Western Scotland.

seek spiritual centres in different, alternative directions, while 'existential' travellers tend to commit to one spiritual centre, residing there permanently or visiting periodically as a form of pilgrimage (Sharpley and Sundaram, 2005).

Although the focus of holistic tourism is largely the self, Smith and Kelly (2004: 4) note that 'it can be no coincidence that many retreats are located in aesthetically pleasing, environmentally lush and culturally rich surroundings' (Fig. 1.1). They suggest that the importance of the outer journey (the chosen destination or landscape) as a location in which to conduct the inner journey is an issue worthy of further research.

Conclusions

In this introductory chapter we have tried to suggest how our conception of 'welfare' and a welfare-centred approach can differ from (but can complement) notions of sustainability within tourism, and how it can articulate the trade-offs, inequalities and imperfections that characterize tourism processes. This led us to argue that, within this role, conceptions of welfare, to be meaningful, need to be underpinned by ethical principles. These in their turn can highlight the fact that tourism development, or, rather, those involved in decision-taking processes within it, may often confront ethical dilemmas. Such an underpinning and the dilemmas that may arise demand from all stakeholders of tourism development a recognition and acknowledgement of their responsibilities. Although 'responsible tourism' has become a marketing cliché, the location of responsibility and accountability is critical in assisting the emergence of a more ethically based tourism that can take a more holistic view of the welfare implications of its development processes.

We rounded this off by highlighting the way in which tourism has embraced notions of health, wellness and well-being. Although such a contemporary trend, building on the historical role of health tourism and travel, may simply reflect good business and the adoption of fashionable terms to promote further niche products, it does reflect a conscious attempt to relate tourism, in this case if only for some tourists, to explicit notions of enhanced welfare.

A welfare-centred approach places tourism within its wider social and global context. If tourism participation is currently viewed as enhancing quality of life, then, quite simply, it should be accessible to all. In the next chapter, therefore, we evaluate access to and participation in tourism and the barriers that may inhibit or prevent certain groups in society – and indeed certain societies – from such participation.

2

Access and Participation

[T]he most important aspect of travelling is that we are able to learn more about ourselves through seeing others.

(el Saadawi, 1991: xiii)

Box 2.1. Chapter aims and summary.

This chapter seeks to: address issues of access to and participation in tourism.
It does this by: examining different levels of participation within and between societies, evaluating concepts of 'social tourism' and discussing the constraints on access for people with disabilities.
Its key concepts are: access, participation, social tourism, constraints and barriers.
It concludes that: a 'welfare paradigm' for tourism suggests that there should be equity of access and participation and that the tourism industry should promote and secure this. Both within generating countries and very obviously at a global level this is far from being a reality.

The previous chapter included a brief discussion on the way holidays are thought to contribute to the quality of life. This chapter examines the question of access to and participation in holiday-taking. A major strand of leisure studies' theorizing and research has taken place within a normative 'citizenship paradigm', in which the predominant concern is not with analysing the

nature of the leisure experience but with addressing issues of inequality within a collectivist welfare perspective (Rojek, 1993a). As a result, much of leisure studies is characterized by normative theorizing (Craib, 1984) about how the world, in which public leisure provision plays a central role in securing social citizenship, ought to be (Coalter, 1998: 23). This tended not to be the case in the academic tourism literature until 'sustainability' debates began to dominate policy ideals. This chapter centrally addresses issues of inequality by focusing on unequal access to and participation in tourism activity.

Current writing on inequalities in access in tourism-generating countries, a theme that tends to dominate the rapidly emerging literature in this area, emphasizes poverty and disability as major factors inhibiting participation. But the tourism literature often fails to bring these two components together analytically (Shaw and Coles, 2004) or to consider the ripple of impacts that the pressures of poverty and disability, separately or together, exert on a wide range of kin, carers and friends.

If we accept the proposition that individual welfare considerations appear to provide an important basis for undertaking holidays – for physical well-being, spiritual uplift, education or simple relaxation – such

©D. Hall and F. Brown 2006. *Tourism and Welfare: Ethics, Responsibility and Sustained Well-being* (D. Hall and F. Brown)

a 'welfare paradigm' for tourism would suggest two basic propositions:

- that there should be equality of access to and participation in holiday-taking for all who wish to take part; and
- the (global) tourism industry should be designed to promote and secure such access.

One caveat is, of course, that the welfare benefits derived from participating in tourism should not be secured at the cost of impaired welfare for others. And this raises an immediate ethical dilemma. If wider participation in (international) tourism is to become a reality – to embrace the hundreds of millions of people living in Africa, Asia and Latin America – it is likely to place an unsustainable burden on an already overburdened planet.

Differential Tourism Opportunity

There is now a significant literature focused on understanding why individuals travel and how they reach specific decisions (e.g. Plog, 1974; Ritchie, 1975; Pearce, 1991; Zimmer et al., 1995; Page et al., 2001; Shaw and Williams, 2002; see also Chapter 3). The range of motivations to travel identified in such research has included the need for social interaction, rest and relaxation, challenge, escape from daily stresses, stimulation, education and learning and to visit family and friends.

In the developed world, even – and often especially – those with an apparently high material quality of life expend considerable time and resources in leaving their everyday environment through travelling, to become 'emigrés from the present' (Rojek, 1993b). In addition to understanding why people choose to travel, it is important to know what factors may act as barriers and constraints to travelling, such as lack of time, poor health, disability, financial limitations, safety and security concerns and a lack of information (McGuire et al., 1986; Blazey, 1992). If the motivation to travel is strong enough, these barriers may be negotiated (Gladwell and Bedini, 2004: 687), so

that tourists may perceive themselves as having the freedom to make choices and having at least some degree of personal control over their own experiences. Without such feelings of freedom and personal control, tourism could not be considered to offer the potential for leisure (Iso-Ahola, 1980; Smith, 1987), and any welfare value is diminished.

The essential role of holidays and travel in human welfare has been formally recognized by:

- governments granting legal vacation rights in most countries;
- the recognition of vacations as a basic human right by the United Nations since 1948;
- international declarations on vacation rights and freedom of movement by the World Tourism Organization in 1980 and 1982; and
- the World Health Organization, which includes 'participation in and opportunity for recreation and pastimes' in its quality of life assessment (de Vries, 1996).

Exercising the rights thus conferred is now seen by many (in the privileged developed world at least) as an essential element of their quality of life. But with such rights also come responsibilities. Roche (1992), for example, has pointed out that few elements of social citizenship are based solely on 'rights' and that all imply some form of obligation or duty. While growing numbers of people are taking advantage of their 'right' to vacations, they are also helping to fuel one of the greatest contributors to climate change. Herein lie a number of paradoxes:

- such a process has been referred to as an apparent democratization of travel (e.g. Richards, 1999), spurred on by rapidly increasing motor vehicle ownership, unprecedented availability of air travel and the relatively decreasing cost to the consumer of both, while subjecting our planet to a process of near irreversible destruction;
- such 'democratization' in practice means that the bulk of those living in the

developed world are able to participate, but those who are unable to do so feel that they are missing out on an important aspect of their quality of life; and

- the concept of 'vacation rights' highlights massive global inequalities: for much of the world's population, and notably those in the least developed countries of Africa, Asia and Latin America – global regions receiving increasing numbers of tourists – the concept is meaningless and irrelevant, by virtue of the majority of people's poverty, powerlessness and immobility. Indeed, their condition may be powerfully expressed when such people are brought into contact with tourists or are dependent upon them for their livelihood.

However, for those of us in a position to regard holidays as an element of our quality of life, vacations are important not just because they provide our only unbroken chunk of leisure time, but also because the very quality of time spent on holiday is different. As Richards (1999: 189) points out, holidays offer relief from time and place, two of the key constraints of everyday life, and people can engage in self-indulgence.

In terms of the welfare impact of holidays, a trend towards more frequent, shorter breaks may be beneficial. Research on attitudes to holidays among women has shown that the key factor in the enjoyment of a holiday is the change in environment or daily routine (Davidson, 1996; Deem, 1996). Short breaks have also been advocated as a solution to 'burnout', which is acknowledged as a common problem for people in professional occupations (Schaufeli et al., 1993), although this appears to run counter to suggestions that many people in work need a least a continuous week away before they begin to unwind (see also Chapter 3).

None the less, most of the world's population do not 'go on holiday' (Wheeller, 1994b: 650), and relatively little space in the tourism research literature has been devoted to the welfare implications of their non-participation. Even in developed countries with high levels of tourist generation,

there may be a significant element of the population that is not participating in tourism for structural or social reasons. Authors such as Urry (1990) have highlighted structural socio-economic influences on tourism and travel participation, while Seaton (1992: 110) has argued that, in post-Second World War Britain, 'differential tourism opportunity' has been one component of socio-economic inequality, suggesting that 'probably 20–30 per cent' of the population, notably the aged and unemployed, have had 'little share' in the growth of tourism.

Yet, in the developed world at least, an inability to go on holiday or to take part in other leisure activities is an inability to participate in a commonly accepted style of life that can bring benefits both to individuals and to society. Involuntary non-participation may be an indicator of (relative) poverty and (perceived) deprivation (Hughes, 1991: 194–195).

The importance of tourism as an element of consumption and well-being is reflected in the movement to gain the right to paid holidays. In Europe, this fell into three general periods (Hessels, 1973; Richards, 1999):

- prior to 1914: a period when employers decided whether to grant holidays to their workers. In practice this meant that many manual workers had none;
- the interwar period: when social and economic demands of most groups of workers were encouraged in 1936 when the International Labour Office of the United Nations (ILO) adopted its first convention on paid holidays. In Switzerland, for example, in 1910 only 8% of the country's factory workers were entitled to holidays, but by 1937 this figure had risen dramatically to 66% (Teuscher, 1983);
- 1945+: with prosperity increasing, the holiday time demands of workers met a more favourable response from employers. Legislation was enacted in a number of European states in the 1950s and 1960s guaranteeing minimum periods of paid holiday for workers. In the Netherlands, the average entitlement rose

from 13 days a year in 1946 to 25 days in 1972. In France the pre-war 12-day minimum vacation allowance was extended in 1956 to 18 days, and in 1969 to 24 days, or 4 weeks (Samuel, 1986, 1993).

International differences

Considerable structural differences exist between countries and continents in terms of holiday entitlement, such that a basic access to holidays is not distributed equally between nations. European surveys undertaken in the mid-1980s within the then European Economic Community (EEC) (Faits et Opinions, 1987) suggested that 44% of the Community's population did not go on holiday in 1985. National extremes in such a figure ranged from 69% in Portugal down to 35% in the Netherlands. About half were classified as permanent non-travellers, who did not intend taking a holiday the following year. They were characterized as being relatively old, manual workers, fishermen, farmers, those in the lowest income quartile and rural dwellers. Social class differences between countries were highlighted in that only 16% of the wealthiest quarter of the populations of Britain and France were non-travellers, while 91% of the poorest quarter of Portugal's population fell into this category. Nearly half (44%) of all non-travellers cited lack of financial ability as the reason for not taking a holiday. Richards (1999) reports levels of annual holiday-taking in Spain at 53% of the population, compared with 78% in the Netherlands.

Not all European nations have formalized holidays as a component of social rights. In the UK, for example, these are subject to collective or individual negotiation, with the result that entitlements are lower than in most continental European countries (Rathkey, 1990). The transatlantic ethic behind this discrepancy was articulated in 2005, when the UK government opposed the European Parliament's vote to phase out the UK's opt-out clause from the European Working Time Directive's ceiling of a 48-h working week (Castle, 2005).

Indeed, the UK aside, the pattern of holiday entitlement in much of Europe contrasts sharply with that of the economies in North America and Japan. Having achieved a 40-h working week in 1940, well ahead of their European counterparts, American workers did not succeed in gaining significant holiday entitlements. Schor (1991) attributes the post-war divergence between America and Europe to the tendency for Americans to invest increases in productivity in greater consumption rather than in an extension of their leisure time. Most US workers can expect 2 weeks vacation a year – less than half the entitlement of workers in some northern European countries (Sunoo, 1996; Richards, 1999).

In Japan, leisure and holiday time has historically been even more scarce, with the apparent Japanese propensity for work being cited as a key reason for post-war economic success (Pascale and Athos, 1986). An average working year of 2300 h was reduced to 2111 h in 1988 and to 1800 h by 1995 (Anon., 1993). Yet annual working time in Japan remains some 20% longer than in the EU.

There are significant differences between the holiday patterns of people in Europe and those of Americans and Japanese. As noted, average incomes in America and Japan are higher than in most European countries, so money should be no constraint on the ability to travel. However, the relative scarcity of leisure time in Japan and America and also the relatively unequal distribution of incomes in the USA arguably create obstacles to vacation-taking. Many Americans and Japanese therefore have comparatively large amounts of money to spend on holidays, but very little time in which to spend it, lending credence to the 'if it's Tuesday it must be Belgium' travel cliché.

Yet vacations make a significant contribution to the quality of life for many Americans: an increasing desire has been demonstrated among workers to trade monetary rewards for leisure or vacation time. Surveys have indicated that 80% of respondents would take 2 weeks of vacation in place of 2 weeks of extra pay (Hilton Hotels

Corporation, 1995). However, Richards (1999) reports that, from an unpublished sample, almost two-thirds said that reducing their work hours would have a negative or very negative effect on their career success.

In Japan, workers may also be afraid to take holidays in case their job is not there when they return. This refusal to take time off is sometimes fatal: in 1995 there were 63 registered cases of *karoshi*, or death through overwork, in Japan (Anon., 1996). But there is a growing importance attached to leisure and tourism consumption, particularly by the younger generation (MacCormack, 1991; Harada, 1996; Richards, 1999).

The shift in attitudes to leisure and vacations is even more evident in Europe. Research in Germany, for example, has indicated that leisure and vacations have become more important life spheres for most people than work or politics (Tokarski and Michels, 1996). In the Netherlands workers have an advantage in that the system actively encourages saving money for holidays. The *vakantietoeslag*, or vacation money, 'saved' for most workers by their employers had increased to 8% of annual salaries by the mid-1990s (Richards, 1996).

For most people in the developing world, the major constraint is low income. Although the elite engage in holiday travel, this is still a luxury that most cannot afford. In India, for example, expenditure on international travel averages €0.50 per head of the population, and in Indonesia €5.50 per head. On the basis of time and money availability, Richards (1999) has identified three broad groups of societies regarding constraints on holiday-taking:

- less developed countries: 'time poor and money poor': most people have relatively little leisure time and lack the financial means to engage in tourism;
- northern Europeans: 'time rich and money rich': with relatively few constraints on their ability to take vacations. Southern Europeans have similar vacation entitlements but generally have lower standards of living;

- America and Japan: 'time poor and money rich': many people have few financial but relatively severe time constraints.

In spite of the increasing spread of tourism consumption, holidays are still a contested element of social rights in many parts of the world. Work is still the most important aspect of most people's lives. Although the holiday time available to many people has increased, Richards (1999) discerned that a ceiling appeared to have been reached in many countries in terms of the proportion of the population who can take holidays in any year. In the UK and France this proportion seems to be around 60%, whereas in the Netherlands participation seems to have levelled off at around 75%. Further extensions of tourism participation are likely to be precluded by the dismantling of the welfare state in many current social democratic and corporatist states.

Differences within countries

The time and money structures that produce significant differences in tourism consumption between nations are also evident to a lesser extent within nations. In fact, the convergence evident in vacation consumption between European countries in some cases masks increasing inequalities in the distribution of leisure time and income within nations.

The driving force for increased tourism consumption has shifted away from the relative income equality that characterized the initial post-war period (de Grazia, 1992) towards income polarization (Sassen, 1991). In the early post-war phase of vacation growth in the 1950s and 1960s there was a rapid extension of the total number of people taking holidays. But, as leisure breaks became an established element of consumption for most people, the focus of growth shifted towards second and third holidays or short breaks (see Box 2.2), taken predominantly by those in higher socio-economic groups. An increasing proportion of growth in demand may therefore be the result of a

Box 2.2. The French lose a holiday.

In May 2005 Jean-Pierre Raffarin, the (soon to be replaced) French prime minister, was required to defend a plan to make employees work unpaid over a holiday. The 'Day of Solidarity' on 16 May was introduced after 15,000 mostly elderly people died in the heatwave of 2003. Employers had to pay a tax for the work, which was to raise €2 bn for health care. M. Raffarin said it was 'a decisive step in the fight against the isolation of fragile people'. Subsequent demonstrations indicated that some workers thought otherwise.

Source: Anon., 2005a.

Social living conditions	Occurrence of obstacles	
	Unconstrained non-traveller	Constrained non-traveller
Satisfactory	Type A	Type B
Unsatisfactory	(Type D)	Type C

Fig. 2.1. Different types of non-travellers (after Haukeland, 1990: 179).

concentration of consumption, rather than extension of consumption to all social groups (Richards, 1999).

In Europe, at least, there is a dual trend towards increasing convergence of tourism consumption between nations, fed by rising incomes in some poorer nations, and increasing divergence of tourism consumption between social groups within nations as a result of income polarization (Richards, 1999).

The consumption of tourism in different regions and between different social groups is shaped by welfare state structures and policies, either directly, through the recognition of holidays as a social right, or indirectly, through redistributive mechanisms (Hamnett, 1996). With piecemeal dismantling of welfare state regimes, the promotion of holidays as an element of the quality of life is likely to become more problematic. Tourism is currently promoted more for its beneficial economic externalities than for the health and social benefits that have justified an extension of vacation rights in the past. An extension of the productivist approach to tourism and leisure is therefore taking place, in which holidays are not only seen as a necessary support for work but become an area of work in themselves (Richards, 1999).

None the less, that opportunities to go on holiday should be treated as an important indicator of social well-being was emphasized by Haukeland (1990), who interviewed non-travellers in Norway to investigate a causal relationship between social welfare and holiday opportunities. He argued that, if one's personal or household living conditions are 'unsatisfactory', these will, in most cases, restrict the quantity and quality of opportunities available to that individual. Similarly, the boundaries surrounding possible alternatives open to any individual often extend into the field of holiday travel. Within the perspective of 'social right', there is a fundamental difference between those persons who are obliged to stay at home and those who actually have the opportunity to take a vacation but still prefer to remain at home. In the latter case, the main question is whether or not a person's decision to forgo travel can be described as an effect of an unsatisfactory social situation (Haukeland, 1990).

In Fig. 2.1 Haukeland's conceptualization views the two dichotomies combined in a four-quadrant model. The simple matrix yields a typology of three different non-travelling characteristics:

- Type A represents persons who are not confronted with any obstacles to going on holiday. Their general social situation is also unproblematic. Nevertheless, these individuals prefer to stay at home in order to maximize their well-being.
- Type B is a little more complex. Here the social living conditions are satisfactory. However, other constraints prevent

these individuals from taking holiday trips. Such obstacles are either temporary or permanent.

- Type C encompasses constrained non-travellers who are placed in an unsatisfactory social situation. The problem here might relate to a welfare issue (such as lack of economic means, health resources or personal freedom) or be more complex. Non-travel under such circumstances reflects social welfare problems, and the additional lack of opportunity to go on holiday can exacerbate (a sense of) social deprivation. In certain cases non-travel can reinforce social problems.
- Type D represents unconstrained non-travel with unsatisfactory living conditions, which is a logical possibility but it probably occurs rarely.

This typology can be employed in conceptualizing non-travelling characteristics within a social welfare perspective, although, of course, the relationship between social welfare and travelling opportunities is not exhausted by this model. Constrained non-travelling (Type B) embraces more than simply the effects of unsatisfactory social living conditions (Type C). On the other hand, the fact that a problematic social situation does not necessarily lead to the forgoing of holiday travel is not reflected in Fig. 2.1, since this paradigm only relates to varieties of non-travelling. Thus an unsatisfactory social situation is neither a necessary nor a sufficient condition explaining the phenomenon of non-travel (Haukeland, 1990).

In the Type C group, an especially complex and, in some cases, diffuse pattern of factors was found to be operating. However, lack of economic means and the need to care for other members of the household were seen to be the most significant inhibitors to travel among this type of non-traveller. A characteristic shared by most of the members of this socially deprived group was an expressed desire to have the opportunity to go on holiday.

What kind of social values does holiday travel represent from the non-traveller's viewpoint? Among the Type C group, a feeling of lack of change in everyday life seemed to be the most important deprivation. Indeed, Smith and Hughes (1999) found that, for families who are rarely able to go on holiday because of personal economic and social circumstances, the meaning and significance of the rare possibilities for holiday-taking emphasized notions of 'change' and of establishing relationships.

Restricted opportunities for rest and relaxation, both mental and physical, were also much emphasized by this group. Other values associated with holiday trips, such as social contacts with other people, getting closer to nature and access to amusements and entertainment, were not emphasized in the same way by the Norwegian group. Push factors therefore appeared to be more relevant than pull factors (Dann, 1977) for the socially deprived in determining the need to take a holiday (Haukeland, 1990: 182).

Overall, however, there appears to be little in the (English-language) literature exploring the welfare consequences of being excluded from tourism and travel as part of 'everyday life'. There is even less on the effects of being restricted to experiencing vicariously some elements of it through reading about other places and cultures, being told about overseas holidays, receiving postcards and holiday souvenir gifts, viewing others' holiday photographs or camcorder videotapes, watching television holiday programmes, receiving advertising for exotic holidays and perhaps viewing websites and webcams (Moore et al., 1995: 81).

Social Tourism

Social tourism has been defined as 'the relationships and phenomena in the field of tourism resulting from participation in travel by economically weak or otherwise disadvantaged elements of society' (C.M. Hall, 2000: 141).

If it is true that there are real benefits to be derived from a holiday (especially for the disadvantaged) and that a holiday is a 'necessity', then there may well be a good case for active financial intervention in order to bring holidays within reach of such deprived persons. From a welfare perspective, access to other goods and services (such as better education, housing and employment opportunities) might receive higher priority in contributing towards an enhanced quality of life for the 'poor' (e.g. Glyptis, 1989). But, if it is the role of government to be concerned directly with the economic (and social) well-being of its citizens, then a case for a direct government subsidy for holiday-taking can be argued – whether a subsidy to the consumer or to the provider firms (Hughes, 1984).

Purely non-profit organizations for social tourism came into existence in the late 19th century. The Cooperative Holiday Association was founded in England in 1893 to provide relaxing and educationally valuable holidays. But, as noted earlier, it took some considerable time for holidays to become customary for large sections of the working populations in developed countries. Since then, promotion of social tourism has been tackled in different ways across Europe. Teuscher (1983) identified three models.

First is the northern European (Britain, Germany, Netherlands, Scandinavia) model. Here institutions of social tourism were essentially holiday organizations for everybody: applying commercial principles they catered for the holiday wishes of people with small budgets on a practical basis. 'Pleasure' was a principal objective, with educational aims and public influence not prominent. Indeed, in Scandinavian countries, the concept of 'social tourism' has meant that everybody, regardless of economic or social situation, should have the opportunity to take a holiday. But, while norms have been established to help remove physical obstacles for disabled persons, more direct wider political measures, whereby socially deprived groups are mobilized into tourism, have not been introduced, but have been the domain of private initiative through charitable organizations and special interest groups (Haukeland, 1990: 178–179).

Second, Mediterranean Europe (France and other Latin European countries): here a special structure of social tourism developed which differed considerably from commercial tourism. These countries contributed to social tourism remaining a distinct tourist activity, even though the ways of life of different socio-economic classes were converging. Non-profit associations grew substantially after 1945 (Troisgros, 1980). Contributions by the state and by social organizations allowed accommodation to be created for people with limited financial means, such that vacationers are able to use them through channels such as the social services, trade unions and similar organizations (Haulot, 1981).

Third, Central and Eastern Europe under state socialism: 'social' domestic tourism and recreation were employed as a means of implicitly improving the health and welfare of the labour force while inspiring them with a sense of local and national patriotic pride (D. Hall, 1991b: 82–89). In societies where both social and spatial mobility were inhibited to varying degrees, such opportunities were heavily subsidized from the workplace by enterprise or trade unions in terms of transport and accommodation provision, although fairly rigid methods of allocation that favoured urban industrial families were employed (Pearlman, 1990). Such a system of assured markets and limited funding available for facility upgrading often resulted in notoriously poor service quality. This characteristic has persisted to this day in some regions.

Outside Europe, similar schemes have been reported from Canada (Moulin, 1983) and South Korea (Pyo and Howell, 1988).

Within the second of the European models, the Swiss Travel Fund (REKA) was founded in 1939 as a cooperative with the purpose of encouraging travel and holidays for those of limited financial means. It was developed jointly by the tourism and transport industries, employees' associations and trade unions, employers and cooperative associations. Public authorities also participated in the early conception of the fund and have been represented on the board but without holding a dominant position (Teuscher, 1983: 216).

Initially the organization did not construct its own accommodation, merely using existing capacity in hotels, boarding houses, holiday apartments and group establishments. But in the 1950s a shortage of family accommodation led to REKA building its own accommodation establishments. A notable feature of the fund has been the 'REKA cheque', created as holiday currency. Cheques flow from the Fund to selling agents and on to consumers, and then via suppliers (over 10,000 enterprises), back to the Fund. Teuscher (1983) quotes a discount rate on tourist services of just under 14% for users of the cheques – about 600,000 Swiss households – in the early 1980s. Further, a graded rental discount of 10–50% is granted to families with lower incomes. Teuscher (1983: 218) argued that one of the prime reasons for a high intensity of annual holiday-taking in Switzerland (around 75%) has been the systematic saving for holidays represented by this system, whereby most groups within the Swiss population use institutions of social tourism at some time in their lives.

Internationally, in 1956 a movement was initiated that subsequently led to establishment of the Bureau International du Tourisme Social (BITS: <http://www.bits-int.org/>), which now has a large number of affiliated organizations scattered around the world. The Bureau seeks to establish the right to a paid vacation and to provide those on low income with subsidized travel. For example, in Spain the government has aided its pensioners to enjoy holidays in off-peak periods in areas like Majorca – a policy that benefits pensioners and enables hotels to retain trained staff and generate income over otherwise slack periods of the year. BITS promotes the concepts of low-cost 'vacation villages', of camping sites and of a form of tourism that benefits the vacationer, the host and the environment within which they meet.

In the 1970s the English Tourist Board (ETB) and the Trades Union Congress (TUC), through a social tourism study group, examined the issue of holidays for the disadvantaged (Social Tourism Study Group, 1976; TUC and ETB, 1980). The study analysed the experience gained from a programme of subsidized holidays by London boroughs designed to give socially deprived people, especially the elderly and handicapped, the opportunity to go on holiday. The study was undertaken among the local authorities responsible, and all boroughs involved in the programme emphasized the importance for social well-being of giving relief to caring relatives.

It was argued that these holidays provided an essential break for members of the family who had to carry the long-term burdens of emotional, mental and physiological stress. In relation to their clients, most boroughs referred to the benefits of a change in environment. Particularly among people who were tied to the home and had limited mobility, the daily routine of activity was often very narrow. Anticipation of and looking back on the holiday were considered to be almost as valuable as the holiday itself. Relief from boredom and a broadening of experience were more deeply felt here than among normal holidaymakers (Haukeland, 1990).

Subsequently, the Holiday Care service was established in 1981 to hold and distribute details of holidays for the disadvantaged. The service is a charity financed by donations which now provides holiday information for those with a physical disability (Holiday Care, 2005). Partly because of the widespread availability of low-cost accommodation in the UK – including holiday camps, caravans, camping and boarding houses – more radical policies for extending holiday participation were not recommended by the group.

Low-income groups in the UK have also been the concern of organizations such as the charity Family Holidays Association (founded in 1975), which provides holiday grants for deprived families under pressure. The Pearsons Holiday Fund (founded 1892) exists to send children from inner cities on seaside and country holidays. Kids Out is a national charity providing special days out for disadvantaged and special needs children as well as financial assistance and breaks for young carers, parents and families across the UK. In 2004 Kids Out helped over 40,000 children and their families (Kids Out, 2005). Splash, an Association of British Travel Agents (ABTA) tour operator, offers low-price holidays for one-parent families. Other initiatives have been pursued to aid single parents and disabled groups. In the 1980s, a pressure group for single parents, Gingerbread, negotiated an early-season (usually pre-Easter) holiday for single parents with one of the major holiday camp/resort chains, Butlins. Butlins charged off-peak prices and used the opportunity to train new staff prior to the start of the main season. In 1998 the Deptford (south-east London) branch of Gingerbread alone ran 15 trips to theme parks and seaside resorts for its membership of solo parents (Ryan, 2002: 18–19). But there remains a lack of both public awareness of and research into such organizations, which are mainly drawn from the charitable and voluntary sector (Turner et al., 2001; Hunter-Jones, 2004: 256).

The advocates of extending holiday participation argue that it should not be seen simply as a charitable, altruistic exercise of inclusion or as just exploiting a hitherto untapped market, but as an investment in the well-being and fabric of society (Hughes, 1991: 195–196). The fact that better-positioned socio-economic groups are taking advantage of increasing tourism opportunities reinforces the notion that holidays are seen as a positive and necessary part of life.

Age, Gender and Responsibility

Attempts to integrate older people into youthful societies have often failed to recognize the qualitatively different yet positive aspects of a holiday in older age and the constraints that older people may face. While the tourism industry has increasingly stressed the financial value of the senior market (see below), poverty is all too prevalent for many elderly persons, especially women. Domestic responsibilities,

caring for others, coping with bereavement (including the loss of a travel companion), physical difficulties or concerns over personal safety represent constraints and responsibilities for older women tourists that have not been well researched (Small, 2003: 37, 31). Factors influencing holiday-taking that have been recognized in more recent studies of senior citizens include increased leisure time after retirement, discretionary spending money and deteriorating health (e.g. Dann, 2001; Fleischer and Pizam, 2002).

Although many older people lead active, busy lives, there are growing numbers of older people also experiencing social isolation and loneliness. Women are more likely to experience this, given their propensity to live longer than men. Lack of awareness about community services and cultural and/or religious or language barriers may contribute to such social isolation. On the other hand, structural ageing may well increase the number of older people wishing to participate in volunteering, and this has the potential to strengthen communities and reduce the risk of isolation for older people (Jackson, 2003: 16–17).

'Demographic compression' – when a number of key life events, such as finding a partner, birth of children, home purchase and caring for aged parents, become compressed into a shorter space of the overall life cycle – is a growing phenomenon, particularly in mid-working and older working age. The demands of caring both for dependent children and for ageing parents are likely to increase as populations continue to age. In Australia, 2.3 million people look after relatives who are elderly or have a disability or illness, in addition to looking after children. More than half of all such carers (59%) combine their caring role with paid work, and the majority work full-time. Most people providing care are in older working age groups, and most of those caring for a parent are women (73%) (Jackson, 2003: 14).

Gladwell and Bedini (2004) suggest that the constraints on leisure travel for informal family caregivers, both with and away from their care recipients, fall into three distinct areas: physical, social and emotional, with the latter being the most notable. They conclude that:

- a particular sense of loss of freedom is felt after commencing caregiving, with reduced leisure travel acting as a symbol of a circumscribed environment;
- while many caregivers still travel, their motivation changes from leisure to more functional purposes; and
- many spousal caregivers are unwilling to travel alone, unfettered, as they would miss and worry about their spouse.

It is clear that tourism and hospitality professionals need to develop methods to reduce the worries and increase the quality of the travel experiences for caregivers and others in similar constrained positions. Gladwell and Bedini (2004) cite as good practice Marriott Corporation's provision of respite opportunities for caregivers: if a caregiver is going on vacation, his/her care recipient can receive short-term respite care at one of Marriott's assisted-living and special needs facilities. These offer medical supervision and assistance with daily living needs by trained staff, as well as socialization with other guests and residents.

Tourism and Disability

According to the Americans with Disabilities Act of 1990 (ADA), a person with a disability is defined as one with a physical or mental impairment that substantially limits one or more major life activities. A major life activity includes caring for one's self, performing manual tasks, walking, seeing, hearing, speaking, breathing, learning, working and participating in community activities (LaPlante, 1991).

About one in five Americans has some form of disability and one in ten has a severe disability (Kraus et al., 1996). The number of people with disabilities is expected to rise to around 100 million by the year 2030 (Burnett and Bender-Baker, 2001: 4). Between 1990 and 2020 the population aged 65 to 74 could grow by as much as 74%, while the population under 65 would increase by only 24% (Lawson and Kinsella, 1996).

Although a number of researchers addressed disability issues in the late 1980s and early 1990s (e.g. Driedger, 1987; Smith, 1987; Murray and Sproats, 1990; Muloin, 1992), until relatively recently, little research had been published examining tourism and disability (Darcy, 1998, 2002; Burnett and Bender-Baker, 2001).

Darcy (2002) illustrates how attitudes to people with disabilities in general, and research about people with disabilities in particular, have evolved significantly over the past 25 years, following a wider discourse on disability that emerged as a coherent theme during the late 1950s (Tregakis, 2002). Initially, attitudes to and research about disability were conceptualized in a framework of personal tragedy, with the focus on the individual's impairment. The person was treated as a victim who has suffered personal misfortune. Since then, the emergence of disability political movements has seen the emphasis shift from a personal tragedy to disability as a form of social oppression. Thus, 'the social model of disability does not deny an individual's impairment but strongly states that the resultant disabilities are a product of socially constructed barriers that exclude or segregate people with impairments from participation in mainstream social activities' (Darcy, 2002: 63).

The way that disability is conceptualized and consequent attitudes have a profound effect on society and people with disabilities:

- attitudes influence individual and public behaviour towards people with disabilities (Antonak and Livneh, 1988). Understanding disability as an 'abnormality' of the person rather than as a societal shortcoming shapes the behaviours that lead to isolation and marginalization (Imrie, 1997, 2000). In many cases the behaviours are not intentional but rather stem from the 'non-disabled bias' of common societal practices (Peat, 1997);

- attitudes inform public opinion, which influences public policy, allocation of resources (Chamberlain, 1998) and access to education, transport and employment (Walker, 1983); and
- the prevailing attitudes influence the self-concept of persons with a disability themselves (Walker, 1983). Surrounded by negative attitudes, people with disability may internalize negative attitudes and beliefs (Beckwith and Matthews, 1995; Imrie, 1997). Their personal identity and social interaction/integration are affected, as are their demands for service and policy development (Wang, 1992).

Importantly, from a tourism perspective, this change in attitude means that the conceptualization of disability involves both the impairment and socially constructed barriers. It is recognized that the nature and severity of the impairment may have an effect on the range of activities a person may participate in and may also influence how the tourism experience is shaped.

It is also recognized that participation in tourism is as much a right of people with disabilities as it is of the able-bodied population. Socially constructed barriers, including attitudes of tourism industry workers, should not dictate an individual's ability to travel. To bring order to this complexity, in 2001 the World Health Organization issued a revised version of the International Classification of Functioning, building on the United Nations (UN) Declaration on the Rights of Disabled Persons (1975) and UN Standard Rules for the Equalization of Opportunities (1993). It recognizes that participation in society is the right of all individuals and that participation is a complex interaction between body function/structure, activity participation and the environment. The environment is conceptualized as both physical and attitudinal, such that either or both can hinder or facilitate people's participation. Responsibility for barriers and/or facilitators within the environment is firmly placed at the societal level. As such, it becomes incumbent on all sectors of the community

to implement strategies to minimize both physical and attitudinal constraints. This has clear implications for tourism stakeholders.

Crude marketing approach

A familiar refrain in the industry literature revolves around the notion that more attention needs to be paid to the disabled, because they, together with family and friends, represent a potentially significant, but often ignored, market (Yau *et al.*, 2004). In the USA, the *Wall Street Journal* has referred to disabled people as the 'next consumer niche' (Prager, 1999): a large and growing 'group' which has more money to spend than often assumed. According to the US Census Bureau (Kahn, 2000), 50 million disabled consumers in the USA have $1 trillion at their disposal (Fost, 1998). Attempting to reach 'this powerful consumer group' represents for Ray and Ryder (2003) good 'handicapitalism' (a term, we are told, first used by Prager, 1999). For them, businesses seen to be reaching out to people with disabilities by removing physical barriers to travel will exhibit apparent concern for diversity and sensitivity (Williams, 1999).

In the UK, the English Tourism Council (ETC, 2000) followed the national government's aim of trying to increase access to tourism for all pursuant to the 1995 Disability Discrimination Act (DDA). It also drew attention to the economic potential of the market for disabled tourists with the explicit intent of defining the business opportunities of widening access. The ETC estimated that there were ten million disabled people in the UK. This was based on a wide interpretation of disability that gave relatively high estimates – accounting for about 15% of the total population – in an attempt to highlight the market potential (Shaw and Coles, 2004; see also Woodhams and Corby, 2003). The ETC (2000) argued that an estimated 2.7 million disabled people in England had a propensity to take domestic holidays. Other reports have strengthened this perspective, identifying a potential spend of around £17,000 million from disabled people who would holiday within Europe if appropriate facilities were available and barriers removed (Deloitte Touche, 1993).

However, the situation is more complex than such a simplistic marketing approach might suggest, because of the range of disabilities and associated physical and economic constraints, partly conditioned by the relationship between age and disability. While in the UK 5% of the age group 15–24 are disabled (e.g. see Aitchison, 2000), this figure rises to 30% for the age group 65–74 and over 80% for those aged over 85. Clearly, the expectations, experiences and meanings of holidays are likely to vary across such age groups, and disabled people represent not one market, but a series of different sub-markets and a range of constraints on mobility. For example, financial restrictions associated with disability restrict access to the world of work, and the experiences of such disabled people are ones of marginalized groups and do not reflect the strong market potential optimistically presented by tourism agencies (Shaw and Coles, 2004). At the broader level, it is necessary to position many disabled people within Haukeland's (1990) so-called group of 'constrained' tourists: people who want to travel, but are constrained through personal circumstance such as illness or lack of money.

Others have argued that the tourism industry should be more considerate of disabled tourism, not only for business purposes or to comply with legal requirements, but for reasons of corporate citizenship in helping to create a more inclusive society (Phillips, 2002). Yet the industry often appears reluctant to engage with the changes required to meet the needs of disabled visitors (AHLA, 2000), and has lobbied governments in the USA (Elliott, 2000) and the UK (*Financial Mail*, 2000) to reduce requirements for the provision of accessible accommodation (Yau *et al.*, 2004). Phillips (2002: A48) suggests that there exists a fear of displacement: that 'too many' disabled customers will deflect core business.

This raises two important and related issues:

- if disabled people are not to be treated differently, then all types of services and destinations need to welcome them and improve access. If this does not happen, then disabled tourists will remain marginalized to varying degrees; and
- certain destinations may be seen as only catering for the disabled, creating concentrations of discrimination. To a limited extent this has started to happen in a number of UK seaside resorts. Notions of corporate citizenship therefore need to become part of the debate within tourism if these problems are to be avoided.

It is therefore possible to recognize a growing interest in disabled people within the tourism industry, although much of this interest is based on a somewhat narrow agenda that increasingly sees the disabled tourist as a potentially lucrative market waiting to be tapped. At the policy level, the main emphasis is increasingly based on unlocking this potential by improving facilities and access.

Constraints/barrier models

Until recently, few studies have explored the usefulness of the leisure constraints framework in the tourism context (Hinch and Jackson, 2000). In recent years there have been a number of contributions to the understanding of constraints on participation in tourism activities (Gilbert and Hudson, 2000; Fleischer and Pizam, 2002; Pennington-Gray and Kerstetter, 2002).

Constraints on leisure were originally defined as barriers to participation (Nyaupane *et al.*, 2004). Francken and van Raaij (1981) viewed perceived barriers to leisure participation as either internal (capacities, abilities, knowledge and interests) or external (lack of time or money, geographical distance and lack of facilities) to the participant. Iso-Ahola and Mannell

(1985) recognized three categories of constraints: social-personal, social-cultural and physical. Smith (1987) also identified three main types of barriers: (i) environmental, including attitudinal, architectural and ecological factors; (ii) interactive barriers relating to skill challenge incongruities and communication barriers; and (iii) intrinsic barriers associated with each participant's own physical, psychological or cognitive functioning level. Of these, intrinsic barriers were felt to be the greatest obstacle. Feelings of incompetence in leisure activity may, over time, lead to feelings of generalized helplessness, resulting in reduced future participation (Murray and Sproats, 1990).

Subsequent research and analysis challenged the use of the term 'barriers', suggesting that 'constraints' are in fact more complex and comprehensive. Further, notions of 'participation' were also challenged, recognizing that constraints influence far more than the choice to participate or not (Jackson and Scott, 1999). Out of such debates, the definition of leisure constraints came to be embedded in the three categories that have been consistently supported by published research: intrapersonal, interpersonal and structural (e.g. Crawford and Godbey, 1987; Smith, 1987; Turco et al., 1998; Hawkins et al., 1999; Jackson and Scott, 1999). The classic hierarchical constraints model (Crawford et al., 1991) established the dynamic nature of the categories while emphasizing the necessity of studying them simultaneously (Daniels et al., 2005):

- intrapersonal constraints are associated with a person's psychological state, physical functioning or cognitive abilities (Smith, 1987) and include areas such as stress, anxiety, lack of knowledge, health-related problems and social ineffectiveness. Intrapersonal constraints have also been conceptualized as antecedent constraints in that certain intrapersonal factors, such as personality and socialization, may predispose individuals to participate in or avoid certain leisure activities (Henderson et al., 1988; Scott, 1991);

- interpersonal constraints are those arising out of social interaction or relationships among people within social contexts (Scott, 1991): they can occur during interactions with an individual's social network, service providers or strangers, or because one lacks a partner with whom to engage in some leisure activity (Crawford and Godbey, 1987). Smith (1987: 381) states that the dependency on others may severely restrict pleasure travel if an individual has 'maladaptive social relationships with caregivers and service providers'; and

- structural or environmental constraints are said to intervene between preferences and participation (Crawford and Godbey, 1987) and include financial challenges, lack of time, transport difficulties and regulations.

The conceptualization of constraints as negotiable emerged in the early 1990s, offering a refinement to the leisure constraints body of knowledge. Scott (1991) asserted that constraints were not necessarily insurmountable; instead, people might find a way to modify behaviours to sustain leisure involvement. This perspective proposed that people 'negotiate around' constraints employing a variety of strategies, 'achieving their leisure goals, but often in a way that differs from how their leisure would have been if constraints had been absent' (Jackson, 1999: 196).

Yet Richter and Richter (1999) contended that, at an international level, neglecting to establish travel standards for persons with disabilities posed growing ethical dilemmas relating to health, security and accessibility. Cavinato and Cuckovich (1992) concluded that services must go beyond what is required by law to fully address the constraints faced by travellers with disabilities. In examining legal measures adopted to facilitate air travel by individuals with disabilities, Abeyratne (1995) recommended 76 guidelines pertaining to individualized services in areas such as flight reservations, airport transport and on-board facilities. He concluded that, while progress had been made in several areas, increased recognition of the disadvantages faced by travellers with disabilities was needed. This included the needs of their carers, as well as international action and commitment to reduce air transport barriers (Daniels *et al.*, 2005): for example, toilet facilities on aircraft cannot accommodate carers with care recipients because of the minute size of the compartments. Many airports have revamped their walkways to accommodate wheelchair users and yet check-in counters have not been modified and remain too high (although there are ways to avoid face-to-face check-in procedures: e.g. see Frary, 2005).

Gladwell and Bedini (2004) found that the primary physical constraints on leisure travel included accessibility of facilities and services, time to prepare, mobility and energy. Despite legislative change, accessibility of services was still a constraint on travel, notably in relation to accommodation. The time required to prepare for a trip or an outing was often a problem, and some tours, for example, did not allow for travellers who required more time to get ready in the morning or for slow walking. Indeed, a significant physical limitation identified was the loss of physical stamina and energy experienced by the disabled when they travel.

Social constraints included the importance of financial, family and human service support. For some, lack of support from family members posed a barrier to their leisure travel. The most prominent theme that emerged within this area, however, dealt with the support of service providers. A significant and arguably critical limiting factor (e.g. Oliver, 1989; Devine and Dattilo, 2001) is the attitude and perceived skill level of the people within travel businesses when serving individuals with varying types of disabilities (Bedini, 2000). Closely related to attitudes of service providers are those of other individuals on tours and in public places.

Sensitivity training is needed to address attitudes (and ignorance) among some service providers in the various facets of the tourism and hospitality industries. The education and training of tourism

services need to keep pace with demographic trends and the needs of increasingly older tourists with disabilities. Providing adequate tourism opportunities and services is not only a legal responsibility but a moral obligation (Card, 2003). Training programmes for providers on how to anticipate and meet the needs of people with disabilities would aid in providing more satisfying travel experiences. A disability etiquette training programme developed by American Airlines for all its airport customer contact staff is an example of such training.

Daniels *et al.* (2005) conclude that:

- the study of travel needs and constraints for individuals with disabilities is clearly still in its infancy;
- the limited breadth of data collection and reporting methods employed suggests a need for greater diversity in forms of information gathering and dissemination;
- research tends to segment tourism constraints, treating them statistically rather than illustrating how they interact. Little is known about how travel constraints interrelate or how travellers with disabilities balance constraint types with negotiation strategies; and
- individuals with disabilities are consistently faced with unique travel constraints that are not being clearly or consistently addressed by tourism managers.

Overcoming constraints

Yau *et al.* (2004) explored the tourism experiences of individuals who develop mobility or visual impairments and recognized five stages in the process of becoming active travellers. They suggested that a better understanding of these stages can help create greater awareness of the tourism needs of people with disabilities.

Personal stage – acceptance and reintegration

Coming to terms with disability is necessary before tourism is seen as even a hypothetical possibility, and is a necessary part of becoming an active member of the family, the community and wider society. However, as a leisure pursuit, travel is not a priority during the rehabilitation process anyway. Rather, the focus is on learning to look after oneself.

Reconnection stage – exploration for future travelling

This entails a process of integration where the individual begins to become established in community life. This can be a challenging period of self-discovery, personal empowerment and growth. Again, little tourism occurs as the individual focuses on learning to live independently, although this varies between cultures (e.g. Tseng et al., 1995). At this stage some people begin to travel again, but efforts are tentative: first experiences expose the person to stereotypes of how those with disabilities are expected to behave. To avoid this, many travel with family members or close friends or join a tour organized for people with disabilities. Some with newly acquired 'hidden' disabilities, such as visual impairments, may even try to disguise their disabilities. Others with obvious disabilities suggest that travel may be a positive experience as they find the public is more willing to help, even to the extent of disrupting their routines and ignoring wishes to be left alone.

Travel analysis stage – search for information

The process changes from tourism as an abstract concept to resolving the practical concerns relating to ensuring a safe and enjoyable experience, such that the tourist must consider and resolve a range of issues. For some, the task may be too daunting, but for others, with increasing experience, the type and magnitude of considerations grow smaller. Detailed pre-planning is often required at a level and extent far greater than required for able-bodied counterparts. There is a constant need to verify the accuracy of published information: the respondents of Yau et al. (2004) often found it to be wrong or misleading. Significantly for the

industry in this respect, Turco et al. (1998) suggested that people with disabilities are more likely to be disproportionately loyal to businesses (such as specific travel agents and hotels) that best serve their needs or provide them with positive experiences.

Physical journey stage – compensation and compromise

People with disabilities must make compromises and adopt a number of compensatory strategies to manage the experience. Some relate to adjusting to unsuitable accommodation, dealing with architectural and ecological barriers, forsaking certain activities in order to allow extra time to return to an assembly point, and not visiting attractions with others in the group because of inaccessibility. In extreme cases, tourists with disabilities are forced to adopt drastic coping strategies. Yau et al. (2004) reported that some of their respondents dehydrated themselves on long-haul flights so that they would have to go to the toilet less frequently. One participant with quadriplegia also indicated he would eat less food before a trip so that he would be less likely to defecate during the journey. Many seek innovative strategies to visit sites that are high on their priority list but they must often rely on the advice of others regarding which places are accessible or not. Yau et al. (2004) suggest that most disabled travellers adhere to the advice even if their abilities are underestimated, and that the perceived loss of opportunities to travel and visit represents an additional real loss the individual must adjust to (Mumma, 1986; Lindgren, 1996). The need for altered strategies when planning and taking a holiday inevitably has an impact on enjoyment of the experience, and relatively inexperienced tourists in particular can feel that compromises significantly impair their enjoyment of travel.

Experimentation and reflection stage – different tastes of travelling

If the person has a positive tourism experience, they will be motivated to do it again.

On the other hand, as was speculated by Smith (1987), if the experience is negative or if the individual is not ready to travel, future tourism activities will be affected. As the person becomes a more experienced tourist, they will learn appropriate strategies to maximize enjoyment. Tourists with disabilities are often forced to accept more expensive arrangements than those of able-bodied travellers. In order to have companions, they may have to make many compromises, in terms of destination, travel mode, time and date of travelling.

Yau *et al.* (2004) conclude that, for those with disabilities becoming active travellers, tourism represents a metaphor of recovery.

Gatekeepers

Despite more than 25 years of political advocacy by disabled groups, much ignorance, fear and discrimination towards people with disabilities continues to exist. Overcoming constraints to pleasure travel requires the coordination of individuals with disabilities, social networks and service providers. Industry service providers act as important gatekeepers to travel participation, both in terms of their attitude and in the quality of information and other services they provide.

Miller and Kirk (2002) explored the extent to which the UK's tourism industry had adopted the 'access for all' standards as set forth in the 1995 Disability Discrimination Act (DDA). Their research suggested that 'the overall picture is one of non-understanding, or misunderstanding' (Miller and Kirk, 2002: 88) of how to address the needs of potential customers with disabilities. They concluded that there is a gap in the quality of services offered to individuals with disabilities in comparison to other travellers. Importantly, their findings reflect an insufficient level of service in a country where strict standards and a commission to enforce those standards are in place (Daniels *et al.*, 2005).

The success of travel agents relies on their ability to provide products that suit clients' needs and wants. An understanding of those needs and wants, coupled with deep product knowledge, is implicit in this assertion. However, a number of sources question both the quality and accuracy of the advice they provide. Travel agents may offer reliable information for mainstream tourists (see Chapter 3) but, for a variety of reasons, they may not serve the needs of special populations particularly well. Indeed, rather than breaking down constraints to travel for people with disabilities, travel agents may actually create an additional obstacle (McKercher *et al.*, 2003).

Further research is needed to explore the training and strategies employed by service providers to assist travellers with disabilities in overcoming constraints. Particular research attention should concentrate on communication. Dattilo and Smith (1990: 10) emphasized the need for professionals to use 'people first' language in order to communicate respect and positive attitudes towards individuals with disabilities. While this is common in therapeutic recreation research and practice, it has not been adopted sufficiently by tourism managers.

In terms of changing attitudes, three strategies need to be more widely adopted by the travel industry if participation in tourism within generating countries is to be rendered more inclusive:

- a deeper experience of people with disabilities and others experiencing constraints (Eberhardt and Mayberry, 1995);
- simulation exercises (Grayson and Marini, 1996; Marini, 1996; Conill, 1998); and
- opportunities to obtain accurate information, for example through training seminars or discussion groups (Marini, 1996; Pernice and Lys, 1996; Timms *et al.*, 1997).

There are strong ethical and industry arguments for facilitating greater access for physically, psychologically and financially constrained groups. However, this needs to be placed within the wider global context of: (i) lack of tourism participation by large numbers of citizens of poorer countries; and (ii) the increasingly dangerous global environmental pressures that existing levels of travel and tourism are contributing to.

A Global Rationing System for Travel?

The first article of the *Tourism Bill of Rights*, based on the *United Nations' Universal Declaration of Human Rights*, specifically mentions 'the right of everyone to rest and leisure . . . and freedom of movement without limitation, within the bounds of the law' (WTO, 1985, Article 1). What the Bill does not acknowledge, however, is the impossibility of exercising such rights if a much greater proportion of the planet's population was in a position to do so. Ironically, true equity would render the right wholly unrealizable. There should also be clearly articulated responsibilities accompanying the rights enunciated. These might include: to use the freedom to travel sensibly, mindful of its potential natural and cultural resource depletion and degrading abilities, and to acknowledge the privileged position that being able to travel for recreational purposes represents.

That international tourism consumption is mainly the privilege of citizens from developed industrial countries would appear iniquitous and contrary to the Bill. Mihalič (1999) has argued that a tourism emission trading programme could provide governments with an efficient tool for obtaining both constraints on and equity in international tourism consumption by offering financial compensation for not travelling. Travellers would hold tourism permits equal to the value of their travel consumption units. If these proved insufficient, they would have to buy permits from participants who travel less. Non-travellers would be compensated for not travelling, and developing world nations would thus gain financial resources in compensation for their lower travel propensity. Such a programme would assist control of the growth of tourism by limiting the total number of certificates.

The most renowned best practice model of tradable permit systems is the case of sulphur dioxide (SO_2) emissions in the USA. The SO_2 allowance trading programme was introduced under the auspices of the Clean Air Act in 1990. Within the European Union, a carbon dioxide (CO_2) emissions trading programme has been suggested (IPE, 1998). Both cases refer to pure pollution certificates that aim to reduce the quantity of pollution emissions. The question of current and intergenerational equity in development, for example the distribution of SO_2 and CO_2 pollution rights among different nations today and in the past, has not been addressed.

The same number of certificates could be issued to everyone, and thus indicate every person's equal right to travel and consume the environment. Basic questions pertaining to their use would include who would be entitled to issue tourist certificates and the extent of their entitlement. Mihalič (1999) argued that certificates must be issued at the international level and their numbers could be determined on the basis of the desired rate of growth in international tourism within a certain year. Certificates could then be distributed among countries according to numbers of citizens.

Obvious issues raised by this include the question of who would act as the distribution agency, how to guarantee the system would not be corrupt or corrupted and the not inconsiderable issue of business travel and tourism. Would the latter case be covered by the distribution to individuals, perhaps allowing for variations in quota based on an individual's employment (a complicated and possibly expensive process), with business organizations trading on those individuals' allocations, or would each business have its own quota? If the former, organizations could outbid individuals such that travel and tourism would be skewed much more towards business as the highest payer and then to bigger and more profitable business. This would see the illogical outcome of further domination of tourism and travel – in this case its consumption – by transnational corporations (TNCs).

Also problematic is the question surrounding the unit of measure of certificates (travel consumption unit), which, Mihalič (1999) suggests, could be an overnight stay, a cross-border visit or even an activity. She then argues that the simplest solution would be the designation of a single overnight stay as a basic unit of measure. But day visitors may inflict high levels of ecological damage. More logically, a formula encompassing distance travelled combined with mode of travel might be the most appropriate in terms of resulting environmental externalities, while not being too complicated to apply. Carbon-equivalent energy notionally consumed would appear the most obvious and potentially the least unrealistic measure.

Further, why, as Mihalič (1999) implies, should this system omit domestic tourism and travel? This is greatest in the most developed and physically largest countries, notably in the USA, where it is accompanied by the greatest levels of fuel consumption.

Mihalič (1999) suggested that certificates could be differentiated according to season: a given year would be divided into three to five seasons, and certificates would apply to a specific season and a specific number of travel consumption units. Certificates valid for the high season would dictate a higher market price in comparison with off-season and low-season certificates, which, in turn, she argues, would contribute to reducing the seasonality of tourist demand. Yet, while one could account for the different timing of seasons in different hemispheres, even within one country different activities have different peak seasons (winter sports compared with summer sun compared with spring/autumn wildlife tourism), thus complicating such an approach.

Clearly any scheme to 'reallocate' access to tourism and travel appears, at the time of writing, not to be on the political agenda as, superficially, its pursuit would not be in the electoral interests of generating-country governments. None the less, this could easily change as a result of:

(i) popular, and thus governmental, appreciation of the urgency to act to reduce climate change and transport's contribution to it; and (ii) current less developed countries (LDCs) flexing their political muscle in seeking greater equitable access to travel and tourism as a basic human right and desirable consumable resource. These arguments are taken up again in Chapter 8.

Summary and Conclusion

Despite the massive growth in tourism over the past few decades and its apparent 'trickle-down' spread from an elite to a mass market in the major generating countries, at a global level taking a holiday remains a minority activity. Lack of income, particularly but by no means exclusively within the less developed countries, physical or mental impairment and a shortage of time – because of either work commitments or the need to provide constant care for others – are some of the most serious constraints on a person's ability to participate in tourism. Although some public authorities (and charities) have made efforts to improve access to tourism for those not currently participating, such efforts are themselves dependent on wider political–economic structures and attitudes to welfare provision. The market potential offered by some sections of the non-holiday-taking population within existing generating countries seems now to be recognized by the industry very much for its profit-generating possibilities rather than because of any ethically driven desire to maximize public welfare. Perhaps it would be naive to expect otherwise.

What is also significant, as explored in Chapter 5, is that governments and aid sources from the developed countries are now putting some effort into encouraging poor people in less developed countries to participate in tourism production, implicitly to serve mostly international tourists from developed countries. Does this suggest a global approach to perpetuate a master–servant relationship while protecting the dominant position of 'Westerners' as tourism consumers?

This chapter has evaluated access to and participation in tourism and the constraints that may inhibit or prevent certain groups in society – and indeed certain societies – from such participation. It can be concluded that:

- current inequalities in access in generating countries, a theme that tends to dominate the rapidly emerging literature in this area, emphasize poverty and disability as major factors inhibiting participation, but often fail to bring the two together or to consider the ripple of impacts that the pressures of poverty and disability, separately or together, exert on a wide range of kin, carers and friends;
- wider global inequalities are reflected in the balance of tourism participation being dominated by generation from developed countries and regions, with little or no participation taking place from the poorest countries; and
- an immediate ethical dilemma presents itself – if wider participation in (international) tourism is a likely outcome of improving living standards in less developed countries, to embrace the hundreds of millions of people living in Africa, Asia and Latin America, this is likely to place an (even greater) unsustainable burden on the planet.

Thus, as academics, teachers, practitioners, tourists and commentators already drawn into tourism processes, we face a potential personal sense of hypocrisy:

- we want to see tourism participation increased and access improved for those currently constrained from doing so;
- in contrast, despite (cynical?) international declarations on rights to tourism and travel, we hesitate to contemplate the broadening of tourism participation globally: (i) because of the ethical dilemma it poses for the already threatened global environment; and (ii) because it may also threaten our own (already unsustainable, over-consuming) privileges in access to and participation in tourism and travel activity.

By adopting a welfare-centred approach to the question of access to tourism, we hope to have highlighted an under-researched area and to have explored how and why many people are not able to enjoy the benefits of taking a holiday. In the next chapter we turn our attention to those who are able to be actual tourists.

3

The Welfare of Tourists: Dimensions, Responsibilities and Implications

Expectations are high, with a year's worth of stress to relieve and the pressure to have a good time.

(Sheila Keegan quoted in Scott, 2005)

Box 3.1. Chapter aims and summary.

This chapter seeks to: demonstrate how a welfare focus can illuminate a variety of policy-related issues concerning the well-being of tourists.
It does this by: employing a tourist welfare cycle framework, within which the chapter discusses some of the health benefits and domestic stresses, risks and responsibilities of taking a holiday.
Its key concepts are: tourist welfare cycle, well-being, responsibility, post-holiday syndromes.
It concludes that: locating responsibility for the welfare of tourists before, during and after taking holidays is a complex and yet critical requirement for improved well-being for both tourists and the tourism industry.

Introduction: Tourism as Well-being?

The common assumption that holidays are beneficial for those taking them appears to be supported by such contentions that 95% of British doctors recommend holidays as an alternative to medication, especially when patients have stress-related ailments. Australian research has indicated that most people enjoy a lessening of tension and fatigue after the first 4 or 5 days of holiday (Norfolk, 1994). Yet we have seen in recent years a marked growth in the literature on tourism and risk, accidents, ill health, terrorism, safety and security (e.g. Smith, 1999; Lepp and Gibson, 2003; Page *et al.*, 2005; Peattie *et al.*, 2005). This might suggest the limited or questionable welfare value of taking a holiday. There are irony and paradox in such apparent threats to tourism, qualities that are reflected in a number of trends:

- international tourism continues to grow, while tourists and the tourism industry continue to seek out new destinations and activities, so that more people are travelling to more and different places while pursuing different activities in those places, seeking out more distant and 'exotic' (and therefore unfamiliar) environments (Habib and Behrens, 2000): thus tourists are penetrating ever more cultures and environments alongside other globalizing processes;
- although tourism has tended to be characterized as largely risk-averse, certain tourism and recreation activities, such

Table 3.1. Components of the tourist welfare cycle.

Cycle elements	Key factors	Key concepts	Implications
Preparation	Availability of information	Security, safety, health, risk	Travel company information and communication practices
Anticipation	Travelling companions	Well-being	More research needed
Travel	Mode, time, distance	Stress, DVT, flexibility	Can be made much less stressful. Can be an important part of the tourist experience
The destination experience	Motivation, behaviour, activities	Common sense	Tourist responsibility is critical
Post-holiday syndromes	Reflection	Recirculation, readjustment	Wider modification of destination perceptions. Readjustment can raise questions of home and work life

as adventure tourism, are becoming potentially more dangerous as more less-skilled and less well-equipped participants seek to share what may be seen as lifestyle-determining activities. Partly as a result, risk assessment and management have become important considerations, to protect the operator as much as the tourist; and

• whether a reality or not, for many, the world has been made to appear a more dangerous place to be travelling in. As such, considerations of safety and security, following major violent incidents involving forms of transport and centres of tourism, have risen dramatically in the list of priorities for the industry and the regulatory frameworks within which it operates.

Tourism is being seen increasingly as an important element in the quality of life (see Chapter 1), as a key component of lifestyle and a crucial element of the work–life balance. But, at the same time, there is a growing secondary reaction to the impacts of tourists' activities, particularly if characterized as self-absorbed and individualistic 'niche' pursuits. There appears to be an inherent implausibility in the claims of sustainability attached to such activities (e.g. Mowforth and Munt, 1998).

In attempting to conceptualize the tourist experience, Gunn (1988) recognized

three key stages: the creation of pre-image, participation and evaluation. The holiday experience begins with the collection of information about likely or possible destinations, before confirming arrangements through making reservations, setting dates and making special purchases (Ryan, 1991, 1994). This chapter recognizes that there are further elements of the tourist cycle with clear welfare implications, and we suggest that the tourist 'welfare cycle' (Table 3.1) can be characterized as being composed of:

• preparation;
• anticipation;
• the experience of travel, transport and the journey;
• the destination experience; and
• post-holiday syndromes.

Although these elements have been subject to unequal levels of attention and research, they are employed to structure the rest of this chapter.

Preparation

Maximizing tourist welfare requires a realistic appreciation of the opportunities and potential threats any destination or experience might offer, and being suitably prepared – physically and mentally – for them. If holidays are to enhance, or to at least maintain, the welfare of those taking them, there follow important considerations:

- What are the welfare consequences of such tourist aspirations for the other stakeholders in tourism processes, including other tourists?
- How far do behavioural, structural and other circumstances of the tourism industry condition such welfare attainment?
- How far do potential tourists receive the reliable and impartial sources of information about conditions in destination countries that they need to optimize both their own welfare and that of those they encounter?

The potential risks to tourists, while not new, have been brought into sharp focus in recent years through terrorist incidents, kidnappings, air disasters, concerns about deep vein thrombosis (DVT) and the incidence of diseases such as SARS. The 1989 Hague Declaration on Tourism states that the safety, security and protection of tourists and respect for their dignity are the preconditions for the development of tourism.

The literature on the (potential/likely/supposed) impacts of terrorism and instability has grown exponentially as a concomitant of the transatlantic 'war on terror'. Reflecting this, and emphasizing an apparent growing tourist concern for security, Lepp and Gibson (2003) identified terrorism, war and political instability, health and crime in their literature review of what they referred to as 'major risk factors' for international tourists.

Individuals are exposed to risk constantly, whether working, at leisure in the home or on holiday, near or far. But there are particular factors relating to travel, and to being in a foreign environment, which make tourists particularly vulnerable (Peattie *et al.*, 2005), and which demand appropriate preparation:

- transport risks: travelling poses specific risks related to transport accidents, hijackings, contracting DVT or driving while jet-lagged (especially on the 'wrong' side of the road compared with home experience);
- unfamiliar environments: finding themselves in a new environment can render tourists vulnerable to unfamiliar bacteria, climatic or traffic conditions (Lawton and Page, 1997);
- targeting of tourists: in some destinations, tourists may be targets for criminal or terrorist activity (Richter and Richter, 1999);
- unfamiliar language: safety warnings and health information in a foreign language create additional risks for tourists. Smith (1999) highlighted the importance of multilingual information and advice in protecting tourist health and safety (see Box 3.2);
- unaccustomed activities: holidaymakers may engage in activities they are unused to, and which increase their vulnerability (Page *et al.*, 2005). These might be a component of the holiday (skiing or hiking) or an activity undertaken 'because you're on holiday', such as excessive sun exposure, binge drinking or unprotected sex. Indeed, excess alcohol consumption can increase other forms of risk such as vulnerability to crime.

Box 3.2. Tourism, language facility and welfare.

Despite observations that significant numbers of tourists prefer to remain within a spatial and psychological 'bubble' partly in order to obviate any embarrassing or potentially risky encounters with the 'host other' (e.g. Jaakson, 2004a; Pi-Sunyer, 2004), our experience of places and cultures – and particularly personal interaction with local people – is, almost without exception, enhanced by a facility with the local language. Yet little research into this phenomenon as a source of tourist experience enrichment and satisfaction – and an articulation of tourist responsibility – appears in the literature (e.g. Basala and Klenosky, 2001). The contribution of language guides, phrase books, audio courses and the like, alongside the increasing number of popularly available guides to customs and etiquette for particular cultures, offers a rich vein for research.

Within this context, the industry's responsibility for addressing welfare considerations, particularly in the period before tourists depart or even commit themselves to a holiday, is coming under increasing scrutiny, alongside the responsibilities of public policymakers and tourists themselves. However, both the industry and policymakers seem reluctant to engage in public discussions about the risks associated with particular destinations or elements of tourism. This is perhaps unsurprising, given the economic value of the industry and its importance as a generator of foreign exchange. For Cartwright (2000), taking responsibility means, in practical terms:

- ensuring a proper health infrastructure in the development of tourist areas;
- operators stipulating minimum hotel standards, backed up by regular auditing;
- tourists taking sufficient responsibility to ensure that they do not expose themselves to unnecessary risks; and
- the application of appropriate monitoring systems in the control of travel-related diseases.

Since tourism quality and visitor satisfaction are intrinsically linked to the experience of a visit (e.g. Ryan, 1991), there are clearly important implications for destinations (see also Chapter 4) in terms of their image, promotion and the encouragement of repeat visits. Thus, for the welfare of tourists and destinations, it would seem logical for the tourism industry to take responsibility for the provision of adequate advice to inform intending travellers of the potential hazards, risks and type of health experiences they may encounter in particular tourism environments and which can ultimately affect their (longer-term) quality of life (Lawton and Page, 1997: 89).

Richter and Richter (1999) highlight a lack of helpful information available, arguing that national, state and local officials rarely warn inbound tourists of health, safety or accessibility issues. But such information provision need not be entirely handled by public agencies. The tourism industry can play an important part in informing tourists about risks to health and safety. However,

given the vertical integration of the tourism industry and the ownership of many travel agencies in generating countries by the travel conglomerates, retail travel agents are required to sell preferred products quickly and efficiently (Richardson, 1996; Hudson et al., 2001). These include those that offer higher commissions or bonuses to agents, cross-promotions or other incentives and, of course, holidays of their parent company (McKercher et al., 2003). There is little incentive for them to alert customers to any health or other hazards present at their destination (except the negative publicity that would ensue should these hazards materialize).

Reilly (1988) and Case and Useem (1996) observed that the nature of the travel agency business is high volume/low margin. As such, there is a narrow gap between financial success and failure for most – ultimately, financial decisions drive agency operations. Further, many of the services travel agents perform are unprofitable. As a result, agencies tend to employ fewer personnel than the volume of business requires, and staff may have to work long hours. Traditional volatility in demand, coupled with recent changes to the tourism distribution system, including the advent of the Internet, capping of commissions and the development of alternative distribution channels (Baum and Mudambi, 1994; Henderson, 1994; Litvin, 1999) have made profitability more difficult (McKercher et al., 2003). Viability depends on the ability to process clients efficiently, and therefore the industry prefers to promote products that are 'worry-free' – that is, the product is well known and can be booked easily in a cost-effective manner (Dube and Renaghan, 2000).

Yet travel agents have been described as the most important information gatekeeper in the travel purchase decision-making process (Middleton, 1994), as experts who are knowledgeable in all aspects of tourism (McIntosh and Goeldner, 1990) and as information brokers whose opinions and recommendations are sought because of their high level of knowledge and involvement in a particular product class (Klenosky and Gitelson, 1998). As opinion formers, their knowledge and information has a significant impact on destination choice (Lawton and Page, 1997), particularly for those lacking knowledge of destinations and those seeking international travel (Baloglu and Mangaloglu, 2001).

Leiper (1995) recognized seven roles for travel agents: motivating, informing, booking, purchasing, planning, organizing, supporting. Older people are more likely to use a travel agent than younger people, and a study of older tourists to Canada identified travel agents as the second most important source of travel information after friends (McGuire et al., 1988). A study in 1993 of British travellers showed travel agents to be the most frequently used communication channel (Hsieh and O'Leary, 1993; Lawton and Page, 1997: 90). Despite the increasing use of direct selling by tour operators and Internet trading (e.g. Boyne and Hall, 2004), travel agents' roles still underpin much of the choice behaviour of potential travellers.

None the less, the widely held assumption that retail travel agents are experts in all aspects of travel is largely a myth fostered by the travel trade. Travel agents may be able to offer generic advice, but they often fail to provide accurate information on special requests tourists may have (Lawton and Page, 1997; McKercher et al., 2003), as anonymous, random visits to agents undertaken for Travel Trade Gazette have often shown.

In studies of UK travellers, up to two-thirds expressed a willingness to take pre-trip health advice from their GP, but, in practice, travellers were twice as likely to consult only their travel agent (Shickle et al., 1998). Indeed, travel agents have been cited in both the USA and the UK as the best channel through which appropriate health advice can be disseminated (Stears, 1996).

The quality of information provided in relation to health-care issues and travel may be poor and not particularly reliable or accurate. Several studies have revealed that few travel agents offer health information spontaneously and, when prompted, they often give advice that is inconsistent with current medical practice and often incorrect (Grabowski and Behrens, 1996; Harris and Welsby, 2000; Lawlor et al., 2000; Leggat, 2000; Provost and Soto, 2001). In Europe, the EC Directive (90-314-EEC) on package travel that came into force (in the UK) in January 1993 made it an offence for travel organizers and/or retailers to fail to provide their customers with necessary information on health requirements (Dunscombe, 1992; Clift and Page, 1994).

The Consumers Association (Zagor, 1995) found that a large number of travel agents gave the wrong answers when asked about the conditions and limitations of their holiday insurance policies, while Wayman (1995) found, in the wake of the Kurdish Workers Party anti-tourism campaign, that none of a range of UK travel agents approached for information on holidays in Turkey mentioned the potential terrorist threat. Sharpley et al. (1996) were highly critical of the information provision for travellers emanating from the British Foreign and Commonwealth Office, both for the welfare of tourists and in terms of ethical considerations for tourist destination societies.

The literature on the quality of travel agent advice focuses on the one-way communication process between the agent and the consumer. But communication is a two-way exchange process. The ability of the individual to articulate his or her own needs effectively must also play a key role in the information exchange process, especially if that person has special needs. McKercher et al. (2003) found that disabled traveller respondents reported great variability in the quality of service provided by different agencies, as well as among different staff within the same agency. A small number described positive experiences, but most expressed low confidence in the sector. Such a failure to provide an adequate service directly affects the ability of tourists with disabilities to participate fully in travel (see Chapter 2).

A great deal of reassurance or uncertainty can rest with the quality and quantity of travel documentation provided. For example, Boxes 3.3, 3.4 and 3.5 indicate material provided by a leading tour operator

Box 3.3. *Action Today.*

Action Today **from Thomas Cook: 10 December 04 – 1600**

US Dollar Transaction in Cuba – No. 21 Updated

On the BBC web site there is an article advising from the 8th of November Cuba is to ban commercial transactions in dollars, in response to tighter sanctions imposed by the US.

The information we have at the moment is as follows:

Dollars will no longer be accepted in shops and other businesses, and tourists and local's [*sic*] exchanging dollars will have to pay a commission, estimated at 10%.

In a statement the Cuban central bank have advised that dollars would not [*sic*] longer be accepted in shops and businesses. Dollars will have to be exchanged for 'convertible pesos' – a local currency that can be used in special shops but has no value internationally – for a 10% charge.

Cuban residents will still be allowed to hold an unlimited amount of dollars and they will be able to exchange them without charge until the new law comes into effect in two weeks. [The 2 weeks had already passed by the time this update was issued.]

Cubans living abroad have been advised when sending money home to relatives to send money in other currencies, such as Euro's [*sic*], Sterling or Swiss Francs.

This information can be found on the BBC News website.

We are urgently waiting for further information from our suppliers, over the recommended cash and Travellers Cheques to take. This message will be updated once this has been received.

Update: From advice from the Cuban embassy customers are advised to take sterling cash or travellers Cheques when travelling to Cuba. It appears that if customers have to encash sterling into the "convertible pesos" the 10% charge does not apply. We are still awaiting final confirmation from our suppliers. For latest information customers can contact the Cuban embassy on 0207 240 2488.

Update: The following information has been sent out from our suppliers: Customers should be advised to take other currency and/or currency travellers cheques such as Sterling or Euro and exchange for the Cuban peso upon arrival. Warning: Tourists who wish to exchange US$ currency or cheques will incur a 10% commission charge.

Update: All tourists leaving Cuba are required to pay a departure tax, not an arrival tax, which is normally $25 (£17.00). This tax is now required to be paid in Cuban Pesos, which travellers will receive when they exchange their currency once in Cuba.

Update on recommendations to take to Cuba:

❑   **Recommend to take Sterling Travellers Cheques and Sterling cash**
❑   **Travellers taking US$ notes or Travellers Cheques will have to convert them into local 'Convertible Pesos' with a 10% charge.**
❑   **Travellers Cheques and/or credit cards drawn on US banks are NOT accepted in Cuba. This includes American Express credit cards and American Express cheques.**
❑   **Travellers have also experienced difficulties using Abbey National, Capital One and MBNA (including Thomas Cook) credit cards and are recommended NOT to be taken.**

Update on encashing Travellers Cheques in Cuba:

❑   **WE HAVE BEEN ADVISED BY OUR CONTACTS OVER IN CUBA TO RECOMMEND CUSTOMERS TO ENCASH TRAVELLERS CHEQUES AT BANKS AND BUREAU [*sic*] ONLY. IF YOU HAVE ANY CUSTOMERS ASK ABOUT ACCEPTANCE AT HOTELS WE SHOULD ADVISE THAT THIS IS LIMITED.**

Nicky Skeels

FE Operations Assistant UK Retail Foreign Exchange

FN: 5000-6225 (01733 416225)

Box 3.4. *Travelling Safely.*

The pamphlet *Travelling Safely*, produced by the (UK) Civil Aviation Authority (CAA, 2001) (CAA Document 477) provides brief advice to air travellers under the headings:

- How should I behave on board an aircraft?
- What happens if I drink too much alcohol?
- Can I smoke during the flight?
- Why should I listen to the safety briefing?
- Why should I wear my seat belt?
- What am I allowed to carry in my baggage? [accompanied by colour-coded boxes: what you can take on board (green) and must not take on board (a reddish ochre, certainly not an advancing red)]
- How much baggage am I allowed?
- What electronic equipment can I use during the flight?

Such advice is summarized on the cover of this pamphlet accompanied by appropriate graphics and the slogan 'The Civil Aviation Authority Ensuring Your Safety':

- NO to abusive behaviour
- NO to excessive drinking
- NO smoking
- LISTEN to the safety briefing
- Keep YOUR seat belt fastened
- CHECK your luggage

The back page offers contact details for further information under the headings:

- Security
- Dangerous goods
- Cabin safety
- Health

Box 3.5. *Keep Your Passport Safe While You're Away.*

In contrast to the *Hitchhiker's Guide to the Galaxy* (Adams, 1979), the UK Passport Service (nd) leaflet *Keep Your Passport Safe While You're Away* declares on its front side, 'Keep it safe – Keep it separate – Keep a copy'. The leaflet provides clear advice in the event of the traveller's passport being lost or stolen. In view of the erstwhile absence of, but public debate concerning, compulsory identity cards in the UK, the leaflet's final paragraph resonates strongly: 'In many countries it is a legal requirement to carry identity documents at all times, so if your passport is missing we strongly advise taking immediate action to replace it.'

accompanying the provision of air tickets 3 weeks before a 12-day holiday from the UK to Cuba in January 2005. The letter featured in Box 3.3 could be particularly confusing as it presents information successively updated as one reads the document, including potentially conflicting advice because the material that has been updated has not been removed or edited. This source of information would appear to be a travel company internal document for sales staff, who should then summarize and present to their clients a clear, unambiguous and digestible message, rather than simply passing on an unedited and potentially confusing message. Further, the travel company's covering letter also included a summary that did not wholly clarify the situation, largely duplicating sections of the internal note as well as introducing additional information.

These examples of documentation received in preparation for one long-haul holiday exemplify the varying quality of literature and the need for the tourists' advisers – still often travel agents – to carefully filter, edit and explain material sourced elsewhere and passed on to the client. The above examples represent both good and not so good practice in this respect.

At least partly because of the perceived vacuum of information, some independent commercial organizations provide a health information service to potential travellers. The UK Medical Advisory Services for Travellers Abroad (MASTA <http://www.masta.org.uk>), for example, runs a travellers' health line telephone service and website (MASTA, 2003), travel shops and clinics, and produces a free guide to malaria protection, which is distributed through a major pharmaceutical retailing chain. A Scottish Executive-supported public access website, fitfortravel (SCIEH, 2005), has been available for some time, providing travel health information for people travelling from the UK. Importantly for the industry, in 2003 a UK government-sponsored National Travel Health Network and Centre was opened in London to provide a public health and specialist travel health service, albeit exclusively to health professionals (UCLH NHS Trust, 2003).

Indicative of the variable level and quality of information available from formal sources, a substantial popular literature that addresses health and safety issues for intending travellers has also been developed (e.g. Dawood, 1992; Elkington and Hailes, 1992; Wilson-Howarth, 1995; Kenyon, 1996; Pelton, 1999; Jones, 2001; Naik, 2003; Wright, 2003; Beech, 2004; Hodson, 2004; Sapsford, 2004; Swan and Laufer, 2004; Vainopoulos, 2004). But, of course, this is no substitute for personalized health requirements and targeted provision.

Social networks and social position are also significant in overcoming the information deficit, although this area appears poorly researched. As a reflection on the attitude of the travel industry to providing information on potential risks, Nolan (1976: 7) found that information from friends and relatives, although low in credibility compared with more formal sources, was the most comprehensive. Francken and van Raaij (1979) also concluded that informal social information was increasingly being used, but noted that the higher the level of education of the tourist, the more information sources were employed (Mansfeld, 1992).

Despite the EC Directive, there remains a fragmentary and at best loosely coordinated provision of pre-holiday information upon which tourists and travellers can base realistic judgements on the likely welfare risks they may face. Although travel brochures are a potentially important source of health information, examination of those available from town centre travel agents showed that only 11% carried prominent health information, 64% placed it at the end and 25% had none at all, leading to the observation that tourist health is the 'silent factor' in tourism customer service (Wilks and Oldenburg, 1995).

Responses to tourism health and safety concerns tend to be reactive and in response to large and newsworthy incidents or health scares. In short, concerns for personal safety may result from a lack of knowledge and/ or conditioning by media images rather than from actual risks. This can lead to an effort to protect tourists from risks which, although serious in terms of their potential

consequences, may be rare (Peattie *et al.*, 2005). But they may be temporarily highlighted by the media's propensity to focus on a dramatic event and then to move on to others before the first has been concluded: the issue attention cycle (Downs, 1972; Iyengar and Kinder, 1987; C.M. Hall, 2002, 2003b).

In this way, when tourism risks are discussed, it is the newsworthiness of the risk and its consequences, more than the probabilities and outcomes involved, that may often drive the debate (Peattie *et al.*, 2005). For C.M. Hall (2003b: 42). Such 'issues highlight the importance for understanding the means by which tourism-related issues and events get onto media or policy agenda. Agenda-setting research focuses not on the opinions surrounding issues, but on issue salience.' Almost half a century ago, Cohen (1963: 13) observed what for Hall has become the central public agenda-setting hypothesis: '[the press] may not be successful much of the time in telling people what to think, but it is stunningly successful in telling its readers what to think about'.

At governmental level, the intricate and often hidden relationship between tourism (and trade) and politics (and international relations) influencing the provision of information, advice and support is not always in tourism's favour (Sharpley *et al.*, 1996). National governments may impose travel restrictions on their citizens (e.g. Ascher, 1984; D. Hall, 1984, 1990; Ascher and Edgell, 1986; C.M. Hall, 1994b). These may be for economic reasons, such as temporary limits on the amount of money that an individual can take out of the country, or ideological, as in the US embargo on Cuba (Box 3.6). In the case of visa or immigration restrictions on incoming tourists, they may result from broader policy decisions.

Political instability in destination areas, as a factor influencing tourist flows (Richter, 1992), may stimulate governments in tourism-generating countries to issue warnings or advice to potential tourists about travel to such destinations. For example, the US State Department issues detailed and up-to-date travel advice to tourists through its Citizens Emergency Center (Edgell, 1990), and the

Box 3.6. Ebookers drops Cuba.

Hundreds of British tourists had their travel plans ruined after Ebookers cancelled all its bookings to Cuba. The travel agency group also owns Travelbag, Flightbookers and Bridge the World, all of which have cancelled every holiday or flight booking they hold to Cuba. The group was bought by Cendant, a large US corporation, in February 2005, and some 3 months later decided it must comply with the US trade embargo prohibiting trade with or travel to Cuba.

In a statement Ebookers said it had acted quickly as soon as the position regarding Cuba 'became clear'. The company was refunding its customers, offering a £100 voucher and 'considering all appropriate options for alleviating the inconvenience'. A spokesperson refused to say if this meant financial compensation would be available even though it would cost travellers significantly more to rebook their trips compared to when they made the initial reservation. Around 400 people were affected.

Lawyers at the Association of British Travel Agents deemed this a case of *force majeure*, an unforeseen circumstance beyond the company's control, even though some bookings were taken after the takeover. In such cases the travel firm would not be liable to pay compensation.

Source: Anon., 2005c.

Travel Advice Unit of the British Foreign and Commonwealth Office (FCO) advises tourists about potential political, health and other problems in over 100 different countries (FCO, 2005). In 2004 the FCO established a standing advisory council representing tourism stakeholders to help inform the production of its travel advisories, following a campaign from Tourism Concern to ensure fair and balanced travel advice.

Such official advice varies in strength from precautionary to virtual bans on travel, the officially stated overriding concern being the health and security of the government's nationals abroad. Notionally this is an important and possibly vital welfare component of tourist preparation, which suggests that the issuing of travel advice should be non-political. However, the potential exists, through travel advice, for the governments of tourism-generating countries to influence, and disrupt, the structure and flow of international tourism, and thereby to exert economic and political pressure on destination countries (Sharpley *et al.*, 1996: 1–2).

Government advice – perhaps transmitted via intermediary agencies – may be just one, albeit crucial, element in deterring tourists from travelling to particular intended destinations. But the presence of (implicit) risk-aversion attitudes and behaviour in relation to the gathering of information by intending tourists before a trip has been recognized for some time (e.g. Nolan, 1976; Francken and van Raaij, 1979; van Raaij and Francken, 1984; Mansfeld, 1992). At a broad level, Carter (1998) examined the social construction of geographical regions by (UK) international travellers attending a specialist travel clinic in Glasgow. In terms of travel health risks, three sets of simple, apparently superficial, constructs were evident:

- Europe and North America were perceived as safe;
- Africa was seen as dangerous and to be avoided; and
- Asia was constructed as simultaneously risky but also exotic and worth experiencing.

Previous studies had shown that large areas of the developing world were perceived in generalized terms as risky (e.g. Cossens and Gin, 1994).

However, while observing that there was a tendency to treat both Africa and Asia as undifferentiated 'others', Carter (1998: 357) pointed out that travellers' accounts perceived danger within Africa as 'linked to random events beyond the control of the individual, such as blood transfusions'. In contrast, the dangers that travellers associated with Asia were perceived as more 'controllable', with two caveats: sexual contact should be avoided and food consumed with care. Through such acts of personal responsibility, travellers deemed that the region could be 'made safe'. Yet for some male travellers these apparent gross stereotypes of place were further reinforced by the stereotyping of Eastern women in terms of their representing 'dangerous sexuality' (although it could be equally argued that, being characterized as 'submissive' and more 'feminine' than Western women, they may also represent a degree of security). Carter makes little of the background characteristics of his sample: were these (introducing yet another stereotype) typical Glaswegian males? But he further suggests that of particular concern were the attitudes expressed by business travellers:

> only male business travellers here construed the risk of Asia to be caused by the 'Other' sexuality of its peoples. This may lead one to believe that business travellers would avoid sexual contact while working abroad. However, the manner in which this group construed the risk, introduced the possibility of ambivalence – a simultaneous fear and attraction.
>
> (Carter, 1998: 357)

The author's previous research indicated that business travellers were more likely to have new sexual contacts than other tourists, and that these contacts were most often drawn from the host population of the region being visited rather than from among other travellers (Carter, 1997a). Yet the scope for the uptake of health promotion aimed at modifying sexual behaviour in this group may be limited by the very ambivalence of these beliefs, particularly that of perceived sexual risk as being a passive threat almost 'beyond' their control. This, together with other research (e.g. Hawkes, 1994), would seem to highlight the need for sensitive pre-travel health promotional material that is targeted especially at business travellers. Such materials should express awareness of the possibly complex interactions between the social construction of risky locations and likely eventual behaviour while visiting these areas. We might add that understanding the apparently underlying moral codes of different (mobile) occupation groups and classes could be instructive.

The fact that travellers readily produced similar social constructions supported Carter's view that a discourse surrounds 'regions' such as Africa that culturally associates them with ideas of danger and ill health for people in the West (Kitzinger and Miller, 1992). He therefore suggested that

this should be of some concern to governments and the travel industry promoting travel to locations outside North America and Europe.

More importantly, the research suggested that the beliefs expressed by these travellers were not static entities, but rather the result of a discursive process. The cultural meanings given to the health threats of remote places is a dynamic process, and therefore this needs to be taken into account in the preparation of information for travellers. If done successfully, Carter (1998) argues that travellers will be in a better position to minimize risks in the knowledge that they are not reinforcing existing myths liable to damage distant countries' images (and economies).

Although not well researched, the quality of a holiday and its relationship with the domestic contextualization of leisure breaks may closely relate to the nature and processes of holiday decision making. The literature suggests that in some cultures there has been a significant trend towards joint holiday decision making compared with earlier 'male-dominant' situations. This may hide actual or subliminal disagreement that finds its voice on the holiday, with potentially negative consequences for the shared and individual welfare experience. Litvin *et al.* (2004) recognize the significance of assumed joint decisions for tourism marketers promoting the family vacation product.

Mottiar and Quinn (2004) suggest that females may have a dominant role in the early stages of holiday planning, possibly making them the 'gatekeepers' to holiday choice. Several studies have also recognized that children play a part in family decision making (e.g. Thornton *et al.*, 1997; Lindstrom, 2003; see also Chapter 6) and that they can enrich the nature of the adult experience (Ryan, 1992). Older children appear to play a greater role in holiday decision making (Pasumarty *et al.*, 1996; Roedder John, 1999), while younger ones have a much greater impact on actual (family) group behaviour while on holiday (Fodness, 1992). We can hypothesize that a greater number of children within a family unit is likely to be significant in at least two ways:

- given that 'pleasing the child' has been cited as an important motive for parents in holiday decision taking (Ryan, 1992), a greater number of children is likely to increase the diversity of holiday demands and thus complicate holiday decision taking, perhaps resulting in family tensions and even conflict; but, perhaps more significantly
- increasing numbers of children may suggest a decreasing financial ability to support a significant holiday experience for all the family, raising issues of access and participation discussed in the previous chapter.

Anticipation

From a welfare perspective, the process of travel is important for the short- and longer-term physical and psychological impacts it may have on the traveller – from travel sickness to DVT, from short-term gratification to lifelong experiential imagery. Some of these effects will, of course, be initiated long before the travelling begins, and may be more intense if the anticipated holiday is repeating a visit to an environment of previous positive experiences. Overall, however, the academic literature on tourist experience anticipation and its physiological and psychological effects is rather thin.

An investigation into what effect the expectation of holiday-taking has on the sense of well-being of UK tourists (Gilbert and Abdullah, 2002) indicated significant differences between a holiday-taking group and a non-holiday-taking control group. This was expressed in terms of current effect and the individuals' life as a whole (their 'global well-being'), and in three specific life domains: family, economic situation and health. The authors found, unsurprisingly, that those who are waiting to go on a holiday are much happier with their life as a whole, experience fewer negative or unpleasant feelings and thus enjoy an overall net positive effect or pleasant feelings. Members of the holiday-taking group were also happier with their family, economic situation and

health domains compared with those in the non-holiday-taking group. The conclusion was that the anticipation of a favourable event (holiday trip) positively affected the respondents' subjective well-being.

Trauer and Ryan (2005: 490) argue that more attention should be given to the dynamics of travelling partnerships, whether of friends, families, spouses or lovers. Although holidays are commercial products, they suggest that what is being purchased in a holiday is not 'a place' but rather time for partners to be together (with place as the implicit background). They therefore contend that a fundamental element of the holiday experience is the degree of intimacy that exists between travellers: 'it is that which permits openness to the nature of the place and the travelled to' (Trauer and Ryan, 2005: 490). Yet they say little about the contribution of such intimacy to the anticipation of a holiday experience. This is perhaps a further area ripe for conceptual exploration. If, as Trauer and Ryan (2005: 490) suggest, 'human to human intimacy on holidays is indeed an important and essential necessity for the health of the human psyche', then its contribution to the home environment both before and following the holiday surely merits further analysis. Issues relating to individual, unattached travellers, of course, are different in this respect.

In his philosophical treatise, de Botton (2002) makes two interrelated points in relation to the anticipation of travel. The first is that the reality of the quality of experience may not match our prior expectations, particularly our anticipatory emotions that have been stimulated by marketing and promotion images. And, of course, the creation of such images is nothing new: de Botton (2002: 9–11) recounts the story of the Duc des Esseintes from J.-K. Huysmans's 1884 novel *A Rebours*. The Duc lived alone in some degree of reclusion but on a whim decided to travel to London. With time to spare en route in Paris, he purchased Baedekker's *Guide to London*. Avidly consuming the guide's terse descriptions, he repaired to a nearby English tavern in the French capital, where he decided that actually travelling to London would only disappoint the dreams he had been stimulated to create by the guide. So he returned home, never to travel again.

The second point is that anticipation, like memory and art, is selective:

> the anticipatory and artistic imaginations omit and compress, they cut away the periods of boredom and direct our attention to critical moments and, without either lying or embellishing, thus lend to life a vividness and coherence that it may lack in the distracting woolliness of the present.
>
> (de Botton, 2002: 15)

Thus, in the personal anticipation and prior imagery of a holiday in Barbados, 'there had simply been a vacuum between the [arrival] airport and my hotel' (de Botton, 2002: 13). This had omitted the tedium of the luggage carousel, the stress and hassle immediately encountered on leaving the airport arrivals area, the negotiation of transport, traffic congestion, ugly landscapes and the impairment of judgement that accompanies sleep deprivation. Arguably the travel industry not only fails to prepare the traveller for such discordance between anticipation and reality but may actually encourage it through selective provision of information and imagery construction, with potentially significant negative welfare consequences, such as the need to drive in unfamiliar circumstances while jet-lagged.

The Experience of Travel, Transport and the Journey

The stress associated with international and, to a lesser degree, domestic travel can be the result of various psychological factors, which can be exacerbated by the effect of congestion on, and of, transport systems. Pre-journey (e.g. flight) anxieties may relate to:

- the degree of stress involved in getting to the final place of departure on time;
- the marketing of travel insurance;
- pre-departure check-in formalities (but see Frary, 2005);
- the complex array of luggage and/or body security checks undertaken by strangers

in an unfamiliar environment: at airports they are a reminder of the risk of hijack and in-flight explosion; and
- overcrowding in terminal buildings, which can overwhelm and disorientate travellers; as a result, premium fare passengers such as business travellers are often provided with access to executive lounges and a more relaxed and welcoming environment.

As Pi-Sunyer (2004: 17) observed, in the immediate post-9/11 US context, the only air travel sector to flourish was that of executive jet hire, whose elitist role of hassle and risk avoidance was emphasized in such promotional straplines as 'no lines, no stopovers, no taking off your loafers'. Yet large parts of travel activity may be accompanied by a degree of 'mindlessness' (Langer and Piper, 1987; Pearce, 1988): 'This might be described as being akin to the state sometimes experienced by drivers when they arrive at their destination with little ability to recall the events of the journey. A process of automatic reactions has taken place' (Ryan, 1994: 297).

Pearce (1988) suggested that there are a number of opportunities for such 'mindless' (lack of conscious) behaviour that induces little recall. Many are highly scripted occasions where a series of familiar steps are followed in a programmed sequence. These include the checking in of baggage, queuing and passing through X-ray examination at an airport. They present little challenge or novelty for the regular traveller and hence little cause for either high or low levels of satisfaction. This may suggest, therefore, particularly for the regular traveller, that repeatedly encountered 'stressful' situations, such as being subjected to body searches and luggage X-ray examinations, become absorbed, through psychological adjustment and adaptation, to be regarded as the norm.

A negative effect on travellers' welfare, trans-meridian disturbance (jet lag), is associated with time zone changes and sleep deprivation during long-haul travel (Iyer, 2004). Confusion in travellers is significantly under-recognised (Habib and Tambyah, 2004).

Movement between hemispheres and thus between seasons can also be disturbing (but also invigorating) – from winter to summer, autumn to spring and vice versa. The use of melatonin is sometimes prescribed under such circumstances. As a naturally occurring neurohormone, its rate of secretion is increased by darkness, causing the individual to feel sleepy, although with possible side effects.

En route anticipatory fears and phobias, which may revolve around the threat of terrorism or hijack, potential language difficulties and likely friendliness of the host population in the destination region, can be ameliorated by in-flight information and entertainment, in addition to pre-journey preparation. In practice this may be very variable in quality and relevance. On a 9-h flight from Paris to Havana recently experienced by the authors, for example, interminable promotions for Parisian attractions, fashions and life in Indo-China on the in-flight television screens were followed, finally, by an 8-min film about arrivals procedures. This was shown at a time when the aircraft was already over land and many passengers were intent on looking out of the window to catch perhaps their first glimpses of Cuba. This was a wholly inadequate preparation for the political and cultural environment about to be encountered.

Of course, many elements of travel psychology can be personal: loneliness and a sense of isolation can contribute to a traveller's feelings of anonymity during a journey, particularly if travelling alone, despite the opportunities for meeting and talking to new people. Media stories of air incidents, although they are rare occurrences, will heighten a general fear of flying (pterophobia), where the passenger has no sense of being in control. A significant increase in treatment centres for this condition is reported (van Gerwen et al., 2004). Up to 80% of regular fliers are said to experience apprehension when boarding an aircraft. This may be heightened by a sense of claustrophobia in the cramped aircraft cabin, further exacerbated particularly for non-smokers if smoking is permitted on board (Ryan, 1994). Equally, the increasing proportion of non-smoking long-haul flights may present regular smokers with discomfort.

Most airlines acknowledge an awareness of potential in-flight health-related problems and include one or two pages in their in-flight magazines devoted to exercises and other ways in which passengers can avoid immobility and the potential threat of deep vein thrombosis (DVT) in the legs, a condition which can travel to the heart or brain and be fatal (Nicholson et al., 2003; Tasker et al., 2004). Reduced air pressure within the flight cabin and dehydration, which may occur because of the recirculation of dry air within the aircraft, can exacerbate this and other potential medical conditions. The phenomenon of DVT amongst travellers, initially and inaccurately referred to as 'economy class syndrome', became an increasing media focus at the start of the decade (Table 3.2), representing an agenda-setting exercise that helped to raise awareness and stimulate some positive response from both airlines and travellers.

It is likely to be some years before research into DVT will have an impact on the ergonomic design and conditions that many air travellers endure on long-, and not so long, haul flights (Lumsdon and Page, 2004: 11). The public policy priority for this area tends to be downgraded in favour of recurrent concern associated with the spread of infection by air travellers. The combination of large numbers of people from many different places locked in close proximity over several hours with other passengers in an environment of recirculated air poses increased risks. Severe acute respiratory syndrome (SARS) has been the most notable recent infection, first emerging in China and Hong Kong in late 2002 and then spreading by air travel to Vietnam, Singapore, Canada and other locations. It caused some degree of panic and short-term economic crisis in the face of cancelled travel and accommodation bookings. For much of the crisis during the first half of 2003, outbound tourism from Hong Kong was reduced by 80% (Henderson and Ng, 2004; Mason et al., 2005).

SARS was perhaps significant also in helping to re-emphasize the relatively unhealthy conditions that people travel in

Table 3.2. Selected UK press reports on DVT and associated travel-related health problems (from Watson, 1999; Laurance, 2000; Milmo and Arthur, 2000; Calder, 2001; D. Hall, 2001; Townsend, 2001; Arthur, 2002a, b; Hannah, 2003).

Headline and source	Content	Comment
'Safety fears as fliers feel the squeeze' – *Scotland on Sunday*, 27 June 1999	Some airlines were accused in a study of reducing seat pitch to an extent that there was insufficient room between seats for tall people to adopt the crash position in the event of an emergency. Seven major regular or charter airlines were shown to have seat pitches of 31 inches or less, and some charter airlines as little as 28. It was suggested that over the past 10 years there had been a downward trend in economy-section seat pitch in order to squeeze more passengers into the same space.	The article was derived from a paper in *The Lancet* by German and Austrian doctors. There is an interesting ethical dilemma here: if squeezing more people into an aircraft is instrumental in reducing the number of aircraft flying, then there would appear to be an environmental gain, or at least reduced loss. The UK Civil Aviation Authority (CAA), which regulates air travel, has a minimum 28-inch seat pitch standard, 'for comfort'. Despite the critical significance of seat pitch and room in which to move legs, nowhere in the newspaper article was there reference to DVT.
'Death after flight triggers calls for air travel inquiry' – *The Independent*, 24 October 2000	Air safety organizations admitted that no records were kept of the number of passengers suffering from DVT after a 28-year-old bride-to-be died at Heathrow following a 20-h flight from Sydney.	The Air Transport Users' Council and others called for a clearly needed large-scale clinical study. Haematologists argued that DVT risk was increased for smokers, those taking the birth control pill or having hormone replacement therapy. The UK Aviation Health Institute began arguing that a seat pitch of 31 inches or less was particularly risky.
'Peers warn of fatal blood clots on long journeys' – *The Independent*, 23 November 2000	The House of Lords Science and Technology Committee report, *Air Travel and Health*, suggested that while there was no explicit evidence to suggest that air travel carries a higher risk of blood clots than other forms of travel or that travellers as a whole are more prone to develop the condition than non-travellers, anecdotal evidence suggested there may be a problem that warranted urgent investigation.	The apparently mixed message that there was no firm evidence and yet urgent action should be taken was rendered more positive by virtue of the fact that the Committee chairman, Lord Winstone, a well-known media figure in the UK, made subsequent pronouncements reinforcing a sense of urgency in the need for generating (i.e. funding) research into the subject (as he would, being a medical researcher himself).

'Airline buys half a million Airogym devices to stop blood-clot deaths' – *The Independent*, 19 April 2001

Dubai-based Emirates airline had purchased 500,000 inflatable foot pads, which help passengers simulate the effects of walking while sitting down. The Airogym was developed by a former British Airways pilot following a DVT incident on his flight from Hong Kong to London. Emirates' head of medical services claimed it was not an admission of the recognition of the threat of DVT.

Since 'the DVT scare became widespread', captains of long-haul flights on Airtours and Virgin Atlantic had been using the 'fasten seat belt' sign to get exercising passengers to sit down so that the cabin crew could carry out their duties.

Emirates had recently been criticized for installing ten seats abreast into the economy class of new Boeing 777s when the industry standard was nine.

What is the relative risk of DVT compared to potential injuries from large numbers of exercising passengers being unbelted when an aircraft hits turbulence?

Doctors at Ashford hospital, which serves Heathrow, had recently claimed that every 6 weeks on average one passenger arriving at the airport was dying as a result of DVT.

'Airlines to be sued over DVT deaths' – *The Observer*, 29 July 2001

Lawyers were about to bring compensation claims against airlines on behalf of 30 British air passengers, ten of whom had died, on the grounds that the aviation industry was accountable for deaths and illness from DVT.

The claimants were from Varda – the Victims of Air Related DVT Association – and were supported by the Aviation Health Institute. They argued that evidence suggested doctors had been aware of the dangers of immobility on long-haul flights since at least 1968 and yet airlines had only recently begun highlighting potential dangers to the travelling public.

'Fear of flying may raise risk of fatal blood clot' – *The Independent*, 24 January 2002

A developer of medical diagnostic equipment claimed that fear of flying could trigger stress incidents leading to clots and, with other medics, sought the airlines' cooperation in undertaking research and generating data.

Claiming that 10% of travellers on long-haul flights could be at risk, particularly the overweight, the elderly and those recently having had surgery, the hypothesis aired here is based on the fact that adrenalin released into the blood when someone is stressed tends to thicken it.

'First-class air passenger killed by blood clots' – *The Independent*, 22 March 2002

A woman who flew first class from Miami to London Gatwick died from pulmonary embolism – a blocked artery in the lungs – resulting from DVT a day after arriving home.

This well-publicized death highlighted that DVT had been misguidedly referred to as 'economy-class syndrome'.

'Long-haul flights can increase risk of strokes in passengers with heart defects, say scientists' – *The Herald* (Glasgow), 24 June 2003

Long-haul flights can increase the risk of people with a common heart defect suffering a stroke. French researchers had found that all passengers who had a pulmonary embolism as a consequence of DVT and then suffered a stroke after a long flight had a patent foramen ovale (PFO) – an opening between two chambers in the heart.

The reported study, published in *Neurology*, had examined 65 passengers taken to hospital with pulmonary embolism on arrival at Charles de Gaulle airport in Paris over an 8-year period. Frederic Lapostolle, who led the study, said the risk of a stroke may be higher than found in the study because researchers did not include people who died during or immediately after air travel.

during long-haul flights. These result from pressurization (which can affect those with breathing difficulties), ventilation and the historical increase in recycled air used in aircraft cabins, the use of pesticides to disinfect aircraft, ozone pollution and solar radiation (Lumsdon and Page, 2004: 14).

Overall, the travel experience, with its delays, (lack of) comfort, travel time and ease (or otherwise) of accessibility to the destination, is important for several practical reasons:

- in the early stages of a holiday, expectations are high, and negative experiences on the outward journey may encourage disproportionate dissatisfaction;
- a long, tiring journey can mean that arrival at the destination is followed by the first day (or more) of the holiday being one of recovery rather than exploration, especially if the time zone difference is great; however,
- if the journey simply goes according to plan and an expected service is delivered, no addition to total satisfaction may occur (Ryan, 1994: 300, 1997: 56–57).

The contention made by some authors (e.g. Fussell, 1982) that tourism is not travel, on the basis that the journey is not an important part of the holiday product when compared to the travel of the past, is to ignore the intrinsic attraction of the spatial movement in travel. This has not been well researched (Sørensen, 1997); further, its welfare implications have been poorly articulated. Travel is a key element of the tourist experience (Pearce, 1992), both in terms of travel to and from the final destination, and in the transport available for circuits and other travel within the destination area. In some circumstances the transport experience can be the exclusive tourism experience (Lamb and Davidson, 1996; D. Hall, 1999; Halsall, 2001).

Moreover, tourists are travelling longer distances, have more flexibility in their modes and routes of travel and thus can better 'control' the journey in terms both of its intrinsic nature (transport mode, geographical dimensions and timing) and the experiences it is likely to generate.

Intermediate place experience

There appears to have been only limited research undertaken and interest shown in tourists' experiences of intermediate places: those stopping-off points on transit routes that may not in themselves be regarded as tourism destinations. While the transit experiences at a hub airport may offer an obvious environment in this respect, there is a substantial under-researching of the welfare experiences of intermediate places on motoring routes.

Jacobsen and Haukeland (2002), for example, examined the responses to and levels of satisfaction with roadside eating places in northern Norway frequented by foreign visitor motorists. Such places may offer a hit-or-miss experience in an environment where choice may be severely limited. This contrasts with the specific objective of travelling to a destination for gastronomic reasons or of being aware of gastronomic choice within a destination area (e.g. Sheldon and Fox, 1988). In the Norwegian survey, landscape views, service quality and the friendliness of staff were seen as the most satisfactory features. Fewer found the quality and range of food to be good, while price level, given high Norwegian costs, was the weakest point. The researchers undertook a factor analysis of these perceptions and isolated three sets of factors:

- physical standard and ambience: air quality and the absence of smoke, hygiene and tidiness, use of resources and the interior ambience of the establishment;
- food: quality and choice of food coupled with location and accessibility of the establishment; and
- staff quality and views: the combination of the human and the physical scenery frame in which meals are taken.

Jacobsen and Haukeland (2002: 5) concluded that 'the experience of food is predominantly related to smell and taste – senses not generally focused on in tourism research' (but see Dann and Jacobsen, 2002, 2003). This suggests further avenues for research in terms of extending the study of sensory perceptions within tourism, more fully embracing gastronomic tourism within the transit experience, and the ability of intermediate places to promote themselves through positive experience-related place imagery.

The Destination Experience

Improvement of our own welfare is a major individual motivation and element of personal satisfaction. Derived from the work of Maslow (1970), Beard and Ragheb (1983: 225) recognized four motivational needs – intellectual, social, competence mastery (competitive) and stimulus avoidance (seeking solitude) – which formed the foundations of their leisure motivation scale, subsequently replicated in other studies (e.g. Sefton and Burton, 1987; Loundsbury and Franz, 1990).

However, such classifications indicate little of the intensity of experience or the welfare implications of 'experience' per se. Partly in this respect, Ryan (1997: 32–33) cites the work of Csikszentimihalyi (1975: 36), whose concept of the 'flow' experience was 'one of complete involvement of the actor with his [sic] activity'. This has been applied in wilderness recreation research (e.g. Mannell *et al.*, 1988; Priest and Bunting, 1993), although it could equally apply to rock climbing, Zen meditation, philately or bus spotting (Fig. 3.1). It can be characterized by seven indicators:

- the perception that personal skills and challenges posed by an activity are in balance;
- the centring of attention;
- the loss of self-consciousness;
- an unambiguous feedback to a person's actions;
- feelings of control over actions and environment;
- a momentary loss of anxiety and constraint; and
- feelings of enjoyment or pleasure (Csikszentimihalyi, 1975: 38–48).

Clearly a wide range of visitor motivations and objectives can generate such an emotional state, and the context, meanings and experiences of tourism can vary considerably between holidays, places and tourists. To talk of the 'tourist experience' implies a consistency of attitude or homogeneity that,

Fig. 3.1. Enthusiasts photographing London's passing transport icons – a Routemaster farewell cavalcade, September 2004.

of course, does not exist in reality. But the 'tourist culture', a characterization of tourism destination zones, whether real or imaginary, has long been identified (e.g. Mathieson and Wall, 1982; Pearce, 1982; Ryan, 1991: 145, 1993: 175) (Box 3.7). The welfare implications of these characteristics are explored in this and the following chapter.

When tourists' welfare at the destination is discussed, safety and security issues relating to terrorism (Sönmez and Graefe, 1998a, b) and crime (Mawby et al., 2000) (Table 3.3) tend to dominate the headlines and policy agendas. In practice, a tourist is far more likely to fall victim to health problems than to violent incidents (Table 3.4). *Holiday Which?* (Nicholson-Lord, 1995) suggested that, while 15% of Britons taking foreign holidays fell ill, an increase in reported illness, injury and crime while on holiday abroad may reflect the role of holiday insurance. There appears to be an increasing eagerness to claim for incidents, however minor, with the associated requirement to obtain official police or health service documentation to support such insurance claims (see also Ryan, 1993).

The scale and nature of tourist health and safety problems has been conceptualized as a continuum (Page et al., 2005): from

minor ailments and problems, which affect a significant proportion of visitors, to more serious and fatal incidents, which affect a small number but which are traumatic in nature.

Where significant numbers of people are gathered for leisure purposes, often each for a relatively short time and from a diverse range of source areas, maintaining a healthy environment is especially difficult. For example, there is usually no effective way to screen visitors to detect the carrying of a contagious disease. It is a commonplace that people on holiday or business trips often sleep less, drink more and may be less cautious about eating food from unfamiliar sources. Transport centres such as airports and railway stations, as well as aircraft, trains and buses, often have large numbers of people gathered in small, confined spaces with poor air quality; and, as individuals' stress derived from travel experiences rises, ability to fight off illness decreases (Tarlow, 2004c).

We have been told for some time that personal safety is becoming an increasingly important issue for travellers (Martin and Mason, 1987) and that tourists expect a destination to be safe and clean (McEwan, 1987; Haywood, 1990). Indeed, by the early 1990s, a number of researchers recognized a shift in tourists' focus from the economic cost of the experience to concern with health and safety issues (Ritchie, 1992; Evans and Stabler, 1995). Empirical studies to support this have focused on Japanese travellers (Nozawa, 1992), retired travellers (Quiroga, 1990), Hong Kong residents (Mok and Armstrong, 1995) and US repeat visitors to Canada (Neiss et al., 1995).

Yet, paradoxically, diverse studies (e.g. Hugill, 1975; Gottlieb, 1982; Machlis and Burch, 1983; Jafari, 1987; Ryan et al., 1996; Ryan and Robertson, 1997) have pointed to the way in which 'common sense' appears often to be abandoned by tourists, particularly when abroad. This is not well conceptualized, however. For example, in theories relating to tourist types, those abandoning 'common sense' might be hypothesized as lying closer to Plog's (1974, 1990) allocentric tourists (risk takers, those seeking the

---

Box 3.7. Characteristics of a 'tourist culture'.

- Large numbers of visitors staying for a short time
- Large numbers of seasonal workers
- Transient relationships between visitors, between visitors and workers (both local and temporary) and between tourists and agencies of the tourism industry within both destination and generation areas
- Leisure is the main motivation of activity
- Tourists are freed from the constraints of their normal lifestyle, and are even more selective as to those norms of their peer groups to which they adhere than normally
- Spending is comparatively unrestrained
- Businesses reflect the importance of tourism
- The cultural expressive symbols are based on stereotypes and caricature
- Superior/inferior relationships exist

Source: Ryan, 1993: 175.

Table 3.3. Relationships between tourism and crime (from Ryan, 1993; de Albuquerque and McElroy, 1999).

Ryan's scenarios	Description
1. Tourists as incidental victims	The tourist is an accidental victim who happens to be in the wrong place at the wrong time, and is specifically viewed as an easy target.
2. The tourist location as a venue for crime	The characteristics of the tourist culture (see Box 3.7 above) make it easy for a criminal to remain inconspicuous. Tourist activities can provide a front for (organized) criminal activities.
3. Tourism, the provider of victims	Tourists are easy targets for certain types of crime, although often the data on which claims of a tourism–crime relationship are based are questionable.
4. Tourists – generators of a demand for criminal activity?	Tourists themselves are generators of crime through their behaviour, which may be more indulgent than at home (e.g. getting drunk and fighting). However, it is not wholly clear how far tourism initiates a demand for illegal services rather than reinforcing factors within the host society that give rise to those services in the first place. Extending the ethical limits of what is permissible raises complex issues: for example, tour operators may use accommodation that might fail the requirements of health and safety legislation in the generating country but which is permitted in the destination country.
5. Tourists and tourism resources as specific targets of criminal action	Taking tourists hostage or even murdering them for political motives because they are considered a legitimate target as symbols of global capitalism and are engaged in a sponsored activity of the state.

Table 3.4. Reported degrees of tourist ill health.

Report	Published source
Common reporting of gastroenteritis among cruise ship passengers (see also Chapter 4).	Werner *et al.*, 1976; Dannenberg *et al.*, 1982
High levels of respiratory problems among cruise ship passengers.	Fitzgerald, 1986; Christenson *et al.*, 1987; Di Giovanna *et al.*, 1992
Up to half of all international travellers are likely to experience ill health as a result of an overseas trip. Diarrhoea rates of 40% were regularly recorded from many European destinations.	Dawood, 1989; Leggat and Goldsmid, 2004
10% of all travellers become ill and 5% have to be hospitalized, often because they fail to take elementary health precautions.	Hunter, 1991
Alimentary problems could exceed a 50% attack rate.	Cartwright, 1992
54% of Australians visiting developing countries reported some form of illness.	Behrens *et al.*, 1994
36% of all travellers returning to Scotland reported illness, especially alimentary (diarrhoea and vomiting) and respiratory.	Cossar *et al.*, 1994
In 1990, 2000 Britons returned home with malaria, while 200 succumbed to typhoid.	D. Hall, 1995
63% of respondents in a survey of 1000 adult travellers had experienced holiday illness.	*Travel Weekly*, 1998
63% of visitors to North Queensland experienced a health problem, ranging from sunburn to fractures.	Peach and Bath, 1999
89% of tourists to the high-altitude Sagarmatha National Park in Nepal suffered some form of ailment.	Musa *et al.*, 2004

unfamiliar) rather than the psychocentric (those seeking the familiar). However, anecdotal evidence has suggested that: 'The tourist may ignore not only the cultural norms of home but also those of the magnet. Breaking the rules is actually one of the principles of "touristhood"' (Jafari, 1987: 153).

One obvious consequence of this element of the 'tourist culture' is that a major source of threat to the welfare of tourists is often the tourist's own behaviour, raising important questions regarding the sharing of responsibility between:

● tourists, for their own behaviour and its impacts on others: tourism workers, residents, other tourists and the environment;
● the tourism and travel industries, deriving profit from establishing the framework in which tourists act out their experiences; and
● destination managers.

Threats to the welfare of tourists from their own behaviour may include:

● insufficient medical prophylactic preparation, especially in the case of malaria (e.g. Hunter, 1991; Carter, 1998; Zuckerman, 2004);
● unwise exposure to sun and the risk of skin cancer (Conway et al., 1990; Grenfell and Ross, 1994; Mihill, 1995);
● undiscerning or excessive intake of food and drink, resulting in exposure to gastrointestinal infection and exposure to risk while under the influence of alcohol;
● imprudent sexual activity, resulting in exposure to potentially lethal infection and unwanted pregnancy (Conway et al., 1990; Black et al., 1994; Clark and Clift, 1994a, b; Taylor, 2001);
● accidents (Johnson et al., 1991; Ryan, 1993; Sager, 1993; Leggat et al., 2005), which kill 25 times more UK travellers abroad than do infectious or tropical diseases (Dawood, 1989: 286), and notably road accidents. These are the leading cause of death for US citizens travelling overseas (Bewes, 1993), while trauma caused by road accidents is a major cause of air evacuations of the

same group (Hartgarten, 1994). A limited popular literature has developed in response to this major welfare threat (e.g. Davies, 2001).

Many holiday insurance policies now have clauses which, for personal liability cover, may deliberately proscribe certain potentially risky activities such as hiring mopeds in Greece (Zagor, 1995), a notoriously accident-prone form of tourist transport. Similarly, policy proscriptions may be imposed on particular countries and regions: securing personal insurance for travel to and in certain regions and countries where perceived risk is high, such as Afghanistan or North Korea, may prove difficult or prohibitively expensive.

Although there exist strong elements of self-induced risk on the part of tourists, how far does the industry on the ground ameliorate or exacerbate such threats to welfare? Governments, tour operators, airlines and resort operators all have responsibilities towards visitors, tourism employees and residents of destinations to provide adequate information and protection to ensure that risks are known and avoided, or are at least minimized (see Chapter 4).

Shortcomings in industry responsibilities have been highlighted in the quality and safety of accommodation, attractions, transport and catering (Spivack, 1994), often generating high-profile media publicity on such issues as:

● deaths by poisoning from carbon monoxide escaping from faulty gas heaters in self-catering apartments;
● underwater obstacles in swimming pools;
● poorly guarded high-rise hotel balconies; and
● poor food hygiene in hotels and restaurants.

But, as Table 3.5 indicates, there is often a wide range of responsibilities involved in tourist accidents. Some may be freaks of chance or individual momentary lapses, others may have significant structural origins, and others again may be a combination of both, but where the first may mask the second.

Table 3.5.   Examples of high-profile media stories highlighting tourist accidents/incidents.

Headline	Incident	Reason/responsibility	Source
'Brits in hol hell trap'	Two British tourists died as a result of a gas leak in apartments in Playa Las Americas, Tenerife, Canary Islands.	Apparently the result of a leaking butane canister. A similar incident had occurred in the same complex 3 weeks previously. The accommodation provider and authorities responsible for monitoring safety standards were clearly at fault.	*The Star* front page (Allen, 1994)
'British tourist killed by bear'	A British tourist died saving his wife from a grizzly bear in Jasper National Park, Alberta, Canada.	Inappropriate behaviour by the couple, who were insufficiently prepared in unfamiliar circumstances.	*The Guardian* (Anon., 1992)
'British tourist killed by performing elephant'	An elephant charged during an obedience display at an animal park in Pattaya, Thailand.	The elephant was 'on heat' and should not have been on display. The animal park had a history of incidents. The park management bore a heavy responsibility for this death.	*The Guardian* (Walls, 2002)
'Holiday Britons killed in Florida as car hits tanker'	Three adults were killed and four children seriously injured when their car was in collision with a petrol tanker.	On the first day of a family holiday, in a hire car, the driver had just missed a turning and took a U-turn into the path of the tanker. In a jet-lagged condition, driving on the opposite side of the road to what would be the norm at home, in an unfamiliar environment, in a probably unfamiliar car, is something many tourists, unwisely, undertake.	*The Guardian* (Scott, 2004)

Perhaps the most serious long-term tourist health risk, but one that goes largely undiscussed within the industry, is skin cancer caused by excessive sun exposure (Peattie *et al.*, 2005) (Fig. 3.2). This is the most common form of cancer, with globally more than three times as many cases as lung cancer, the next most common form. It is the second most common form of cancer in the UK (perhaps the most common, given under-reporting), and also the fastest growing, with its incidence having doubled in the past 15 years. In some key tourism destinations it is reaching epidemic proportions: in the US, risk has increased from 1 case per 1500 in 1935 to 1 in 75 by 2000 (Edmunson, 1997).

Growth in international tourism is one of the factors viewed as contributing to this increase, and particularly the rise of family holidays to sunny destinations. Single incidents of severe sunburn, particularly during childhood, can determine eventual skin cancer risk, posing challenges for the awareness and behaviour of both parents and children (Hill and Dixon, 1999).

The risk of melanoma (the form of skin cancer accounting for most of the fatalities) can be doubled by even one incident of serious childhood sunburn (Crane *et al.*, 1993). Such a risk to young tourists is demonstrated in a sample of New Zealand students (Table 3.6), 56% of whom had been sunburnt during their summer holidays, with almost half having suffered to a moderate or severe degree (Ryan *et al.*, 1996; Ryan and Robertson, 1997). The classification of student tourists in Table 3.6 emphasizes that attitudinal data are important in identifying categories of travellers who are more at risk than others. In these cases, those groups designated as a consequence

Fig. 3.2. The expanse of Copacabana beach, Rio de Janeiro, crowded with sunbathers at a subtropical midday.

of their stated behaviour and attitudes as 'vibrant voyagers' and 'experiential socializers' appear to be most generally at risk. (However, compared, for example, with Carter's (1998) findings with business travellers, the 'vibrant voyagers' are more likely to confine their social and sexual explorations to other travellers rather than extending them to the 'other' of the host population.)

In the nature of response to and sense of responsibility for the cancer risks posed by holiday sunburn, two key factors tend to dominate. The first is the time lag between a sunburn incident and the resulting skin cancer, which could be a matter of months or more than 30 years. Thus, although it is a significant risk associated with travel, sunburn lacks the immediate consequences linked to most other tourism health and safety risks.

The second is the degree to which sun exposure is often the central point of a tourism experience. Carter (1997b), for example, has emphasized how, among young Glaswegian tourists visiting the Mediterranean, sun exposure represents a complex social process within which the tan may act as a critical emblem of tourist consumption. However, from focus group discussions, Peattie *et al.*

(2005) believe that such attitudes are changing. Within Australia, teenage respondents showed that health communication and concerns about skin cancer were beginning to change attitudes, since a deeply tanned appearance was increasingly viewed as a badge of stupidity and recklessness rather than of achievement (Garfield, 2004). On the other hand, lack of exposure to sun can result in vitamin D deficiency. Thus, as in other aspects of behaviour and lifestyle, individuals need to maintain a sensible balance: overreaction can sacrifice the physical and psychological benefits of moderate sun exposure claimed by many within the medical profession (Ness *et al.*, 1999).

Perhaps reinforced by aspects of the 'issue attention cycle', these factors may explain why, despite being highlighted as a growing risk within tourism (Clift and Page, 1996; Carter, 1997b; Ryan and Robertson, 1997; Segan *et al.*, 1999), sunburn and skin cancer have received relatively little attention compared with terrorism, DVT or sexually transmitted diseases (Peattie *et al.*, 2005). Yet skin cancer is preventable: simple behavioural changes, such as avoiding the strongest sun and making appropriate

Table 3.6. New Zealand student tourists (derived from Ryan *et al.*, 1996; Ryan and Robertson, 1997).

Category	Description	Characteristics
1. Moderates	Largest group – over one-quarter	Close to various scale midpoints
2. Reflective cruisers	These enjoy the company of others, are not risk-takers and are reflective, looking for a new life perspective	• Second largest group • Do not party hard or strongly seek romantic liaisons • Above average for socializing • Below average for relaxing • Generally enjoyed holidays but surprised at the risks that others took • Tended to be more reflective
3. Vibrant voyagers	A relatively large group who seek relaxation and excitement in active social life	• Social life based on nightlife and search for romantic and sexual encounters, although with the implication that this is likely to be with other travellers rather than members of the host population • Tend to be heavy drinkers • They party hard and have a 'great time' • They view such behaviour as broadening their outlook on life
4. Comfortables	Enjoyed themselves more than the average	• Did not see themselves as antisocial • Their holiday did little or nothing to influence their perspectives on themselves or on life • Did not consider romantic encounters an important element of their holiday
5. Isolates	Relatively antisocial: enjoy themselves very much but prefer their own company	• Low desire for an exciting social life • Little interest in seeking romance or drinking • Tended to be reflective
6. Experiential socializers	Small group: highest scores on relaxation and enjoyment	• Look for exciting social and varied nightlife • Drink more on holiday than when at home • Different from 'vibrant voyagers' in being more reflective on life, themselves and social relationships • Experienced social activities as a means of intellectual development
7. Woebegone wayfarers	Smallest group: enjoy themselves least when on holiday	• Did not have time to relax • Felt their holidays did not offer any life-enhancing experiences • Relatively uninterested in an exciting nightlife or a romantic encounter

use of suncreams/sunscreen, hats and 'long' clothing, would prevent up to 90% of cases. A key question is whether those within the tourism industry and those within public health are doing enough to make tourists aware of the risks and of the appropriate protective strategies.

Tourists can be more vulnerable to health and safety risks when travelling to unfamiliar destinations (Lawton and Page,

1997). This applies to the dangers from sun exposure, since the risks vary depending on latitude, season, time of day and weather. Local variations in topography can have a major influence, since highly reflective surfaces such as sand, snow and water – all common ingredients in popular holiday experiences – may increase ultraviolet (UV) exposure by as much as 90% (Robins, 1990). Altitude also increases risk: radiation levels increase by 4% with every 300 m of elevation – clearly relevant for those taking a holiday in mountainous regions. Ozone depletion has further complicated the environmentally related variations by introducing seasonally related fluctuations in UV intensity not directly related to the apparent intensity and warmth of the sun (Peattie *et al.*, 2005).

Such variability clearly creates responsibility challenges for:

- tourists, in terms of avoiding excessive sun exposure;
- those working in public health: promoting maximum protective behaviour in all circumstances might eliminate risk in theory, but may be counterproductive in practice as it could destroy the *raison d'être* for many holidays while also increasing the likelihood of vitamin D deficiency;
- the media and advertising industry, which tend to reinforce unsafe behaviour in relation to sun exposure; and
- the marketing communications campaigns within the tourism industry itself.

Peattie *et al.*'s (2005) observation of travel industry promotional materials revealed that images of people engaged in critical sun-safe behaviours (wearing hats, long clothing or locating themselves in the shade) are still strongly outweighed by images of 'sun worship'. However, they highlight an apparent trend towards increased use of brochure cover photographs featuring models in hats and long clothing for long-haul sunshine-oriented destinations. This perhaps reflects a stereotypical targeting of a more upmarket clientele who are perceived to be likely to be more responsive to and to associate with images of 'responsible' behaviour. But the extent to which brochure images reinforce stereotypes of risk behaviours remains a potentially interesting avenue for research.

Keeping healthy, avoiding accidents and other welfare-critical factors would appear to be essential ingredients for tourist satisfaction, if only because failure to do so reduces satisfaction levels. Yet such factors have tended to remain implicit rather than explicitly articulated in theoretical formulations. For example, Ryan (1991, 1994) has suggested that the relationship between motivation, performance and resultant satisfaction invites consideration of a number of variables, including:

- the expectation and perception of the place and its attributes;
- the importance of the activity to the individual in meeting personal needs;
- the expected outcomes of the activity;
- the role of intervening variables: internal, personal factors such as perceived ability to bring about a desired outcome; and external factors that affect the probability of a desired outcome such as the availability of human and other resources;
- the presence of significant others and the importance attached to them; and
- the degree to which an individual is able to adopt adaptive behaviour, such as goal adjustment and search behaviour, given the frustration of initial objectives (Ryan, 1991, 1994; see also Trauer and Ryan, 2005).

But Ryan does not develop the welfare implications of such variables.

Some travellers may delight in recounting horror stories of bad tourism experiences or of travel to potentially dangerous and hostile destinations (e.g. O'Rourke, 1989; Fraser, 1993; Pelton and Aral, 1998). Others, through the pursuit of so-called 'dark tourism' (e.g. Lennon and Foley, 1999, 2002; Breech, 2000; Henderson, 2000; Tarlow, 2005), specifically seek out attractions, activities and destinations that have a morbid dimension. Sites associated with war and conflict have become particularly popular (Smith, 1998). Decrop and Snelders (2005) have suggested a typology of tourists, based on a combination of socio-psychological processes and decisions, that can help us better understand evolving and divergent trends in tourist behaviour. Yet most tourists still seek safety, security, comfort and emotional uplift. A significant popular literature has developed to assist tourists and to warn them of the potential problems and dangers of travel (e.g. Moynahan, 1983, 1985; McPherson and MacFarlane, 1992).

Prentice *et al.* (1994) employed the term 'endearment' to express the tourist's relationship with a destination area. As an expression of 'the experiences and benefits tourists gain from being tourists', 'endearment' has a number of potential welfare implications, which were largely not explored. However, Prentice *et al.* emphasized that, while for most leisure tourists 'endearment' is effected through various activities and interaction with local people, at least two caveats are important in segment identification and destination marketing. First, repeat tourists have different perceptions from those of first-time visitors and may establish an explicit endearing relationship with an aspect of place or person(s) that contributes to the desire to return. Second, specifically in respect of those visitors with (pre-existing) friends or relatives, 'endearment' may be expressed towards those friends or relatives rather than to the destination area itself. This is no doubt often the case, although a detailed study of 'visiting friends and/or relatives' (VFR) tourism in Scotland did find evidence of relatively infrequent visitors motivated for the opposite reason: using the residential location of a friend or relative specifically to be able to visit a particular destination area or attraction (Boyne *et al.*, 2002).

Post-holiday Syndromes

A number of authors (e.g. Gunn, 1988) have distinguished the period immediately after returning home from holiday as evaluative and a time to reflect on the holiday and travel experiences in order to inform future holiday choice decisions. A number of commentators (e.g. Dann, 1995, 1996; Norton, 1996; Jenkins, 2003) have embraced this conceptually within a 'circuit of culture', whereby, having been exposed to promotional material and then to the destination experience itself, the tourist returns home to reflect on and to modify her/his understanding and thence to circulate such a re-evaluation within their own society. In this way, as Norton (1996) argues in relation to colonial imagery of safari tourism in East Africa, by recirculating their experience, tourists are able to modify perceptions of the destination within a pre-existing framework of 'discursive indicators'.

Yet many holiday images and experiences fade quickly, skewed for perpetuity by the visual images retained in photographs, videotape/DVD, postcards, brochures and souvenirs. Research on the timing of subsequent holiday choice decisions appears limited, suggesting that the effective function of post-trip cognitive evaluation may be less an accurate reflection of 'feedback' than some models of linkage might suggest. Service industry received wisdom suggests that negative consumer experiences, such as a bad holiday, are likely to be circulated by word of mouth and in writing to up to ten times more people than are positive experiences.

Numerous post-holiday surveys have been undertaken of tourists' reflections on their experiences, quality of services and overall aspects of 'satisfaction'. From a welfare perspective, the importance of these lies in their ability to be absorbed into a conceptualization of tourist experience and in their practical value in being fed back to the industry in order to improve the destination welfare experience. In this respect, Ryan's (1997) sampling of 1127 UK 'holidaymakers' was potentially useful. He categorized their most common holiday experiences, relating them to higher aspects of Maslow's (1970) hierarchy of needs. Ryan found sources of dissatisfaction for his sample to be wider in range but lower in number than the sources of satisfaction (Table 3.7).

Generally, the material and spiritual experiences of a holiday all too soon become reabsorbed into 'normal' everyday life, diluted and subsumed to a minimal (shared) corner of our consciousness. In material terms, for example, the CD of the music that meant so much on the holiday may be absorbed into the rest of the collection and played with rapidly declining frequency.

Post-holiday tension (PHT) or 'post-holiday blues' can be a significant psychological state following a holiday. In the UK at least, it has been found to be experienced by 79% of men and 74% of women, with 10% taking a day off to recover before returning to work. It is suggested that a week's holiday may provide insufficient time to recover from workplace stress, particularly as the stress generated by preparing for the holiday itself can follow the traveller. A UK survey revealed that 76% of returning employees estimated that their stress levels were back to pre-holiday levels within a week of returning to work (BBC News, 2000b). Doctors report a marked increase in visits from their patients complaining about minor ailments such as backache and irritable bowel syndrome after a summer break (Ripley, 2003).

Being back at work can be difficult for many people: problems of having limited freedom and fitting in again with work relationships can lead to frustration:

> You soon find out who's genuinely interested in what you've done, seen, visited. It's alarming how quickly you do absorb into your 'former' life and how the novelty of being back wears off within days, and the novelty of me being back for other people wears off too. The single most depressing thing I've found adjusting to is not actual work itself but going from living spontaneously and doing something different every day to a restrained, routine-driven life where only two out of every seven days give you the chance to do something 'out of the norm'.
>
> (Grover, 2004)

Factors that commonly contribute to this syndrome tend to fall into three major categories:

- psychological: for example, having unrealistic expectations of employment

Table 3.7.   The main concerns of Ryan's sample of 1127 UK 'holidaymakers' (from Ryan, 1997: 60–63).

Item of dissatisfaction	Number of mentions
Poor weather	192
Long journey there and back	68
Airport delays	57
Having to go home/back to work	55
Insufficient income/high prices	42
Poor food	35
Insects	28
Cramped/basic accommodation	24
Intrusive noise	24
Being ripped off/hassled	23
Poor hotels/accommodation	19
Long journey back	17
Being rushed/too much to do/see	16
Overcrowding/too many people	14
Long journey there	13
Cramped flight/poor flight	11
Local people not friendly	11
Traffic jams	11

and colleagues, and feeling disappointed when those expectations fall short;

- financial: perhaps as a result of paying for the holiday; and
- physical: the strains of commuting combined with a lack of exercise at work, perhaps coupled with having gained weight on holiday from too much food and alcohol (Langley James, 2003).

To manage the adjustment between holiday and work, a number of employers, encouraged in the UK by the quality agency Investors in People (IiP), provide guidelines for their returning workers (Box 3.8).

The 'embodiment' of post-holiday syndrome has been recognized in a growing demand for body contouring surgery. This may involve breast enlargement, 'tummy tuck', liposuction or the removal of thread veins in the legs, all apparently fuelled by the growing phenomenon of 'beach envy'. A private hospital in Glasgow reports a disproportionate number of its clients wanting such surgery during September and October on returning from holiday. Claiming that this is not confined to the wealthy, the hospital indicates that many clients start saving as soon as they return home and then schedule their operation for a month later. 'In warmer climates, like in Italy and Australia, people spend more time looking after themselves, and when Scots go on holiday it suddenly dawns on them' (BBC News, 2000a).

However, return to the familiar is perhaps more positive for some, if only for relatively negative reasons. This may be returning from a foreign country to the free use of the traveller's own language again and the ability to articulate and convey communication in precise verbal terms (and not having visual signals misinterpreted) instead of in a fractured, pidgin version of the host or traveller's tongue.

The post-holiday period may also bring the returnee into contact with those not encountered at other times of the year, such as the retail staff who help to develop the holiday print film. On returning the photographs following processing, does

---

Box 3.8. Advice to avoid or minimize post-holiday syndrome.

At work

1.   Do not abandon the holiday rhythm altogether: don't try to catch up with everything at once; set a work exit time and stick to it; and try to maintain a physical activity enjoyed during the holiday such as swimming.
2.   Prioritize work: only tackle the really important tasks during the first few days: for example, end the tyranny of the email inbox and avoid feeling pressured into responding to every item.
3.   Take a regular break: thinking time can enhance creativity and effectiveness.
4.   Reduce any feelings of isolation at work.
5.   Plan more leave: especially planning the next holiday can provide something to look forward to.
6.   But do not plan all the spontaneity out of life.
7.   Do not feel guilty about being away from work.

At home

1.   Seek support from family or friends, especially if they can help recall of the good times while on holiday.
2.   Share responsibilities at home.
3.   Be realistic: tackle one action at a time.
4.   Budget: plan around financial pressures.
5.   Continue healthy habits: food, fluid intake, sufficient sleep and exercise.
6.   Certain foods can also be mood boosting. Eat regular portions of lean meat, cheese and eggs, which are rich in the amino acid tryptophan, which converts to the mood-enhancing compound serotonin in the brain. Several studies have also found a link between a low intake of omega-3 fatty acids, such as those found in fish, and higher levels of depression.
7.   Seek the light: improve mood by spending time in daylight or near windows.

Sources: BBC News, 2000b; BUPA, 2004; Johnston, 2004.

---

the processor's sincerely conveyed, more than service encounter cliché 'enjoy your pictures' hint at having shared the experience of some of the depicted locations and activities that pass through their hands? Is this non-digital encounter one that will

disappear with rapidly changing photographic technology?

Further, holiday photographs prove or
validate the fact that the tourists involved
have experienced something beyond the
everyday, and, if sufficiently 'exotic', may
be perceived to confer status. Representing
the 'recollection' element (Fridgen, 1984) of
the post-holiday stage in the tourist welfare
cycle, photographs both enhance and dis-
tort trip memories. As well as abstracting
from their context (perhaps uncharacteris-
tic) captured moments in time, the imperfect visual nature of photographs – perhaps
under- or overexposed, out of focus, blurred
or poorly framed – will also colour (even
monochromatically), and perhaps come to
dominate over a period of time, reflections
on and recollections of the experience or
situation represented. Is it true, as Little
(1991: 156) suggests, that 'photographs are
personal signs that come associated with a
story that serves as mnemonic for the experience'? We may, for example, be great lovers but poor photographers (or vice versa),
with our physical, photographic representations of an otherwise well-remembered
romantic holiday providing an emotional
anticlimax. Ironically, good-quality photographs might be being collected after
processing and viewed for the first time
against the backdrop of a holiday romance
turning sour in the cold light of post-
holiday reality.

Haldrup and Larsen (2003) suggest that
much tourist photography revolves around
(re?)producing social relations rather than
consuming places. It is a 'theatre of life',
where people in concert perform places,
scripts and roles to and for themselves. However, little is said of those actors involved in
the processing of tourists' photographic
images. Perhaps their incorporation into a
conceptualization of the exchanges involved
in the realization of holiday photographic
imagery would highlight a wider web of
post-holiday (social) relations woven around
such personalized representations of 'holiday'. This might, in turn, help us to better
understand some of the welfare dimensions of the post-tourism transition back to
'normality'.

A crucial factor is that for most of
us the holiday experience is not our norm
and, however much, particularly in retro-
spect, we may wish it to be or while on holiday subconsciously assume it to be, we are
cruelly reminded with immediate force that
it is not. This in turn causes us to reflect
on our own lives, our perceived (relative)
success, happiness, relationships and other
major qualities that for the rest of the year
we cannot – or will not – contemplate for
fear of depressing ourselves further.

But, equally, what if we are happy and
content with most of our lives? And, if we
have bad holiday experiences or find the
country we visit has a poor standard of
living or an oppressive political or cultural
environment, we may just be tempted to
appreciate our own circumstances a little
more positively. Or the experience may spur
us to act to modify our circumstances.

Looking to the next holiday is the obvious psychological escape mechanism from
our 'ordinary' lives, renewing the tourist
cycle, revitalizing the welfare revolution. In
this sense, tourism is very much both a personal and a religious pursuit, more about
'self' and less about the 'other'. But, rather
than being the oft-characterized process of
pilgrimage, it is the conscious moving from
one festival, one holy week, and anticipat-
ing the next in the religious calendar of
tourism. It is, like the opium of the people,
addictive for those who have access to its
recreational, welfare-enhancing properties.

Summary and Conclusion

Following from the introductory factors
summarized in Chapter 1 and the constraints
on access and participation emphasized in
Chapter 2, we began this chapter with the
proposition that individual welfare considerations appear to provide the basis for
undertaking holidays and leisure travel and
that the tourism industry should be designed
to promote and secure such welfare.

In the chapter we employed a tourist
welfare cycle framework to evaluate some
of the key welfare dimensions of holiday-
taking for the tourists involved and those

facilitating the experience. Several factors can enhance welfare and the chapter has also examined those that may compromise it, while suggesting where responsibility for preparing for, avoiding or coping with such factors lies. Indeed, it is clear that there are several aspects of the activities of tourists, industry facilitators (such as travel agents) and destination authorities that could improve the welfare of both tourists and those they encounter, through a greater assumption of responsibility for those shared welfare outcomes.

In the next chapter, the perspective of the welfare of those living and employed in tourism destinations is taken.

4

Living and Working in Tourism Destinations

Flexible is a polite word for low pay. In service industries, this has nothing to do with global competition. Shelves can't be stacked in Singapore nor grannies bathed in Bombay, nor airline food packed anywhere but Heathrow. Cheap service-sector jobs do nothing much for the wider economy: they only provide the better-off with services that are cheaper than the true cost.

(Toynbee, 2005)

Box 4.1. Chapter aims and summary.

This chapter seeks to: take a welfare-centred perspective on those living and working in tourism destinations.
It does this by: addressing issues of 'community', ethical relations, crime and health, employment welfare, restructuring and labour migration, within frameworks emphasizing trade-offs, competition and complementarity.
Its key concepts are: community, trade-offs, employment conditions, labour migration.
It concludes that: industry fragmentation diffuses authority and responsibility, and most stakeholders currently lack the ethical motivation to raise much of the industry above its dependence upon a relatively low-wage, 'flexible' workforce.

Introduction

Krippendorf (1989: 115–119) discussed the need for those involved in developing tourism to pay special attention to the ways that it can benefit destination resident populations. A welfare-centred approach to the question of tourism destinations, their residents and employees can assist an evaluation of both the benefits and disbenefits, the trade-offs between them and between residents and those involved in tourism.

This chapter will take such an approach by focusing on those living and working in tourism destination areas. We address issues relating to notions of local 'community' within destination residents, and its inadequate conceptualization. The role and significance of tourism vary considerably within and between different local areas, and tourism interacts with other aspects of a destination's development sectors in diverse ways. The frequent associated use of 'community' and 'tourism sustainability' may not reflect such a situation adequately and may be a way of obviating the need for a more holistic consideration of the needs of all stakeholders. Within this context, a focus is placed upon the ethical nature of interactions between the major tourism actors within the destination, with trade-offs, competitive and complementary roles being examined. Second homes, crime and health are addressed in this context. A number of aspects of tourism employee welfare are then evaluated, including the position of women, the effects of post-communist restructuring, the complex issues surrounding labour migration and the specific case of employment in the cruise line industry.

Residents as 'Community'

Lash and Urry (1994) argued that the notion of local place-based community had been threatened for half a century or more as a result of the increasing mobility of society and growth of global communications. But it has actually re-emerged as a vehicle for rooting individuals and societies in a climate of economic restructuring and growing social, cultural and political uncertainty. As political, social and economic structures based on the nation state are questioned, so 'local community' has joined the rhetoric of the sustainability literature to be seen as an essential building block in the 'new sociations' and political alliances of the emerging 'third sector' (Richards and Hall, 2000).

Place-based communities have become central to a holistic concept of sustainability, with an implicit recognition that protection of the 'natural' environment must be grounded in the communities and societies that exploit and depend upon it. Natural environments are culturally constructed (Eder, 1988; Green, 2005; see also Chapter 6), and local communities and economic systems may hold the key to their survival or destruction. But this raises questions about the nature, scope and function of 'community'. Community-led 'sustainable development' requires an understanding not just of the relationship local communities have with their environment but also of their internal political, economic and cultural tensions and conflicts.

This has created a growing literature on community-based tourism and community development in tourism in recent years (e.g. Pearce *et al.*, 1996). Murphy's (1985) classic review of community tourism formed the basis for many later studies. It emphasized the necessity for each community to relate tourism development to local needs. Some destination communities seek to empower themselves by developing successful tourism products that reflect and promote their goals and values (e.g. Moctezuma, 2001). This often needs to draw upon expertise and funding sources available locally, including universities, local and regional government, NGOs and other consultants, and on partnership opportunities with public, private and NGO bodies (Murphy and Murphy, 2004: 28).

Nevertheless, the concept of local community needs, as a key dimension of a welfare paradigm for tourism, remains both elusive and contested.

The word 'community' implies a common interest, possession or enjoyment (*Collins Westminster Dictionary*). However, the interests of those living in a local area do not always coincide. The literature on the bounding of 'community', conflict versus consensus and questions of inclusion and exclusion is considerable. Different groups or individuals may benefit or suffer disproportionately from tourism development (e.g. Prentice, 1993). This leads to tensions, sometimes open conflict, not least over the aims or outcomes of tourism (see, for example, Kamsma and Bras, 2000). But industry assumptions of consensus imbue 'community' with implicit ideological underpinnings. In some cases, however, there may be an 'altruistic surplus' effect, which leads individuals to recognize the communal good derived from tourism and therefore to lessen opposition to tourism development, even among those who may not benefit directly (Richards and Hall, 2000).

But Butcher (2003: 3) sees the search for 'community' in other societies as representing tourists' disillusionment with their own. Singh *et al.* (2003: 6, 7) argue that community-based tourism is an amorphous concept, and that 'in the tourism literature, communities have usually been researched and described in the form of case examples . . . rather than being defined'. Thus Jackson and Morpeth (1999: 5) point out that, even in documents such as Local Agenda 21, 'community' is employed inconsistently and without definition. Although Murphy and Murphy (2004) offer a more comprehensive strategic management approach, their case studies are largely restricted to the New World.

Early models of resident perceptions of tourists (e.g. Doxey, 1975) were quick to suggest that feelings were unidirectional. Others recognized the fluidity of destination residents' experiences (Hottala, 2002; Fisher, 2004). Within a destination area there can exist a range of views from acceptance to avoidance, and these in turn change over time. Factors that account for this range of reaction include physical distance between where residents live and work compared with tourist spaces and the ratio between hosts and guests, as well as the extent of support for tourism that exists within the host community. Lankford and Howard (1994) developed a tourism impact attitudinal scale that identified ten variables that could influence a resident's opinion about local tourism. These were: length of residence, economic dependency on tourism, distance of tourism activity from resident's home, resident involvement in tourism decision making, birthplace, level of knowledge, level of contact with tourists, demographic characteristics, perceived impacts on local outdoor recreation opportunities and rate of community growth.

Derived from Elkington's (1999: 397) notion of a 'triple bottom line', Murphy and Murphy (2004: 261–262) suggest that residents have three general objectives in relation to tourist arrivals: a financial return for the community, enhanced environmental resources and attractions, and social equity through local planning and management. But Howie (2000) points out that disadvantaged local communities may not be able to identify with tourism development because they view it as an exogenous development with benefits that largely accrue to outsiders. Inability to identify with tourism development in turn may lead either to resistance or to indifference. Research in a variety of locations and in different tourism circumstances has tried to articulate such resident attitudes (Table 4.1; see also Box 4.2).

Jackson and Morpeth (1999, 2000) suggest that Local Agenda 21 (LA21) does offer the potential for marginalized communities to be involved in tourism development, but this is often frustrated by lack of awareness or divided responsibilities in local authorities. Policies relating to different aspects of sustainability are often not integrated (e.g. tourism and transport – see D. Hall, 1999, 2004d), constraining the exchange of information within policy-making bodies and between different policy levels. The lack of stability in communities in transition may undermine participative models. Ironically, however, conditions of instability may also provide windows of opportunity for community involvement which may not be apparent in more stable communities (e.g. D. Hall, 2000).

In many cases, however, the development of tourism may only serve to highlight existing inequalities and differences in the community. Communities themselves are unequal, and the fashionability of research into social exclusion has re-emphasized the inequalities within and between self-recognized groups (e.g. Cloke and Little, 1997; Milbourne, 1997). Yet the variables of race, gender, sexuality, age and (dis)ability and their role as determinants of tourism power dimensions are still poorly researched, despite one or two key critical studies (e.g. Morgan and Pritchard, 1998; see also Chapter 2).

The failure of existing institutions to address problems of inequality and deprivation has led to the growth of the 'third sector': grass-roots organizations, NGOs and other associations that operate outside existing formal structures of governance. The objective of these alliances is 'empowerment', an ideal that is based on the concept of generative, rather than distributive, power (see also Chapter 5). Most current power structures are distributive, in the sense that they presuppose a scarcity of resources that must be distributed. They are therefore forced to compete with each other for resources. The generative view of power, on the other hand, assumes that everyone has power, or skills and capabilities. The aim of individual and group empowerment, therefore, is to combine everyone's power in collective action for the common good (Sofield, 2003). In many cases it remains at the level of

Table 4.1. Typologies of resident attitudes towards tourism (% of research samples) (from Davis *et al.*, 1988; Ryan and Montgomery, 1994; Williams and Lawson, 2001; cited in Murphy and Murphy, 2004: 191).

Florida (Davis *et al.*, 1988)	Bakewell, Derbyshire (English Peak District) (Ryan and Montgomery, 1994)	Ten New Zealand towns (Williams and Lawson, 2001)
Lovers 20%: no negative opinions of tourism	*Enthusiasts* 22%: support tourism but not excessively	*Lovers* 44%: approve of tourism the most and believe the benefits are distributed fairly throughout the community
Love 'em for a reason 26%: less strongly pro-tourism	–	–
Cautious romantics 21%: although being positive towards tourism also recognize some negative features	–	–
In-betweens 18%: hold moderate opinions, agreeing with statements to a lesser degree than *lovers* or *haters*	*Middle-of-the-roaders* 54.3%: between the other two	*Taxpayers* 25%: who do not feel very strongly about anything to do with tourism except how it has a bearing on their taxes, both good and bad
Haters 16%: have extremely negative opinions regarding tourism and tourists	*Somewhat irritated* 23.5%: have negative opinions about tourism's impacts and are sceptical about its benefits	*Cynics* 10%: who approve the least, and think that tourism has changed their town for the worse
–	–	*Innocents* 20%: who seem to be missing both the benefits and the problems of tourism because of their lack of direct contact with the industry

---

Box 4.2. Residents of 'real' destinations.

Finding local opinions is a dangerous game. A friend visiting relatives in Barbados said they didn't understand why he wanted to go and lie on the beach like a dumb tourist.

Last week, in unpretty Gretna Green, a local confided that he could not imagine why anyone would go there for romance, before stopping, sensing he'd gone too far.

As one reader responded to a recent Sunday newspaper piece on 'the real Spain', the article's author had done little more than 'cloak this land where I am happy to live with his own ridiculous, totally unrealistic fantasies'. The real 'real Spain' is, she said, full of people doing things like going to offices.

Source: Topham, 2005.

---

rhetoric, and may unrealistically raise expectations that are unable to be met. As Mowforth and Munt (1998, 2003) have emphasized, analysis of power relationships is crucial to an understanding of the impact of tourism on the community. Not all members of the community, however defined, are equally able to influence the decisions that affect them.

Although empowerment is a concept that is implicit in most versions of 'sustainable tourism', it is usually a distributive form of empowerment to local communities from above, rather than generative empowerment from within (Richards and Hall, 2000). Smith and Duffy (2003: 138–139) argue for distributive justice based upon the development of 'dynamic and enthusiastic institutional arrangements'. Yet they point to the fact that few ecotourism projects, for example, have sufficiently strong institutions to support this. The 'empowerment' of local groups through participative planning and development presupposes, as any democratic process should, that there are substantially different options available for people to choose freely between. Yet, in the poor rural areas where community tourism is often advocated as a central plank of development planning, these choices rarely exist. Instead, agendas are set by those offering aid or investment (Butcher, 2003: 122; see also Chapter 5). Further, Gössling (2002b) argues that tourism, as an agent of modernization, decontextualizes and dissolves the relationships individuals have with society and nature, undermining the very conceptual basis of community tourism as a plank of sustainable development.

Destinations, Stakeholders and Ethical Behaviour

A welfare perspective seeks to identify optimum outcomes and to highlight the trade-offs and compromises required to achieve them. As noted in Chapter 1, the ethical nature of tourism stakeholders' behaviour represents a key factor in this process. Thus Fennell and Przeclawski (2003) argue that the roots of the negative consequences of tourism can be found in the behaviour of three main groups of actors: tourists, inhabitants of the visited localities and 'brokers' (including those involved in tourism administration, marketing, tour operation/guiding and hotel and tourist information staff). This is exemplified in Table 4.2.

Of course, interactions between stakeholders are not so clear and straightforward in reality, and it could be argued that the compilation of such ethical perspectives is inevitably driven by the compilers' own cultural perspectives. Even an apparently simple concept such as timekeeping and the mutual obligations it demands is subject to cultural reinterpretation (Box 4.3).

Welfare of Residents and 'Host–Guest Relations'

Our next contentious cliché is 'host–guest relations' (Sherlock, 2001). In any destination residents may not feel that they are acting as 'hosts' nor may tourists consider themselves as 'guests'. Similarly, visitors may not regard local residents as 'hosts', nor may local people think of tourists to their area as 'guests'. There may be no direct relations – economic transactions – between significant proportions of these two sets of 'stakeholders' (Aramberri, 2001; Singh et al., 2003: 10). Yet the welfare of tourists who are able to visit, enjoy, relax or be stimulated in places where other people live may be gained at the expense or enhancement of the welfare of those residents. A normative welfare paradigm would argue that successful tourism should be able to enhance the welfare of both, as would Local Agenda 21 and any interpretation of sustainable tourism.

Reality is, of course, more complex: destination policymakers and decision-takers are often faced with trade-offs that will benefit one or more groups at the (relative) expense of one or more other groups. But, even if a company seeks to be ethical and responsible, the imposition of its ethics and practices on a destination community can be problematic if these are not consonant with the ethics and practices of the local community (Murphy and Murphy, 2004: 257). Baldacchino (1997), for example, has identified a 'small-scale labour syndrome', whereby incompatibilities arise between small island communities and multinational operations that establish businesses in these communities. Within this syndrome, corporations send expatriates to exercise 'gunboat diplomacy' by imposing the corporate line on local employees, while local communities subvert the corporate rules and regulations through the application of their own culture, experience and values.

Within the context of ecotourism development, Erlet Cater's (1994) 'winners and losers' framework provides a useful starting point in evaluating distributive aspects of welfare benefits derived from tourism. Reiterating this more recently, Boyd and

Table 4.2. Tourism–actor interactions (after Fennell and Przeclawski, 2003: 142–149; also Ayala, 1996; Fennell and Malloy, 1995, 1999; Timothy and Ioannides, 2002).

Actors/stakeholders	Ethical perspectives on interactional behaviour
Tourists	
1. The tourist as self	The tourist has the opportunity to become better acquainted with: (i) her/himself; (ii) residents and their customs; and (iii) the natural world of the visited region.
2. Behaviour towards residents	Tourists should respect the basic values of the inhabitants as well as the social order of the destination community.
	Thus local inhabitants should be viewed on equal terms, and not as objects to be manipulated, humiliated or taken unfair advantage of.
	Tourists need to be considerate of the fact that local people with whom they interact are often working.
	Tourists thus need to be conscious of the way their own behaviour may influence how residents formulate opinions about their source country.
3. Tourist–tourist interactions	Tourists should avoid inducing other travellers into behaviours that contradict their ethical beliefs, and they should not follow such behaviour.
	Information about the destination should be shared.
	Other tourists should be respected, for example in relation to time-keeping (see Box 4.3).
4. Interactions with nature/culture	Tourists are responsible for respecting and caring for the environment they are visiting.
	It is important for visitors to understand the concept of relative carrying capacities.
	Tourists need to appreciate the importance of their choices – e.g. of transport, accommodation, attractions – for the actions of others and for their (collective) global impacts.
Residents	
1. Towards tourists	Tourists should be valued beyond their financial contributions, and these values need to be consistently communicated and reinforced through culture, mission and vision statements of public and private organizations.
	Thus tourism needs to be viewed as a vehicle to broaden the horizons of residents – as an open window to the world to promote education, tolerance and positive attitudes towards others.
	Residents should protect their cultural identities.
	Visitors should not be discriminated against in regard to race, nationality, beliefs or gender (or age, or by being a tourist).
	Tourists should be offered good medical aid and high-quality services.
2. Towards own 'community'	'Communities' must be made aware of how the industry is planned, developed and managed to help prevent loss of control.
	The host population should therefore actively participate in decisions on the type of tourism appropriate to their own lifestyles, cultures and natural resources, and be free to reject tourism.
	The 'community' must protect itself and its citizens.
	The direct and indirect benefits of tourism should be spread fairly across the 'community'.
	Residents should recognize and react positively to the desire of many tourists to meet and interact with local people.
3. Towards own environment	The local population should value and take care to protect the natural and cultural heritage in which they live and work, and thereby provide a better home for themselves and visitors alike.
4. Towards brokers	There need to be clearly defined lines of communication between providers and residents, allowing residents to voice concerns over development that affects their lives.

Continued

Table 4.2. *Continued.*

Actors/stakeholders	Ethical perspectives on interactional behaviour
	Residents will be interested in employment opportunities within the industry, and to benefit directly or indirectly from other aspects of tourism development.
Brokers	
1. Behaviour towards tourists	They should critically examine the economic, social, cultural and educational consequences of their policies. They should strive to secure appropriate levels of certification and accreditation to enable them to structure the best and safest programmes, convenient and safe transport, hygienic conditions, and to protect the safety and rights of their clients. Operator programmes need to be sensitive to the ecological and social conditions of the attractions that are central to their itineraries. Operators need to be sensitive to the fact that different categories of tourists have different needs and desires, and that programmes must be adjusted accordingly. Information provision should be full, objective and impartial, and should support mutual understanding and dialogue through the provision of information on local culture, customs, beliefs and ethics.
2. Behaviour related to residents	Tourism administrators and governments should strive to promote tourism based on social, cultural, ecological and educational well-being. The rights of the inhabitants and their interests therefore need to be taken into account in tourism planning and development. Residents must be allowed to know how they are benefiting, directly and indirectly, from tourism development in their region. Local people should be prepared for contact with tourists, and be informed about the culture, customs and behaviour of visitors. Residents should be supported in developing an attitude of hospitality and tolerance. Mechanisms should be developed to promote the authentic local traditions and values of resident and indigenous populations. The physical planning of tourism must take into account the rights and interests of the local population, and notably cultural heritage and the natural environment. If possible the everyday life of the inhabitants and their customs should not be disturbed. Developments should not aggravate the living conditions of the local population.
3. Towards other brokers	Within the spirit of competition, an atmosphere of respect and cooperation should be fostered. Industry organizations and associations should share information, technologies and expertise, especially as success is often contingent upon many externalities outside the scope of the operator. Governments should provide leadership in marketing and promotion and be equitable in their dispensation of information. Tourism organizations need to include corporate ethical values in marketing, promotion and programming.
4. Towards the environment	Ethical conduct in planning and development should be applied across all aspects of tourism and not confined to ecotourism. All brokers involved in the planning, development, management and delivery of tourism, in association with other industries, should share the task of creating the cleanest and most efficient product possible through the newest and best technologies available.

Singh (2003) suggest a fourfold typology ('scenarios') of 'tourism–host community [sic] relationships' (Table 4.3), which represent, in crude and generalized terms, a

Box 4.3. Timekeeping and cultural (re)interpretation.

During a recent visit to Cuba, the authors took a 2-day motor-coach excursion that involved spending more than an hour at the beginning of the first day, and a similar time at the end of the second, cruising the hotels of Havana and Playa del Este picking up and dropping off the various participants (from around a dozen nationalities) of the excursion.

During the varied and many stops over the 2 days, national stereotyped characteristics soon became apparent. German and Nordic travellers would return to the bus on time or before, British would amble and be within a few minutes of the scheduled time, while Mediterranean and Latin American tourists would engage the guide in conversation – over a second or third ice cream, to which she did not object – to well beyond: (i) the previously announced departure time; and (ii) the point (usually 10–15 mins after (i)) when the Cuban driver began to get restless, an emotion usually expressed by his testing the range of the bus engine's throttle.

Doubtless such roles and attitudes would have been modified and melded had the excursion been of longer duration.

welfare interpretation of such relations. 'Relations' or 'relationships' may not be an appropriate term, given the often substantial lack of interaction between these two groups. 'States of (well-)being' may be more apposite. Of course, such typologies overlook winners and losers within stakeholder groups and, as noted earlier in the chapter, most notably differential impacts among destination residents (e.g. Lindberg *et al.*, 2001).

We would suggest, however, that a more holistic and realistic appraisal of destination dynamics should embrace the general welfare impacts of at least three groups of stakeholders within any such representation of destination relationships and tradeoffs. Examples of this approach are shown in Table 4.4. This acts to draw together the focal groups of Chapters 3, 4, 5 and 6 in this volume.

Welfare Frameworks for the Destination

Drawing on a wide interpretation of 'destination resident' to include those working in the destination but not living there, we can conceptualize five types of 'states of (well-)being' that residents may experience in relation to tourism-related activities. These can be designated:

- *competitive*, where residents, tourism workers and tourists compete for spatial

Table 4.3. A typology of 'tourism–host community relationships' (from Boyd and Singh, 2003: 26–30).

Designation	Scenarios	Examples
Win–Win	Community-based tourism	CAMPFIRE projects, Zimbabwe (Chalker, 1994; Potts *et al.*, 1996)
Win–Lose	Community benefits at the expense of mass tourism through restricting tourist numbers, emphasizing quality tourism, minimizing leakages	Bermuda (Conlin, 1996)
Lose–Win	Tourism gains at the expense of the community, which may be destroyed both socially and physically	Gambling tourism, Atlantic City (Morrison, 1989; Eadington, 1999)
Lose–Lose	Tourism and community both lose, such as where short-term, uncontrolled, mass, coastal, resort-based development takes place	A number of Mediterranean resorts (Klemm, 1992)
Modifications	Lose–lose has been reversed in some Mediterranean resorts	Benidorm and Mallorca (Curtis, 1997)

Table 4.4. A typology of destination welfare trade-offs between residents, tourists and tourism workers.

Trade-offs: residents–tourists– tourism workers	Scenarios	Indicative examples (yes, some of these are contestable)
Win–Win–Win	Development of an enjoyable product providing decently paid employment and stimulating the development of appropriate infrastructure and facilities that can benefit residents	Regenerated quayside, Newcastle–Gateshead, River Tyne, north-east England
Win–Win–Lose	Tourists and residents gain services and more accessible attractions at the expense of exploited (migrant?) workers	Rapid development of Dubai, UAE*
Win–Lose–Lose	Residents gain assets by exploiting both tourists and workers	Unlikely to obtain
Win–Lose–Win	Tourists are exploited by a socially damaging product that nevertheless provides economic benefits for employees through wages and residents through taxes	Gambling casinos on US Native American reservations
Lose–Win–Lose	Tourists gain at the expense of both exploited labour and destinations, which suffer negative impacts but few of the benefits of tourism	Ocean cruising in the Caribbean
Lose–Lose–Lose	Uncontrolled development with high levels of leakages and a product that soon loses its attractiveness	Antalya on the Turkish Mediterranean coast
Lose–Lose–Win	Tourists are exploited by a dubious product that makes the promoters wealthy but does social harm to residents	Timeshare rip-offs, generating a negative image of particular destination areas
Lose–Win–Win	All-inclusive resorts that are physically and economically isolated from local residents	Many Mediterranean, Black Sea, Caribbean, etc. enclaves; Center Parcs

*UAE, United Arab Emirates.

and social resources, such as transport, including road and parking space, water and other natural resources, accommodation and property. Specific competitive engagements can be the focus of media attention (e.g. Boxes 4.4 and 4.5);

- *complementary*, whereby the activities of tourists and the tourism industry complement those of residents, for example offering appropriate employment opportunities, helping to raise local skill levels or enhancing the quality of and access to local amenities;
- *complicit*, where the values and aspirations of residents and mass tourism would appear to converge in opposition to external (often environmental) values, as in the case of the Akamas peninsula

in Cyprus, where locals, including landowners and developers, wanted to share the perceived benefits of mass tourism in opposition to environmental conservationists and governmental muddled thinking on 'sustainable tourism' (Ioannides, 1995);

- *subverted*, where destination residents' values and practices are undermined to the detriment of both their cultural and social welfare, for example as expressed through health and diet (see below); and
- *subordinate*, whereby destination residents are explicitly subordinated to the tourism industry and may be unable to express a dissenting voice to its presence and practices.

Box 4.4. Competition for beach territory in southern Spain.

Frustrated with finding local beaches covered with parasols left by tourists who turn up hours later to claim their spot on the sand, the residents of Almuñécar – a popular holiday destination, especially among young Spaniards from the north – took the issue to the local council.

Council officials agreed the practice had to end, and for 2004 authorized a ban on people leaving beach parasols on the sand in the morning as place-holders. They ordered the police to patrol the beaches and seize any parasol left unattended, reclaimable for a fine of €36.60.

In response, a group of angry tourists surrounded a police vehicle containing parasols and blocked the road for 2 h. Local opinion suggested that most of those who got up early to place parasols were from Granada, the largest city in the region, but that having claimed the best spots they often did not use them until after lunch.

Source: Heckle, 2004.

Box 4.5. Competition for access to the surf: Cornwall, south-west England.

A group of anonymous Cornish surfers, who style themselves as guerrillas, have campaigned against the influx of often amateur surfers and partygoers, who, they claim, pollute beaches, show disrespect to the local community and do not abide by surfing etiquette, crowding their 'line-ups'. The faction has undertaken local patrols, attempting to tape beaches off to visitors who have been in the area for less than 3 weeks and to enforce the locals-only message using 'guerrilla tactics'. One gang member was reported as saying that:

> I think there are too many floaters in the water. They have no respect: they hold illegal beach parties and crowd the waves. The beaches need someone to take control so local people can enjoy them too. We are not against tourists but against the abuse of the countryside and beaches.

The growing antipathy to strangers threatened to spread from villages such as St Agnes, known as 'the badlands', and Portreath to the heart of Newquay, Britain's surfing centre. But the local Restormel council's tourism department and the British Surfing Association (BSA) condemned the campaign, which could have a significant local economic impact. Surfing is the largest contributor to the Cornish tourism industry, believed to be worth £64 million (c. €95 million) a year. Newquay's main surf school has seen a surge from 200 clients in 1994 to 8000 in 2003.

The BSA's national director said the 'locals only' concept was contrary to the surfing ethic, which makes it so easy for British enthusiasts to surf in international waters. 'Anyone who is a credible surfer travels to catch the surf. We respect other people's waves and they respect ours. I don't think this issue is about the environment. These people seem selfish,' he said.

A worker at Aggie's Surf Shop thought the hostility could be fuelled by issues other than crowded waves:

> There's resentment among young people who can't buy homes in their own town because city people buy up the property as second homes which are left empty for 10 months a year. When you live here, you surf all the poor waves every day and when it gets good for a few days a year, every learner and his dog gets in the water.

Though some in the wider community are keen to play down the growing tensions, there were reports of similar clashes on the south-west coast of Wales in 2003 when, in Pembrokeshire and Gower, Welsh surfers felt more should be done to publicize a code of conduct for the amateur enthusiast. Others believe the tensions are inherent in the sport: 'surf wars' have plagued American and Australian coasts as well as surf spots in Hawaii – notably Waimea Bay – and Europe. Indeed, in Hawaii, in addition to the problem of crowding, surfing has become commodified for passing tourist groups and for Hollywood film-makers.

Sources: Akbar, 2004; Martin, 2004.

In practice, of course, these categories may overlap and merge; situations are fluid, changing over time and, whether or not considered as a 'community', residents' welfare interests and values can be far from uniform and consensual. We now take three phenomena to articulate briefly some of these issues: second homes, crime and health.

Second homes and lifestyle migrants

Changes in global economic production systems have seen landscapes with high amenity value becoming increasingly attractive for temporary and permanent migration (Williams and Hall, 2002; Gallant *et al.*, 2005; Kuentzel and Ramaswamy, 2005). Growth in spatially and temporally flexible teleworking, discretionary leisure time and increasing proportions of retired households have all intensified demand for attractive living environments (Müller, 2005). In areas of second-home ownership and lifestyle migration, the discordance in perception of amenity between incomer and long-term resident may be considerable, leading to competing, different demands on the same resources (Hall and Müller, 2004).

The conceptualization of competition for living space and unequal access to property and services that may exist between residents, tourism workers and tourists is most graphically expressed in the growth of second homes in destination areas. During the height of the tourist season, certain parts of cities, towns, villages, campsites, beaches, cathedrals and museums can be dominated by tourists from a specific country, region or culture, and locals can be made to feel aliens in their own home area. This can be exacerbated if language and other cultural differences establish barriers to mutual understanding and fan flames of potential mistrust. This is certainly exacerbated if outsiders buy local property, inflating local prices and excluding locals – particularly younger potential house buyers or renters – from gaining access to the local housing market, while leaving holiday homes empty and reducing demand for local services for significant periods of the year.

But this simplistic picture may be complicated considerably by second-home owners becoming semi-permanent or permanent residents, perhaps even working in tourism, by their renting property to other holiday-makers who use local services, and local people themselves becoming second-home owners. Thus guests may stop visiting and become hosts; hosts may be longer-term visitors themselves, such as seasonal migrants. Anthropological research in more developed countries (e.g. Kohn, 1997) has pointed to the increasingly blurred boundary between the identities and roles of hosts and guests, particularly where there is little or no cultural difference.

Residents' attitudes to tourism and tourists may change over time, either positively or negatively (e.g. Lindberg and Johnson, 1997; Teye *et al.*, 2002). As a result, the sense of place and of 'community' become blurred, and perhaps even lost (e.g. Gössling, 2002b). In this respect, Sørensen and Nilsson (1999) produced a typology to suggest that, far from there being a host/guest dichotomy, there exists a continuum (in this case specifically relating to rural areas) within which some nine types of residential and visiting positions can be identified (Box 4.6).

For German second-home buyers in Sweden, Müller (2002: 182–183) distinguished three consumption-led categories, each with different impacts and implications for local residents: *circulating*: having access to a place that can be visited regularly during the weekends, typically located within 'nature'; *seasonal*: exclusively using the second home once or twice a year, drawing on an almost global supply of destinations; and *permanent*: with initial intentions the same as the other groups, but deciding to move permanently to the second home, perhaps after retirement or simply to start a 'new life' abroad. Thus second-home ownership may be seen as a possible stage towards permanent migration, implying a potential long-term change of local demographic composition and a 'Trojan Horse' effect for the local community (Box 4.7).

In Norway, Flognfeldt (2002: 201) found increasing recognition of the contribution that second-home owners were able

Box 4.6. A rural residents–visitors continuum.

- *Holiday tourists*: holiday tourists staying in the area, e.g. in a cottage, an inn, or at a farm.
- *Transit tourists*: holiday tourists who consume the experiences and recreational values of the area but are accommodated outside the area.
- *Day visitors*: visitors having their permanent residence within day-trip distance, using the area for recreation.
- *SFR (staying with friends and/or relatives)*: visitors with socially defined connections to the area.
- *Weekend visitors*: regular users of rural residences who 'go rural' at weekends.
- *Permanent tourists*: two-home residents who reside in the countryside on a part-time basis. Alternation between urban and rural residence is beyond a work/holiday distinction.
- *Resident tourists*: persons who have moved to the countryside for reasons rooted in aesthetics and ideology. The countryside is perceived as a more authentic, real and aesthetically attractive place for life and family.
- *Other incoming permanent residents*: persons whose residence is based on tangible matters (e.g. employment). Aesthetic or recreational qualities of the area are less important.
- *Local-born and raised residents:* persons born and raised in the area. Not necessarily residing there always, their stays outside the area have a temporary character.

Source: Sørensen and Nilsson, 1999: 8–9.

Box 4.7. What about the locals?

There is a large popular literature on the practicalities of living in another country. About 500,000 Britons now own homes in France, a figure that is estimated to be rising by 20,000 annually, and which has stimulated an increasing trend in cross-channel commuting (e.g. Hetherington, 2004).

The popular literature for the UK market on the purchase (Igoe and Howell, 2002; de Vries, 2003; Hampshire, 2003; Kristen, 2003; Laredo, 2003; Davey, 2004), ownership (Pybus, 2002; Hart, 2003) and restoration (Everett, 1999; Laredo, 2004; Whiting, 2004) of property in that country is now immense. There is also a growing popular literature to meet demands for retiring to another country (e.g. Hampshire, 2002; Holbrook, 2004), and for setting up small businesses such as B&Bs (e.g. Hunt, 2003; de Vries, 2004). Speculative property purchase within the new EU accession states is also catered for (e.g. Pownall, 2004).

We are not aware of a popular literature for long-term residents on ways of coping with second-home owners and lifestyle in-migrants.

to make to business knowledge development amongst residents and (potential) tourism workers. He cited examples of second-home owners taking seats on boards of local companies, being a contact person for sales of local products in their permanent home area, being a mentor for local youth undertaking education in urban areas, and buying local handicrafts and equipment for use in the areas where they permanently lived or for their own businesses. Thus, emphasizing the complementary social, economic and cultural contributions to local communities that such temporary residents make,

Flognfeldt argued that, for their mutual benefit, longer-term residents needed appropriate mechanisms through which to express to the second-home dwellers that they were welcome to participate in local development policies. Other studies have focused on the stresses and psychiatric problems that lifestyle migrants have faced. These may come about because the migrants may have been trying to escape problems only to find that their difficulties had travelled with them (e.g. Kimura *et al.*, 1975; Streltzer, 1979).

The different quality of contributions and relationships that such incomers (in this case lifestyle in-migrants) have with long-term residents has been summarized by Fountain and Hall (2002) (Table 4.5). Although relating to a specific geographical context, these issues have resonance in many other locations that have attracted second-home owners and lifestyle migrants (e.g. Chaplin, 1999). However, the authors emphasize that such impacts need to be viewed within a consideration of how far local people are actually involved in and can relate to such processes. This would

Table 4.5. Implications of lifestyle migration for the local residents, Akaroa, South Island, New Zealand (from Fountain and Hall, 2002: 165–166).

Supportive implications	Potentially divisive and destructive outcomes
Financial support through local spending and payment of local government taxes	Substantial difference in socio-economic status and lifestyle choices from local people
Playing a leading role in many of the town's organizations	Environmental protectionist values, reflecting their economic independence from the community
Helps to maintain or increase property prices – a mixed blessing	Significant population turnover – incomers having found their dreams unfulfilled
–	Skewed demographic structure – usually with increased older age groups and a decline in school-aged children – leading to questionable viability and sustainability of certain local services and an ensuing downward spiral fuelled by families with children leaving

seem particularly important not only in less developed countries, where power relations usually see local people reduced to onlookers (see Chapter 5), but also in 'developed world' locations on the geographical power peripheries of such expanding blocs as the EU (Box 4.8).

We agree with Williams and Hall (2002: 42) that:

> The challenge for any community is how to harness these tourism and migration channels, which constitute fundamental globalisation processes. How can places use the innovative capacities of the different forms of tourism-related migrants, how can they extract further economic benefits from VFR tourism, and how can they enhance their place image?

Crime and destination areas

Much attention has been paid within tourism management and the tourism academic community to tourists' experiences and fear of crime (Chesney-Lind and Lind, 1986; Harper, 2001; George, 2003; Lepp and Gibson, 2003), but much less to residents' experiences. According to earlier research (e.g. Jud, 1975; Fujii and Mak, 1980; de Albuquerque, 1981), tourist areas appeared to suffer disproportionate amounts of crime, and within such areas tourists appeared to be victimized more frequently than local residents (de Albuquerque and McElroy, 1999). Reasons suggested for this included the fact that tourists are seen as an easy target – they may typically carry more than usual sums of money (although use of credit cards and hotel safe boxes might be thought to obviate this). They may also engage in 'risky' behaviours, may be ignorant of local languages, signs and customs and lack local support groups (Pizam et al., 1997).

A dichotomy in patterns of (US) crime victimization has been observed, where tourists may be more susceptible to property crime and robbery, while residents of destination areas are more likely to be victims of aggravated assault and murder (de Albuquerque and McElroy, 1999). While, for example, Pizam (1982) found little linkage between tourism and crime in a US-wide survey, a later cross-cultural study (Pizam and Telisman-Kosuta, 1989) suggested that tourism was perceived to lead to an increase in organized crime (Ryan, 2003; Cirules, 2004).

British tourists' experiences of crime while on holiday and their perceptions of safety (Brunt et al., 2000; Mawby et al., 2000) appear to confirm high victimization rates. Yet, while many from a sample surveyed took notions of safety into account when they chose a holiday destination, few saw crime or disorder as a problem when they

Box 4.8. On the cusp of the EU: property purchase for second homes in Bulgaria.

Bulgaria has liberalized its property law to allow direct purchase of land by citizens of EU states from the moment of formal integration. Until then, the direct purchase of land by foreigners theoretically is not allowed, but in practice many already own land and other property through intermediary companies set up jointly with a Bulgarian citizen, or by contracting the use of land through specialized agencies. In order to meet demand British banks have included Bulgaria on the list of countries where a loan is available for buying property. In many places, Britons, Greeks and smaller numbers of Scandinavians, Dutch and Germans have bought or rented property at relatively low prices.

But prices are rising rapidly due to both external and internal factors, and the appearance of foreign speculators has contributed substantially to the rise in prices and their geographical differentiation.

For example, foreign buyer interest caused a rapid increase in the price of property in the village Galata near Varna, where the price per m² rose from €7 to €20, and in the ski resort Bansko, where it rose from €40 to €70 in a year, from 2003 to 2004 (<http://www.dnevnik.bg>). It is expected that the price of property in Bulgaria will double on confirmation of EU accession.

This is likely to have the effect of:
(i) excluding most Bulgarians from the high-amenity-valued areas; (ii) stimulating the mobility of many existing residents out of such areas; and (iii) inducing relative immobility in those residents not living in amenity areas.

Source: Bachvarov, 2006, with additions.

replicable, should fear and perception in such circumstances be less than one might expect, and can this be turned to advantage for destination well-being as well as tourist satisfaction?

There are two problematic issues here: different modes of crime exist, and tourism is difficult to isolate as an independent variable. First, within tourism destination areas, four overlapping categories of crimes are often recognized:

- activities directed against tourists: the perpetrators may be local residents, tourism workers, criminals attracted to the area by tourism or other tourists themselves;
- crimes committed by tourists: these may be aimed at residents, tourism workers or fellow tourists;
- crimes that occur through the illegal servicing of demands created by tourists; and
- criminal activities that relate to the growth and development of a destination that has a tourist-dependent economic base.

Ryan (1993) suggested a fivefold refinement of these categories:

- tourists are incidental victims of criminal activity that is independent of the nature of the tourist destination: most crime is directed against the resident population;
- a venue is used by criminals because of the nature of the tourism location but the victims are not specifically tourists;
- a location attracts criminal activity because tourists are easy victims: most crime is opportunistic (including that of tourists themselves) and is motivated primarily by the acquisition of property;
- criminal activity becomes organized to meet certain types of tourist demand (e.g. sex, drugs, illegal forms of gambling);
- organized criminal and terrorist groups commit specific violent actions against tourists and tourist facilities (also reinterpreted by de Albuquerque and McElroy, 1999).

subsequently went on holiday. This led to the conclusion that, while the criminological and tourism literature suggests – and sometimes assumes – that fear normally exceeds risk, in the case of tourism and crime, at least from the UK sample, it appeared that risk may exceed fear (Mawby *et al.*, 2000). This clearly raises critical questions concerning pre-trip information on crime and measures to avoid it, tourists' perceptions of such hazards and their tolerance levels (see Chapter 3). Why, if the UK findings are

---

> **Box 4.9.** Tourism and 'structural violence'.
>
> In East Africa tourism has expanded to dominate much of the coastal area of Kenya and subsequently Tanzania. Closely linked to this has been an expansion of sex work and heroin use. An anthropological study of the lives of women heroin users has illustrated the ways in which economic and social forces of globalization carried by international and regional tourism have negatively affected their health and social welfare. Violence is seen to be an everyday feature of their lives as the women service particular requirements of tourists seeking the pleasures of 'tourist paradise'.
>
> Although the literature on tourism, sex and sex work is now extensive, there continues to be a need for the development of a theoretical model of sex tourism that can accommodate the diversity of tourist-related sexual economic exchanges, particularly in less developed countries, their wider societal context, not least in relation to migration and people trafficking, and the power relations that underpin them.
>
> **Sources:** Ryan and Kinder, 1996; Oppermann, 1999; MacKay, 2001; Taylor, 2001; Jeffreys, 2003; Beckerleg and Hundt, 2004.

Second, despite these self-evident truths, it is often difficult to actually distinguish the influence of tourism, if any, on trends in crime and 'antisocial behaviour' in any particular place (although see Box 4.9). There are perhaps three basic reasons for this:

- tourism is part of wider social and economic development processes and often cannot be separated out: such processes may mask a significant or negligible tourism-related contribution;
- statistics are often poor, exacerbating the problem of identifying cause and effect; and
- conflicting trends tend to be reported from different destinations, for reasons possibly unclear because of the previous two factors.

For example, work in Queensland, Australia, has resulted in mixed research findings. Reported crime rates in Cairns and

the Gold Coast – both popular tourist centres – over a 10-year period suggest that criminal activity has grown faster than the overall rate for the state as a whole and faster than population growth. In contrast, the Sunshine Coast, just 200 km north of the Gold Coast, with almost identical attractions, has crime rates much lower than the state average. Prideaux (1996) offers two explanations for this. First, Cairns and the Gold Coast have much higher levels of drug offences, and drug use is often associated with additional criminal activity. Second, promotional advertising for Cairns and the Gold Coast has often focused on images of semi-naked women and men, active nightlife and suggestions of uninhibited behaviour. The Sunshine Coast has not done this and caters largely for families. Brunt and Agarwal (2004: 13) also found an apparent link between 'resort marketing and levels of deviant tourist behaviour' in south-west England. Although other background factors, such as local social deprivation, were contributory, they noted that the marketing style of the resorts of Torquay and Newquay, which had higher recorded rates for theft and drug offences, appealed more to a younger adult market than others in the region.

This again suggests the need for destination residents to (be able to) take a more active part in decisions affecting the promotion and image formation of their home area in order to be able to influence tourism impacts on their own social and economic welfare (e.g. Pizam *et al.*, 1997). For example, Bloom (1996: 99–101) suggests several initiatives to combat tourist-related crime in South Africa amongst disadvantaged groups:

- empowering community role players in regional tourism structures: clearly demarcating the roles and functions of tourism bodies at regional and local levels to ensure the proper delegation of tasks to community leaders;
- formulating tourism-linked human resource development objectives: to include meeting basic needs, developing human resources, building the economy and democratizing state and

society, as strategic levers in alleviating the problems of crime and violence;

- reconstructing sub-sectors of the tourism industry in terms of future challenges and opportunities: to emphasize the contributions communities themselves can make to their economic development, shifting the emphasis to an integrated and coordinated approach that is inclusive;
- compiling fast-track programmes for capacity-building in human and financial resources: with extensive training and education programmes that focus on the benefits of tourism involvement and the use of tourism resources for disadvantaged communities (see also Chapter 5);
- providing guidelines for potential tourism entrepreneurs to become part of the tourism industry: particularly in terms of funding possibilities and mechanisms, education and training and business networking opportunities. Initiatives to accommodate poorer communities may include the development of particular attractions, accommodation facilities, tour operation and guiding services in and around townships and villages;
- stipulating community responsibilities and self-initiatives: through full participation of disadvantaged groups in initiatives; and
- addressing transparency and control issues: to bridge the psychological and cultural gaps that have separated people of different ethnicity and economic positioning.

Such ideals are, of course, partly based on wider considerations. When tourists' safety and security appear to be compromised, and particularly when this receives media attention, the knock-on effect of tourists' staying away can affect destination residents and workers substantially. The impacts of reduced levels of receipts and negative welfare implications for tourism workers may be felt both locally and nationally (e.g. Box 4.10) (see e.g. Faulkner, 2001; Tarlow, 2004a).

Cooperation and coordination between local authorities and the tourism industry

---

Box 4.10. Crime and negative publicity for Rio de Janeiro.

Security was increased in the tourist areas of Rio de Janeiro after four muggings were reported to police in one weekend. Visitors from Germany, Italy and Argentina were among the victims. A 61-year-old Japanese woman was in hospital after being stabbed while fleeing her attackers. The Rio de Janeiro Hotel Association expressed its concern that the authorities were not doing enough to protect the US$1 bn annual tourist spending in the city, which could easily be deflected as a result of negative publicity from such activity. Earlier, gunmen held up a bus taking 17 Germans to a hotel from the airport. The next day two Americans were robbed on the same motorway. There were claims that 1 million tourists had been lost in the past year because of crime.

Source: Davies, 2004.

---

are vital in such circumstances. Yet, when a high crime rate in New Orleans in the 1990s was clearly drawing attention and negative perceptions from potential tourists and conference planners, there was an apparent lack of tourism industry concern and cooperation in trying to overcome it. This was considered to be a major constraint in alleviating the situation, threatening the well-being of a strong tourism sector in the city (Dimanche and Lepetic, 1999).

From a large-scale visitor survey undertaken in Anaheim, part of the Los Angeles agglomeration and home to Disneyland, Tarlow (2004b) concluded that destinations and visitor accommodation providers need to include a tourism security component in their marketing to remain competitive. Those places that choose to ignore security concerns risk losing business and facing legal action. Respondents made it clear that, in this 'era of terrorism' and in places where there is a high level of street crime, a highly visible police and security presence makes them feel more comfortable.

The deterrent effect of conflict and civil unrest on tourism development is generally well documented (Smyth, 1986; Cater, 1987; Pizam and Mansfeld, 1996; Theocharous, 2004). The rapid recovery of tourism activities following cessation of threatening activities has been noted in a range of destinations, including Cyprus (Andronicou, 1979), Sri Lanka (Richter and Waugh, 1986) and Northern Ireland (Sharrock, 1994). Turkey, the second most popular destination for UK foreign holidays, ironically partly thanks to hyperinflation fuelled by military spending, has been subject to a sporadic anti-tourist terrorist campaign since the mid-1980s, and this continues to pose a number of ethical questions for the industry (Wayman, 1995; Bowcott, 2005). The supervision of media coverage of crisis and crisis management has become a core issue for the tourism industry (Beirman, 2003: 13). This was expressed when, following the bombing of a *dolmuş* taxi-bus used by tourists and locals in the resort of Kusadasi, it was reported that angry shop owners tried to prevent television news crews from filming the scene for fear of the images discouraging other tourists (Nalbantogly, 2005).

In Egypt a 'self-induced' welfare threat to the tourism industry was emphasized by Aziz (1995), who argued that Muslim terrorist violence against tourists was a reaction to irresponsible tourism development. Safier (1994: 4) placed this within a wider societal context by arguing that: 'When the forces making for inequality, division and disrespect reach a certain point, then the reactions can be correspondingly cumulative and ultimately dangerous to all.'

While such a context has been overtaken by world events since September 2001, the rhetoric of 'the war against terror', military intervention in Afghanistan and Iraq and the bombing in London of international tourists and workers by UK citizens have added extra layers of complexity to the host–guest, East–West, Islamic–Judaeo-Christian dichotomies influencing attitudes towards the perceived role and imagery of international tourists and the international tourism industry. None the less, the fragility of international tourism under such circumstances can also provide the context for expanding the industry's ethical underpinnings. As the globalization of tourism encounters social, economic and political inequalities, resource conflicts and expressions of ethnic

identity in many of its more popular locations, the industry will be required to express in concrete terms its desire to maintain and enhance the welfare of destination environments. If this is not the case, the welfare of tourists and of the tourism industry itself will be threatened as they and it are held to ransom by those viewing the important economic role of tourism as a valid target through which to attack national governments and as a symbol of dependent development through which to confront the current world order.

Tourism, disease and destination health

Tourism is an important factor in the spread of disease (Rodriguez-Garcia, 2001). It can increase opportunities for genetic exchange among microbes and enhances the selection and spread of resistant strains, as well as the evolution of viruses in new environments, which makes the treatment of a growing number of diseases more problematic (Moennig, 1992; Goldsmith, 1998; WHO, 1998a, b; Gössling, 2002a).

Locally in destination areas, tourism infrastructure may substantially alter the habitats of disease-carrying insects and animals. The irrigation of hotel gardens, for example, may create puddles that provide breeding grounds for malaria-carrying mosquitoes.

The indirect contribution of tourism may be equally important (Gössling, 2002a). Tourism has been shown to contribute to climate change, which in turn is leading to the diffusion of old, new and re-emerging infectious diseases (Kumate, 1997; WHO, 2000a), and it is also believed to lead to continued El Niño Southern Oscillation (ENSO) phenomena (Houghton *et al.*, 2001). These have strong effects on the climate of some of the world's poorer regions: southern Africa, parts of South America and South East Asia. In these areas, the number of people killed, injured or made homeless by natural disasters caused by ENSO is increasing and there has been growing recognition of links between El Niño and disease. The El Niño cycle is also associated with increased risks of some of the diseases transmitted by mosquitoes (malaria, dengue and Rift Valley fever). This can result from these vectors increasing substantially after heavy rainfall in dry climates or as a result of drought in humid climates (where, for example, rivers may turn into strings of pools) (Gössling, 2002a). Warmer temperatures may also allow disease to spread in highland areas (WHO, 2000b).

Tourism may also indirectly increase health problems because reports of epidemics may be suppressed or ignored to avoid the negative impacts that bad health news might have on the tourism industry (Goldsmith, 1998) (Fig. 4.1).

There appears to be relatively little information on the impact of diseases brought by travellers to destination populations (Gössling, 2002a). But local residents are clearly vulnerable to death and disability as a result of accidents, violence and injuries caused directly and indirectly by tourism (Fig. 4.2). They also have to bear the consequences of undesirable behaviour,

Fig. 4.1. Risky destination with suppressed information? Pyongyang, North Korea.

such as over-indulgence in alcohol and other toxic substances, sex tourism and the potential dangers of organized crime competing for resources and markets.

Further, tourists are also responsible for changes in ideas, values and norms, which may affect health. For example, perceived demand from tourists visiting developing countries may contribute to the increasing provision and local consumption by residents of 'fast food', alcohol, tobacco and other toxic substances (Rodriguez-Garcia, 2001). All these changes may exacerbate already existing health and social welfare problems, particularly in developing countries. More positive changes (for some), such as greater personal freedom (for women) and increased mobility, may also occur and are discussed below.

The exchange of values, ideas and conceptions through tourism and travel also leads to changing human–environmental relations, which have wider health and welfare implications. This may assist a loss of attachment to place, result in changing resource use patterns and encourage the increased consumption of (industrial) goods and products (Gössling, 2002a, b). Separation from traditional cultural norms may lead to psychological disorientation and alienation. This may reinforce, in both individual and collective behaviour and attitude, the Cartesian separation between 'nature' and 'culture' that characterizes 'modern' societies, albeit without the support systems of a welfare state.

A loss of knowledge about local ecological limits, the alienation of lifestyles from the capacity of ecosystems to provide functions, goods and materials and decreasing attachment to place are interacting processes that contribute to personal and global welfare problems. They are considered by a number of analysts to be a major factor in the global environmental crisis and thus detrimental to sustainable development (Borgström-Hansson and Wackernagel, 1999; Hornborg, 2000; Gössling, 2002a).

Tourism is a major agent in global environmental change, and it will in itself be affected by this change: health and disease are just one aspect of the welfare dimensions

Fig. 4.2. Heavy tourist traffic and atmospheric pollution from exhaust emissions, Ming Tombs road, north of Beijing.

of this interrelationship (Gössling, 2002a) (see also Chapters 3 and 8).

Working in Tourism: Satisfaction, Motivation and Opportunities

Until relatively recently, the welfare considerations of destination employment in tourism have been represented in a somewhat fragmentary literature within conceptualizations of the international division of labour (Mackie, 1988) and class relations (Ireland, 1993).

Welfare can be expressed in a number of ways within tourism employment. The satisfaction and retention of front-line employees is a particularly useful indicator (Rust et al., 1996; Karatepe and Sokmen, 2006). In the literature, front-line employees have been shown to be:

- underpaid and highly stressed (Weatherly and Tansik, 1993);
- the initial recipients of a high proportion of customer complaints (Tax and Brown, 1998); and
- susceptible to high levels of work–family conflict (Boles and Babin, 1996; Netemeyer et al., 2004).

Although the literature on workplace stressors has a considerable history (e.g. McGrath, 1970; Warr and Wall, 1984), employees in tourism have been underrepresented in stress and coping research, particularly in the area of stress management (Law et al., 1995). Yet food service outlets and hotels have ranked highly on the list of stressful environments for both employees and managers (e.g. Sarabahksh et al., 1989).

Factors regularly cited as contributing to stress have included antisocial work hours and conditions, insufficient pay, relationships with co-workers, poor management, and front-line roles where there is a requirement to deal with the public on a continuous daily basis (KPMG, 1991; Ross, 1993b). Yet it has been argued that few companies learn from the mistakes and failures of others in being aware of and successfully managing the welfare issues of their key service employees (Johnston and Mehra, 2002).

Ross (1993a) found that individuals with low work satisfaction were less likely to approach their manager or supervisor for support or assistance, reflecting the fact that management was often at least part of the problem. From a study of front-line employees in Australian attractions, Law *et al.* (1995) determined that stressors originated from two main sources: one relating to the organization as a whole, the other to the immediate role characteristics and work demands. They therefore emphasized the need for appropriate management strategies to help alleviate the amount of stress experienced by employees at work, which should include the provision of incentives and explicit recognition and acknowledgement of employees' work value and achievements. Law *et al.* (1995) concluded that the identification of managers and management behaviour as a principal source of stress may reflect on the lack of training and/or education of managers in the attractions sector (e.g. Littlejohn and Watson, 2004).

The key to raising motivation lies with managers' understanding of what their employees want from work (Simons and Enz, 1995). The competitive business environment requires, as an imperative, strong management and stable, eager to serve and highly committed employees, working as a team to run the business. Yet high turnover and employee morale problems appear to some commentators to be an inalienable feature of the industry worldwide (Woods, 1992; Lam *et al.*, 2001). None the less, labour turnover is a significant burden for most organizations, resulting in additional recruitment and training costs as well as decreases in productivity. Further, the intangible costs of turnover are notable in the areas of employees' morale and the reputation and goodwill of an organization (Hogan, 1992).

Employees' work satisfaction has been considered and defined in a variety of ways. Locke (1976) defined job satisfaction as a pleasurable or positive emotional state resulting from the appraisal of one's job or job experiences, while Robbins and Coulter (1996) saw it as an employee's general attitude towards his or her job. Of significance to tourism labour turnover rates is research that suggests that an employee's satisfaction with an organization is closely related to length of service (Smith *et al.*, 1996). Higher satisfaction levels of new employees with

less than 6 months of employment have been found, which might be related to the pleasure of obtaining a new job, but satisfaction drops for employees of more than 6 months, and the greatest level of job turnover occurs during this period. Smith *et al.* (1996) drew the obvious conclusion that high turnover may be the result of lack of job satisfaction among employees.

Research has shown that married employees are more satisfied with their jobs than their unmarried co-workers (Keller, 1983). It may be that conscientious and satisfied employees are more likely to be married or that marriage changes employees' expectations of work. It may also be that marriage brings a degree of fulfilment and contentment with broader aspects of life, which is reflected in employment orientation and attitude.

From their employment satisfaction studies within the hotel sector in Hong Kong, Lam *et al.* (2001) concluded that well-educated hotel employees were not satisfied with their jobs, feeling that they had made a greater investment in their education and that their pay-off should be greater. The implication is supported by equity theory (Ronen, 1986; Scholl *et al.*, 1987): that employees' return should be commensurate with their investment, otherwise they will be dissatisfied. Indeed, half a century ago Vollmer and Kinney (1955) found that the higher an employee's educational level, the greater likelihood there was for dissatisfaction.

Such employees expect more in terms of favourable working conditions, more understanding supervision and higher pay. To trade off a higher level of unmet expectations, hotels can provide job rotation opportunities for well-educated employees with potential. New environments and the accruing of additional knowledge, skills and experience as a result of a job rotation programme may produce high motivation. Importantly, the exposure to different job functions can help development and preparation for future promotion. Employees require some degree of a sense of personal responsibility, together with the freedom to use the authority which should be commensurate with it (Lam *et al.*, 2001).

Conditions for entrepreneurial success may include task-related motivation, appropriate skills and expertise, expectation of personal gain, familiarity with and employment of new technologies, and a supportive environment (Lordkipanidze *et al.*, 2005). That new forms of production and organization have flourished in some regions and not in others can also be attributed to 'certain imperfectly understood and difficult to quantify (sociocultural) environmental characteristics known as "regional milieu"' (Williams and Copus, 2005: 307). Important aspects of such milieux may include:

- 'social capital' and 'local capacity', which emphasize cultural, educational and attitudinal characteristics (Bennett and McCoshan, 1993);
- the role of 'institutional thickness' (Amin and Thrift, 1995) and the 'associational economy' (Crooke and Morgan, 1998), both of which emphasize the importance of the quality of agencies and organizations involved in regional development, and the interaction between them; and
- 'untraded interdependencies' – the network of links between firms, development agencies, educational institutions and research establishments, which, if well developed, can facilitate the rapid diffusion of information (Storper, 1995) in 'learning regions' (Morgan, 1997).

More specific social factors that may contribute to the supply of entrepreneurs include an entrepreneurial tradition, family position, social status and level of education. Yet

> one of the most valued aspects of the local business environment is the aggregate skills and knowledge base of the local labour force, though much of this 'human capital' is associated with 'tacit knowledge', practical skills and experience, rather than formal education.
> (Williams and Copus, 2005: 318)

But the role of governments in stimulating and creating an appropriate entrepreneurial climate may be critical. This may be accomplished most explicitly by the adoption of an entrepreneurship policy (Nylander, 2001). The EU enterprise policy, for example, emphasizes the need for a regulatory climate favourable to entrepreneurship. Such policy should encourage corporate social responsibility (CSR) (see Chapter 7), the integration of environmental and social concerns with business objectives, and interaction with stakeholders, with the aim of contributing to sustainable development (Lordkipanidze *et al.*, 2005).

The increasing diversity of both tourists and workers in the tourism industry and the growing competitiveness of destinations and businesses mean that there is greater need for internationally transferable skills (Aitken and Hall, 2000). But, while there is a recognition of the need for such skills in the industry as a whole, there is often a reluctance to acknowledge its importance within individual businesses, with implications for human resource policies, education and training. In their comparative analysis of regional entrepreneurial activity, Williams and Copus (2005: 318) found a clear 'training deficit' between dynamic and lagging regions. A key element in regional transformation and restructuring has been the need to establish and consolidate 'new mentalities', even though an underlying continuity and resistance may persist through pre-existing business/political ('survival') networks, for example in parts of the former Soviet Union supporting forms of crony capitalism (e.g. see D. Hall, 2004c).

This may be reflected in poor service quality, inadequate or inappropriate information and poor or non-existent market research. For example, in Bulgaria, aspiring to EU accession, Bachvarov (2006) argues that tourism quality is still regarded as that necessary to satisfy demand as it is perceived by the providers. The diversification and upgrading of services should be one of the strategic objectives of Bulgarian tourism, with high-quality training for those in the industry as a priority. According to Bachvarov (2006) the existing system of professional education is outdated. Higher educational institutions offer theoretical teaching but little practical implementation, and work experience in companies is particularly weak.

In contrast, the Lithuanian Rural Tourism Information and Development centre provides professional advice for current and potential rural tourism entrepreneurs in this recent EU-member Baltic state. The centre organizes seminars and training courses about rural tourism services, business organizations and related issues, undertakes marketing analysis and oversees service quality. The centre thus acts as an intermediary between tourists and rural tourism providers (Lordkipanidze et al., 2005).

More remote regions may have suffered in the past from problems of access to training, although comprehensive online provision has largely removed this barrier. Yet in the eastern Alps low productivity resulting from the small business structure of tourism here requires the development of new skills for strategic cooperation in order to help entrepreneurs to develop flexible and market-oriented destination management companies (Pechlaner and Tshurtschenthaler, 2003).

Other constraints may reflect the need for a revision and updating of curricula and training methods. In Tanzania, a country well placed to offer tourism experiences centred on wildlife, unique landforms and rich cultures, Barron and Prideaux (1998) found a lack of environmental awareness by members of staff of a key hospitality educator, resulting in the absence of such issues in the curriculum. They viewed this as a direct threat to the ability to manage a balance between the conservation of the country's natural assets and income generation.

Barriers to training and skill development may have cultural roots. The Goldfields Tourism region of western Victoria has a rich Aboriginal history, but one which has been largely ignored, even though indigenous perspectives can be developed and Aboriginal people involved in the interpretation of the region's history with appropriate training and support (Clark and Cahir, 2003).

Particularly in developing societies, the arrival of tourism employment opportunities can exert profound structural and social, as well as economic, impacts on the resident community. Evidence appears to be contradictory as to whether tourism employment merely reinforces existing social and structural differentiation – based on gender, class, race or age considerations – or allows new socio-economic groups to emerge to reduce socio-economic inequalities. Dogan (1989) and Verbole (2003), for example, have shown that previously homogeneous 'communities' that consciously adopt a particular response to tourism can become diversified, such that local groups arise exhibiting very different responses to tourism development and emerging as winners or losers from tourism development processes.

Enhanced welfare opportunities can result from being located in an advantageous structural position. For example, those owning land in key locations can reinforce their structural position or sell to developers for substantial financial gain. For those with more education or training, tourism may provide new opportunities in managerial positions and thereby open further fractures in local stratification systems. For example, Moore's (1970) study of a Canary Island village revealed a class of new entrepreneurs that had emerged as a result of modest tourism development to pose a challenge to the power of local political leaders. On the Canary Island of La Gomera, Macleod (1999, 2003) showed this role of entrepreneurialism to have been consolidated with the development of ecotourism there.

The demonstration effect – an emulation of the values and lifestyles of tourists – may follow. The self-perceived increased status of tourism workers and those gaining economically from tourism development may be reinforced by access to locations and amenities which are otherwise inaccessible (perhaps as a result of tourism development) to the resident population as a whole (e.g. Seaton, 1996, 1997). In Malta (Boissevain, 1977; Boissevain and Inglott, 1979), young adults experienced considerable social mobility as a direct result of tourism. Family ties were loosened and intergenerational conflicts emerged. In such circumstances where young adults probably feel that their welfare has been enhanced, local people may find it difficult to respond to such challenges to their collective welfare, while the tourism 'industry' may be ambivalent in wishing to acknowledge its responsibilities towards local social structures.

Welfare, tourism employment and gender

Tourism employment opportunities for local people in developing areas may be typically unskilled, low-paid roles that are seen to reinforce the gendered horizontal segregation of occupations (e.g. Bagguley, 1990; Levy and Lerch, 1991). Men are often over-represented in professional, managerial and supervisory positions, while women are often recruited into work that is deemed to represent an extension of their traditional domestic responsibilities (Kinnaird and Hall, 1994, 1996, 2000; Swain, 1995). This is reinforced by assumptions that, if the best jobs and highest rewards are linked to an accumulation of human capital, women are inevitably disadvantaged because their process of accumulation is interrupted by marriage, birth and child-rearing (Coppock et al., 1995). These may be further reinforced or refined through ethnic and cultural differentiation (e.g. Scott, 1995, 1997; Devedzic, 2002). None the less, Ghodsee (2003) argues that, in the case of Bulgaria at least, state support for viable economic sectors such as tourism, with relatively high wages and employing a 'critical mass' of women, can help to ease women's burden within transition processes.

Despite the potential improvements in economic status that women may attain as a consequence of involvement in tourism-related employment, a wide range of social, cultural and political barriers may constrain them from aspiring to leadership roles. In Sri Lanka (Samarasuriya, 1982), for example, even women who owned and managed their own guest house or restaurant did not gain increased status, because of the low value ascribed to women's work.

Within the Maltese souvenir handicraft industry, Robson (2002) found identity to be promoted by the gendered images of local handicraft workers making textiles or forging metal and glass and by gendered

practices in the production, promotion, depiction and retailing of tourism crafts. Stereotyped ideas of authenticity reinforce patterns of gender inequality. Men tend to be wage earners, working in public occupations, while women's work is often informal and based in the home. Women dominate low-technology, nimble-finger craft production, such as lacemaking and knitting. Geographically they are atomized and scattered. In contrast, men dominate the crafts employing technology, such as glass-blowing and metalworking, and are located in formal workplaces, which are, in turn, more accessible to the tourist gaze.

In the rural sector, tourism development can provide women with employment opportunities and support for self-determination. This can take the form of managing the provision of bed and breakfast accommodation (although, again, this can be viewed pejoratively as simply an extension of the domestic role), management of farm-based attractions or establishing one-person, family or collaborative small and medium-size enterprises (SMEs) (Verbole and Mele-Petric, 1996; Kulcsar and Verbole, 1997).

A basic need, particularly in less developed countries, is women's unfettered access to land and property (Bob and Musyoki, 2002; Hartl, 2003). The pivotal role of women in tourism, and of tourism in this process, places a considerable responsibility on the industry's development and management, and its collaboration and partnership with other social and economic development sectors to recognize the specific needs of women, and the specialized training and access to credit required in order to encourage women's entrepreneurial activity (Weiner, 1997).

Restructuring effects

Even within developed societies structural change can exert profound effects on the welfare of tourism workers. The rapid privatization of the tourism industry in former communist Central and Eastern Europe in the early 1990s, for example (D. Hall, 1991a; Harrison, 1993), brought substantial unemployment with the 'downsizing' of large former state enterprises. But at the same time this provided the political and legal freedom for the opening up of many small- and medium-scale private enterprises and entrepreneurial opportunities, as witnessed by the early growth of private guest houses in Hungary and the Czech Republic. In this way, residents have been drawn into the industry while others have been removed.

In Hungary, Szivas and Riley (2002) found that new entrants to the tourism industry appeared to have transferred from a wide and unconnected set of occupations. They argued that, while the tourism industry appeared to facilitate post-communist labour market adjustment, the tourism sector remained one of the lowest-paid sectors of the Hungarian economy. This irony, Szivas and Riley suggest, may have come about because change was so widespread in Hungarian society from the mid-1980s onwards that it became a societal norm to accommodate what would have appeared to be radical and perhaps unwelcome change in other circumstances. They also recognize that, with tourism enterprises often operating within the informal economy, the actual earnings and benefits from tourism jobs may be significantly greater than official data might suggest.

Within this process of structural re-adjustment, Szivas and Riley (2002) detected for Hungary a relatively low level of spatial mobility. They suggested that it may have been substituted by occupational mobility, with workers changing job sectors but staying in the same area, rather than attempting to pursue their original employment in a more prosperous region. This then led them to raise an important methodological issue in relation to the shortcomings of 'snapshot' research and the importance of synchronous studies for societies undergoing prolonged periods of restructuring: 'if people move into tourism as a contingency or because they lack a better alternative, will they stay there or will they move on at the first opportunity?' (Szivas and Riley, 2002: 70).

The influx of labour from a wide range of industries raises the question of how tourism itself is affected by such a level of diversity and what mechanisms are in place to assist the necessary adaptation and socialization processes to accompany or precede training and education. Sector newcomers bring experience that may be very different from the requirements of their tourism jobs. The literature on the psychological effects of occupational change from production to service indicates that a considerable degree of adaptation is required (Szivas and Riley, 2002). In the short to medium term, the use of such labour may act to prolong the persistence of poor service attitudes (e.g. Airey, 1994; Airey and Shackley, 1997).

The degree to which restructuring processes arising from transformation adversely or positively affect the role and identity of women is a matter of some debate. Weiner (1997) pointed to the effects of such processes in marginalizing and/or excluding women through reductions in state-funded health and child care, family planning and education, as well as heavy reductions in the administrative employment positions that women can find. Somewhat diffuse research has suggested that generally women are less well positioned to take advantage of new economic opportunities under such conditions. In tourism, acting in such roles as guides and as hostesses in newly privatized or new companies often means being paid a poor basic wage and having to depend on tips and other favours to sustain an adequate income (Buckley, 1997).

For entrepreneurial women, one response is to start their own business, despite the difficulties of obtaining credit and the risks of trying to survive alongside the grey economy, particularly when they often do not have the appropriate connections and, in post-communist societies, access to 'survival networks'. But some have been supported by aid-assisted business incubators. Such facilities can provide low-rent office space, access to information and communications technology and provision of business training courses and advice. In Russia, women have received nearly half of all loans made to small businesses by a $300 million fund of the European Bank for Reconstruction and Development. In

Hungary about 40% of new businesses there were being started by women in the late 1990s (Medvedev, 1998).

Small-scale, 'community'-based, 'sustainable' rural tourism projects have been a notable element of European-aided projects in a number of post-communist countries. In the case of Albania, women have been targeted, through the employment of participatory rural appraisal (PRA) in collaboration with local NGOs. Schemes to reduce the danger of villages becoming impoverished in the backwash of large-scale coastal tourism development have sought to enhance local economic and social capacity and encourage financial institutions to support rural 'self-help' schemes (Fisher, 1996). But community involvement and ownership of tourism development have often been inhibited by the legacy of minimal local experience of bottom-up development and lack of opportunities to participate in local decision making. This has been superimposed upon a tradition of male dominance, thereby doubly marginalizing women in decision-making processes.

Further, tensions may arise as the result of misunderstanding and incompatibility of objectives. The promoters of 'ecotourism' projects, for example, may wish to present the absence of infrastructure as providing a pristine environment appealing to rural and ecotourists. Yet, for local people, and especially women, participation in such schemes may be pursued on the assumption that tourism development will help improve their local infrastructures and services, such as a clean water supply, piped sewage disposal facilities, electricity, an access road and telecommunications, and thereby reduce their daily burden (Holland, 2000).

Tourism Workers as Incomers

Until recently, the relationship between tourism and migration had not been well researched (Williams and Hall, 2002). But it raises important issues concerning the definitions of tourists and migrants, and the politics of migration, refugees and citizenship. Different, often blurred, categories of temporary mobility that embrace the spectrum of notions of 'migrant' and 'tourist' may see individuals and families enjoying varying rights in respect of access to health and welfare facilities, property, legal status and educational provision (Urry, 2000).

The positions that tourism labour migrants take up may be classified as skilled managerial, intermediate posts such as tour guides and agency representatives, and unskilled labour with low entry thresholds (King, 1995). This simple categorization is complicated by the gender stereotyping of certain roles and by ethnic differentiation, which may be place-specific. In their overview of the interrelationships between tourism and migration, Williams and Hall (2002) recognized the series of economic and cultural mechanisms that influence the search spaces, demand and investment of such groups. They adopted an idealized four-phase model of relationships that could become locked into a circle of growth under certain conditions (Box 4.11).

Williams and Hall (2002: 11) argue that, although the model in Box 4.11 is simplistic, it emphasizes the fact that not only does tourism lead to migration, but migration may generate tourism flows, in particular through the geographical extension of friendship, ethnic and kinship networks. Although not new, the scale, intensity and geographical scope of such linkages have increased significantly in recent decades (Dwyer et al., 1993).

Thus tourism development processes may involve the movement not only of large numbers of tourists, but also of people who relocate to work in the tourism industry, either wholly or partly. The potential complexity of such flows may reflect core–periphery dependency and other spatial and structural inequalities or reasons that may be highly personal. Specifically, labour migration flows to tourism destinations have embraced several spatial characteristics:

- from an interior to a coastal location – for example, within Spain and Yugoslavia in the 1960s and 1970s (Poulsen, 1977; Lever, 1987);

Box 4.11. Four-phase model of tourism–migration relationships.

1. The flow of tourists into an area leads to the creation of a tourism industry that, initially at least, recruits labour locally, and the provision for tourism employees of accommodation and other welfare facilities remains small-scale and informal.

2. As tourism develops there is a continuing growth in demand for labour, particularly with certain specialized skills. This is likely to outstrip local supply, creating the need for labour migration (Monk and Alexander, 1986). The origins and composition of such flows are likely to be highly differentiated (e.g. King, 1995). They are also likely to be seasonal, reflecting both the temporal nature of tourism demand and the migrants' perceptions of the relative uncertainty of employment and unfamiliarity of the environment.

3. The tourism–migration nexus becomes more complex. As tourism continues, earlier tourism flows will have generated migration flows. These are of two main forms: consumption migrants, including retired people, and production migrants, responding to employment opportunities, although the latter may also be influenced by lifestyle goals, such as the setting up of a small tourism business on a Scottish island based on good information and computing technology (ICT) links (e.g. Kohn, 1997). There are also changes in the nature of labour migration from third countries, with seasonal flows being complemented by permanent labour migration. The growth of permanent migrant communities generates VFR tourism, both inbound and outward. These may be more frequent for the consumption-led migrants, on the assumption that they have more free time and potentially higher incomes.

4. Two additional forms of mobility characterize this phase. First, 'permanent' migrants may reach a point where they decide to leave. In the case of labour migrants this may be for personal reasons or in response to declining economic opportunities if tourism is stagnating or declining. For consumption-led migrants it may reflect booming economic conditions forcing up prices and depressing their real incomes, and/or increasing frailty of retirement migrants, leading them to return home to seek the support of their families (King *et al.*, 2000). The second type of new mobility is where earlier VFR tourists to migrants at the destination decide to become migrants themselves, stimulated by both their tourism experience and the existence of local social networks.

Source: Williams and Hall, 2002: 8–12, with additions.

- from a rural to an urban context – as in many developing countries (e.g. Smaoui, 1979);
- from urban to rural locations, for example associated with processes identified as counter-urbanization in New South Wales in the 1980s and early 1990s (Sant and Simons, 1993);
- intra-regional within the same country (e.g. Cukier and Wall, 1994); or
- international – e.g. southern Europeans to northern Europe and vice versa, and, following EU enlargement, citizens of new accession states to western Europe (e.g. Coles and Hall, 2005).

Any destination may experience combinations of these flows. For example, Salvà-Thomàs (2002) identified two main flows of labour immigrants into the Balearic Islands: a north–south flow from European Union countries, and a south–north component, partly unregulated, related to labour demand in certain pressured sectors such as construction. But the attitudes of local people may be significant for the availability of such employment roles. In more developed societies, locals may shun tourism-related jobs as poorly paid and demeaning, particularly where the economy is strong. In contrast, within destinations in less developed countries, such as Fiji and Vanuatu, tourism positions may be highly sought after. This is because of perceived high wages, job security and opportunity to interact with tourists and gain gratuities and other benefits, thereby improving social and gender roles and status (Williams and Hall, 2002: 27–28).

The motivation for such migration is often presented in terms of push and pull factors, and the cultural disparities between source and host region are important for the welfare implications of such activity. Often tourism migrant workers are segregated from the local population in terms of their physical activities and activity spaces, such as accommodation and working hours, and by their ethnic and religious backgrounds. But in the literature on tourism destinations, compared with wider migration studies, such as those on gender-related mobility (e.g Phizacklea, 1983; Barbieri and Carr, 2005; Iredale, 2005; Norman et al., 2005), relatively little research has been undertaken on:

- the welfare of tourism migrants;
- the impacts of such movement on family life, particularly when employment is seasonal;
- the socio-economic consequences for the source areas; and
- the implications for subsequent service provision in both source and host regions.

In one of the few studies to examine, albeit in passing, in-migrant tourism employment, Lordkipanidze et al. (2005: 792) point to migrants being one of the most dynamic sources of entrepreneurship in rural areas. They cite the growth of around 250 enterprises, mostly restaurants, operated by Middle Eastern, Chinese and Vietnamese entrepreneurs in the Söderslätt region of Sweden. Such success may reflect or mask a complex web of possible relationships between labour migrants and destination residents in terms of unequal superior/inferior structural positions or of complementarity through differentiation.

A hierarchical inferior–superior structural relationship may become explicit between migrant workers and residents in the destination region. Cukier and Wall (1994) found that the majority of street traders in Bali were in-migrants from other Indonesian islands. Ironically, in the light of the island's emphasis upon cultural tourism, they shared neither the Balinese language nor its Hindu religion. Seeking skills to enter the formal sector, these incoming street traders took up low-paid and low-status jobs that were none the less more remunerative than employment back home, reflecting significant income and employment opportunity differentials between Indonesian islands. In such cases, migrants were seen not to be supplanting the indigenous workforce, as they were filling low-status

cultural roles and economic niches in which locals chose not to participate. Thus, socially, economically and structurally, such tourism workers were placed in a position of inferiority in relation to the resident population.

In contrast, multinational control of large-scale tourism development is often characterized by an influx of outsiders to fill high-status and high-income managerial and skilled positions (e.g. Ankomah, 1991), potentially reversing hierarchical positions.

In some cases lower-grade skills can still be employed as a (temporary) access route to a 'superior' role. In the Albanian capital Tirana, for example, in the early 1990s a Slovenian construction firm, contracted to build a hotel owned by Austrian interests and part-financed by the European Bank for Reconstruction and Development, drafted in fellow countrymen as construction workers for the project. This policy was pursued in a country with one of the highest unemployment rates in Europe because the company claimed it could not rely on local skill availability, thereby reinforcing the negative self-image and lack of access to appropriate training of the local Albanian labour pool (D. Hall, 1994).

In other circumstances, the internal migration of a national majority group to minority areas may both prejudice the welfare opportunities of the minority and dilute its cultural role in tourism. Within the context of rapid tourism development and social change in China – the 'unrivalled leader of Asian tourism' (WTO, 2002: 4) – issues relating to the tensions between the local and the global, and endogenous and exogenous development factors, have been emphasized by Yamamura (2004) in the World Heritage Site (WHS) of Lijiang, in an ethnic minority area of Yunnan Province. Until the late 1970s, during a period when tourism was severely restricted, the handicrafts and traditions of Chinese ethnic minorities were largely suppressed. From 1978 an 'open-door' policy increasingly drew foreign capital into tourism (Zhang et al., 1999; Huang, 2004), and allowed a revival of ethnic minority traditions, which were portrayed to tourists as examples of the diversity of Chinese culture (Sofield and Li, 1998).

Previous research (Swain, 1990) had emphasized how ethnic groups were differentially placed to take advantage of their newly discovered tourism roles in response to the Chinese government's 'commoditizing' such ethnicity (Harrison, 2001: 38–39). Following an earthquake in 1996 and designation by the United Nations Educational, Scientific and Cultural Organization (UNESCO) as a WHS in 1997, Lijiang experienced a dramatic increase in tourism businesses, largely driven by an influx of Han Chinese majority peoples from outside the region selling goods largely devoid of local character. This exogenous, inauthentic dominance has been exacerbated by the local Naxi people's tendency to lack business and management know-how and their inability to draw upon government support policies. As a consequence they have been placed at an economic and cultural disadvantage. Yamamura (2004) argues that there is therefore a need for policies to promote local entrepreneurial endeavour through support for indigenous organizations and networks to help stimulate high-added-value goods and services that can draw upon and illuminate local culture and heritage and thereby improve the welfare position of the Naxi.

Complementarity through cultural differentiation may be expressed in other contexts. Thus, in northern (Turkish) Cyprus, Scott (1995, 1997) found that, although local (Muslim) women's participation in the tourism labour force had increased in recent years, migrant, and notably Romanian and Russian, women were being employed in those occupations considered culturally 'unsuitable' by locals (in this case as croupiers in the casino). This division of female labour was seen not to represent 'inferiority' or 'superiority' in the dichotomy between the indigenous and incoming groups, but it helped to highlight women's dual role and identity.

Gössling (2002b) argues that long-distance travel disrupts the sense of what is a person's home and their sense of attachment and care. In destination areas where there may be both long-haul tourists and long-distance migrant tourism workers, this may have important implications. Gössling suggests that, without this sense, citizens do not perceive themselves as part of a place any longer, and lose their understanding of the ecological limits of and the responsibility to care for places.

Tourism employment migration can act to postpone long-term rural or regional development in the migrants' source areas, although they may regularly send back significant amounts of money in remittances to their families. Yet often such potential capital is used for consumption to (self-)build a larger house or buy a new car rather than being invested to help upgrade local infrastructures or improve employment opportunities. In Albania, for example, recipient of an estimated $615 million in remittances in 2001, a building boom has taken place in recent years. But the country's banking system needs substantial reform to enable it to become a venue for the transfer of remittances and a source of credit for enterprise development, as few remittances are currently invested in productive activities (Martin et al., 2002).

Return migrants may be coming back to a home area that itself acts as a tourism destination. Unskilled migrants may return with financial capital in the form of savings and human capital in language acquisition, work experience and possibly some training. European research on return migrants emphasizes the importance to personal status of being able to be self-employed and setting up a small business such as a hotel, restaurant or bar (King, 1986; Kenna, 1993).

Particularly in developing areas, employment generated by rural tourism can discourage rural to urban migration flows, and represents an intervening opportunity that, nevertheless, requires careful planning if it is to be integrated into a national or regional plan for socio-economic transformation. In Tunisia, where planned tourism has been an important part of national development policy since the 1960s (Gant and Smith, 1992; Poirier, 1995), Smaoui (1979) found farmers and farm workers being drawn into tourism and being replaced in agriculture by migrants from elsewhere. This resulted in disruptions to food production and unforeseen consequences for income distribution and local service provision.

In contrast, in Venezuela the establishment of a free port on previously marginal Margarita Island reversed an existing pattern of predominantly male emigration (Monk and Alexander, 1986). The free port stimulated considerable domestic shopping tourism, and, while local men returned to take up new employment opportunities, local women continued to migrate as many of the new jobs in free port shops and hotels were taken by incoming women. Thus the tourism destination is portrayed as both generator and absorber of tourism migrant labour, in this case differentiated by gender, with significant social and welfare implications.

The NGO Tourism Concern (2004) reports that

> Many tourism workers who migrate to the tourist hotspots suffer social alienation, the disintegration of families, and abuse of alcohol and drugs as a result of poor living standards, stressful working conditions, and displacement from their own families and original communities.

But more detailed studies are required to examine the structural positions of incoming tourism workers in relation to the provision of services such as housing, health and education (e.g. Hautzinger, 2002), which affect their welfare. Studies are also needed to explore how the distribution of welfare gains and losses interposes between (migrant) tourism workers and the resident population. How far, and in what circumstances, can these groups share the values on offer to be consumed by tourists and the benefits derived from such consumption? The migration consequences of EU enlargement, for example, should spawn interesting research in this area (e.g. Hall *et al.*, 2006). Their implications extend far beyond tourism into considerations of potentially strategic importance.

Tourism Working Conditions: Cruise Line Employment

Tourism Concern pursues a number of campaigns, including that supporting improved conditions for mountain trek porters, examined in the next chapter. Under the campaign banner *Sun, Sand, Sea and Sweatshops* (Tourism Concern, 2004), the organization has undertaken research into tourism employment conditions in five popular holiday destinations – Bali, Mexico, the Dominican Republic, Egypt and the Canary Islands – in an attempt to seek fairer conditions and remuneration for workers. This has revealed a range of examples of labour exploitation, including: long working hours, unpaid overtime, over-dependence on tips, stress, lack of secure contracts, poor training and lack of promotion opportunities for locally employed people. While it is difficult to generalize from specific cases and there is as yet insufficient research to draw firm conclusions, certain sectors of the tourism and travel industry clearly depend upon low-wage, informal, casual, part-time and intermittent labour sources.

One important element of tourism's formal sector, dominated by ownership within the world's richest countries, is the ocean cruise line industry. Research into working conditions within this sector has been undertaken both by relatively dispassionate academics and by vested interests in labour unions. Their findings tend to be similar.

Cruise line employment represents a separate, relatively coherent sector, to a large extent defined by a specific and identifiable working environment. Yet for purposes of analysis this presents a paradox. On the one hand, the discrete and explicit working environment should permit meaningful generalizations to be drawn on cruise line employment. But, on the other hand, possibly for reasons of access, relatively little has actually appeared in the tourism literature on the conditions of cruise line employment and the consequent welfare of crew members, despite the fact that there is a growing literature on the nature, behaviour and perceptions of cruise tourists (e.g. Teye and Leclerc, 1998; Kester, 2003; Petrick, 2003; Jaakson, 2004a; Yarnal, 2004).

Although ocean cruise tourism is a rapidly growing sector, only temporarily set back by the events of '9/11' (Miller and Grazer, 2002), in terms of their administration and location of responsibilities, ocean cruise industry operations represent explicit elements of globalization constrained by only marginal accountability. As Wood (2000, 2004) and others have pointed out, this raises a number of equity issues, not least for the people employed by the cruise lines. The ships' very size symbolizes high concentrations of multinational capital: they spend much of their time in non-territorial waters, only briefly visiting favoured ports of call, and make cost savings by taking advantage of destinations that have cheap or low-tax fuel bunkering (Bull, 1996). Ocean cruise lines thus replicate the behaviour of land-based multinational companies (MNCs) by driving down costs through playing off one low-cost supplier against another.

Cruise ship crews may represent highly diverse labour forces, originating from up to 50 countries on a large ship (Wood, 2000). Such globally recruited labour is usually stratified into three groups – officers, staff and crew – who have separate living quarters, segregated dining areas and different rules of engagement concerning interaction with passengers. They also enjoy vastly different pay levels, usually with a clear racial distinctiveness attached to the hierarchical divisions. Crew are often drawn from less developed countries, where pay rate expectations are low: 'Captains from traditionally European sea-faring nations are extolled in cruise industry marketing, while below the almost exclusively white officer class is an increasingly global crew' (Wood, 2004: 140).

The pattern is replicated on most cruise lines, although some recruit more heavily from specific markets: Holland America Line, for example, relies heavily on Filipino and Indonesian crew members. Of the 114,000 who work on cruise ships around the world, about 70% are hotel/catering staff. They include cabin stewards, bar staff, waiting staff, laundry workers, cleaners, chefs and kitchen crew, as well as receptionists and clerical staff. Also within this group are sound and light technicians, social hosts and play organizers for children. All of these are usually directly employed

by the cruise lines, on fixed-term contracts, usually for between 6 and 10 months at a time.

A further 20% comprise the officers and crew, who work in the deck and engine department. They include the greasers, fitters and mechanics, motormen, plumbers, deck cleaners and other non-officer ratings. Most of these are usually experienced seafarers whose working life is in the merchant marine, even if their repeat contracts are short. Other crew members, such as those working in the on-board shops, gyms, spas and beauty salons, or as entertainers and musicians, are not the direct employees of the cruise companies but work for concessionaires or independent contractors (War on Want and ITF, 2002: 11).

Within these global and 'domestic' contexts, cruise line employees are confronted by a number of welfare-related issues. First, avoidance of national or international regulations is a major characteristic of cruise lines (Wood, 2000, 2004). 'Open registry', better known as the use of flags of convenience (FOCs), circumvents home-country employment, wage, health, safety and environment laws, taxes and maritime regulations. Indeed, cruise development has been explicitly assisted by the climate of deregulation and availability of pools of flexible and cheap migrant labour. FOC ship crews are subject to the laws of the country in which the ship is flagged, and in most FOC countries employment laws protecting the rights of workers are virtually non-existent.

This has been exacerbated by the fact that companies have responded to increasing competition by attempting to squeeze greater value from their workforce, who experience:

- insecure, short-term contracts;
- low wages and high costs, including illegal agents' fees to get the job: money often has to be borrowed at high rates of interest and, if anything goes wrong with the contract, the cruise ship worker and their family may find themselves in a spiral of mounting debt;
- long working hours and high work intensity, leading to fatigue;

- poor management practices, including bullying and favouritism, racial and gender discrimination;
- high labour turnover, fatigue and inadequate training, giving cause for concern about safety; and
- employers who are hostile or resistant to trade union organization and collective bargaining (War on Want and ITF, 2002: 1–2).

Royal Caribbean Cruise Lines, for example, although based in Florida, is registered as a Liberian corporation and it has been estimated that the company saves around US$30 million annually in avoiding payment of US taxes by registering its ships under FOCs (Frantz, 1999). Such savings, Wood (2004: 137) suggests, enable cruise ships to offer accommodation, meals and entertainment for substantially less than such a package would cost in most of the ports that they visit. In 2003, for example, North American cruise lines enjoyed a cabin occupancy rate of 95% compared with an average hotel room occupancy rate of only 59% (Toh *et al.*, 2005).

Wood (2004: 142) argues that since '9/11' the flag of convenience regime has come under closer global scrutiny, and suggests that the 'war on terrorism' could threaten its existence. Long-existing campaigns against the system, waged notably by organized labour, such as the International Transport Workers Federation (ITF), alongside campaigning NGOs, such as War on Want, had previously achieved limited success, with just a few cruise ships signing agreements with the ITF (War on Want and ITF, 2002). These agreements fall far short of negotiated union contracts – virtually the entire cruise sector being non-unionized – but seek voluntary compliance from companies in relation to the treatment of crew.

Second, the government of China has been trying to gain access to overseas ship employment as a means of raising the country's maritime skills to international standards (Fong, 1997). By tapping a virtually inexhaustible source of cheap labour from the People's Republic, the cruise line industry could drive down crew wages and conditions further.

Third, being concentrated within a limited space with large numbers of people from different environments over a period of time, ships' crews are exposed to a greater risk of contagious diseases than many other tourism sector workers. For example, in 2002 many tourists and employees on board several ships owned by Carnival Cruise Lines, Holland America Line and Disney Cruise Line were infected with a Norwalk virus (Charatan, 2002; Boorstin, 2003). Norwalk results in acute gastroenteritis (AGE), of which there are some 23 million reported cases annually in the USA (Mead *et al.*, 1999). The confined quarters of a cruise ship provide ideal conditions for such viruses to multiply and be transmitted (Bond, 2003).

In the 2002 outbreaks, of which there were 21 affecting 17 cruise ships, although several companies removed ships from service in order for them to be disinfected, a major source was found to be tourists, who had been infected before they boarded the ships. Once on board, they spread the virus both to other passengers and to crew (Grady, 2002; Bond, 2003). Weaver (2005: 357) suggests that a noteworthy aspect of these outbreaks was that the virus spread rapidly within a controlled environment where it was believed that sufficient precautions had already been taken.

The welfare environment of cruise line employees on board ship remains ambivalent. The International Council of Cruise Lines (ICCL), which represents the interests of the most dominant cruise lines in the North American market, issued a 'Shipboard Workplace Code of Conduct' in 1999. This was promoted as a measure of its members' 'commitment to providing passengers and employees alike with the optimal levels of safety and security while cruising'. But the code is entirely voluntary, its contents are limited and no monitoring or verification procedures have been put in place. Significantly, it does not incorporate workers' rights to freedom of association (War on Want and ITF, 2002: 25).

Ironically, a popular literature (e.g. Bow, 2002) has developed for those seeking employment in the cruise line industry. It is, of course, aimed exclusively at those potential employees from developed countries looking for managerial and service roles, rather than the considerably less-well-paid, ethnically separated, manual labour sectors.

Conclusions

In this chapter we have focused on welfare aspects of living and working in tourism destinations. One of the much-touted mantras of sustainable tourism, that it needs to involve the local 'community', fails to acknowledge the often inadequate conceptualization and, importantly, the practicality of the latter term. The role and significance of tourism will vary greatly within different local areas, and tourism will interact with other aspects of a destination's development sectors in different ways.

Tying notions of 'community' to 'tourism sustainability' may not reflect such a situation adequately, and may be a way of obviating the need for a more holistic consideration of the needs of all parties. With this in mind, a focus was placed upon the ethical nature of interactions between the major tourism actors within the destination, with trade-offs and competitive and complementary roles being examined. The examples of second homes, crime and health were addressed in this context. A number of aspects of tourism employee welfare were then evaluated, including the position of women, the effects of post-communist restructuring and the complex issues surrounding labour migration and the specific case of employment in the cruise line industry.

Industry fragmentation diffuses authority and responsibility, a theme taken up again in Chapter 7. This makes it difficult both to locate points of responsibility and to establish realistic norms for addressing destination welfare in terms of the well-being of its residents and workers. For various reasons, most tourism stakeholders currently lack the ethical motivation to raise much of the industry above its dependence upon a relatively low-wage, 'flexible' workforce. This renders much of the industry, including destinations, their residents and employees, vulnerable.

The employment dimensions of this discussion in particular provide an appropriate context for the following chapter, in which we address the apparently ethically driven issue of pro-poor tourism development.

5

Pro-poor Tourism?

We are so far behind achieving what we promised – what we swore we would do five years ago in the UN millennium development goals – that the targets for 2005 will not be met until 2150. We're a joke, we are a complete and utter disgrace and we perpetrate this falsity and this lie on the head of the already trodden upon, mute and weak.

(Geldof, 2005)

Box 5.1. Chapter aims and summary.

This chapter seeks to: evaluate the nature and role of pro-poor tourism (PPT) in enhancing the welfare of residents and tourism workers in destination areas.

It does this by: examining the recent emergence of poverty-reduction development strategies and the growing role of tourism within them.

Its key concepts are: poverty reduction, development (goals), pro-poor tourism.

It concludes that: PPT, although flawed, has the potential to be an important tool in assisting poverty reduction and in the generation of more just tourism development processes in poor destination areas.

Introduction

In Chapter 2 we addressed the nature of and constraints on widening access to tourism participation, essentially from a consumption perspective. In Chapter 4 our welfare focus was concentrated on the tourism destination, in terms of both its residents and the workforce. In this chapter we take the debate forward by evaluating the role of tourism in alleviating poverty – essentially through employment and its economic diffusion effects – through a policy mechanism that has come to be known as pro-poor tourism.

People in extreme poverty are taken to be those who continue to live on an income of less than US$1 per person per day. When this standard for a global poverty line was proposed by the World Bank and the UN in the late 1980s, it was a far more generous standard than it is approaching two decades later. A more realistic figure now is $2, and even this is 'mean' (Remenyi, 2004: 193). The economic and social constraints that such poverty imposes are summarized in Table 5.1. Almost half of the world's 6 billion inhabitants live on less than $2 a day, and a fifth on less than $1 a day. While the number of people living below this line is declining in some regions, it is increasing in much of Africa. Poverty is particularly acute in sub-Saharan Africa and South Asia. In light of these statistics, some analysts believe that the tourism industry can play a significant part in poverty reduction (Cattarinich, 2001: 1).

Table 5.1. Major constraints of poverty (from Remenyi, 2004: 204).

Economic constraints	Social constraints
Absence of access to cash	Being dependent
Low productivity	Subject to violence and duress
Few assets	Vulnerability to misadventure
Low absolute savings capacity	Feelings of hopelessness
Low income	Behavioural passivity
Chronic unemployment	Alienated within one's community

Tourism Development and Less Developed Countries

But the above is to ignore two critiques:

- that of development policy for LDCs, arguing that, until recently, such policy has promoted modernization at the expense of equitable poverty reduction; and
- that of tourism in LDCs, which views the industry as an extension of exploitative dependency (e.g. Britton, 1982).

Tourism and 'development'

Poverty reduction as a development goal was subordinate to 'modernizing' 'economic development' policies for much of the second half of the 20th century. Remenyi (2004: 197–198) suggests that this reflected three key factors:

- a (Western) post-war development strategy based upon a fear of mass unemployment and poverty in the world's most mature economies;
- a concept of modernization that demanded the diversion of national production from consumption to investment, and even required a period during which poverty increased before it fell; and
- advisers setting development priorities that would encourage LDCs to import.

But since the early 1990s mainstream development thinking has begun emphasizing the importance of 'pro-poor' growth over economic growth, and development strategies founded on information and priority-setting processes that are 'participatory'

(Greeley and Jenkins, 2001; Remenyi, 2004: 198–199). Strategies for improving individual welfare and capacity for self-reliant escape from poverty are concerned with ensuring that the poor have a voice that is heard in the corridors of power. They are also designed to increase the opportunities for poor people to graduate to better jobs, achieve higher levels of consumption and participate in the process by which wealth creation and accumulation are realized (Remenyi, 2004: 190).

Pro-poor growth is growth that is the result of poverty-reducing economic activities (Box 5.2), and its importance was reflected in the publication of the first issue of UNDP's *Human Development Report* in 1990, and production of the first *Poverty Reduction Strategy Paper* (PRSP) by the World Bank and the International Monetary Fund (IMF) for their African 'clients'. But it was only at the September 1999 annual meetings of the World Bank Group and IMF that ministers endorsed the proposal that country-owned poverty-reduction strategies should provide the basis of World Bank and IMF concessional lending (Remenyi, 2004: 191).

The common goal of participatory poverty reduction and pro-poor growth strategies is to enhance the creation and accumulation of six major types of capital:

- financial capital: savings;
- human capital: skills, quality and vulnerability of labour available;
- institutional capital: education, health, governance;
- social capital: sense of community and mutual support;

Box 5.2. The goals of pro-poor growth strategies.

To loosen the constraints that keep people poor by:

- reducing unemployment and underemployment;
- raising poor households' capacity to save;
- enabling entrepreneurship and innovation to flourish;
- facilitating poor households' realization of their savings-investment plans;
- allowing new markets to be explored and served;
- enhancing risk management to avoid misadventure, ill health and economic loss;
- removing vested interests that limit economic opportunities of the poor;
- addressing gender equity issues that contribute to institutionalized poverty;
- compensating for the impact of market failures on economic opportunities of the poor;
- augmenting access to assets that the poor need for growth in self-reliance and productivity;
- attending to environmental issues critical to the sustainability of livelihoods above the poverty line; and
- ensuring that procedures are in place to achieve good government and the absence of corruption.

Source: Remenyi, 2004: 202.

- natural capital: the resource base of a village or household;
- liquid capital: money (Remenyi, 2004: 199–201).

The subsequent success of PSRPs and the growing adoption of inclusive participatory processes in development programmes are indicative of a spreading recognition of the need for effective poverty-reduction planning (Hulme and Shepherd, 2003).

Tourism and dependency

D'Sa (1999) argued that contemporary tourism is a justice issue, requiring governments of developing countries to provide basic protection for powerless communities and their environment; organized religion to exercise moral authority, particularly for supporting the poor and vulnerable; and

the establishment of solidarity between Western tourists and local communities, probably through tourism NGOs. They should find ways of channelling some of their money away from the coffers of the travel operators and agents, for example, by funding community projects in the poorer tourism destinations. Yet the capitalist system, or indeed any political–economic system threatened by unconventional or potentially rival models, soon adopts, absorbs and re-channels those forces, as, for example, in the case of 'charity challenges'.

As colonies became independent after the Second World War, they found themselves lured into the Western capitalist system by three institutions set up in the 1940s: the World Bank, the IMF and the General Agreement on Tariffs and Trade (GATT) (D'Sa, 1999). The developing world was advised to modernize – build new facilities, go for technology, aspire to the Western way of life. The emphasis was on economic development. The World Bank offered loans, which, in the 1960s, were extended to tourism projects, with 1967 being declared tourism year by the United Nations. Structural adjustment policies were imposed by the supranational actors to keep LDC economies open to imports from the developed world and to the indebtedness that resulted from the loans required to manage structural adjustment and to purchase those imports (Mowforth and Munt, 1998: 291).

In 1975 the World Tourism Organization (WTO) was set up with the mission 'to develop tourism as a significant means of fostering international peace and understanding, economic development and international trade'. The emphasis here was clearly in favour of industry, with 'peace' and 'understanding' appearing almost as afterthoughts or palliatives, especially in the absence of social concerns. With this reinforcement of an economically driven First World industry, D'Sa (1999) recognizes three categories of stakeholders:

- Northern investors (such as tour operators, hoteliers), who dictated the standard of tourist facilities to be built in developing country destinations;

- local elites (government and business), who were taken on as junior partners to provide the land, natural resources and labour; and
- local resident communities, who were left to pick up the pieces.

For D'Sa (1999) tourism is a product of the prevailing unjust economic and social order underpinned by global capitalism, as a consequence of which international tourism in LDCs is characterized by three 'negative' components:

- an imbalance in global tourism generation, reflecting the fact that developed countries, with 20% of global population, possess 83% of world income and consume over 80% of the world's resources. The power centres of the North set the agenda and define the rules of engagement, whereby LDCs in the global economy essentially provide resources for Northern industries. While the North is awash with food, over a billion people in the developing world suffer crippling poverty, 800 million are chronically hungry and 40,000, half of them children, die from hunger each day. Many LDCs still labour under heavy debt repayments, often owed to the richest countries, and as a consequence have to compromise health and education programmes in order to pay up;
- racism: many tourists may arrive in a developing country with a power consciousness derived from a sense of economic and racial superiority, and may, as a result, express little respect for local culture and traditions. A master–servant relationship has developed in the developing world tourism industry;
- the 'new world order', constructed on the 'right' of the powerful and their TNCs to force open the economies of the weak, leading inevitably to the continued enrichment of the elites and the immiseration of the majority. This new order is characterized by resurgent corporate power, global mobility of capital and labour, and greater power vested in

supranational institutions – the World Bank, the IMF and the World Trade Organization.

D'Sa (1999) asks, rhetorically: since the 'wealthfare' of investors overrides the welfare of the ordinary people, what hope is there for a people-centred tourism? He argues two points.

First, respect for autonomy and concern for justice are regarded as core ethical principles in the West. By these principles, local communities should be left alone to lead their own lives and have priority over their own resources, but, in practice, the development paradigm of the profit-seeking elites takes precedence. The poor have to be modernized for their own good. Common lands are expropriated, scarce resources (like water or electrical power) are diverted for the comfort of tourists. The developers, in fact, may simply be implementing master plans designed by foreign advisers and consultants.

Second, while the civil and political rights of individuals at risk from repressive state power are stoutly defended, the economic, social and cultural rights of powerless groups and communities are consistently downgraded in the face of corporate objectives. The rights of individuals to subsistence, education and health care have been subordinated to the rights of investors. Although a Tourism Bill of Rights confers 'the right of everyone to rest and leisure', in practice it is largely tourists from developed countries who exercise this right, while poor, indigenous communities remain vulnerable both to the intrusions of tourists and to the depredations of investors demanding open and 'free' markets (Fig. 5.1).

In a series of meetings and declarations chronicled by D'Sa (1999) (Box 5.3), voices representing residents and other stakeholders of LDC destinations have been raised.

Can Tourism be Pro-poor?

This might suggest that the tourism industry per se may not be the most favourable

Fig. 5.1. Contrasting images in a tourism economy: Bizerte, Tunisia.

environment for employment of the poor, particularly in the poorest countries and regions. This is apparent for a number of reasons:

- a high reliance on part-time and seasonal labour can suppress or at least constrain regional income levels and employment structures;
- particular sectors, such as the cruise industry, reflect rigid racial and gender stratification, conditions of near exploitation and little opportunity for those from poor backgrounds to gain access to promotional ladders;
- there continue to exist high levels of economic leakage from most destinations in the less developed countries;
- to prevent early failure, new entrepreneurs require empathetic financial institutions and other institutional support mechanisms (training, networking, tax incentives), a reasonable local

infrastructure and (information on) market opportunities, all elements that are in short supply in the poorest countries and regions.

Can tourism therefore, realistically, be an effective economic and social mechanism for alleviating poverty? The rather simplistic arguments underpinning pro-poor tourism, as interpreted by UK development agencies, can be summarized as:

- a recognition of insufficient progress in existing poverty-reduction programmes;
- acknowledgement that tourism is a major economic sector with relatively rapid growth rates in less developed countries, and is thus potentially important for pro-poor growth; and
- limited evidence suggesting that the pursuit by tourism companies of business in pro-poor ways can make commercial sense (Ashley and Haysom, 2005) (Figs 5.2 and 5.3).

Counter-arguments might suggest that trying to achieve two objectives with the same tool is suboptimal. Initiatives that have sought to involve poor people from less developed countries in tourism-related activities to help reduce their poverty have tended not to be (initially) generated from within the tourism industry, but from international development agencies and NGOs. For example, Tourism Concern was funded by the European Commission (EC) and the UK government Department for International Development (DfID) in 1999 for a 3-year project examining the tourism industry's commitment to developing countries' communities. To do this, Tourism Concern set up an international fair trade in tourism network. It concluded that the industry must look towards ethical trading practices. The main objectives of this should include: encouraging fair trade partnerships between tourism and hospitality investors and local communities; seeking a fair share of benefits for local stakeholders; fair trade between tourists and local people; fair and sustainable use of natural resources; and fair wages and working conditions (Tourism Concern, 2001).

Box 5.3. Organized responses to tourism from residents of poorer countries.

1. Manila Declaration (1980)
A groundbreaking people's Tourism Workshop held in Manila (ECTWT, 1988) was attended by 30 participants from 18 countries. It pointed to tourism jobs generated being minimal, seasonal and highly exploitative, arguing that economies, cultures and social structures had been disrupted by the long-term effects of tourism. The workshop called for a comprehensive reorientation of the tourism industry, taking as its basic premise the fundamental spiritual and human development of peoples everywhere.

2. The Bad Boll Conference (1986)
140 people from 30 countries met in Germany to discuss Third World tourism (ECTWT, 1986). Organized by the Ecumenical Coalition on Third World Tourism (ECTWT) and the European Tourism Network (TEN), the conference brought together NGOs, churchmen, tour operators, funding agencies, social scientists, educators and journalists. It envisioned a 'new tourism order' – just, participatory, culturally sensitive, benefiting both sides economically and providing support for its 'victims', such as sex workers.

3. Asia–Pacific Workshop on Tourism, Indigenous Peoples and Land Rights (1995)
Held at Sagada, Mountain Province, Philippines, participating indigenous groups from Hawaii, Papua New Guinea, Australia, Taiwan, Irian Jaya, India, Bangladesh and Nepal issued a declaration arguing for reversal of the processes whereby 'the tourism industry designed by transnational corporate interests turns our ancestral homes and sacred grounds into playgrounds for the pleasure of the few' (Anon., 1995).

4. Joint Declaration by Goa NGOs (1997)
This Joint Declaration, put out by a number of Goa's People's Groups (NGOs) on Goa tourism (Goa Foundation, 1997), deplored the despoilation of much of the state's natural ecological assets, which had been squandered on the 'wrong' type of tourism, whose presence had brought neither money nor pleasure to the locals. The brunt of the tourism burden was being borne by ordinary people in whose name development was promoted.

5. May 1997 Manila meeting organized by the WTO and the Philippine Department of Tourism
President Fidel Ramos spoke for the masses of the developing world when he declared that some of tourism's problems were serious enough to threaten the social cohesion of communities. Tourism in less developed countries cannot comprise a world-class resort for affluent tourists with thousands of unemployed and hungry people outside the gates (WTO, 1997).

Source: D'Sa, 1999.

In the face of such increasing pressure and activity from outside the industry, only recently has the WTO begun to take a pro-poor initiative (Box 5.4). Current approaches are predicated on a growth and poverty-reduction strategy whereby businesses are meant to deliver growth and redistribution while public investment facilitates poverty reduction and equity (Ashley and Haysom, 2005: 1–2).

Evolution of PPT

For some time a lack of focus on poverty has been identified within the tourism agenda (Ashley *et al.*, 2000, 2001). Despite widespread interest in 'green', 'eco-' and 'community' tourism from the mid-1980s, emphasis on environmental and cultural protection often failed to consider the full range of impacts on the livelihoods of the poor in destination regions (Neto, 2003). This has been even more the case in the context of mass forms of tourism development (WTO, 2004).

The 1999 United Nations' declaration on tourism and sustainable development, which made explicit reference to the potential of tourism for eradicating poverty (Goodwin, 2005), set the context for an

Fig. 5.2.   Sandal assemblers and repairers working in the shadow of the Taj Mahal, Agra.

Fig. 5.3.   Heavy manual labour by the young in Kathmandu, Nepal.

increased emphasis on pro-poor tourism following the United Nations' Millennium Declaration. Adopted by 189 nations in 2000, this set out eight International Development Goals (IDGs, also known as Millennium Development Goals: MDGs) to be achieved by 2015. These included halving the proportion of people living in extreme poverty – on the basis of the global situation in the 1990s (Box 5.5).

Development agencies have been evolving sustainable livelihoods (SL) approaches largely in response to these targets (DfID, 1999). Tourism has been adopted by a number of governmental and non-governmental bodies as part of this process, leading to the fear that tourism might be seen unrealistically as a 'quick fix'. But, somewhat ironically, progress has been painfully slow (Sahn and Stifel, 2003; United Nations, 2005).

Is it realistic for tourism to be 'pro-poor'? In the face of a complex industry driven by private-sector profit, governments have relatively few tools with which to influence direction, particularly in developing countries, where fiscal and planning instruments for capturing non-commercial benefits may be weak. Nevertheless, tourism

Box 5.4. The World Tourism Organization's ST-EP initiative.

The World Tourism Organization, the UN agency responsible for tourism, launched an initiative to 'creatively develop sustainable tourism as a force for poverty elimination' at the 2002 World Summit for Sustainable Development in Johannesburg (United Nations, 2002).

The programme was launched in collaboration with the United Nations Conference on Trade and Development (UNCTAD), the UN agency focusing on the world's poorest countries, and was to be extended to other partners as it evolved.

ST-EP (Sustainable Tourism – Eliminating Poverty) focuses on long-term activities designed to encourage 'sustainable tourism' that specifically alleviates poverty, bringing development and employment. It has four components:

- an international foundation to attract new dedicated financing from business, philanthropical and government sources;
- a research base to identify linkages, principles and model applications;
- an operating framework to 'incentivize' and promote good practice among companies, consumers and communities;
- an annual forum to bring together stakeholders from public, private and civil society, and sources for information, exchange and active participation.

At the WTO's assembly in Beijing in 2003 a resolution was passed mandating the Secretary General to pursue aggressively the implementation of ST-EP.

Source: WTO, 2004.

would appear to possess several potential advantages as a sector to support pro-poor economic growth (Box 5.6).

In 2004, less developed countries (Africa, South and South East Asia, Caribbean and Latin America, Middle East) received 21.5% of world international tourist arrivals (WTO, 2005). Of this total, Africa received just 4.3% of the world total and, for sub-Saharan Africa excluding South Africa, the figure was just over 2% (Box 5.7). Nevertheless, among the 12 countries that are home to 80% of the world's poor, tourism is significant or growing in all but one (Ashley et al., 2000). This is an important consideration

for the proponents of PPT since it cannot be developed without linkages to an existing tourism product or transit market. Both domestic and regional tourism are also significant and growing in Asia, Africa and South America, and can be important markets for the poor: small-scale, informal tourism-related services can act to expand economic participation (Goodwin, 2002).

Despite the problems associated with 'community'-based strategies (discussed in Chapter 4), 'community tourism' is often thought of as the main avenue for the poor to participate in tourism, for example through community-run lodges, campsites or craft centres, which are often supported by NGOs. In order to achieve greater sustainability in such employment, innovative means of participatory planning have needed to be adopted. The Dutch development NGO SNV, for example, has employed appreciative participatory planning and action (APPA) methodology in Nepal to draw out ideas and 'dreams' from villagers in developing local tourism action plans (Hummel, 2002).

Poor individuals engage in all types of tourism through self-employment (e.g. hawking, or small enterprise) and casual labour. But there is a lack of data on how participation of the poor varies by market segment (see Table 5.2), which could be employed in helping to build past experience and best practice into such local development plans.

PPT within the wider context

Emerging trends indicate the importance of domestic/regional tourism, although there have been relatively few analyses of the spatial distribution and internal movement of tourists within developing countries (e.g. see Oppermann, 1992; Ghimire, 2001). This reflects national tourism policymakers placing importance on achieving targets in total tourist numbers and income, and also the difficulties of data collection. Studies focusing on the spatial movement and residency patterns of tourists within poorer countries are important because they provide clues to the regional distribution

---

Box 5.5. The Millennium Development Goals.

1.   Eradicate extreme poverty and hunger:

- halve, between 1990 and 2015, the proportion of people whose income is less than $1 a day
- halve, between 1990 and 2015, the proportion of people who suffer from hunger

2.   Achieve universal primary education:

- ensure that, by 2015, children everywhere, boys and girls alike, will be able to complete a full course of primary schooling

3.   Promote gender equality and empower women:

- eliminate gender disparity in primary and secondary education, preferably by 2005, and in all levels of education no later than 2015

4.   Reduce child mortality:

- reduce by two-thirds, between 1990 and 2015, the under-5 mortality rate

5.   Improve maternal health:

- reduce by three-quarters, between 1990 and 2015, the maternal mortality ratio

6.   Combat HIV/AIDS, malaria and other diseases:

- have halted by 2015 and begun to reverse the spread of HIV/AIDS
- have halted by 2015 and begun to reverse the incidence of malaria and other major diseases

7.   Ensure environmental sustainability:

- integrate the principles of sustainable development into country policies and programmes and reverse the loss of environmental resources
- halve, by 2015, the proportion of people without sustainable access to safe drinking water and basic sanitation
- by 2020, to have achieved a significant improvement in the lives of at least 100 million slum dwellers

8.   Develop a global partnership for development:

- address the special needs of the least developed countries, landlocked countries and small island developing states
- develop further an open, rule-based, predictable, non-discriminatory trading and financial system
- deal comprehensively with developing countries' debt
- in cooperation with developing countries, develop and implement strategies for decent and productive work for youth
- in cooperation with pharmaceutical companies, provide access to affordable essential drugs in developing countries
- in cooperation with the private sector, make available the benefits of new technologies, especially information and communications.

Sources: Devarajan *et al.*, 2002; United Nations, 2005.

---

of income generation, employment creation and economic multiplier effects (Brohman, 1996).

Yet unless these positive impacts are managed carefully the poorest may gain few direct benefits from tourism, while bearing many of its costs. Benefits depend on the nature of society and the extent to which the poor can participate economically in a sector that is influenced by a wide range of local, policy, environment and commercial factors (Goodwin and Pender, 2005).

O'Hare and Barrett (1999), for example, analysed the regional distribution of international and domestic tourism in Peru using local and regional databases.

Box 5.6. Tourism's potential advantages for pro-poor economic development.

1. The consumer comes to the destination, thereby providing opportunities for selling additional goods and services.
2. Tourism provides an opportunity to diversify local economies, assisting poor and marginal areas that may possess few other export and diversification options.
3. It offers labour-intensive and small-scale opportunities compared with other non-agricultural activities.
4. The service nature of the sector and high proportion of low-skill domestic-type jobs increase accessibility to women, although not always in a way that increases their status, as noted earlier. Often women are most involved in informal-sector activities, particularly hawking.
5. It values natural resources and culture, which may feature among the few assets belonging to the poor.

Source: Ashley et al., 2000.

International, more than domestic, tourist distributions were found to be highly concentrated (and persistent) in a relatively small number of local authority areas and locations. Such concentration was seen to be linked to complex regional variations in tourism attractions, transport access, basic tourism services and government regional promotion of the industry. Tourism, particularly the hotel and restaurant sector, was seen to bring important benefits in terms of gross domestic product (GDP) and employment creation. However, a regional distribution analysis of hotels and restaurants revealed that the industry was benefiting the already better-off local authority areas rather than the poorer ones. Continuing investment patterns and government laissez-faire policies indicated that diffusion or dispersal of the tourism sector to new areas was unlikely under these circumstances.

Tourism is a relatively fragile business, often small-scale and dispersed and yet requiring a range of diverse skills to be successful, and these may not be easy to develop or attain in one person or a family unit. Particularly important skills that are likely to

be initially lacking amongst the poor include language knowledge and a realistic understanding of tourist expectations. Financial capital is critical for the poor to be able to expand informal-sector activities within tourism: those who become entrepreneurs have usually managed to generate their own capital over time, by starting small and re-investing profits over several years or perhaps as migrant labourers, possibly in tourism. But they can be easily marginalized if outside investors drive rapid growth in the industry, as occurred, for example, on Boracay Island in the Philippines (Shah, 2000). Where tourism is stimulated by outside agencies, it may be championed by those who do not share the values and identity of, and attachment to, the local area held by long-time residents.

Where the poor have access to micro-credit (e.g. through institutions such as the Grameen Bank in Bangladesh) and to dynamic and flexible forms of social capital, the potential for participation may be greater. For example, in Bali, most restaurants are managed either by families or by *Sekaha* – voluntary associations with clear principles for division of work and revenue. This system is also used for car and bicycle rentals and running minibuses and restaurants. At Indonesia's Bromo Tengger Semeru National Park, activities such as horse and jeep rides are organized through associations that try to ensure fair access to the market for all their members. In contrast, tourism in the Upper Mustang region of Nepal is organized by outside interests. The Tour Agencies of Nepal Association (TANA) has helped to frame rules that make independent travel difficult, thereby reducing opportunities for local entrepreneurs (Shah, 2000).

Tourism is generally an additional diversification option for the poor, rather than a substitute for their core activities. Its ability to complement or conflict with the seasonality of agriculture, livestock management or fisheries is often a critical issue. Risks have to be low: capital is in short supply and the timescales for success are short. Evaluation of such risks may lead to small-scale options with few trade-offs and low risk.

Box 5.7. Ignoring Africa.

In the 1960s geography and development texts on Africa barely acknowledged tourism. That by Pollock (1968) made no mention of it, while, in Hodder and Harris's (1967) important edited work, tourism was relegated to three paragraphs within the chapter on the Maghreb (Harris, 1967: 86–87).

   More than a decade and a half ago sub-Saharan Africa was being referred to as a massive region with unrealized tourism potential (Ankomah and Crompton, 1990), which could be realized particularly through regional cooperation (Teye, 1988). Yet relatively little has been written about tourism here since, and what has been published has tended to concentrate on a handful of countries: South Africa, The Gambia, Kenya, Mauritius and Seychelles. In most of these cases, traditional notions of trickle-down and diffusion effects through society may have been limited, both socially and geographically. For example, although the Maasai of Kenya and Tanzania may live close to major international tourist destinations (Thompson and Homewood, 2002), their participation in the tourism industry is extremely low (Coast, 2002). Similarly, local levels of support for tourism development may differ notably between regions, places and differently positioned socio-economic groups (e.g. Sirakaya et al., 2001).

   Successful tourism development in Africa requires attention to a range of issues such as clear tourism development objectives, integration of these into national plans, local involvement and control, regional cooperation and integration, and tourism entrepreneurship. Dieke (2003) has again emphasized the need for intra-African cooperation to assist the provision of an enabling environment and the mobilization of strategic resources. In Kenya, for example, a number of systemic shortcomings in tourism training that would be improved by regional collaboration have been identified, including curriculum deficiencies and the inadequate development and enhancement of workplace skills (Mayaka and King, 2002).

   In Tanzania, while the tourism sector's share of GDP has increased in recent years, contributing to employment generation, economic gains have come at the cost of environmental degradation, social hardship and the breakdown of social norms and values (Kulindwa, 2002). In the case of staging mega-events in Africa, for example, factors such as the unequal nature of the global contests to stage them and broad infrastructural and resource incapacities often mean that such events bear greater costs than benefits for African countries (Cornelissen, 2004).

   Further, the construction of nation and identity, as portrayed and projected through the websites of national tourism and travel bodies, often represents a struggle to create a cohesive image that can be attractive to Western tourism consumers, but at the same time raises questions of self-identity and the commodification of cultural distinctiveness and 'exoticism' (Fürsich and Robins, 2004).

   As a basis for nature tourism generation, community wildlife conservation initiatives are an important economic and environmental tool. In the case of Namibia, for example (Barnes et al., 2002), they generate an important contribution to national income and to wider development processes. They also provide a channel for the capture of international donor grants, which can be important catalysts in promoting land-use change for conservation.

   Local economic development (LED) is a common response to changes in the economic fortunes of a locality. Various economic strategies are associated with LED, some of the most prominent being those of place marketing and attempts to refocus economic activity along new or previously underused avenues, with tourism promotion being an increasingly common option. Nel and Binns (2002) examined the responses of the small community of Still Bay in Western Cape Province, South Africa, to economic crisis and the absence of vital social facilities. Critical to the success and sustainability of this LED initiative was the establishment of various development projects, in which certain key actors took a leading role in bringing the community together. Local cooperation, linked with successful place marketing and tourism promotion strategies, has laid the basis for the economic revival of the town and empowerment of historically disadvantaged groups. None the less, Rogerson (2002) identifies tourism-led LED initiatives failing to benefit Black communities in South Africa.

On the other hand, inappropriate tourism development pursued without professional advice, but based on the false assumption that it is easy to generate markets and thus income and employment, may result in a negative image for the local area or region and a permanent negative reaction from local people. Such a situation may apply almost anywhere, and will be the result of a number of typical 'implementation gaps' (Box 5.8)

Table 5.2. Participation by the poor in different market segments (from Ashley *et al.*, 2000; Shah, 2000).

Market segment	Participation by the poor
Domestic or regional tourists	Research studies in Yogyakarta (Indonesia) and elsewhere in South East Asia show that domestic and other Asian tourists tend to buy more from local vendors than do Western tourists.
Budget and independent tourists	Are more likely than luxury tourists to use the cheaper guest houses, home-stays, transport and eating services provided by local people. They tend to stay longer at a destination than group tourists and interact more with the local economy, but spend less per day, often bargaining hard over prices.
Nature-based tourism	Does not necessarily provide more opportunities for the poor than 'mass tourism', but offers four advantages: (i) takes place in less developed areas; (ii) often involves smaller operators with more local commitment; (iii) has a higher proportion of independent travellers; and (iv) if marketed as 'ecotourism' may stimulate consumer pressure for socio-economic benefits.
Mass tourism	Is highly competitive and usually dominated by large suppliers with little destination commitment. It generates employment while negative impacts may not spread beyond immediate localities. Thus it is crucial to determine how local economic opportunities can be expanded and negative impacts minimized.
Cruises and all-inclusives	Rapidly growing segments likely to generate few economic linkages. The Gambian government has banned 'all-inclusives' in response to local demands.
The informal sector	Where opportunities for small-scale enterprise or labour by the poor are maximized. For example, at Bai Chay, Ha Long Bay in Vietnam, almost a dozen local families run private hotels, with local involvement in tourism spreading to an estimated 70–80% of the population, running noodle stalls, being ambulant vendors and hiring boats and motorbikes.

(see also Chapter 1). These emphasize the conventional wisdom of the need for local cooperation and partnership.

Where they own land, local residents are less likely to be forced out, although they may sell up early in tourism development to outside speculators and, as a result, become employees in the industry rather than owners or decision makers. Otherwise, retained tenure over land and natural resources can give the poor market power and enable them to negotiate and secure benefits from tourism, including the ability to secure the confidence of potential investors (e.g. Mahony and van Zyl, 2001). Such tenure needs to include rights of exclusion, so that access can be charged for. For example, at Mahenye in Zimbabwe's south-east low veld in the 1990s, the local community gained significantly from a lease agreement for two lodges. This was only possible because the community and local authority controlled the lease rights, the local council used its power to support community interests and the CAMPFIRE programme provided a supportive policy context (e.g. Chalker, 1994; Potts *et al.*, 1996).

But there are many other examples where a few private entrepreneurs have managed to exclude local people in order to gain key assets, often through unauthorized land-grabbing. For example, Sabang is the gateway town for St Paul's National Park in the Philippines, and until the 1970s contained much public land, almost all of which has now been privately exploited. The local authority lacks effective power to prevent breaches of planning regulations. This raises questions concerning the role of central government. Where the poor lack rights to negotiate directly with tourism developers, government authorities should be in a position to promote their interests, for example, through planning approval being contingent upon investment benefiting local communities. Within South Africa's Strategic Development Initiative one important criterion for selecting between bids for

> **Box 5.8.** Typical 'implementation gaps' in small-scale tourism development.
>
> **1.** Mediocre knowledge of tourism: perhaps reflecting a precipitate sector entry based on false assumptions.
> **2.** Low-quality farm accommodation: possibly indicating low investment capital and a lack of forward planning.
> **3.** Lack of information about the requirements of guests: exposing poor market awareness and information flows.
> **4.** Lack of time to spend with guests: possibly indicating poor time management and a lack of prioritization and commitment.
> **5.** Lack of finance to start or adequately sustain a business: perhaps indicating insufficient recognition by, and lack of provision of appropriate investment instruments from, the banking and financial sectors.
> **6.** Low levels of village infrastructure: but this can be turned to advantage in attracting small-scale ecotourism.
> **7.** Low levels of information about tourism activities and opportunities in villages: which may reflect both poor networking activities and a lack of support from public bodies.
> **8.** A lack of complementarity with local government and other agency objectives: reflecting poor communication, perhaps an absence of trust and a lack of common vision.
>
> **Source:** Nylander and Hall, 2005: 27–28.

tourism concessions was the nature and extent of investors' plans for boosting local development (Koch *et al.*, 1998).

Regulations covering tourist activities, qualifications of workers or service standards are often geared to formal-sector requirements and may impinge most on those lacking contacts and capital. For example, near Sa Pa in Vietnam and in Upper Mustang in Nepal, regulations ostensibly designed to protect ethnic minorities from sociocultural intrusion by keeping tourists away from them have also prevented them from participating in and benefiting from tourism (Shah, 2000). In contrast, in Namibia, accommodation classifications that excluded very basic but clean campsites and home-stays have been revised, as have guide training systems that were suitable only for those equipped with the

English language, a formal education and access to the capital city (Ashley *et al.*, 2000).

Tourists often stay in accommodation that is owned by outsiders and local elites, and spend time at attractions from which local poor people, such as suppliers of goods and services, may be excluded. Access to the tourism market is most constrained where 'enclave tourism' and all-inclusive packages develop. Often the only option for local people in these circumstances is hawking, perhaps at the enclave entry and exit points, at roadsides or at known excursion destination drop-off points. However, organized markets, particularly at prime sites, can greatly facilitate local sales to tourists. For example, women craft-sellers have sites within some parks in Kwazulu Natal (Ashley *et al.*, 2000).

Formal-sector tourism enterprises can provide a market for the labour and products of the poor. But often labour and luxury goods are imported from outside the locality. Leakages of tourism expenditure may range from as little as 25% for large economies such as India, to 75% in The Gambia and parts of the Commonwealth Caribbean. Important from a welfare perspective is how much actually stays within the destination and is spent on the goods and services of the poor. There is some evidence to suggest that, where a local – rather than external – elite owns formal-sector enterprises, they are more likely to engage local suppliers (Shah, 2000).

In summary, pro-poor tourism can generate four types of local cash income, generally involving distinct categories of people:

- wages from formal employment: waged employment can be sufficient to lift a household from insecurity to security, but may only be available to a minority, and not to the poor(est);
- earnings from selling goods, services or casual labour (e.g. food, crafts, building materials, guide services): casual earnings per person may be very small, but much more widely spread (Ashley, 2000; Shah, 2000), and may be sufficient, for example, to cover school fees for one or

more children; guiding work, although casual, is often high-status and relatively well paid;

- dividends and profits arising from locally owned enterprises;
- collective income: this may include profits from a community-run enterprise, dividends from a private-sector partnership and land rental paid by an investor. It may be particularly significant for communities who do not have other options to earn collective income, although such enterprise can be problematic to manage (Ashley, 2000).

Tourism development can change poor people's access to assets and to related livelihood options in a number of ways. Positively, it can:

- generate funds for investment in health, education and other assets;
- stimulate the provision of necessary infrastructure;
- assist the development and consolidation of social capital in individuals and families;
- help strengthen the sustainable management of natural resources; and
- generate a demand for improved assets, such as education.

Negatively, it can:

- act to reduce local access to natural resources;
- draw heavily upon local infrastructure to the possible exclusion or marginalization of local people; and
- disrupt local social networks.

As an example, Il Ngwesi lodge in Kenya was developed by members of Il Ngwesi group ranch (a registered group of around 500 pastoral households with collective tenure rights over their land). A participatory assessment of livelihood impacts revealed that impacts on natural capital, particularly grazing resources, and access to physical infrastructure are more important to most members than the nearly 50 new jobs. The wildlife/wilderness area around the lodge provides emergency drought grazing. The lodge's physical presence, radio and vehicle help to keep others out and provide emergency access to a hospital, which was previously lacking.

However, there are more numerous examples where local residents lose access to local natural resources (Ashley et al., 2000). For example, on Boracay Island in the Philippines, one-quarter of the island has been bought by outside corporations, generating a crisis in water supply and only limited infrastructure benefits for residents (see also Smith, 1994). Similarly in Bali, Indonesia, prime agricultural land and water supplies have been diverted to large hotels and golf courses, while at Pangandaran in Java, village beach land, traditionally used for grazing, repairing boats and nets and festivals, was sold to entrepreneurs for a five-star hotel (Shah, 2000).

Local residents often highlight the way tourism affects other livelihood goals, such as cultural pride, a sense of control, health and reduced vulnerability. Sociocultural intrusion by tourists is often cited as a negative impact. Certainly sexual exploitation particularly affects the poorest women, girls and young men. The poor themselves may view other types of cultural exchange as positive. But, of course, the overall balance of positive and negative livelihood impacts will vary enormously between situations, among people and over time, and in the extent to which local priorities are able to influence the planning process. It is important to consider the many ways in which tourism affects different components of livelihoods, and a 'sustainable livelihoods framework' (Carney, 1998), now adopted by a number of development agencies, helps to provide a checklist (Table 5.3).

The poor are, of course, far from being a homogeneous group. Impacts are inevitably distributed unevenly, reflecting different patterns of assets, activities, opportunities and choices. The most substantial benefits, particularly jobs, may be concentrated among a few. Net benefits are likely to be smallest, or negative, for the poorest. It is acknowledged that pro-poor economic growth strategies give rise to economic opportunities that favour the non-poor more in absolute terms than they benefit those below the

Table 5.3. Tourism impacts on livelihood components (adapted from Ashley and Roe, 1998; Carney, 1998; Ashley, 2000).

Tourism effects	Possible positive impacts	Possible negative effects
Livelihood goals	Supporting economic security, cultural life, health, e.g. by • increasing cash income of workers/ entrepreneurs; • contributing to cultural restoration; • catalysing improvements in hygiene.	Undermining economic security, self-determination and health, e.g. by • creating dependency on a volatile industry among workers; • creating local inflation; • disempowering residents from decision making; • exacerbating the spread of disease.
Livelihood activities	Expanding economic options, e.g. by • creating employment and small-business options for the unskilled and semi-skilled; or • complementing other activities, e.g. earnings in agricultural lean season; and • developing transferable skills.	Conflicting with other activities, e.g. • constraining fishing, gathering, or agriculture if land and natural resources are taken away; • clashing with busy agricultural seasons; • increasing wildlife damage to crops and livestock.
Capital assets	Building up assets (natural, physical, financial, human, and social), e.g. • enhancing physical assets, if earnings are invested in productive capital; • enhancing natural capital, if sustainability of natural resource management is improved.	Eroding assets, e.g. • losing access to natural assets if local people are excluded from tourism areas; • eroding social capital if conflict over tourism undermines social and reciprocal relations; • overburdening the physical infrastructure (sewage, water supply).
Policy and institutional environment	Improving the context or residents' ability to influence it, e.g. by • expanding local markets, focusing policymakers' attention on marginal areas; • participating in tourism planning and enterprise, providing residents with new status, information and skills to deal with outsiders.	Exacerbating policy constraints, e.g. • diverting policymakers' attention, resources and infrastructure investment to prioritize tourism over other local activities; • improved transport access and markets can undermine local production.
Long-term livelihood priorities	Complementing people's underlying long-term priorities, e.g. • diversifying against risk, or building buffers against drought, by developing an additional source of income which continues in drought years.	Creating or exacerbating threats to long-term security, e.g. • physical threats from more aggressive wild animals as a result of disturbance by tourists; • economic vulnerability can be exacerbated due to dependence on volatile tourism.

poverty line. A 10% growth rate equally distributed will always be more advantageous for the person on a higher income in absolute terms (Remenyi, 2004: 196). A review of 24 case studies in Asia indicated economic gains for all sections of the community, but with those already better off gaining most (Shah, 2000). Gender impacts may see women being the first to suffer from loss of natural resources, such as access to fuel wood, and from cultural/sexual exploitation. But they may benefit most from physical infrastructure improvements, such as piped water, where this is a by-product of tourism.

D'Sa (1999) argues that the employment of focus groups as community representation is a compromise, and often 'community' participation/representation is through elites, perhaps hand-chosen for their views and manipulative abilities, armed with contacts and information that the rest of the 'community' lacks.

Where a local elite does not exist, migrants may move in to exploit new opportunities. The poverty impact of this may depend on whether migrants are poorer groups, more willing to work for lower returns to escape conditions elsewhere, or skilled entrepreneurs seizing new opportunities before local skills have a chance to develop (Ashley et al., 2000). On the other hand, D'Sa (1999) questions whether investors can be realistically expected to be interested in the welfare of the masses, who have little to offer besides their labour. He sees a fundamental impasse here between market values (profits, competition, survival of the fittest, acquisition, individualism) and family/community values (sharing of wealth, cooperation, support for the weakest, spirituality, harmony with nature), and wonders how, for example, a code of ethics is able to resolve such a contradiction.

Gender mainstreaming

The processes for and constraints on empowering women within pro-poor tourism strategies have parallels with the efforts to mainstream PPT within tourism and development policy. Gender 'is mainstreamed

when the development process and frameworks are transformed in ways which ensure the participation and empowerment of women as well as men in all aspects of life and especially in decision-making structures' (Taylor, 1999: 7). But most institutions have found gender mainstreaming difficult to achieve (Kabeer, 2003; Hunt, 2004), as a consequence of which few nations or development agencies have formally implemented this approach.

The work of Boserup (1970) was important in pointing out that, contrary to contemporary belief, women did not take jobs from men but helped to expand the available labour force and thus opportunities for economic growth. A decade on, as efforts were under way to make development policies more gender-sensitive, many LDCs were facing enormous problems of indebtedness. Subjected to World Bank and IMF 'structural adjustment' policies from the early 1980s, the governments of Mexico, the Philippines and many African countries had to reduce spending, devalue currencies and open their economies to foreign investment (Beneria, 1999; Hunt, 2004: 250).

As formal employment shrank for both men and women, the latter increased their activity in the informal sector, working long hours in petty trading and craft production (de Pauli, 2000). In Zambia, for example, the informal-sector workforce almost doubled between 1986 and 1996, with women making up over two-thirds of the 3.4 million informal-sector workers by the end of that period (Floro and Schaeffer, 2001).

Within such a context, several factors are required in order to achieve gender-equitable development:

- a legal and institutional environment that promotes gender equity, rather than reinforcing gender discrimination;
- women being organized and vigilant at national, regional and local levels to ensure that laws, policies and programmes are consistent with gender equity, and to promote proactive approaches to improving the situation of women;

- individual women having the self-esteem and confidence to actively participate and negotiate on their own behalf at the level of the household, community and nation; and
- men who are willing to recognize that gender oppression affects them too, and are able, reflexively, to subject 'masculinity' to critical scrutiny in terms of how it affects them, as well as being willing to change the way they benefit from their gendered privilege, from the household to the international level (Hunt, 2004: 259).

Within PPT processes, 'community participation' approaches such as participatory rural appraisal (PRA) can easily lead to a false consensus being derived from the views of those with power and influence in a local area; they certainly do not guarantee that poor people will benefit (Renard, 2001). For women, such approaches can overlook issues that are difficult for them to raise in front of men. Thus facilitators of 'community participation' approaches need to be sensitive to gender and power dynamics within a local area and have strategies to address them. Indeed, it is important in such contexts to identify different qualities of power (Rowlands, 1995):

- power *over*: a relationship of domination and subordination;
- power *to*: having decision-making or problem-solving power;
- power *with*: people organizing together to achieve their goals; and
- power *within*: the self-confidence to act.

The women's movement has tended to emphasize the last two forms of empowerment, noting that empowerment is not simply about offering opportunities for participation in decision making, but encouraging people to have confidence and a sense of entitlement to participate (Hunt, 2004: 258). Again this mirrors the wider requirement of poorer groups generally.

However, in gender-mainstreaming development, the concept of empowerment has been interpreted largely to mean economic empowerment of individual women

through credit programmes (Oxaal and Baden, 1997). While these may have been valuable, the social aspects of empowerment may have been equally, if not more, important to women than the economic benefits alone. As articulated by women from Indian self-help groups, such social aspects include:

- mobility – the capacity to go beyond the house independently;
- increased respect and dignity – within the family;
- assertiveness – women becoming bolder within the family and in dealing with officials; and
- solidarity and support – the mutual support received from self-help groups (Kilby, 2001).

Nature-based tourism

As indicated in Table 5.2 above, relatively small-scale nature-based tourism may offer limited employment opportunities for the poor. 'Optimum conditions' considered necessary for community-based natural resource management (CBNRM), which can support conservation and reduce economic leakage, suggest ownership should be as small-scale as is practicable. The development of nature-related tourism has seen some local African communities gaining more control over the wildlife safaris and parks in their areas. Yet fragmentation and lack of coordination may result in local people finding it difficult to voice their environmental concerns in the face of top-down policy initiatives. Despite the employment of 'participative' development models, in reality, often few choices are available to local people. They may be encouraged to follow, perhaps uncritically, official recommendations, undermining ideals of active and effective participation (Twyman, 2000: 232; Butcher, 2003: 122).

Further, 'wildlife tourism' has taken on mass tourism characteristics in a number of African, Asian and Latin American countries, with control passing out of local hands. Mbaiwa (2005a, b) cautions with experience from the Okavango Delta, Botswana, where wildlife tourism is dominated by foreign safari companies and has failed to contribute significantly to rural poverty alleviation. Akama (2004: 151) notes in respect of wild-life safari tourism in Kenya that over 60% of the sector is under foreign ownership and management.

In some cases there may be good ecological and human welfare reasons to promote consumptive forms of wildlife tourism. For example, Novelli and Humavindu (2005: 178) report that locally managed trophy hunting in Namibia creates employment for the rural poor as trackers, skinners, cooks, cleaners and drivers. It also stimulates the take-up of educational opportunities, including language acquisition and training as hunting guides and taxidermists. Discussion of access to management roles – either now or in the future – is, however, notable by its absence.

By the late 1980s, with the impacts of IMF/World Bank structural adjustment policies unravelling, African development planners needed to reconsider their post-independence strategies for tourism development as an economic motor. International tourism was proving to be more capital-intensive than anticipated. Agriculture and other local linkages had not developed as fully as envisaged, nor had domestic management and entrepreneurship. At the same time, the growth of international development NGOs was encouraging some African countries to move towards natural habitat conservation (D.O. Brown, 1998: 71) in the face of growing international concern about tropical deforestation.

These conservation-oriented NGOs adopted 'ethical' brands such as ecotourism as a way to achieve their conservation agenda in LDCs, while claiming to offer innovative development opportunities based on nature-based niche markets. Butcher (2003: 3) argues that this greening of aid through 'sustainable tourism' has reflected profoundly low horizons for addressing poverty and inequality. Basing local economic development around guardianship of the natural environment, for Butcher, eschews the transformative economic development that could make a significant difference to poorer societies. Although, for example, the CAMPFIRE projects in

Zimbabwe were held up as making a virtue out of not separating people from their natural environment, Butcher (2003: 117) argues 'why not . . . separate people from their environment? Why not offer them something better than a life close to nature?' He suggests that encouraging groups of people to remain in a traditional relationship with their land reflects 'a narrow development agenda that should be challenged rather than lauded as innovative and even moral'.

By the early 1990s, a number of LDCs were 'caught in a web of alternatives' (D.O. Brown, 1998: 69) to potentially alleviate their debt burdens. One of these was a programme of debt-for-nature swaps (DfNSs): 'an innovative market approach to the dual problems of Third World debt and tropical deforestation' (Chambers et al., 1994: 142). These swaps notionally assisted economic growth through the vehicle of nature-based conservation and 'sustainable tourism' (Patterson, 1990; Mahoney, 1992). They involved at least a three-way set of relationships between the debtor government and its financial institutions, the World Bank and appropriate development NGOs. The debt was exchanged for bonds with a longer maturity period than the original debt. These were passed to the NGO and the interest earned by the bonds was used to support a variety of local conservation programmes and projects involving the NGO (D.O. Brown, 1998: 72).

Claimed benefits of debt-for-nature swaps included the attraction of development FDI and the ability to develop increasingly popular ecotourism. The development of small-scale enterprises or zones surrounding nature parks and reserves was also envisaged. These could provide the environment for generating 'quality tourism' through highly controlled development and selective marketing (D.O. Brown, 1998: 75–76).

But such schemes had only a nominal impact (Sarkar and Ebbs, 1992) and were poorly taken up in the 1990s, partly because of their complicated logistics and bureaucratic processes. Rather like criticisms of PPT, the dual objectives of DfNSs were viewed by some as an unrealistic compromise, resulting in very limited outcomes:

- proportions of debt relieved were miniscule, often less than 1% of a country's total;
- areas of (usually) tropical rainforest conserved were minimal; while
- several commentators argued that the swaps were not legally binding (e.g. Hrynik, 1990; Deacon and Murphy, 1997).

Further, Butcher (2003: 129) suggests that debt-for-nature swaps have expressed the broader inequalities between North and South and have further diminished the development concept. Not least this is because swaps (further) compromise national sovereignty, requiring debtor governments to accept a number of conditions imposed by international financial institutions while needing to delegate major responsibilities of environmental management to NGOs (Potier, 1991).

One relatively positive element of the programme has been the way in which Costa Rica has been able to take advantage of both its ecological and financial elements to firmly establish itself as a major (albeit long-haul for many) focus of ecotourism. Perhaps the most important longer-term outcome of the swaps programme has been an increased international awareness of tropical deforestation and the international agreements that have followed from that. Despite earlier criticisms, major international development agencies have continued to pursue swaps in varying ways (e.g. OECD Phare, 1998; OECD EAP Task Force, 2002; Thapa and Thapa, 2002).

Supporting PPT: Strategic Action Required

On the basis that the concept of pro-poor tourism is realistic in appropriate environments and has practical value within development policy, the following key issues would appear to require attention:

- Putting poverty issues on the tourism agenda: this requires proactive and strategic intervention. Trade-offs may be necessary, such as between attracting all-inclusive operators and maximizing informal-sector opportunities, or between faster growth through outside investment and slower growth building on local capacity (Ashley *et al.*, 2000).
- Expanding poor people's economic participation by addressing constraints (see Chapter 2) and maximizing employment opportunities (see Table 5.4).
- Incorporating wider concerns of the poor into decision making, such as employing tourism to create beneficial physical infrastructure.
- Pursuing pro-poor interventions at three levels:
    - at destination level – proactive practical partnerships can be developed between operators, residents, NGOs and local authorities to maximize benefits;
    - at national policy level – policy reform may be needed on a range of tourism issues (planning, licensing, training) and non-tourism issues (land tenure, business incentives, infrastructure, land-use planning); and
    - at the international level – to encourage responsible consumer and business behaviour and to enhance realistic commercial codes of conduct.
- Working through stakeholder partnerships, including business, to ensure that initiatives are commercially realistic and integrated into mainstream operations. NGOs and donors can facilitate training, organization and communication to enable businesses to use more local suppliers.
- Changing the attitudes of domestic and international tourists is essential if PPT is to be commercially viable and sustainable: for example, integrating pro-poor approaches into voluntary codes and certification systems and educating tourists on socio-economic issues. It may be more difficult to raise interest in poverty issues among industry and consumers than has been the case in relation to

Table 5.4. Actions to enhance economic participation of the poor in tourism enterprise (after Ashley *et al.*, 2000).

Constraints on participation of the poor in tourism	Actions that can reduce constraints
Lack of human capital	Education and training targeted at the poor (particularly women) to enable uptake of employment and self-employment opportunities
Lack of finance, credit	Expand access to micro-finance (e.g. Grameen Bank). Gradual pace of tourism development – avoiding crash development relying on outside investment
Lack of organization. Exclusion by organized formal-sector interests	Recognize and support organizations of poor producers. Recognize organized tourism interests as just one voice to be heard among others
Location – far from tourism sites	Develop new core tourism assets and infrastructure in relatively poor areas but where a potentially commercially viable product exists
Lack of market power. No ownership/ control over resources of market value. No bargaining power with investors	Strengthen local tenure rights over land, wildlife, cultural heritage, access to scenic destinations and other tourism assets. Use planning gain to encourage potential investors to develop their own strategies for enhancing local impacts for the poor
Regulations and bureaucracy. Exclusion from registered and promoted categories of tourism facility/service	Minimize red tape, revise or remove regulations that exclude the least skilled, ensure that necessary tourism regulations embrace sectors and activities operated by the poor with appropriate standards and processes
Inadequate access to tourist market	Enhance vendors' access to tourists through e.g. siting resorts near public access routes and vice versa, supporting organized markets for informal and small-scale sellers in towns or adjacent to national parks
Limited capacity to meet requirements of tourism market	Business support to improve quality, reliability of supply, transport links
Underdevelopment of domestic/ regional/independent tourism in comparison with international tourism and all-inclusives	Incorporate domestic/regional tourism and independent tourism into planning strategies. Avoid excessive focus on international all-inclusives
Government support targeted to formal sector	Recognize the importance of the informal sector; support it in planning processes
New tourism opportunities conflict with existing livelihood strategies	–

environmental issues, although the 'Make Poverty History' campaign might suggest that more people are becoming aware of global inequalities.

- Incorporating PPT approaches into mainstream tourism: PPT should not just be pursued in niche markets.
- Reforming decision-making systems to permit local livelihood priorities to influence tourism development through

enhanced participation by the poor in decision making. Three ways can be identified:

- strengthening rights at the local level so that local people have market power;
- developing effective participatory planning;
- using planning gain and other incentives to encourage private investors

to enhance local benefits (Ashley et al., 2000).

However, Mahony and van Zyl (2001) caution against over-optimism by emphasizing two key issues arising from pro-poor development in South Africa:

- the long lead time needed for local people to realize substantial benefits can cause disillusion arising from unrealized expectations: this emphasizes the need to demonstrate the short-term benefits, if any, of such projects;
- the extent of a project's benefits will relate to the size of the local community involved: they can be diluted if they need to be shared by a large number of local people. This demonstrates the need for PPT to be a component of larger (rural) development programmes.

Pro-poor Tourism: the Welfare of Trek Porters

The above suggests that it is possible to establish tourism that benefits the poorest, provided stringent conditions are followed. Current examples of tourism in very poor communities, however, suggest that implementation may be problematic. One example, that of porters' conditions, raises a major ethical concern relating to the welfare of an apparently tourism-dependent vulnerable group. The issue has been the subject of a campaign championed by Tourism Concern (2002), focusing on Nepal, Peru and Tanzania. It was further highlighted in June 2004 when five porters, serving with an Italian trekking team on the mountain K2, drowned in a stream (Ecotourism Society Pakistan, 2004).

Porters carrying trekkers' equipment are an essential part of treks, accompanying thousands of tourists each year (see Frohlick, 2004, for a gendered approach to this). In the Himalayas, while Sherpas are from high-altitude areas, most Nepalese porters are poor farmers from lowland areas and are unused to the high altitudes and harsh conditions, subject to frostbite and altitude sickness. Indeed, Nepalese porters suffer four times more accidents and illnesses than Western trekkers, and reports tell of porters being abandoned by tour groups when they fall ill. There appear to be a number of key welfare issues relating to porters.

Loads carried

The load carried by porters varies according to the location and type of trek. Legal limits range between 15 and 30 kg maximum. In practice, the weight of the load should take into consideration such individual factors as difficulty, altitude and duration of the trek and the porter's physical ability.

A problem highlighted on Mount Kilimanjaro in Tanzania is that of guides abusing porters' rights (Tourism Concern, 2002). Legally, porters climbing Mount Kilimanjaro in Tanzania should carry a maximum of 25 kg including their own gear, but there have been reports of guides bribing the rangers who weigh the porters' loads and of guides choosing porters on the basis of payments and bribes. Porters who complain may fear for their livelihoods. As a consequence, during 2004 the Kilimanjaro Union was set up to ensure that porters who are members are protected and have adequate working conditions.

In Peru, legal prescriptions are such that adult male porters should carry a total maximum of 25 kg, and female and adolescent porters 20 kg. On the Inca Trail to Machu Picchu, regulations introduced in 2001 prescribe which licensed operators can manage tours along the trail, and a maximum of 20 kg for porters' loads. Concerns have been expressed regarding the effectiveness of government weighing, and in 2002 the Inka Porter Project (IPP) – a non-profit organization – was established in part to overcome this problem through the provision of education on such issues as health and the environment. For 2004/5 a training and drop-in centre was being created at the foot of the Inca Trail for porters and other indigenous people working in tourism. Supported by Tourism Concern,

IPP has a website providing advice for travellers (<http://www.peruweb.org/porters>).

For all treks with porters, pre-trek weighing provides a good opportunity for trekkers to get to know their porters and to make sure they are properly dressed and have the appropriate equipment. It should also provide operators with time to monitor for unsafe carrying practices, ensuring that porters do not carry loads with woven blankets and ropes unsuitable for sustained walking.

Qualifications, training and income

At present, there are no formal systems in place (with the exception of Peru) to ensure that candidates undergo a health check before undertaking porter's work. In Peru, a successful medical examination and the ownership of a certificate from the Ministry of Health have become necessary to be able to work as a porter. Robinson (1994) found that a large share of travel and trekking agencies in Nepal are controlled by Sherpas, who are able to move through the hierarchical structures in Nepal's trekking industry. But Tourism Concern (2002) suggests that most porters are farmers between 30 and 50 years old looking to supplement their income. They are usually judged fit to work as porters by physical appearance alone. In Tanzania, experience in climbing seems to be the only criterion for becoming a porter.

That portering is perceived as seasonal work usually means porters do not receive adequate training in first aid, health and safety issues, including the symptoms of altitude sickness, management of emergency situations and general health and hygiene. Porters' organizations have begun to change this: for example, in 2003 a porter association based in Kathmandu began providing training.

Providing fair compensation for porters is essential to fostering an ethical and sustainable trekking tourism sector. It has been emphasized by porter protection groups that operators should encourage their ground partners to hire porters on a semi-permanent or permanent basis to create a more sustainable source of income. Yet, in situations such as those in the Himalayas, where some ten porters are available for every job required, the market tends to drive wages down.

Clothing, health and security

Tourism Concern (2002) has reported that Nepalese porters die annually from altitude sickness, frostbite and hypothermia after facing extreme conditions clothed only in cotton jackets and light canvas shoes, or even flip-flops. Many more lose limbs to frostbite. Organizations such as the International Porters' Protection Group (IPPG) (<http://www.ippg.net>), the Himalayan Rescue Association (HRA) and Porters' Progress (<http://www.portersprogress.org>) now work to address the worst problems. In Nepal, for example, IPPG, the Himalayan Explorers Connection (<http://www.hec.org>) and the Porters' Progress office have a clothing bank, where donated clothing and equipment are loaned out to porters.

Tour operators should be responsible for ensuring that the local/ground agents supply suitable clothing and equipment at the destinations and allocate the funds. Appropriate warm, windproof trek suit, boots, socks, gloves, hat, snow goggles and blanket should be provided when required and collected when no longer needed, to ensure there is no loss. One UK operator in Peru has organized a partnership with a clothing and trekking equipment company to get donations or discounts on equipment and clothing for their porters.

In the Himalayas porters at altitude appear to be more at risk than other trekkers from altitude sickness because of their extra exertion, higher tendency to dehydration and reluctance to carry the weight of extra water. Responsible staff members (under the direction of the trek leader, who should have funds to cover emergencies) need to take responsibility to escort porters down to safety. The trek leader should also be qualified to provide first aid care. Trekking agents normally insure porters, but insurance coverage is only for the period of the trek. In Pakistan, the majority of porters work without adequate insurance. Tourism Concern (2002) has lobbied for porters to receive full insurance, sickness and disability pay, and for porters not to be dismissed without pay because of illness.

Monitoring and evaluation

Implementation of good and fair practices by tour operators requires developing and maintaining close working relationships with ground agents. Tourism Concern (2002) was made aware of only one UK operator that conducted unannounced spot checks on its local partners. Some operators have set up charities to provide basic medical and educational services for porter communities. Some operators have formalized a process to get feedback from porters, encouraging them to report on each trek. All operators should include porters in decision-making processes, and should regularly consult with them as well as with porter protection groups and local agents.

Responsibilities

Trekkers can play an important role in helping to ensure that fair practices are implemented. Being aware of porters' rights and fair working conditions should be a responsibility that comes with signing up to a trip.

Operators have an important role in continually raising awareness among travellers – which should be perceived to be in the latter's own interests – and educating them before they go. The clients and potential clients of such operators need to ask questions of tour operators – their policies on porters' working wages, loads, equipment, health and medical provision. Following the trek, clients should let the tour operator know that porters' welfare was an important factor in the quality and value of the trip experience.

Independent travellers should hire a porter to help support local communities. In doing so, they should maintain a code of responsibility whereby they get to know their porter, pay them an adequate rate of pay and ensure they carry no more than 20 kg.

In their survey of UK tour operators with policies on porters' rights and working conditions in Nepal, Peru and Tanzania, Tourism Concern (2002) acknowledged 44 operators that were demonstrating proof of their policies on porters' rights and working conditions. The organization also identified 37 operators who either did not have such policies or could not demonstrate proof of them.

Most tour companies without porter policies appear to leave responsibility to the companies that they work with in the destination country, but many appear to know little about the working conditions of their porters. In response to this, Tourism Concern (2002) has drawn up guidelines for (UK) tour operators to observe on porters' rights and working conditions, which embrace the points made above.

The conditions of trekking porters help to exemplify some fundamental issues surrounding the welfare of relatively vulnerable, relatively poor groups, located in marginal areas of relatively poor countries, engaged on the margins of the tourism industry. While the issues raised may be specific to portering at high altitude, they are none the less salient to wider welfare issues concerning the relationship between tourism and poor, marginalized social and employment groups.

Volunteer Tourism – Do the Poor Benefit?

One direct form of pro-poor tourism would appear to be the growing fashionability of being a tourist volunteer for charitable work. Encouraged by the increasing number of charities and ready availability of information (e.g. Pybus, 2003), such work has grown from being dedicated to nature conservation (Ausenda, 2003) to charitable work with and among local people in a number of both developing and developed countries (Wearing, 2001) to 'charity challenges'. In the latter, volunteers travel to less developed countries to raise funds in support of charities often based in the source country (e.g. Guide Dogs for the Blind), which may have nothing to do with the community in which the challenge takes place.

As noted earlier in the chapter, this trend partly reflects the growth of transnational development NGOs working in poorer countries. The harnessing of information technology has permitted the rapid transmission of information and images that attract more funding and legitimacy to NGOs. However, financial management and uneven levels of accountability have raised a number of ethical issues, including negative outcomes of the audit culture, transparency and legitimacy (Townsend and Townsend, 2004).

Thus, with NGOs being driven both by financial considerations and by the need for profile raising and image improvement, volunteer tourism (VT) has become increasingly ambiguous, both in definition and in setting. Reflecting this, Callanan and Thomas (2005) apply the terms 'shallow', 'deep' and 'intermediate' to the spectrum of both volunteer tourists and VT projects. The 'shallow' volunteers are ego-enhancing and participating in projects of short duration, while the 'deep' prioritize altruistic motives, drawing on acquired skills or qualifications.

The 'shallow' charity challenges end of the spectrum has become by far the most popular for participants and an important source of charity fund-raising. Participants pay a registration fee and then raise a minimum level of sponsorship for a charity in order to be able to take part in an energetic 'challenge' for a relatively low cost. Such challenges include hiking along the Inca Way in the Peruvian Andes, climbing to Everest base camp in Nepal, walking along the Great Wall of China, trekking up Mount Kilimanjaro in Tanzania or cycling across Cuba (Bedding, 2004). But questions are raised concerning who really benefits, as the challenges generate a considerable amount of income both for charity and for the travel companies that organize them (see Box 5.9). Part of the funds participants raise are used to pay the cost of the trip, such that the volunteers are in effect getting a cheap holiday. But the word 'holiday' is not employed in any promotional literature, even if the process involves people travelling to an exotic destination in their own free time.

Box 5.9.   Case study: cycling in Malawi.

'For me as a gay man, HIV is a big issue. I'd seen a documentary on the HIV crisis in Malawi, and when I found out that ActionAid had projects there, I got in touch.' Ten participants – friends and family – went, all from the Manchester area. The fund-raising target was £25,000. The gay scene in Manchester provided much support, with several celebrity supporters. Manchester United football club provided a free venue for holding a ball that raised £10,000 on one night. In total £40,000 was raised, about £25,000 of which was net profit for ActionAid.

The trip was 10 days in all, of which 5 were the cycling – around Lake Malawi, from Lilongwe to Mzuzu. In Mzuzu the group visited one of the projects they were supporting – the St John's Support Project, for about 200 children orphaned by AIDS.

'After all that physical challenge, seeing some of the kids who would benefit from what we'd done – there we were, seven gays, a lesbian and two straight men, all in tears.'

Source: Pratt, 2004; also see <http://www.mission-malawi.org.uk>.

Several charities raise funds specifically to benefit local people in the destination country. ActionAid, for example, ran three trips in 2005: each raised about £150,000 (c. €220,000). Classic Tours, which refers to itself as the initiator of charity challenge events, claims to have taken nearly 25,000 participants since 1992, raising £25 million (c. €36 million) for more than 80 charities. Charity Challenge, which was launched in 2000, has supported 500 charities. It offers over 100 departure dates on more than 40 challenges annually, with a target of raising up to £4.2 million (c. €6 million). Scope, which campaigns for equality for disabled people, began offering challenges in 1998, and 750 participants from across the UK have raised more than £1.25 million (c. €1.8 million) (Bedding, 2004).

In response to criticism that donors were being misled into assuming that all their money would go to the charity, a code of practice was drawn up in 1999. Charities and the tour operators they use have to be transparent about the full costs of the trip – which must be no more than 50% of the funds raised.

Of greater concern is the question of what effect the challenges have on the destinations themselves, as they may be little different from any other form of tourism. Charity Challenge (<http://www.charitychallenge.co.uk>) claims that its tours benefit local people as a result of:

- employing local staff – as guides, support teams, doctors;
- using small, family-run accommodation wherever possible;
- purchasing produce locally;
- keeping group sizes small;
- awareness of and support for trickle-down effects: for example, all groups heading for Kilimanjaro spend their first night in a tented camp run and managed by Maasai, who receive the profits; and
- supporting local charities, which may be the main objective or a subsidiary goal.

Yet several elements of charity challenges and other elements of the VT spectrum appear problematic:

- they represent charity rather than empowerment, and, although some aspects of the activity do appear to be pro-poor and empowering, they also appear tokenistic, perpetuating the appearance of a colonial, dependency culture: as such they may appear little different from other forms of international tourism in LDCs;
- who benefits? Apart from the experience and insight gained by the travellers, many challenges are raising money for source-country charities. Volunteers are travelling to developing countries to raise money that will be spent on people with particular needs in developed countries, who will often be substantially more affluent than those who live in the places where these challenges take place. There is little evidence of consequent sustained poverty alleviation in the poor host regions; and
- organizations and individuals involved in these activities need to consider

more carefully their responsibilities to host destinations: travel companies have tended to be overly positive about the impact they exert on the communities they pass through.

Conclusions

In this chapter our welfare-centred approach has focused on the concept, nature and efficacy of pro-poor tourism (PPT) as a policy tool for unlocking employment opportunities for the poor. Increased economic benefits, positive non-economic impacts and policy/process reform are the three central tenets of the PPT model (Roe and Urquhart, 2001; Andrade, 2002; Font and Harris, 2004). But the appropriateness of tourism-related employment as a mechanism for levering citizens of some of the most impoverished countries in the world out of poverty is variable. General principles would seem to apply here (e.g. Boyd and Hall, 2005: 279–280):

- tourism will not be the most appropriate tool for poverty alleviation in many areas;
- only exceptionally should it take priority over (other) traditional activities available;
- there is a need to think beyond just exploiting local natural resources even in a non-consumptive mode;
- tourism production should be both appropriate and distinctive; and
- development should take place within the framework of the region's institutional arrangements, particularly in terms of encouraging collaboration and partnership.

By implicitly suggesting that, through greater participation in tourism employment, tourism should therefore be expanding in the poorest countries, we also confront the tension between local livelihood provision and global resource consumption.

There are a number of welfare conclusions to be drawn from the promotion of pro-poor tourism. First, tourism development has not, to any significant degree, incorporated poverty elimination objectives, despite recent apparent industry 'conversions' to it. Tourism remains driven by economic, environmental and/or cultural perspectives at national and international levels. Given the impact that tourism has had on many of the world's poor, the nature and extent of pro-poor promotion need to move much more towards the centre of the tourism agenda.

Being promoted by Western development NGOs and government departments, does PPT simply provide another route for the perpetuation of long-standing economic imperialism and dependency through tourism? If tourism is to be a part of 'Third World' development processes, it needs to be accompanied, or preferably preceded, by good-quality health and welfare provision for those countries' citizens. This should be to severely reduce incidence of disease and the simple killer conditions such as dysentery and dehydration, and thereby modify the perceived need for large families that often flows from high infant mortality rates. At the same time, this needs to be complemented by example-setting from the developed countries through a reduction in resource-intensive activities, so that we are ethically better placed to be able to encourage employment within low-resource-using activities in less developed countries.

The poverty impacts of tourism embrace a wide range of livelihood/welfare aspects, not just employment or incomes, with differential costs and benefits. Yet participation by the poor in tourism and the benefits they may gain will depend on a range of critical factors, including the type of tourism, planning regulations, land tenure, market context and access to capital and training. Many of these can be influenced by changes in policy or external support. Clearly there is much scope for adapting tourism interventions to enhance livelihood benefits to the poor.

Further, Butcher (2003: 129) argues that rather than attempting to liberate people from the constraints of their environment, PPT 'organises around these constraints'. He thus views PPT as lacking imagination in not explicitly broadening the employment horizons and livelihood aspirations of the poor to beyond their own local area. But is such an 'on your bike' conception realistic in the short term for the vast majority of immobile poor people in the poorest countries?

Finally, PPT strategies must be commercially realistic. The private sector cannot be expected to prioritize poverty objectives, and will not invest in projects it does not believe will create at least some profit. Yet it must be included in the process of developing PPT if only as an aid to identifying products and programmes that are likely to be truly viable (see Ashley et al., 2000; Cattarinich, 2001).

In theory at least, PPT – a broader approach to development than 'community tourism', and prioritizing links between the poor and the formal sector – could be a powerful tool for poverty reduction and the empowerment of the poor in appropriate environments. It can appeal to the anti-poverty, liberal wing of the holiday-taking public. At present, however, most people who holiday (and many working in the tourism industry) in areas of poverty and social dislocation are usually cocooned from, and thus probably ignorant of, its most harrowing effects, and thus seem not to have their consciences pricked by it (D'Sa, 1999). Indeed, by a curious inversion of values, tourists and the tourism industry may express more concern for the preservation of wildlife (Chapter 6) than the welfare of human communities.

6

The Land Ethic? Tourism's Non-human Actors

'There is a phrase . . . current in the occiden-
tal world – "self-interest". The component of
that which is not thought out so closely is
"What is the self?" If you define your "self"
in the smallest possible way, your "self"-
interest is just for today. If you define your
"self" just to include your family, your children, then your "self"-interest goes one generation ahead. If you define your "self" to mean
human beings, your "self"-interest embraces a
thousand years. If you say mammals, vertebrates, multi-cellular creatures, entities with
existence, you embrace the cosmos'.

(Beat poet Gary Snyder quoted in Eyre,
1979: 267–268)

Box 6.1. Chapter aims and summary.

This chapter seeks to: examine from a welfare
perspective the role of animals in tourism
and recreation and the relationship thereby
highlighted between animals and humans.
It does this by: addressing the nature, roles and
relationships of animals employed for leisure
purposes within captive situations and as 'wildlife'.
Its key concepts are: animal welfare,
ecotourism, wildlife.
It concludes that: if ecotourism is to be
effective in the modification of environmental
beliefs, a more ethically effective tourism
encounter with the 'natural world' is required.

The philosophy of this chapter is consonant with the 'land ethic' of American
ecologist Aldo Leopold (1949/1968), which
conceives of enlarging – both spatially and
morally – the boundaries of the 'community' to include such natural elements as
soil, water, plants and animals. Its ethical
implications are important in emphasizing
the need for people to extend their social
conscience from humans alone to a respect
for fellow (non-human) animals and the
wider natural environment and to embrace
the sense of being a fellow citizen of the
'land-community' (Fennell and Przeclawski,
2003: 146). This 'ecosystemic morality'
(Lea, 1993) therefore presents an underpinning ethical principle for nature-based
tourism.

Most people probably do not currently
feel that their self-interest embraces the cosmos, but many do want to spend their holiday time in nature and/or interacting with
animals in some form. In this chapter we
examine welfare dimensions of nature- and
animal-based recreational attractions to
highlight ethical dilemmas, the trade-offs
that exist, for example, between education,
entertainment, conservation and economic
viability, and their management and policy
implications.

Animal Welfare and the Extension of Ethical Concern

The substantial growth and impact of international tourism has coincided in human history with a (Western) re-evaluation of our relationship with the natural world. In particular, our attitudes towards animals have experienced a quantum shift. In the developed world, urbanization has distanced the majority of people from everyday working relationships with animals, while media information and images have both sanitized and sentimentalized the animal world for mass consumption. The ownership of pets has tended to further reinforce the perception of animals as 'safe' and 'cuddly', while also acting to inculcate in many, not least the young, a sense of concern for animals (Tuan, 1984; Ritvo, 1988; although see also Serpell, 1986).

Orams (2002: 287) recognizes three different philosophical approaches to the relationships between humans and other animals:

- the basic Judaeo-Christian view, predominant in most Western cultures, that animals are subordinate to humans and that, as a consequence, humans have the right to utilize animals for human benefit;
- the arguments of 'deep ecologists', animal rights activists and some Eastern religions that (at least some) animals have an equal or equivalent status to humans – they have rights and needs that should be afforded power or position in human decision making; and
- reverential spiritual elements of many indigenous cultures whereby an animal is seen as superior – as when animals are worshipped as gods – and where people pay homage and make sacrifices to animals in order to invoke favour or good fortune, to pay penance or to ensure salvation.

Recorded explicit concern for animal welfare goes back a long way in human history. Around 500 BC Pythagoras was maintaining that humans should treat animals well (Sorabji, 1993). However, the Judaeo-Christian tradition of regarding human animals as masters rather than as members of the natural world – despite the efforts of St Francis of Assisi (Sorrell, 1988) – has contrasted sharply with Eastern religions that assume the oneness of all things natural (Chapple, 1993). Certainly, there has been a long-standing negative tradition in relation to animals in both Judaism and Christianity (Linzey and Cohn-Sherbok, 1997), which animal rights supporters have emphasized (e.g. Linzey, 1976, 1987; Singer, 1985). Aristotle's expressed view that animals were our slaves heavily influenced subsequent Western attitudes towards animals.

Within Christianity, in the 13th century St Thomas Aquinas, deeply influenced by Aristotelian philosophy in seeking to harmonize Christian faith with Greek philosophy, drew on notions of natural ordering and particularly the idea that the 'lower' creation existed to serve the 'higher'. He argued that, because of the lack of community between humans and animals, there was no human duty to love animals as such (Clarke and Linzey, 1990: 104). Such an Aristotelian/Thomist view of animals, incorporating elements of non-rationality, non-community and intellectual inferiority, became the dominant, albeit not unchallenged, Christian voice on animals. The emergence, in the 18th and 19th centuries, of strong humanitarian movements that were inclusive of concern for animals would begin to change this (Thomas, 1983; Linzey and Cohn-Sherbok, 1997: 7).

The culmination of this instrumentalist tradition was reached with the 'father of modern philosophy', Descartes. Cartesian philosophy argued that the absence of rational soulfulness in animals also meant the absence of a subjective self, and animals became compared to machines, albeit acting by 'nature'. The denial of animal sentience provided the framework for insensitivity towards animals, not least in experiments upon them (Regan and Singer, 1989). The tradition of placing animals outside the realm of morality or ethical significance on the grounds that they do not possess rational minds has also been referred to as the 'absolute dismissal' argument (Vardy and Grosch, 1999: 211).

By 1817 Schopenhauer was criticizing the apparent attitude of Christianity and Judaism towards animals as barbaric and morally defective (Payne, 1965). The emergence of anti-cruelty movements around this time saw the establishment in 1824 of the Society for the Prevention of Cruelty to Animals (SPCA) in England, which embraced many prominent Jews and Christians (e.g. Gompertz, 1824). The 19th century's widening sense of justice and obligation to charity complemented well the growing sense of the need to embrace animals. Indeed, a half-century previously, Humphry Primatt (1776), in arguably the 'first systematic theological study of our responsibility to animals' (Linzey and Cohn-Sherbok, 1997: 9), damned cruelty to animals as atheism and 'the worst of heresies' (Linzey and Regan, 1989: 127–130). Not convinced, as late as the mid-19th century, Pope Pius IX forbade the opening of a society similar to SPCA in Rome, on the grounds that humans had duties towards other humans but not to animals.

White (1967) is credited with initiating a debate evolving an 'ecoethology' that recognized a sort of spiritual democracy of nature (Nash, 1989: 6). Thus the focus of ethical thought (if not ethical behaviour) has gradually expanded outwards from self-interest to encompass the family, region, nations and, latterly, animals. Indeed, for many, the welfare of animals has taken on a symbolic role as a barometer of human ethical considerations: 'the greatness of a nation and its moral progress can be judged by the way its animals are treated' (Gandhi, 1959, quoted in Rowan, 1988: i).

In the UK the Endangered Species Acts of the 1970s are seen as significant in heralding an ethical incorporation of the role and rights, or at least welfare, of animals, an approach adopted in a number of Western countries. Indeed, Nash (1989: 4, 7) has considered that the emergence of environmental ethics – whereby the human–nature relationship is treated as a moral issue conditioned or restrained by ethics – might be seen as the most dramatic expansion of morality in the evolution of intellectual thought. Nash credited much of this modern awareness to Leopold's (1949/1968) 'land ethic'. In it the role of *Homo sapiens* changed from 'conqueror' to that of fellow citizen of the 'land-community' alongside, and with respect for, fellow animals and the natural environment.

The term 'speciesism' was adopted by Ryder (1975, 1989), Singer (1990) and others to refer to the disproportionate moral weight given to members of one species – in this case humans – compared with others: 'those I would call "speciesists" give greater weight to the interests of members of their own species when there is a clash between their interests and the interests of those other species' (Singer, 1993: 58).

Historically, humans have enjoyed close relationships with animals, and this has been represented in a wide range of cultural artefacts, from cave paintings to mass-produced birthday cards (e.g. Dembeck, 1961; Toynbee, 1976; Clark, 1977). Notably, across a variety of cultures, particular species such as dogs, horses and cats have been specifically bred and 'tamed' for domestic use as companions, pets or transport. Animals have also been put to work as motive power (pulling anything from ploughs to subterranean mining trucks to double-decker trams), as means of communication (carrier pigeons) and for use in hunting and retrieving, including mountain rescue and anti-crime operations. Budiansky (1992, 1997) has argued that some species were compliant in the domestication process because it was their best route to survival and further evolution. Emphasizing the reciprocity of animal–human relationships, Engel (2002: 4) suggests that we have much to learn from the ways in which animals keep themselves healthy.

For humans, interaction with animals has been essential as a source of food. Many indigenous peoples continue to interact with wildlife for spiritual and cultural reasons as well as for sustenance. Although hunting animals for food and for sport has existed for millennia, the recreational concept of visiting and observing animals as a tourist attraction is a much more recent phenomenon.

Moral debate

The contemporary moral debate concerning animal–human relationships generally revolves around five controversial areas:

- animals being bred and killed for food;
- animals being used for medical experiments;
- animals used for the testing of cosmetics, detergents and other non-medical goods;
- breeding and killing animals for their fur; and
- animals as recreation: the hunting and killing of animals for sport, and the breeding and training of animals for entertainment (Vardy and Grosch, 1999: 208–209).

In this chapter we confine ourselves to the fifth of these areas of concern, albeit within a context acknowledging the range of controversies surrounding humans' use of animals.

Animals and animal products contribute in several significant ways to tourism and recreation experiences. These include:

- the enhanced experiential welfare provided, particularly for children, from interacting with both tame and relatively wild creatures (e.g. Katcher and Beck, 1988), whereby a sense of respect, understanding and compassion can be generated. Conversely, if animals are seen to be 'exhibited' in poor conditions and/or manifest aspects of behaviour that reflect boredom, frustration or pain, then the experience can be negative and possibly traumatic;
- the potential threat, however small, of the transmission of disease or other physical harm, arising from poor animal welfare provision, from animals to humans (with the threat usually greater for children), through interaction at visitor attractions; or
- through the food chain, where food-producing animals are concerned. This is significant not least for a tourism industry looking to food as a means of: (i) enhancing local economic back-linkages and value-added niches for

rural economies; (ii) raising the quality of gastronomy as a means of tourist attraction; and (iii) emphasizing local and regional identity through the promotion of local cuisine, specialist and quality produce; and

- the negative (psychological) experience of seeing animals exhibiting distress as a result of having their welfare harmed through inappropriate captivity.

A growing awareness in society of the disruptive influence that human activity might have on the health and welfare of animals has accompanied increasing interest in the way animals 'naturally' lead their lives. This presents a potential contradiction and conflict between:

- a sanitized view of animals and the desire of visitors for close contact with (certain, relatively safe and appealing) animals (such as feeding); and
- a wider concern for the survival and welfare of those animals.

This is heightened by the trend towards the 'presentation' and commodification of captive animals as 'edutainment' within a context sanitizing 'wildlife'. It raises a number of welfare-related issues, which, in turn, focus on the welfare of animals as objects of human recreation, the welfare of humans experiencing 'wildlife' and the management ethics embracing the welfare of both. First, this area is characterized by relatively little empirical research, inconsistent management and differing views of the role of animals in humans' lives, thereby suggesting a number of contested welfare positions. Second, partly as a result of this, it is clear that greater attention needs to be paid to developing effective management strategies based upon appropriate knowledge and the precautionary principle (Orams, 2002: 281). For example, surveys in Kibale National Park in Uganda found a high prevalence of disease symptoms – notably diarrhoea – among visiting tourists. With high numbers of habituated chimpanzees in the park, this poses major challenges for visitor management in the face of humans being a potential source of infection for vulnerable chimpanzees (Adams et al., 2001).

Animals, Wildlife and Tourism

A prime aim of 'nature-based tourism' is for visitors to get in touch with nature, escape the stresses of daily life and see landscapes and wildlife (Blamey, 2001). It has been claimed that such tourism has been growing at rates generally much higher than the industry average, of between 10 and 30% per annum (Buckley, 1994; Young, 1998; Campbell, 1999; TIES, 2003; Nyaupane et al., 2004). It has become a major component of domestic and international tourism (TIAA, 2002; TIES, 2003), accounting for 7% of all international tourism expenditures (Lindberg et al., 1997). However, its importance varies greatly from one region to another. Filion et al. (1994) reported that, in some countries, this segment embraced between 40% and 60% of all international tourists. In the USA, participation in nature-based tourism is the second most important purpose for trips, accounting for 17% of all trips (TIAA, 2002).

The tourism industry mostly regards 'wildlife' (which includes captive animals – Box 6.2) as a resource for sustaining business, aimed at providing visitors with the experience they desire through a spectrum of animal-oriented activities such as observing, feeding, touching and photographing them. Such an approach includes a concern for animal welfare, but this is placed largely in the context of the need to sustain the viability of the attraction.

A number of writers consider the growth in nature-based tourism, and more specifically animal-based tourism, to be a potential saviour for 'wildlife' (Davies, 1990; Borge et al., 1991; Burnie, 1994). Others are at best sceptical about the environmental sensitivity or sustainability of 'ecotourism' (e.g. Butler, 1990; Wheeller, 1991, 1994a, 2005). And there are many cases that illustrate the negative impacts that may result from tourist–wildlife interaction (e.g. Hanna and Wells, 1992; Burger and Gochfield, 1993; Griffith and van Schaik, 1993; Ingold et al., 1993; Muir, 1993; Viskovic, 1993; Orams, 1995).

'Visitors need to behave in a fashion acceptable to wildlife, not the other way round' (Shackley, 1996: 36) (e.g. Box 6.3).

Box 6.2. 'Wildlife'.

The term 'wildlife' implies creatures in the wild – living in their natural habitats and being able to act out their natural behaviour patterns unfettered. Yet it has been adopted and adapted by the tourism and recreation industries to refer to any animals in almost any situation, including severely constrained captive circumstances, that can be subjected to visitor gaze.

Is this another instance of the widespread use and tacit acceptance of an industry propaganda term, whereby 'wildlife' offers a comforting image of us humans being able to commune with 'pure nature' thanks to the tourism and leisure industries, and thus being able to feel reconnected to our ecological roots, feeding our self-deluding sense of environmental rightness? In short, is 'wildlife' the faunal equivalent of 'authenticity', even though the animals involved may not be 'wild' or be having much of a 'life'?

Box 6.3. Conflicts with saltwater crocodiles.

As a major attraction of World Heritage-listed Kakadu National Park in Australia's Northern Territory, man-eating saltwater crocodiles have grown to 5000 in number since becoming protected in 1971, having faced virtual extinction. But the number of 'crocodile incidents' (with humans) has grown comparably, and park management faces a delicate balance in protecting the 170,000 annual visitors while encouraging them to have a positive experience and at the same time ensuring that the crocodiles thrive in their natural environment.

A plunge pool at Twin Falls, an iconic area of the park, was closed in 2004 because of fears that swimmers could be attacked. Tourism operators, frustrated at having to remove the Falls from their itineraries, accused park rangers of being overly cautious. But an inquest found a tour guide to have been 'grossly negligent' in allowing a German woman to take a fatal moonlight swim in 2002.

Debate continues on how to control the animals. Six hundred are legally culled by landowners each year, but a proposal to permit a limited number to be hunted by wealthy tourists has drawn opposition from local people and animal welfare groups.

Source: Marks, 2005; see also Ryan, 1998.

As such, a range of potentially adverse visitor impacts need to be kept in check to avoid: (i) disturbing or harassing wildlife, and particularly disrupting feeding or breeding behaviour; (ii) polluting the natural environment; and (iii) inadvertently harming wildlife through direct contact. For example, if a human makes physical contact with a member of the rare Chillingham cattle breed – now confined to one site in northern England and another in Scotland – the animal is ostracized by the rest of the herd and left to live out an isolated existence.

Major visitor management principles may involve any of five key elements:

- separation, to physically separate visitors from wildlife (e.g. see <http://www.seabird.org> webcams);
- integration, to mix visitors and wildlife by careful management of their interaction;
- participation, allowing visitors to participate in wildlife management schemes;
- education, providing more information about the consequences of adverse impacts; and
- interpretation, applying information to enhance appreciation and mutual experience.

Many adverse visitor impacts result from ignorance of the consequences of certain actions, such as lighting fires.

The overall impacts of wildlife/nature tourism are difficult to assess without long-term studies, and such recreational activities have only become popular on a large scale in the past 20 years (e.g. Sinclair et al., 2005). This is further complicated by at least four intrinsic factors:

- different animals experience different levels of popularity and public concern. Likes and dislikes are culturally determined, affecting a species' public image and the potential to protect it. For example, small furry animals, such as rabbits or guinea pigs, and sea mammals, such as dolphins and whales, are popular, in contrast to reptiles, such as snakes and lizards. An animal with a poor image in one culture may be portrayed negatively internationally, for example in popular media such as film, as with the African brown hyena;
- different animals' ecosystems possess varying levels of fragility;
- visitor activity can affect different types of animals in different ways: some species have no tolerance of people and are therefore not seen – e.g. mountain lion, wolf; others need to hide some of the time; others dislike being directly approached or having eye contact – e.g. gorillas; and some are very tolerant and may become habituated to human presence: this, usually gradual, conditioning modifies their behaviour; but
- the deliberate 'staging' (commodification?) of encounters with wildlife for tourists is common in many areas, for example through feeding wild animals (Box 6.4). Here the 'accidental' habituation of wildlife can occur, for example, with animals, some potentially dangerous to humans, looking for food in waste bins and elsewhere (Fig. 6.1) (see also Shackley, 1996).

Few attempts have been made to quantify levels of wildlife disturbance from the perspective of the animals' welfare. Some zoological studies have measured changes in captive animals' heart rates, and such information can be useful if employed for a visitor management strategy, where visitor levels can be controlled to below the animals' stress levels.

Although the tourism literature has placed increasing emphasis upon animals in the 'wild' as opposed to those in captive or semi-captive situations, the number and range of 'captive' animal attractions have been growing rapidly. These include animals living in (semi-)natural environments, such as nature reserves and safari parks, and in more domesticated environments, such as farm parks, zoos and riding schools.

This trend and the tourism and recreation industries' responses to it have resulted in something of a paradox:

- an emphasis on 'wildlife' derived from ethical considerations to emphasize

Box 6.4.   The feeding of wildlife (from Orams, 2002).

This widespread practice is used as a means by which tourists and tourism operators can facilitate close observation and interaction with wildlife. But most research shows negative impacts.

For the animals, deliberate and long-term provision of food:

- alters natural behaviour patterns and population levels;
- results in dependency;
- stimulates intra- and interspecies aggression in efforts to obtain food; and
- causes injury and disease from artificial food sources.

There are psychological, social and economic benefits for humans, and sharing food is a natural and deep-seated instinct. In a limited number of cases the animals can be shown to have benefited as well.

However, with the obvious exceptions of deliberate feeding to aid the rehabilitation of injured or sick animals, the use of supplemental feeding to aid the recovery of an endangered species and the feeding of garden birds to aid their survival with diminishing natural habitats (as well as providing domestic entertainment), it is difficult to find any biological justification for the feeding of wildlife. Management approaches range from complete prohibition, to active promotion and management, to ignoring the practices.

For some animals and in some settings, feeding seems widely accepted and yet in others many, particularly biologists and resource managers, are vehemently opposed to it, especially where it intrudes into the few remaining vestiges of the 'uninfluenced' natural world.

If such activities are permitted, feeding should only be undertaken with careful consideration and an obligation to accept the implications and impacts of those activities.

tourism's ability to sustain the 'natural' environment; but also

- the need to meet demand for a high-quality, desirable interaction experience within 'tame' and 'domesticated' circumstances.

Certainly, animals and their welfare have gained a much higher profile within tourism and recreation in the past 20–30 years for the simple reason that they represent a key resource for sustaining business (Box 6.5). The roles of animals in tourism and recreation have become integral to the 'greening' of tourism and the industry's use of vague and often propagandist terminology in promoting its activities. This embraces such terms as 'wildlife tourism' and 'ecotourism', the use of which has led consumers to assume implicit ideals of sustainability. Yet both terms have embraced an area of contested ethical worth – the use of animals as human recreation.

Such development appears to have been based at least partly on the questionable industry presuppositions that:

- 'wildlife tourism' can be 'sustainable';
- the welfare of wild animals and nature is not harmed by 'wildlife tourism'; and
- if 'wildlife tourism' is an 'alternative' to mass tourism, it should not assume characteristics of mass tourism.

Yet much tourism and recreation involving animals has taken on a mass character involving large numbers of visitors and package-type holidays (Weaver, 2003). Such mass activities include wildlife safaris in the tropics, cetacean (whale) watching in a number of the world's oceans, and farm park and safari park visits as recreational day trips.

Duffus and Dearden (1990) and Reynolds and Braithwaite (2001) view the relationship between animals and humans as one of consumptive or non-consumptive use: strongly anthropocentric terminology. Until recently, the non-consumptive dimension of human relations with wildlife had received much less attention than using animals as sources of food, clothing and trophies. Duffus and Dearden (1990: 214) define non-consumptive wildlife-oriented recreation (NCWOR) as 'a human recreational engagement with wildlife, wherein the focal organism is not purposefully removed or permanently affected by the engagement'. Crucially, they suggest that non-consumptive use provides an experience rather than a product.

Yet the literature suggests that interaction with nature has been fundamentally

Fig. 6.1. Habituated coatis at a tourist cafe, Iguaçu Falls, Brazil.

important to humans, with authors suggesting significant psychological and physical health benefits (e.g. Hendee and Roggenbuck, 1984; Rowan and Beck, 1994). It also indicates that visitors are becoming more sophisticated in their requirements, demanding higher-quality and valuable learning experiences (Turley, 1999; Roberts and Hall, 2001). Certainly, human interaction with animals has the potential to encapsulate four realms of (human) experience (Pine and Gilmore, 1998): entertainment, education,

Box 6.5. The importance of 'wildlife' in tourism.

'Wildlife' is employed by the tourism and leisure industries in a number of ways:

Recreational: for entertainment and/or spiritual uplift:

- *viewing*: close by or at a distance, or even by video link;
- *physical interaction:* touching, holding or feeding; and
- *hunting/fishing.*

Scientific: as a means of improving knowledge and ecology:

- *conservation*: the claimed roles of zoos and some farm parks; and
- *education*: such as school visits to zoos and national parks.

Promotional: employed for promoting the tourism industry:

- *marketing and destination imagery:* such as on brochures, websites;
- *commodification*: such as the use of reindeer and wolves as iconic symbols on T-shirts from Finland; Famous Grouse Scotch whisky;
- *a combination of the above*: for example promoting a safari company or an aquarium on baseball caps, T-shirts, mugs and other 'souvenirs';
- *mythical*: for example, the Loch Ness Monster, which tends to be 'sighted' just prior to the start of each summer season, and is thus employed as a promotional emblem as well as being a commodified icon.

Of these, the first two at least have welfare implications and raise ethical issues.

non-consumptive use should meet certain criteria to be of sustained interest to tourists:

- they should be easily and predictably approachable with relatively little effort, and
- ideally should display attractive or interesting behaviour, such as maternal and social behaviour, hunting and feeding.

But such an approach, expecting animals to behave in certain ways, raises issues of anthropomorphic expectations of unnatural behaviour that go some way towards commodifying the role of animals. Indeed, as revealed in an exploration of dimensions of non-consumptive activity in Scotland, such commodification may represent a complex web of roles pursued within any one attraction or activity, with the animals themselves having more than one role or having different combinations of roles within the same attraction. For example, in wildlife parks, some animals may be employed as 'wild' creatures for discovery, while others may be 'tame pets' for interaction, but both may be acting as 'objects' for exhibition. The range of types of attractions and roles indicated in Table 6.2 is based both on empirical observation and on an evaluation of marketing material produced by the visitor attractions themselves.

Animal Welfare in Tourism and Recreation: Management Ethics

Two types of management issue appear central to the welfare debate concerning animals in tourism and recreation:

- attitudes and responsibilities taken towards the role of animals in captive entertainment (such as in zoos, bullfighting, circuses); and
- the ethics of ecological relationships enmeshing humans, animals and the natural environment within such contexts as the pursuit of 'ecotourism'/wildlife tourism/nature tourism.

Taking a somewhat utilitarian scientific approach to the definition of animal welfare, Broom (1992: 90–91) argued that the term

escapism and aestheticism. Such interaction can present a unique experience (for humans), and such an experience can provide the main objective of a visit or can be employed to positively transform recreational activities within a visitor attraction. Reflecting this, a number of attempts to classify and categorize animal-related attractions have been made (Table 6.1).

In their earlier identification of 'consumptive' and 'non-consumptive' uses, Duffus and Dearden (1990) argued that animals for

Table 6.1. Categories of animal visitor attractions.

Authors	Categories	Description
Orams (1996, 2002)	Captive	Animals kept in a fully enclosed, artificially created and human-controlled environment where little or no physical interaction between animals and visitors takes place – e.g. zoos, aviaries, aquaria.
	Semi-captive	Maintain animals in more natural areas, which can be partly or fully enclosed and tend to still be mostly human-controlled – e.g. safari/marine parks, urban parks, wildlife sanctuaries/centres and managed forests or estates.
	Wild	Exist naturally without human management and do not restrain or enclose animals in any way – e.g. access to migratory sites, wildlife safaris in national parks or marine environments. Encounters with animals cannot be guaranteed unless manipulated in some way by the tourist industry, such as through the provision of food.
Reynolds and Braithwaite (2001)	General access	Where animals live in their natural habitat and display undisturbed behaviour, although some habituation to human visitors may occur – e.g. national parks and other wilderness areas, urban parks.
	Limited access	Natural habitats containing rare or unique animal species, which may be accessible only for limited periods of time – e.g. turtle breeding sites, whale migration routes.
	Restricted access	Focus on animals that are endangered and difficult to approach, and the viewing of which requires substantial effort at any given time – e.g. designated wildlife sanctuaries.
	Contrived attractions	Where animals live in artificial environments fabricated and controlled by humans – e.g. zoos, circuses, wildlife parks, aquaria.
D. Hall *et al.* (2002)	Wild creatures for discovery	Animals set in 'natural' or semi-natural environments, often at a distance from visitors and with little contact. An underlying attraction may be the potential 'danger', 'wildness' and 'threat' of such animals, in response to which appropriate animal and visitor management schemes will be in place.
	Tame creatures for interaction	Aimed particularly at children: animals are 'safe' – both in their anticipated behaviour and in freedom from communicable disease – implicitly 'cuddly' and 'attractive'. The animals involved may be relatively familiar to children through media images, although they may not normally come into contact with them on an everyday basis.
	Objects for exhibition	While creatures in either of the above categories may also be regarded as exhibition objects, it is more obvious where animals are presented in restricted surroundings, often 'arranged' in a systematic, if arbitrary, scheme according to genus, ecological niche or geographical origin. Zoological gardens are the most common example of this.

Continued

Table 6.1. *Continued.*

Authors	Categories	Description
	Targets for shooting and fishing	Recreational game hunting – the shooting (or otherwise killing) of birds and animals – usually requires highly prescribed legal and environmental circumstances and, as such, is often a collective activity (Fig. 6.2). In contrast, fishing, in its various forms, is often a solitary pursuit. Such animal-related activities are often characterized by the strong social class identity of their human participants, and indeed may act as symbols of that (self-perceived) identity.
	A source of education, training or science	Although many attractions will claim a visitor education role for the animals they employ, the extent and value of that role is likely to vary considerably. Equitation and fishing course centres may have education and training functions, while zoos claim a scientific dimension to their activities, particularly in relation to species conservation.
	Mythical or symbolic representation	Images of creatures in museums and other displays, on handicrafts and other recreational goods are widespread. More specific is the 'Nessie' Loch Ness 'monster' representation and the visitor attraction industry surrounding it.
	Ancillary roles	Animals or their visual and/or aural representation play various minor, ancillary roles at a wide range of attractions. Such roles may vary from, for example, being represented in a visual display to providing a means of transport for visitors at or to an attraction.

refers to an animal's 'state', and particularly its ability to cope with its environment. Such welfare can be measured scientifically on an individual basis and employed to inform subsequent ethical decisions (e.g. Wemelsfelder, 1997, 1999). But should animals be used for human recreation? As noted earlier, opponents argue that the use of animals is often cruel and thus unethical. There are two relatively polarized positions in this respect:

- that of animal welfarists, who support the notion that humans should provide the best possible conditions for and treatment of animals, opposing, for example, circuses and factory farming; and
- the animal rights movement, which has an altogether more radical agenda (Regan, 1988), flowing primarily from the concept of universal justice. Early inspirations were Thomas Taylor's 1792 *Vindication of the Rights of Brutes* and Henry Salt's classic *Animals' Rights* a century later. This position claims, essentially, that animals have rights,

similar to humans, although issues relating to the nature of sentience and degrees of awareness between species can be philosophically divisive.

In contrast, arguments in favour of the employment of animals for human recreation emphasize that, as part of the 'experience economy' (Pine and Gilmore, 1998), they can provide entertainment, education and emotional enrichment and be part of the conservation and protection of rural and wilderness environments and values (Clough and Kew, 1993: xiii, 3). Emblematic, and by far the most popular form of animal 'edutainment' globally, is the zoo. Applying a welfare lens allows us to observe how far its presentation of (information about) animals can be justified as ethical.

The zoo

One consequence of the European exploration of the New World in the 18th and

Table 6.2. Roles of animals in visitor attractions (from authors' fieldwork).

Types of attractions	Categories of roles						
	Wild creatures for discovery	Tame creatures for interaction	Objects for exhibition	Targets for shooting and fishing	Education/ training/ science	Mythical and symbolic representation	Ancillary, as a minor part of
Wildlife parks	*				*		
Marine wildlife viewing (seabirds, seals, dolphins, porpoises, whales, otters)	*	*	*		*		
Nature reserves	*	*	*		*		
Wildlife centres	*	*	*		*		*
Country parks	*	*	*		*		
Open farms		*	*		*		
Farm parks		*	*		*		
Rare breeds centres	*	*	*		*		*
Agricultural fairs		*	*		*		
Equitation centres		*			*		
Heritage centres		*			*	*	*
Zoos/zoo parks	*	*	*		*		
Insect (butterfly) centres		*	*		*		
Birds of prey centres	*	*	*		*		
Game: field sports				*			
Fisheries/game fishing/coarse fishing				*			
Sea angling				*			
Model-making studio					*	*	*
Museums/exhibitions			*		*	*	*
Garden centres			*				
Wildlife conservation centres	*				*		
Fishing centres				*	*		
Parks							*
Leisure transport							*

Fig. 6.2. Hunting by foreigners is a lucrative element of Mongolia's tourism industry, and is notionally highly regulated. This anti-hunting poster in a protected area makes an obvious point in a strangely sentimental way.

19th centuries was the bringing back of specimens of (usually dead) hitherto unseen, often strange creatures. A curiosity developed in the upper classes of Western Europe and, as a result, 'safaris' to view and hunt wildlife, particularly in Africa, began to grow in popularity (Norton, 1996). Subsequently 'zoological gardens' began to be developed to provide a context for the live specimens the early wildlife tourists began to bring back. In the past century and a half, the growth of facilities that hold wildlife captive and the creation of specific locations that protect wildlife (such as national parks) have been substantial. Worldwide there are around 1000 attractions holding zoological collections, which are visited annually by an estimated 600 million people (Block, 1991; de Courcy, 1995; Hunter-Jones and Hayward, 1998; Beardsworth and Bytman, 2001).

In the UK an estimated 250,000 animals are held in zoological collections. Since 1984, these zoos have been regulated by the Zoo Licensing Act of 1981, which aims to promote minimum standards of welfare, meaningful education, effective conservation, valuable research and essential public safety. In 1993 the World Zoo Organization published a strategy calling on zoos to clarify their commitment to conservation, to establish global minimum standards and to encourage governments and other bodies to appreciate the role of zoos (IUDZG, 1993).

Such roles raise a number of ethical issues (e.g. Bostock, 1993). Supporters of zoos have argued that they play an important role in research, conservation (Bostock, 1987) and education (Robinson, 1989; Block, 1991), and are vital for the conservation of endangered species, helping to increase the public's awareness of the environment and its fragility (Serrell, 1981). Hunter-Jones and Hayward (1998: 98) argue that this provides an underused opportunity for the development of environmental education. They see the zoo having a particular role to play in the process of providing effective education and personal observation for young people. Lifelong attitudes and behaviour towards all animals tend to be based on childhood experiences (Kidd *et al.*, 1995), and thus longstanding positive attitudes towards animals and nature can be instilled in young people by zoo education programmes. Yet zoos were originally created as places of entertainment (Turley, 1999), and only in the past 30 years has the question of conservation and environmental education seriously arisen (Ormrod, 1994). The efficacy of such conservation is contested:

- a decade and a half ago, Tudge (1991) could argue that a globally cooperative zoo conservation programme could save around 2000 species of endangered land vertebrates;
- but at much the same time the World Society for the Protection of Animals (Urry, 1995) was suggesting that only 16 projects had successfully returned endangered species to the wild and that

only a further 20 species were being seriously considered for zoo conservation programmes.

Indeed, such programmes are constrained by a number of factors:

- many species are unable to be reintroduced into the wild, in some cases because their habitats have already been destroyed;
- breeding from a small genetic pool can lead to inbred deformities; and
- zoos can become convenient breeding grounds for diseases, which may then be introduced into the wild (Clough and Kew, 1993: 26).

A more conceptual criticism of zoos is that their animals are taken out of context (Pickersgill, 1996: 351; Turley, 1999: 347) and, as such, the animals lose much of their meaning and value, inevitably diluting the educational role of the zoo. This may be exacerbated because zoos are often poorly financed and continue to have a low political value, which in turn handicaps their ability to lever finance and influence and to innovate.

The role of the often more popular and profitable wildlife or safari park is at best ambivalent; for most animal species from the tropics and subtropics the climate in the developed countries of the northern hemisphere is generally unsuitable. Further, Tarlow (2003) suggests that wildlife and safari parks contribute to a sense of 'hyperreality' (Eco, 1983). This is the state in which the false becomes real and the real is seen as false, and guides report that some tourists travelling to the Serengeti in East Africa find it hard to believe that they are not in an artificial safari park in Europe or North America. Little (1991: 156) reports an interesting variation on this: 'Once when entering Amboseli Game Reserve I noticed a young male tourist standing in the pop-up section of a safari van excitedly whistling the *National Geographic* theme song while taking pictures of a Masai woman dressed in traditional clothing.'

Rapid political change and economic restructuring in Central and Eastern Europe in the early 1990s left many zoos, particularly in the former Soviet Union, in an even more parlous state than they had been previously (Vitaliev, 1993; Bristow, 1994). Elsewhere, the plight of large mammals in Kabul zoo received global publicity.

Deteriorating conditions resulting from a shortage of funds were also the reason that Glasgow Zoo (Fig. 6.3) closed in 2004 after a long period of negative media reporting, diminishing attendance and low employee morale. More than a decade ago, de Courcy (1995: 29) noted the irony that: 'As the education programmes of the urban zoos sensitise city people towards the interests of the animals, they are creating a body of informed people who may not tolerate the present style of zoo indefinitely.'

In addition to the broad ethical argument that it is simply wrong to exploit animals for human entertainment, zoos face the charge that, despite often radical improvements in the past few decades, animals are still 'unnaturally' restricted. Zoo animals inevitably suffer from confinement, and stress or boredom is often reflected in observably abnormal behaviour (e.g. Morris, 1964; Mitchell and Hosey, 2005) (Table 6.3). Yet a problem for the entertainment value of zoos is that the exhibits' normal behaviour may be unattractive to consumers conditioned to assume that animals are perpetually active and engaging. Television nature films tend to focus on the more spectacular parts of an animal's behaviour and ignore the fact that many animals rest for most of the day. Thus, particularly through the deployment of high-quality, engaging and imaginative interpretation, zoos, and indeed other animal-related attractions, need to address the inevitable sense of disappointment and to explain to visitors that sleeping is an essential part of life.

An additional problem is the fact that many visitors are looking for interaction between the animal and themselves. When they feed they expect a show of gratitude, or they try to provoke the animal into action by shouting, knocking on the bars, climbing on fences, taking photographs with flashes or even hurting the animal itself (van Linge, 1992: 116). Different enclosure structures generate different types of behaviour amongst

Fig. 6.3. Glasgow Zoo, shortly before its closure.

human viewers to attract the animals' attention (e.g. Bitgood *et al.*, 1988; Finlay *et al.*, 1988; Kidd *et al.*, 1995). Many enclosure designs allow the animal to remove itself from public view (Mitchell and Hosey, 2005: 9). Visitor effect studies are still needed for a number of species to examine removal behaviour in detail to determine if the animal is recoiling from the audience or whether it only comes into view when the public is present. The distance of the animal from the audience may be critical, and the vertical dimensions of an enclosure are important for a number of species. Overall, however, much still needs to be understood about how design innovations have affected animals' responses to human visitors, and indeed how they have influenced those visitors' perceptions of the animals (e.g. Reade and Waran, 1996).

Published research that aims to determine the effects of visitors on zoo animals has tended to focus on non-human primates (e.g. Hosey and Druck, 1987; Cook and Hosey, 1995; Hosey, 2000; Birke, 2002; see also Cousins, 1978). There is a pressing need to know more about visitor effects on other mammals (e.g. O'Donovan *et al.*, 1993), birds and the less charismatic reptiles and fish: for example, we

are largely ignorant of the effect on reptiles and fish of people tapping on glass-fronted tanks. Such gaps are partly a result of what Wheeller (2005: 266) refers to as the 'cult of the cuddly' – the industry and media focus on apparently appealing creatures to the relative neglect of scaly, ugly, unanimated and other less consumer-friendly species.

There is still much to know about the implications of the presence of visitors for the welfare of zoo animals as one of a number of factors influencing that welfare. The importance of this is underlined by the fact that many zoos rely on the revenue generated by visitors to provide other aspects of animal care that are key to welfare, such as veterinary care and food (Mitchell and Hosey, 2005: 4).

Management responses to raise the quality of animal welfare and visitor experience may be varied but can include:

- the (enhanced) provision of information, interpretation and education materials;
- codes of behaviour for visitors and employees alike;
- the use of video and webcams to minimize intrusion when viewing animals: for example, rare ospreys on their nest, or the gannet and puffin nesting sites

Table 6.3.   Animal behaviour in response to visitor presence (from Mitchell and Hosey, 2005).

Positive behavioural indicators: visitor presence may induce positive behavioural changes and so may be described as enriching	Undesirable behaviour: visitors may stimulate the expression of undesirable behaviours
Play behaviour: this is a clear sign of good welfare as animals perform it if other conditions are good (e.g. if they are not stressed). However, it occurs mainly in young animals and therefore it may not be a very useful indicator for older animals.	*Stereotypes*: repetitive, non-functional behaviour, which can take many forms.
Non-aggressive interactions: in circumstances where animals are housed with conspecifics, non-aggressive interactions between them, such as social grooming, may be essential to the physical and psychological well-being of the individuals. Care must be taken when interpreting these behaviours, though, as in some species social grooming may also occur more frequently after periods of aggression as reconciliation.	*Locomotion/inactivity*: inappropriate levels of locomotion (e.g. repetitive pacing) or inactivity can indicate a problem with welfare.
Signs of interest in the visitors: vigilance and other information-gathering behaviours aimed at visitors, without signs of fear, aggression or begging, may indicate an enriching effect. For example, watching visitors play on a climbing frame may be interesting to animals.	*Vigilance*: repeatedly looking towards the visitors may indicate that the animal is not comfortable with the situation (care should be taken to define between this and vigilance towards the visitors that may indicate general interest).
Greeting behaviour: if shown in response to visitors could indicate that there is a benefit to the animal.	*Avoidance (hiding, turning back, covering, fleeing vertically)*: actively avoiding the visitors may show a need to escape from this stimulus.
Natural behavioural repertoire: if the repertoire is more natural in visitor presence it could be argued to be enriching. This not only includes general activity budgets and a broad behavioural repertoire, but may include body postures, facial expressions and vocalizations.	*Infant shielding/clinging*: being overprotective of youngsters or constantly seeking reassurance from conspecifics can indicate fear.
–	*Aggression*: tension caused by a stressful stimulus can result in increased intra-group aggression, or even aggression directed at humans.
A decrease in such positive behavioural indicators would be indicative of a negative impact of visitors.	*Scent marking*: inappropriately high levels of scent marking can indicate poor welfare in some species.
–	*Urination/defecation (acute)*: if suddenly frightened, animals may urinate or defecate.
–	*Self-directed behaviour*: increase in scratching in some species (e.g. primates), as well as other less frequent behaviours such as excessive grooming or self-biting, would be considered to be negative.
–	*Fear vocalizations*: may be emitted if suddenly frightened by the appearance of visitors.

on Bass Rock, an island off the east coast of Scotland (Scottish Seabird Centre, 2005);

- opening when animals are active – for example, the Singapore Zoo night safari, when it is cooler and the animals are more active (although artificial lighting impacts are a potential problem), was opened in 1994 and has 900,000 visitors a year (Singapore Zoo, 2005);
- the provision of 'behavioural enrichment': encouraging animals to perform an activity that is similar to what they would do in the wild, such as having to search for their food, to stimulate the animal and stop it becoming bored and to provide the animal with exercise, while possibly also entertaining and educating visitors (e.g. Tudge, 1991; Hunter-Jones and Hayward, 1998). The value of such enrichment techniques is the subject of some debate (Born Free Foundation, 2005).

From 2003 all EU member states need to have fully implemented the EU Zoos Directive, which requires all zoological collections to abide by strict standards in animal welfare. Turley (1999) suggests that increasing cooperation with those traditionally opposed to the zoo concept should be in the interests of both parties. However, many countries around the world lack any kind of legislation protecting the welfare of animals in captivity, and thus welfare NGOs are placed at a disadvantage.

Managing for (human) welfare: interpretation and education

Hunter-Jones and Hayward (1998: 105) view the relative lack of good interpretative material available as a constraint on zoo development. They suggest that zoos should pay more attention to presentation and interpretation, not just of particular exhibits but of the wider environment enmeshing both animals and humans and nourishing the relationships between them. By employing the medium of appropriate interpretation, the (human) experience of interacting with animals has the potential to be substantially enhanced through:

- being more aware of an animal's behavioural and welfare needs, and acting accordingly; and
- being closer to the experience of 'communication' with a sentient member of another species (e.g. see Wemelsfelder, 1997, 1999).

As Pine and Gilmore (1998: 104) put it: 'The more senses an experience engages, the more effective and memorable it can be.' And the range of senses drawn upon in the experience of 'appropriate' interaction with animals can transform an attraction visit. Interpretation can transform experience by trying to represent the interaction from the animal's perspective and by regarding the animal as a 'partner' for interaction, rather than as an object of curiosity and manipulation. This implies a stronger emphasis on:

- regarding animals as individuals;
- the need for 'appropriate communication' between human visitor and animals; and therefore
- the need for more natural behaviour of the human visitor: for example, walking through wildlife areas rather than driving or using other mechanical means of motion.

This requires good 'interpretation' of the animal's actions and expressions to the visitor, so that the visitor can understand these and adjust his/her response adequately – for example, not staring directly at primates in zoos or staring head-on at a horse.

Growing evidence suggests that the more 'control' the human visitor exerts over an animal, the more the visitor is inclined to humanize the animal and incorrectly interpret the animal's needs and feelings. This can lead to an unnatural (and probably uninspiring) experience for the visitor, who is left with little understanding either of the animal's behaviour in relation to the visitor gaze or of the animal's welfare needs. Through interpretation, the replacement of 'control' with 'interaction as partners' and 'communication' may serve to convey both the 'otherness' of the animal and the uniqueness and meaning of interaction with it.

It is important to recognize, therefore, that value-added experience enhancement through an interpretation for visitors of what is 'appropriate interaction' differs substantially from the forms of information and 'education' – about the animal's habitat and statistics on its survival as a species – usually provided at animal-related attractions.

Appropriate interpretation can emphasize the experience of personal contact and the need of the visitor to learn to interpret the animal's actions and expressions correctly. Quite simply, two different (body) languages need an interpreter. And the interpretation of those languages can substantially enhance both the visitor experience and the dignity of the animal (D.R. Hall *et al.*, 2002).

Stewart *et al.* (1998) argue that interpretation should have the capacity to take visitors one step beyond where they are when they arrive at a site so that an empathetic sense of place is developed towards the conservation of that place and to similar places throughout the world. This can occur through well-conceived and managed interpretation exerting a cumulative effect. Similarly, Schänzel and McIntosh (2000) suggest that 'increased understanding' gained during a visit to the Penguin Place on the Otago Peninsula in New Zealand may lead to greater environmental awareness off site.

It may not be unreasonable to suggest, therefore, that this development of a sense of place may be translated for interaction with a particular animal as a sense of species. Thus effective interpretation should have the capacity to take the visitor one step beyond their existing conscious relationship with an animal so that empathy is developed towards its behaviour and welfare, and, by extension, to those of other animals.

For successful value-added experience of human–animal interaction, it is therefore essential that the animal's needs and motivations are central to interpretation. Interpretative materials therefore need to contain communication strategies that create links between visitors and, in the case of animals, species, and enable the visitor to establish personally meaningful connections within the interpretative experience while maintaining, and preferably enhancing, the dignity of the animal. This requires that material be targeted at different types of visitor (Mason and Mowforth, 1996; Ballantyne *et al.*, 1998), their social settings and levels of attention that can be achieved.

The influences of the leisure context add a further dimension to interpretation. The further removed from visitors' expectations the experience of interacting with animals may be, the more intensely the interpretative materials will be tested. Importance and enjoyment are essential prerequisites to sustained involvement (Dimanche *et al.*, 1991). One purpose of effective interpretation should be to provide interactive modes of delivery of relevant and provoking material that can attract and engage visitors and increase learning (Moscardo, 1996), thus contributing to a mindful visitor state and potentially, therefore, to an enhanced sense of species. There is a clear need to better understand the visitor–animal relationship in the various types of animal-based visitor attractions.

Circuses and Other 'Entertainments'

While (some) zoos and related organizations can legitimately claim to have conservation and education roles, the presence of animals in many other recreational contexts may be purely for the purpose of human entertainment. The ethical issues arising from these are wide-ranging. In this section we address some of the more important of these.

The use of animals in circus acts is now considered by many as unjustifiable, because it is claimed that circus acts trivialize animals, that animal training is hard and may be cruel, that most animals are actually captured from the wild, thus diminishing the natural breeding stock, and that circus animals often experience poor living conditions. Circuses can serve to illustrate the animal rights maxim that not all harm hurts, with the animals' humiliation, degradation and loss of freedom constituting a harm as great as the physical pain incurred in their training.

But this does raise issues relating to the extent to which (ethical) attitudes towards animals may be culturally determined. Most circuses in the UK have stopped using animals or have closed, thanks to a combination of external pressure and dwindling audiences. Indeed, the new breed of animal-free circuses, such as Cirque de Soleil and Circus Oz, have reinvented and reinvigorated the circus concept (Moriarty, 2000). Now less than a dozen remain, most not employing animals. The famous Blackpool Tower Circus closed in 1989 after 84 years, and more than 150 local authorities have banned circuses using animals. None the less, the popularity of circuses with performing animals remains high in many parts of the world (Fig. 6.4).

The first true circus was established in 1768 in London. Wild beasts were made to perform alongside jugglers, acrobats and clowns, performing tricks that bore little relation to their natural behaviours. Circus animals still spend much of their lives in small cages in beast wagons, only leaving their cells for the performance or for training. Training of these animals can be harsh, sometimes involving the complete domination of the animal by its handlers, which may involve physical abuse (Kiley-Worthington, 1990).

Organizations such as the Born Free Foundation claim that there is no educational value in performing animals. Unlike most other captive animal establishments, legislation covering circus animals and their facilities is often inadequate, outdated or non-existent. In the UK, for example, circus animals are afforded minimal protection under the Performing Animals Act 1925, and the commitment towards conservation, education and high-quality animal welfare required of zoos does not apply to circuses.

Cultural spectacles and recreational animals

Bullfighting is undertaken as a spectator sport mostly in Spain (where the bull is killed), Portugal (where the bull is not killed) and Latin America. Some 30,000 bulls are killed every year in Spanish bullfights, which are specifically excluded from the country's welfare laws. Odberg (1992) reviewed the welfare implications of bullfighting (for bulls and horses), and concluded, unsurprisingly, that much unnecessary suffering took place. Webster (2005: 225) argues, in a somewhat dismissive way, that it is unlikely that bullfighting will ever be permitted in any society other than those where it is already embedded within the culture.

Fig. 6.4.   Performing yaks in the Mongolian State Circus, Ulan Bator.

Supporters of bullfighting argue that it is a traditional, integral part of Spanish (and Portuguese) culture. Indeed, here is an example of a traditional cultural element, markedly commodified, which is under threat as a consequence of the reaction of foreign tourists (Boseley, 1995; *The Guardian*, 1995) and from increased pressure exerted on the Spanish government since the country joined the European Union.

Indeed, many foreign tourists and foreign residents have protested against bullfighting and have tried to get it banned. In other circumstances, such a stance might be considered as ethnocentric: representing a particular, perhaps sentimental but certainly altruistic, concern for animals that several cultures do not appear to share or wish to embrace (Box 6.6).

On the spectacle of a Peruvian bullfight in the 1950s, Che Guevara (2003: 136) could only conclude: 'The fiesta closed with the almost unnoticed death of the sixth bull. Art, I see none; courage, a certain level; skill, not much; excitement, relative. In summary, it all depends on what there is to do on a Sunday.'

Perhaps most (in)famously, in the city of Pamplona in northern Spain, 150,000 people gather every 6 July for the Fiesta de San Fermin, officially a celebration of the life and works of the patron saint of wineskins. The fiesta, an essential element of Pamplona's heritage, is best known for its running of the bulls through the city's streets, a ritual that is performed every day of the week-long event, 'and offers adrenaline-lovers the chance of being chased through narrow, twisting streets by 600-kilogramme fighting bulls, which have been bred to kill on sight' (Gately, 2004: 137–138). The Romans are thought to have introduced bull killing to Spain, and it is possible that it was practised in the settlement that was established in 73 BC and named in honour of General Pompey. The 'sport' was reintroduced after the Christian re-conquest and was first recorded in 1385 (Gately, 2004), and now attracts large numbers of tourists. While the most famous, the bull-running is far from being the only 'entertainment' available during the fiesta, with nightly bullfights, firework displays and a non-stop round of drinking, singing and dancing through the streets.

According to Gately (2004), entertainments that feature animals are common spectacles at festivals: events such as agricultural fairs, rodeos and horse races offer their audience pleasure by matching animals against their own kind in contests of beauty, strength or speed. Horse racing, for example, praised by the Roman emperor Nero as the 'sport of kings', is usually associated with gambling: 'the key purpose of most spectacles involving animals is to provoke their human spectators into a state of excitement, whether by appealing to their sense of aesthetics, or to their primal lust for contest' (Gately, 2004: 159).

The Palio in Siena, for example, is a spectacle held within a superb medieval environment on every 2 July, in honour of the Madonna of Provenzano, and on 16 August, when it celebrates Our Lady of the Assumption. After prolonged preliminary activities, ten horses are finally frantically ridden three laps around the Campo in the city centre. Although the race itself lasts less than 90 s, the spectacle as a whole 'is possibly the most intense and corrupt sporting event in the world, which is simultaneously a showcase

---

Box 6.6. Intervening with tradition.

Notorious in Spain as the rescuer of Blackie the donkey and saviour of several goats from death during a fiesta, Vicki Moore, the co-founder of the animal welfare direct action group Fight Against Animal Cruelty in Europe (FAACE, 2005) suffered a punctured lung when she was caught and tossed on the horns of a bull in Coria, Estremadura, during the Festival of St John in 1995.

The goats she saved were traditionally thrown from the 20-m-high belfry in Manganeses de la Polverosa. Following her interventions local people reluctantly agreed to lower the goats part of the way and catch them in a blanket.

The husband of the campaigner suggested that she constantly risked her life 'not just from these fearsome animals but also from hostile crowds. She is infamous in Spain. Villagers hate her for trying to stop their barbaric fiestas.'

Source: Boseley, 1995.

for medieval pageantry and Italian *brio'* (Gately, 2004: 159). Ecclesiastical support since the festival's 14th-century origins has ensured its perpetuity. Praised by Pope John XXIII, in 1958 the Archbishop of Siena observed 'telling the Sienese not to take part in the Palio is like telling fish not to live in the sea' (Gately, 2004: 179).

At a more mundane level, street traders (Westacott, 1962) have used animals as entertainment for centuries, and performing bears – usually immature Himalayan bears captured as cubs – can still be seen on the streets in southern Europe, Turkey and India. Although such use of animals is now illegal in many countries, laws are often flouted, as in the case of chimpanzees and tiger cubs used by street photographers in Spanish tourist resorts (Clough and Kew, 1993: 8). But one animal's threatened welfare is another person's livelihood: why are street hawkers positioned in this way? Clearly there is a requirement to provide encouragement/incentives to assist their securing of alternative, preferably more remunerative, employment, and thereby improve their welfare as well as that of the animals (Frean, 1992). It might be considered a joint responsibility of both the location's authorities and the local tourism industry that such employment, if available, should be rendered more secure, both ethically and financially.

Are cultural traditions that are not seen as inherently good by those culturally removed from them fair game for destruction by tourism and the pressures of international opinion? The tourism industry may sustain or erode the role of animals as objects of recreation, but it surely cannot ignore its responsibilities in this field.

Many animals previously exploited for 'entertainment' have been rescued and allowed to live the remaining years of their lives in relative peace in refuges and sanctuaries. Monkey World (2004, 2005), in south-west England, for example, was established in 1987 to provide a permanent home for abused Spanish beach chimpanzees. Subsequent arrivals have been rescued from beach photographers, exotic pets shops, laboratories and circuses from a number of countries. At the rescue centre the primates are rehabilitated into social groups and live in large natural areas. Visitors are not permitted to touch the animals. However altruistic the intent, some might argue that employing the inmates of donkey sanctuaries, ape rescue centres and the like as recreational objects is a form of recycling animals for human entertainment.

Ecotourism, Ecocentrism and Eco-welfarism

The emergence of 'ecotourism' as an industry phenomenon during the 1980s and 1990s might be attributable, initially at least, to the recognition of 'welfare' ethics by its 'inventor' Hector Ceballos-Lascurain (1996), who maintained that tourism could assist preservation of rainforest ecosystems in Costa Rica.

> The term was initially coined exclusively for travel to natural realms, and those practising it were ecotourists, who were said to possess a dedicated love of nature . . . Nature-dominated ecotourism was essentially a 'green' panorama in which residents were denied access, particularly in protected areas, since they did not fit in with the 'colour scheme'.
>
> (Singh *et al.*, 2003: 5)

Subsequently, however, within the penumbra of 'ecotourism' as a high-profile vehicle and shorthand cliché for the apparent mass greening of tourism, such trade-offs between nature and local people were deemed to be reconcilable, and local (implicitly 'indigenous') cultures were embraced within its concept and practice. Optimistically,

> Nature could not be saved at the expense of local people, and economics was identified as a viable binding force between the two. Conservation, preservation and development later became implied facets of ecotourism, which now began to be pursued for the well-being of local communities.
>
> (Singh *et al.*, 2003: 5, after Ceballos-Lascurain, 1996)

Yet, following such strong initial altruistic and honourable intentions, 'ecotourism' as a concept, activity and brand, particularly as an aspect of 'responsible' tourism, has been driven by industry considerations of public image and profit – through the attraction of high-spending, lifestyle-influencing, self- and (self-perceived) environmentally aware clients (Wheeller, 1991, 1994b, 2005). Thus, according to Stark (2002), the strong dimension of 'rational trust' apparent in ecotourism's value as projected by industry requires a corrective if ecotourism's ethical role is to stand up to real-life conflicts.

Further, terms such as 'eco-colonialism' and 'green imperialism' have been employed to suggest that the West's 'recognition' of sustainability and environmentalism – personified by ecotourism undertaken in less developed countries – represents the use of new terms and frameworks to sustain old forms of political and economic dominance (Mowforth and Munt, 2003: 54). Such an approach represents a colonial mentality that is arrogant, often disdaining indigenous values and practices (Hinch, 1998, 2001). It appears to assume that 'the land and its resources belong to those who are best able to exploit them according to the values of a western commercial and industrial system' (Spurr, 1993: 31). In short, and representing conceptual continuity with attitudes to animal exploitation, 'ecotourism', rather like concerns for 'animal welfare', is framed in ethnocentric terms and values which many cultures may not recognize.

Through their social construction and systematization of nature (e.g. Eder, 1988; Macnaghten and Urry, 1998), ecotourists perceive the animals and nature they encounter in culturally and historically specific ways (Russell and Ankenman, 1996). If certain species of animals are seen only as a commodity, a resource for human consumption, there exists the danger that, once the value of the commodity decreases, so will the industry rationale for their conservation (e.g. Livingston, 1981).

The management of animals and their environments for recreation therefore requires philosophical underpinnings based upon values of ecocentrism and eco-welfarism. An ecocentric philosophy may embrace many elements of the recognition of the need for 'natural', ecosystemic balance between the (global) environment and our place as a dominant animal species within it.

Ecocentric or 'deep ecological' approaches argue, for example, that, for 'sustainable tourism' to be meaningful, all stakeholders need to agree to live by a 'greener' code at all times, not just when it is convenient (see Chapter 1). As such, ecocentrism tends to reject market-economy-based relations and technological fixes. Within this ethic, the World Conservation Union's *Caring for the Earth* (IUCN, 1991) emphasized the requirement for more sustainable lifestyles, particularly in wealthier, developed countries.

Technocentric or 'shallow ecological' approaches, in contrast, support a modification of existing behaviour rather than alternatives to it. Thus, for example, they argue that promotion of economic growth leads to more opportunities for research into and development of better technology, which can reduce the adverse impacts of economic activities such as tourism. The Brundtland Report on sustainable development (WCED, 1987) (see Chapter 1) has been criticized for taking a 'Western technocentric development through economic growth' approach to a global issue.

In contrast again, eco-welfare represents an ecological approach expressed through the quality of relations (Chapter 1).

If ecotourism is conceptualized as promoting ecological balance between the (dynamic) natural environment, the local population and tourists, concern for the complementary welfare of all three elements should be a clear priority. Both ecocentric and eco-welfare philosophies reinforce this. Further, through the enmeshing of ecological, social, cultural and economic considerations, education, in pursuit of this goal, can be a central concern for ecotourism. Ideally, therefore, ecotourism could act as a fulcrum for the welfare education of the industry itself, for tourists and for the local and national populations of the targeted regions.

The education component of ecotourism has the potential to facilitate change in the environmental (and cultural) beliefs of ecotourists through the advancement of environmental literacy (Kimmel, 1999). Such literacy can be defined as the capacity of an individual to regularly recognize environmental issues, gather and evaluate information, examine and choose among alternatives, and take positions and actions that work to sustain and develop the foundations of environmental knowledge (Roth, 1991).

However, Price (2003) argues that, while ecotourism should be fulfilling this role in being environmentally (and culturally) educative (and thus, implicitly, encouraging ecotourists to think in terms of sustainability), major barriers to effective environmental learning exist. This is the result of adherence by most in Western society, including a significant proportion of those who might engage in ecotourism experiences, to the dominant Western paradigm of progress and modernization. If ecotourism is to be effective in the modification of environmental beliefs amongst travellers, this major conceptual barrier needs to be addressed centrally and overcome in the quest for more ethically effective ecotourism (Price, 2003).

The issue is thus not only of the role of tourism in advancing or reducing the 'welfare' of the natural environment but also in bringing about the enhanced welfare of tourism stakeholders through environmental education and enlightenment, and thus, by projection, enhancing global environmental welfare. If such tourism is to be performing an educational role, it is best targeted at younger members of society, who will be the opinion-formers and decision makers of subsequent generations. Yet the industry construction of 'ecotourism' as a semi-elitist, self-aware lifestyle pursuit has rendered it relatively child-unfriendly. As a result, both education authorities and those with vested interests in appropriate visitor attractions have a responsibility to facilitate and encourage school and young people's educational visits to animals and animal-related environments. However, this apparently simple objective is not without its problems.

Animals and Environmental Education

Rural areas provide an important educational environment for young people, and particularly for urban children divorced from the non-urban environment. Encouraging children to appreciate the countryside can also help in stimulating their parents and friends to take a greater interest in rural affairs, the nature of animals and the provenance of the food they eat. This can thereby assist rural economies and encourage animal-related attractions to generate education programmes that emphasize the role of animal welfare and wider environmental concern.

However, with the continued presence of the verocytotoxin-producing bacterium *Escherichia coli* (*E. coli*) O157 (infection from which can result in acute renal failure) and other potentially transmissible infections, such as the gastrointestinal cryptosporidiosis, such programmes may be constrained. Young people's interaction with animals requires sensitive but effective and consistent visitor management policy, particularly in the face of such risks.

The role of farms as a school journey experience has been debated in the UK for more than a century. *Schools and the Countryside* (Ministry of Education, 1958) emphasized the importance of farm studies and the need for children to make several farm visits at different stages during their school life for their cumulative value. Young people raised in cities, for example, may have misperceptions about the origins of the food they eat, with consequent health and welfare implications. Partly for such reasons, the UK Policy Commission on the Future of Food and Farming (Curry Commission) argued that a key objective of public policy should be to reconnect consumers with what they eat and how it is produced (PCFFF, 2002: 6). The need for schools to develop stronger links with farms was made explicit. The UK government responded that it recognized the importance of young people experiencing the 'outdoor classroom' and noted that 'children benefit from hands-on experiences of plants and animals, within school grounds, through visits to farms, woodlands or field study centres' (House of Commons, 2002: 47).

Research into (urban) young people's knowledge and appreciation of the environment and of animals within it has not been encouraging. Dillon *et al.* (2003) found that school-age students' environmental knowledge and understanding appeared to be poor. Studies of students' awareness were not integrated into any wider conceptual framework such as the food chain, and there was a strong case for improving teaching and learning concerning food, farming and land management and their interrelationships.

Loughland *et al.* (2003), in support of earlier findings (Gonzalez-Gaudiano, 2001; Hicks and Bord, 2001), also emphasized the need for a more integrated approach to environmental education. For young people to have a well-developed relational view of the environment, it is important for them to appreciate the interrelationship between environmental and social issues. Currently they are 'subjected to an education system underpinned by the anthropomorphic values of liberalism and modernity' (Loughland *et al.*, 2003: 14), within which animals are organized into hierarchies, both plants and animals are regarded as pets or pests (Marshall, 1992) and nature is constructed as an object of gaze. Myers *et al.* (2003) argue that curriculum change, and implicitly a greater engagement with animal-related environments, can help children of all ages be more aware of and articulate about values underlying environmental care.

Teaching and learning initiatives need to recognize the complexity of young people's views and understandings, and particularly the impact of their cultural identity on learning needs in relation to out-of-school experiences. In reconnecting young people to the origins of their food, to animals and their working environment, farm and other rural visits can be integrated with classroom learning through:

- geography and environmental science (land use and mapping, environmental practices, climate and seasons);
- biological science (life cycles);
- history (of the farm and changing land use);
- language acquisition (writing activities about farm visits, new vocabulary);
- mathematics (measuring and counting activities); and

- art (drawing, collage-making) (e.g. Lavine and Kraus, 2001).

Several studies have indicated that children can be a catalyst in generating a family visit to a particular attraction or destination (e.g. Swinyard and Sim, 1987; Seaton and Tagg, 1995; Thornton *et al.*, 1997; Nickerson and Jurowski, 2000). They can also enrich the nature of the adult experience (Ryan, 1992). Older children appear to play a greater role in group holiday decisions (Madrigal, 1993; Pasumarty *et al.*, 1996; Lindstrom, 2003); younger children exert more influence on actual tourist behaviour while on holiday. In the UK, under-16s account for almost one-third of all trips to visitor attractions (BTA/ETB, 1998), with figures up to 39% for leisure parks and 47% for farm-based attractions. The latter would suggest at least that the presence of a child, if not their articulated wishes, encourages adults to visit such attractions and environments. Although Turley (2001) suggests that the influence of children on the demand for tourism and recreation experiences is under-researched and undervalued (Howard and Madrigal, 1990; Cullingford, 1995; Thornton *et al.*, 1997; Roedder John 1999), in her own study of zoo visits, she was able to highlight the important part children play in influencing demand for day-visit destinations and recreational activities.

Myers *et al.* (2003) suggest that the perception of what animals need is a rich nexus for environmental education. There are good arguments, therefore, for encouraging children to appreciate relational environmental values, and especially those relating to animals and their environmental context. This has implications both for education policy towards school visits to rural areas and for the providers of farm-based and other animal-related attractions (e.g. D.R. Hall *et al.*, 2002).

But interacting with animals exposes humans to zoonoses (diseases transmitted from vertebrate animals), such as *E. coli* O157 and cryptosporidiosis, which can be harmful if basic hygiene measures are not followed. In 1999 hundreds of rhesus macaque monkeys in a number of safari parks across Britain had to be killed as they had contracted the herpes B virus, which can infect humans. The outbreak demonstrated the actual and potential significance of zoonoses in animal attractions, and raised questions regarding the risks to both humans and animals of contact between them. Risk areas include 'petting zoos' and the increasing number of 'meet the animals' sessions, where members of the public, and particularly children, are encouraged to stroke, hold or feed an animal. Attraction management has an obvious responsibility to provide and require the use of adjacent washing facilities both before and after contact, in order to minimize the risk of cross-infection.

The UK Health and Safety Executive (HSE, 2002a, b, c) advises all farmers and owners of animal attractions to assume that all their ruminants (cattle, sheep, deer and goats) carry *E. coli* O157 and *Cryptosporidium*. It also suggests that at least 45% of all cattle herds may carry the *E. coli* bacterium (HSE, 2002a). Simply carrying the bacterium does not normally cause an animal harm or illness. Indeed, a difficulty in identifying animals that carry the organism is that they usually exhibit no signs of disease (SOEID, 1996). If contracted by humans, however, the toxins that *E. coli* produces can cause illness ranging from diarrhoea to kidney failure, with possible fatal consequences. Young children and the elderly are at greatest risk. Infection can occur through a number of routes, including direct contact with animals, contact with animal faeces and the consumption of contaminated foods, as well as person-to-person contagion.

A number of outbreaks involving children have been associated with educational and recreational visits to open farms (HSE, 2001), although individual cases are reckoned to be substantially under-reported (Payne, 2003). The bacterium can also be carried by pets and wild birds: rabbits were blamed for an outbreak at a wildlife park in England in 2001 (Meikle, 2001). It is a particular risk for children visiting farms during lambing in spring. As a physical threat to rural visitors themselves, therefore, *E. coli* is much more damaging than foot-and-mouth disease (FMD), which, although

able to be spread by human activity, does not affect humans. Controlling the risks from *E. coli* O157 helps to control risks from most other zoonoses such as cryptosporidiosis, which can cause diarrhoea and abdominal pain with flu-like symptoms for up to 6 weeks (HSE, 2002a, c). Clearly, if *E. coli* O157 in particular were to develop into a major threat to rural visitors, such as schoolchildren, this would have profound implications for policy relating to educational visits, for the nature of children's learning and understanding of rural and animal environments, and for many rural tourism and recreation-related businesses.

Following the FMD crisis of 2001/2, managers and policymakers were much more aware of the risk involved in children's interactions with animals. But managing wildlife tourism as education overlaps the boundaries of education, health, recreation and agriculture policy domains. The potential strengths of interdisciplinary, functional integration are constrained by the potential for fragmentation and incoherence.

During 2002 and again in 2004, Scotland's local education authorities (LEAs) were surveyed on their policy approach towards school visits to farms and other animal-related attractions in rural areas. Key issues to emerge included the differences in apparent levels of awareness, response and departmental responsibility between local authorities, raising issues of policy consistency, partly derived from the fragmentation of responsibility. Despite the common use of key central government advisory documents, there appeared to be a critical need for revising and updating policy guidelines – some of which had been issued 15 years previously – in the face of the growth of animal attractions and visits to them.

Clearly difficult questions confront the sustainability of some rural tourism businesses in the face of policy inconsistency and continuing perceived hazard. But these surveys reinforce one of Ritchie's (2003) arguments that, without adequate research and management, the potential impacts and benefits of educational tourism will not be maximized. The evidence would suggest a requirement for closer collaboration between education administrators and those involved in the management of recreational resources to facilitate safe and educationally rewarding visits, to enhance an ethically grounded environmental education.

Summary and Conclusion

This chapter has taken a welfare-centred approach to the non-human animals involved in tourism and their wider captive and 'natural' environments. The human–animal relationship, its management and ethical context were explored. The expression of responsibility through codes of conduct and behaviour was related to the ever-broadening scope of the concept of 'ecotourism'. Social constructions of animals and their environments, and the perception of animals' relative merit and value, not least as 'edutainment', appear strongly culturally determined. This has important implications for their welfare and for the quality of human interactions with them within a recreational context.

The spiritual dimension of 'wilderness' has long been regarded as a key contributor to the development of ecological appreciation. The educational importance of interacting with animals, particularly in more 'natural' environments, is that it has the potential to contextualize and modify perception of and behaviour within our global ecosystem: what Kimmel (1999) refers to as the advancement of environmental literacy.

Others contend that, while 'ecotourism' should be fulfilling this role, major barriers to effective environmental learning exist through the adherence by most in Western society to the dominant paradigm of progress and modernization. If ecotourism is to be effective in the modification of environmental beliefs, this barrier needs to be addressed centrally and overcome in the quest for a more ethically effective tourism encounter with the 'natural world' (Price, 2003).

This leads us to consider in the next chapter the responsibility of the 'tourism industry' and its responses to the tourism-related welfare issues raised in previous chapters.

7

The Tourism Industry: Responses and Responsibilities

Contemporary business organizations do not so much disable people's moral faculties as crowd them out . . . But we do need to trust businesses to be open and honest about their interests and activities, and we do need them to engage in constructive dialogue around the relationship between those interests and the interests of society at large.

(Hendry, 2004: 258, 260)

Box 7.1. Chapter aims and summary.

This chapter seeks to: explore the nature of the tourism industry response to the growth of ethical concern.

It does this by: examining the tools that the industry has adopted, such as interpretations of corporate social responsibility, ethical codes and the explicit rewarding of 'responsible' business. This is compared with some of the realities of the welfare of tourism and travel stakeholders.

Its key concepts are: responsibility, accountability, ethical codes, sustained well-being.

It concludes that: it is contestable whether the patchy and inconsistent trajectory of responsibility within the tourism industry can actually enhance the welfare of stakeholders.

As we have seen in previous chapters, some destinations' apparent over-reliance on tourism has led authors to question the ethics of wider development processes, of which tourism is one part (Goulet, 1973), and the ethics of tourism development in particular (Lea, 1993). The structure of the sector's operations has also attracted criticism. The global tourism industry is fiercely competitive and dominated by transnational corporations, mainly based in developed countries. These organizations leverage power over the suppliers of the tourism product, potentially creating unequal exchange and power relationships (Peet, 1991; Barrett-Brown, 1993). Operators are forced to compete through international mergers and acquisitions, and they survive on small margins because of the substantial economies of scale derived. This results in continuous new product development and aggressive marketing through lower prices (D'Aveni, 1998). The ensuing instability of the sector makes it difficult for companies to plan for a more sustainable future, and Miller (2001: 590) argues that 'against such a background taking steps to behave more responsibly has traditionally received a predictably low priority'.

In this chapter we therefore focus on the tourism industry's response to the welfare and ethical issues raised in the previous chapters and examine the nature of responsibility exhibited.

©D. Hall and F. Brown 2006. *Tourism and Welfare: Ethics, Responsibility and Sustained Well-being* (D. Hall and F. Brown)

Locating Responsibility and Accountability

Some time ago Sims (1991) pointed out that the volume of scandal and abuse of power in business indicated a need for closer scrutiny of corporate activities. Fennell (2000) suggests that a result has been that those working in the commercial world have increasingly found it prudent to put their faith in centres and organizations designed to instil ethical values in business, such as the Canadian Centre for Ethics and Corporate Policy (1999). This independent centre seeks to both: (i) encourage organizations to take account of the ethical dimension in making their business decisions and developing their policies and practices; and (ii) promote ethical values by encouraging and contributing to public, professional and organizational awareness and knowledge (Fennell, 2000: 65).

Corporate social responsibility (CSR) represents the objective of forging stronger connections between business and society and allowing companies to take a direct role in improving the business environment (Laing, 2004). It is 'the continuing commitment by business to behave ethically and contribute to economic development while improving the quality of life of the workforce and their families as well as of the local community and society at large' (World Business Council for Sustainable Development, quoted in Kalisch, 2000: 2).

Acknowledgement of CSR and the perceived need to respond to ethical considerations are increasingly evident in business practice and in the texts produced for business schools (e.g. Hendry, 2004; Jones *et al.*, 2005; Kline, 2005). Free-marketeers may argue that CSR is nebulous and interferes with businesses' prime aim of making profits (e.g. Henderson, 2005). Yet there are important questions relating to the choice of social responsibilities that businesses can sensibly undertake and the ways in which they can be measured and justified (Fletcher, 2005).

In tourism, a number of specialist operators have expressed discomfort with such terms as 'ethical' and 'responsible',

believing that the former is too vague and difficult to define, whilst the latter, if employed in promotional literature, can falsely raise tourist expectations (Weeden, 2005: 238). Kalisch (2002) argues that CSR represents a recognition that tourism sustainability cannot be achieved unless corporate bodies take responsibility to society in general, as well as to their stakeholders. Accountability should be based on more than financial interest. The World Travel and Tourism Council (WTTC, 2002: 1) has articulated the *raison d'être* of CSR in tourism partly in terms of poverty alleviation and social equity: 'growing concern about poverty and the widening gap between rich and poor . . . while profit is the foundation on which business is constructed, many companies are now seeking ways to create value for society while creating value for their business'. Corporate social responsibility is in danger of becoming just another fashion and a cynical means of conveying the impression that the corporate world willingly embraces ethical concern and acceptance of its moral responsibilities (Briedenham, 2004). At its widest, CSR encompasses all the ways in which an organization and its services and products interact with society and the environment. It is also promoted as needing to be an attitude of mind that should inform behaviour and decision making throughout an organization (Laing, 2004: 5–6).

Can consumers and companies negotiate a responsible path towards enhanced welfare or is there a need for independent or regulatory organizations to guide and exert pressure for the collective good? The CSR literature gushes that, rather than being led by consumers, companies should learn to be inspired by them – and combine this inspiration with the confidence to take socially responsible products beyond niches and into the mainstream. Once these products are in the mainstream, we are told, the evidence shows that consumers are unlikely to reject them, and other companies may well imitate them (Burgess, 2003; Laing, 2004: 58). These aspirations are based on a number of contested observations and assumptions (Table 7.1).

Table 7.1. CSR aspirations and reality (from Burgess, 2003; Laing, 2004: 58–60).

Aspirations	Reality
The trend towards ethical consumption is identifiable, growing and diversifying. It is linked to a desire for quality products and services and is not constrained by socio-economic boundaries.	The rhetoric of consumer enthusiasm for buying from companies with responsible practices is in conflict with the reality of a widespread desire for low prices and convenience.
Beyond ethical purchasing, mainstream consumer forces can be powerful drivers of CSR.	Indicators are ambiguous.
Many major companies have moved to meet limited consumer pressure for greater responsibility. In some cases, companies' commitments to CSR have gone beyond the level their consumers are demanding. Rather than being punished commercially for this, they have gained in reputation and activated latent consumer enthusiasm and buy-in. Relatively limited consumer pressure can therefore inspire wider-ranging beneficial effects.	For consumers to be significant drivers of CSR, they need information that is manageable, consistent and authoritative: most information available to consumers on CSR is imperfect and their decisions are not well informed by evidence of the ethics and sustainable practice of producers and retailers. Little company CSR communication is targeted directly at consumers.
Independently verified information on products generates a positive response from consumers and has benefits for companies. It allows them to win consumer trust and dispels accusations of CSR 'spin'.	Different cultures in which business – not least tourism – takes place have varying conceptions of ethics and responsibility (Box 7.2) (see also Wright *et al.* (2003) on business ethics in China, and Pomeranz (2004) discussing Islamic perspectives on business ethics). This renders the concept of 'independence' somewhat arbitrary.

Box 7.2. Inspiring values.

In Finland, Lindfelt (2004) has recognized an environment of growing ethical pressure from customers, investors, global analytical institutions and competitors, all relying on a 'jungle' of various recommendations and norms. Businesses are confronted with a mixture of national regulatory laws, regional norms and international initiatives, in reaction to which some develop their own ethical codes. Yet Lindfelt noted that few Finnish firms used them, and that there was confusion surrounding such terms as 'value', 'corporate responsibility', 'social responsibility' and 'ethics'. Ironically, in a country deemed the least corrupt in Europe, companies in Finland have been uncomfortable employing moral rhetoric to market themselves. Interestingly, Lindfelt argues that the use of explicit ethical codes may be at a low level in such an ethical country because the actual need to spell out ethics is not consonant with the national culture, within which it is implicit and almost innate.

Pro-poor and fair trade in tourism (Chapter 5) represent important elements in the CSR debate, where the emphasis has shifted from short-term 'doing good' to finding 'win–win' situations, in which companies can profit by doing good (Ashley and Haysom, 2005). Within this paradigmatic shift, Locke (2003) recognizes a fourfold typology of CSR approaches (Table 7.2): PPT approaches, for example, would ideally see companies shift from 'philanthropic' to 'encompassing'. For Font and Harris (2004: 1002), concerned with the amenability of CSR to certification, 'the main challenge is turning social issues into measurable and meaningful metrics'.

Fisher (2003) draws a distinction between surface and deep approaches to ethics in understanding the difference between the rhetoric concerning ethics and actual business practice. She argues that a surface approach to ethics, which is associated with self-interest, will not promote ethical

Table 7.2. Approaches to CSR (from Locke, 2003; Ashley and Haysom, 2005).

Minimalist	Philanthropic	Encompassing	Social activist
• Basic stakeholder support • Addressing aspects that are generally human-resource-oriented • Tokenistic	• Project-specific • Related to specific issues relevant to the particular organization • Donations and gifts • Seeks to change	• Looks beyond the immediate business stakeholder group to the broader community • Embedded in company values and management style • Seeks to lead change	• Approach is the foundation of the business • Business is a catalyst for change • Seeks to effect change in others

behaviour, while a deep approach, motivated by the desire to do the right thing, does have the potential to do so. The difference between the rhetoric and business practice suggests that most businesses either intentionally or unintentionally adopt a surface approach to ethics. From the standpoint of public-sector experience, Wheeler (1993, 1995) emphasizes the need for marketeers to balance their individual ethic (an individual's beliefs and values), their professional ethic (as dictated by the marketing profession) and the organizational ethic of their employment context.

The tourism industry in many respects mirrors the way in which contemporary business organizations represent a wide range of forms, activities, linkages and senses of corporate ethos, from the highly rigid and bureaucratic to the highly flexible and adhocratic (Mintzberg, 1996). Scales and structures are embraced that range from one-person, rural micro-businesses to global conglomerates such as TUI, Sheraton Hotels and News International. Irrespective of the presence or otherwise of an ethics code and of organizational structure or function, a company should be able to be assessed against a number of criteria in order that its ethical position and sense of (social and environmental) responsibility can be determined. Such ethical benchmarking criteria are indicated in Table 7.3. It should be borne in mind, however, that few elements of social citizenship are based solely on

'rights' and that all imply some form of obligation or duty (Roche, 1992).

Taking a more lateral view, Hendry's (2004: 252–253) approach to the relationship between business and wider society is based on the argument that we live in a 'bimoral' society in which people govern their lives by two contrasting sets of principles:

• those associated with traditional morality, which, while embracing a modicum of self-interest, emphasize duties and responsibilities, honesty and respect towards others and, ultimately, put their needs above our own; and

• those associated with entrepreneurial self-interest. These also impose obligations, but of a much more limited kind: their emphasis is upon the competitive rather than the cooperative – to advance our own interests rather than altruistically to meet the needs of others. Until recently, behaviour according to the morality of the market was accepted as necessary for economic growth and development, but was seen also as a potential threat to the traditional moral order and was permitted only in carefully circumscribed circumstances and subject to a number of regulatory safeguards.

Hendry (2004: 253) argues that, although both sets of principles have always been present in society, in recent years, and very rapidly, traditional moral authorities – organized

Table 7.3. Ethical benchmarking criteria for tourism companies (adapted and developed from Winch and Watson, 1992: 12–13).

Criterion	Issues
Access and equity considerations (Chapters 2, 3, 4 and 5)	• Can the company represent, facilitate and accommodate a wide range of disabilities? • What is the company's policy on maternity rights and childcare facilities? • Does the company pay men and women equally? • Is there positive discrimination in favour of any particular (minority or disadvantaged) group? • Is there an equitable promotions policy? • Does it have a scheme to monitor the number of people it recruits from traditionally disadvantaged sections of the population? • Does it positively encourage survival and physical access for such groups? • Are its premises accessible to the (variously) disabled?
Client rights (Chapters 2 and 3)	• Does the company fully respect the rights of its clients – tourists – as recognized by international conventions? • Does it endeavour to provide full and impartial information? • Does the company make available client surveys and questionnaire responses? • Does the company respond promptly and effectively to client complaints?
Employees' rights (Chapters 4 and 5)	• Does the company respect its employees' right to belong to a trade union? • Is there a constructive dialogue with the workforce? • Does management receive disproportionate benefits? • Are employees asked to work unacceptably long hours? • Are employees asked to work in unhealthy conditions or put at risk of injury? • Does the company have a proportionate part-time and seasonal workforce complement? • Is there encouragement and support for employee mobility?
Human rights (Chapters 4 and 5)	• Does the company trade with countries or organizations with a poor human rights record? • Does the company research how tourism planning and development processes are executed? • Does the company positively support the participation of local people in deciding the nature and scale of tourism developments?
Exploitation of developing countries (Chapters 4 and 5)	• Does the company exploit developing countries, for example, by driving down wage and price levels? • Does the company ring-fence employment roles in developing countries for Western nationals?
Environmental considerations (Chapters 5 and 6)	• What is the company's attitude to local sourcing, energy saving, renewable energy and recycling, conservation, organic agriculture, pollution and climate change? • Does the company have ethical codes of behaviour for its employees and clients?
Animal welfare (Chapter 6)	• Does the company respect animal welfare and avoid inflicting suffering on animals? • Does the company positively contribute towards species conservation?

religion, state, family, community, education – have lost much of their force. The morality of self-interest has acquired a much greater social legitimacy, and over a much wider field of behaviour, than ever before.

Working within business organizations is thus fraught with moral tensions as obligations and self-interests conflict, and managers are pulled in a number of different directions. The key role of management becomes a political and moral one of determining purposes and priorities, reconciling divergent interests and nurturing trust in interpersonal relationships.

Within an increasingly competitive business environment (despite now familiar academic calls for cooperation, collaboration, partnership and networking), companies have continued to demand loyalty from their employees while no longer being able to afford to reciprocate (Hendry, 2004: 254–255). Often what is actually required is for the company itself to realize that it needs to be guided in its business conduct (Winch and Watson, 1992: 11). For example, Farrell *et al.* (2002a) found in relation to employer and employee behaviour amongst eight large Australian enterprises that there was no discernible association between stated ethical strategies and ethical activity, and argued that the strongest ethical culture affecting behaviour came from external sources.

Tour Operators: Pivot of Responsible Practice?

As an intermediary, the tour operator acts as an important link between tourism supply and demand, facilitating the circulation of products and information between the two (Curtin and Busby, 1999). As such, tour operators represent a critical pressure point of the mass tourism system and can trigger responsibilities and actions of other tourism stakeholders (Budeanu, 2005), in terms of both supply chains and consumer behaviour. Many would suggest that tour operators could do a lot more in this respect. For example, in response to clients of UK tour operators seeking redress for a substandard product, the Association of British Travel Agents (ABTA) administers its own arbitration scheme, which covers more than 7000 travel retail outlets. In 2003 it received 16,258 complaints, and 1103 of these went to arbitration, where the complainant and the travel company agree to accept the decision of an independent referee as legally binding. *Holiday Which?*, the Consumers' Association's magazine, compared and contrasted

the experience of 11 groups of tourists travelling with ten different tour operators who had grievances about their holiday experiences. It found that arbitration judges made higher awards than ABTA in eight of the 11 claims (Robins, 2004). This suggests that the industry itself is less than fair when dealing with clients' compensation claims.

With WTO support, operators established a *Tour Operators Initiative for Sustainable Tourism Development* website (<http://www.toinitiative.org>). This details company case studies of claimed 'sustainable' and 'responsible' activity under six major headings: integrating sustainability into business, supply chain management, internal management, product management and development, customer relations, and cooperation with destinations. This could be seen as a response to the UN Commission on Sustainable Development's 1999 call for 'voluntary initiatives' in support of sustainable tourism development that would 'preferably exceed' any relevant standards (CSD, 1999). However, when last viewed in May 2005, the site still carried a 2001 copyright date.

As part of an examination of the role of corporate social responsibility in the global tourism industry, Miller (2001) identified and evaluated some five factors influencing the responsibility of tour operators' positions.

1. Industry structure

Historically low and competitive prices (Evans and Stabler, 1995) and low consumer loyalty result in low profit margins. This in turn reduces the stability of the industry and thus discourages long-term investment. Against such a background, taking steps to behave more responsibly has tended to receive a low priority. A lack of responsibility on the part of tour operators may also be a function of their lack of ownership and therefore control over the tourism services provided. This enables tour operators to blame destination overdevelopment on local authorities and private developers (Ashworth and Goodall, 1990). Miller (2001: 590) contends, therefore, that, by virtue of the unique middle ground occupied, tour operators can claim to be simultaneously the innocent victim in satisfying existing consumer demand while helplessly responding to the existing supply stock.

Yet the trend within the inclusive holiday sector for takeovers, vertical integration and structural consolidation into a smaller number of increasingly large conglomerates suggests that both the previous points are becoming less convincing. This is because the few large oligopolistic companies are in a position to introduce greater stability and more selective competition and to exert more influence on destination development.

At a general level, Miller (2001) found from his interviews that smaller companies better understood the destinations to which they took their clients and so had a heightened awareness of destination issues and problems, despite their impotence in providing solutions to them. The larger tour operators were seen as being financially able to take steps, but were so removed from the destination that they lacked awareness of the issues and problems found there. This somewhat simplistic view was modified by the fact that many of the large companies had champions who were driving through a change in attitude amongst staff, just as some of the small companies were guilty of being complacent and not tackling the issue of responsibility.

2. Legal requirements

The European Community Package Travel Directive, implemented between 1993 and 1995, requires that tour operators have legal minimum responsibilities, primarily to the consumer and particularly regarding health and safety (Downes, 1996). Yet such responsibilities appear either too minimal or easily circumvented (e.g. Forsyth, 1996). Certainly Miller (2001: 594) reports that representatives of national tour organizations were of the opinion that tour operators 'acted to the minimum point that they could get away with'.

The UK government, for example, seems to have been ambivalent about the level of regulations surrounding tourism, looking for a more cooperative system of guidelines and frameworks to shape the behaviour of companies. None the less, increasing pressure from campaigning groups has resulted in an almost mandatory requirement for companies to adopt codes of responsible behaviour and practice. But this in its turn has seen large companies adopting a code and passing on the ethical requirement to its suppliers in a ripple effect, resulting in a proliferation of codes, as noted in Chapter 1. A minimum degree of regulation is therefore seen to be desirable, if only to avoid duplicating effort and wasting resources by developing yet further codes.

3. Market advantage/negative public relations

Although market surveys repeatedly indicate that consumers regard the environment as an important consideration, not least for travel company policy, as with similar surveys undertaken with motorists, the gap between what respondents idealize and their actual behaviour is often substantial. Yet, for at least a decade and half, we have been told that:

> Consumers are switching allegiances, challenging traditional ethics, and actively seeking out products that are perceived to fulfil their needs, even if more costly . . . Tourists as consumers, are asking questions, seeking creative travel alternatives, and are willing to pay extra to obtain the travel experiences they desire.
> (Wight, 1993: 8)

Whether real or illusory – and quite clearly with substantial cultural divergences – such a perception has been taken on board by the industry. Thus Berry and Ladkin (1997) cite examples where the view is held that destination marketing that promotes 'sustainable tourism' probably results in more business. As noted earlier, received wisdom suggests that market advantage forces companies to improve their ethical performance (e.g. Curtin and Busby, 1999).

Technology has a role to play in speeding the process through which responsible companies can be rewarded for the position they take and consumers can find out about companies that perform poorly. Miller's (2001) interviewees cited a particular television consumer watchdog programme as a source of motivation for companies not wishing to be exposed on it. Yet, as more companies adopt greater social responsibility, so the concept loses its ability to provide market advantage, merely helping companies to remain competitive, and is thus seen as a necessary extra cost.

4. Cost savings

Often it appears that companies are more willing to spend time and money trying to diminish public sensitivity to the negative effects of their short-termism than to adjust to a longer-term behaviour and outlook (e.g. Tibbs, 1993): there is often deliberate economic reasoning behind this. Any business is likely to adopt a course of action until it is cheaper or more beneficial to take up an alternative. Thus, if it is less costly to abuse the environment and pay any fines that are incurred than to adopt a policy of pollution control, then, Miller (2001) argues, the environment will be abused (moral obligation aside).

Indeed, this was a familiar approach in the later stages of state socialism in Central and Eastern Europe, whereby state enterprises were willing to pay pollution fines to local governments rather than pursue more costly and difficult pollution technology upgrades. Those local governments appeared content for this to continue because in some cases such fines became an important component of local income. This continued to the point where complicity between local government and state enterprise was essential for the funding and functioning of local services, and thus an element of resource redistribution from central to local coffers. In practice, while this may have permitted civic dignitaries to purchase more prestigious official cars and build larger municipal palaces, the health and well-being of local residents and workers were severely diminished by the resulting dangerous

concentrations of atmospheric and terrestrial industrial pollutants (e.g. Carter and Turnock, 2002).

The negative behaviour (polluting) will be stopped when the marginal cost of doing so becomes greater than alternative courses of action (disposing of the waste properly). While this is indeed rational, the level at which this is reached will be dependent upon the elasticity of demand and supply for the product. Thus, Barrett (1991) predicts a carbon tax would need to raise taxes far beyond existing levels to see any tangible reduction in non-renewable resource use, and so, similarly, any green taxes to reduce negative behaviour would by definition have to be introduced at a prohibitive level.

The message that conserving resources saves money has been a difficult one to sell, often because of the high initial investment required to produce long-term returns. Although the existence of cost savings and the need to protect long-term investment should be sufficient incentive for companies to adopt the principles of more responsible tourism, in practice this has not been the case and the concept needs (external) intervention to ignite interest (Forsyth, 1995).

5. Moral obligation

Middleton and Hawkins (1998: 107) cited ten reasons for the private sector in the tourism industry to adopt more sustainable practices, but they deliberately excluded an ethical or moral argument on the grounds that it was the least considered factor for most tourism businesses, and especially small businesses. Haywood (1993: 235) concurs: 'Business and society are still seen as separate from each other, and the language of rights and responsibilities, which attempts to link the two, remains irrelevant to the world of the practising managers.'

However, there are tour operators that achieve a necessary profit and act beyond the 'moral minimum' (Smith, 1990). But, as Miller (2001: 592) argues:

> while in the case of several companies
> the morality shown is due to the
> personal sense of obligation felt by the

owner/manager, more commonly the extent of the morality shown is a function of the responsibility that consumers expect companies to have.

Such consumer concern stimulating moral obligation is predicated on the availability of accurate information on company performance. But until recently there has existed a notable lack of such information in general, and about the behaviour of tour operators in particular (see Table 7.3 above). Now the Internet is assisting in gradually rendering some information available in the public domain. But what may be taken as a silent endorsement of a company policy could be simply a lack of knowledge. Greater accountability and information are required to help shift society's perception of where the moral minimum rests.

The far from coherent responses from stakeholder interviews led Miller (2001) to different sets of implications. While the largest group argued that consumers would need to provide the initial trigger for the industry to take more responsible action, others suggested that all stakeholders would need to act in unison for there to be any progress. Some thought it was via the local or destination government that the tourism industry would display greater responsibility in the future. Certainly opinion was divided over the role of large tour operators: some believed that it needed a large operator to set an example and lead the rest of the industry, but for others this seemed unlikely. What was clear was that very few tour operators were about to take action without any external pressure to do so. Gordon and Townsend (2001) found that a number of operators claimed that barriers such as tourist attitudes and health and safety liability stood in the way of doing more for the benefit of destination stakeholders.

Tour operators need to monitor in much greater depth their company performance and provide accessible information resulting from such monitoring to validate their claims about their holidays and provide assistance to a growing number of aware consumers in their choice of operator, thereby potentially increasing consumer loyalty (Miller, 2001).

Yet much of that consumer loyalty may not be the result of a code that clients may not even be aware of, or of a company mission statement that they will immediately disregard. It will be based on personal relationships that (potential) travellers can trust and believe will safeguard their welfare. This is where the role, nature, training and nurturing of a range of 'front-line' workers involved in a diversity of tourism-related activities are so important and yet all too often overlooked. For, although information technology and communication have displaced personal contact in a number of aspects of travel and holiday provision, there remains a wide range of contexts where face-to-face interaction is still central.

Diffuse Responsibility with Individual Initiative and Endeavour

Tourism activity to and at destination locations involves a wide range of people who, because of the part-time, seasonal and relatively ephemeral nature of their employment, as well as the individuals' own residential and career mobility, may have multiple loyalties and responsibilities and a need to weigh up trade-offs. Let us consider three similar, but ethically contrasting, tourism employment roles.

The tour representative

The tour representative ('rep') usually works on behalf of a mass package/inclusive holiday company, and is based in a particular resort/hotel complex. As such, 'reps' come into first contact with tourists when they meet and greet them on the tourists' arrival at the destination airport. After the first day or morning's information meeting with the new group, contact may be sporadic and specific – for example, if a particular problem arises that requires local resolution. But a 'rep's' key role, and the function of the introductory 'get-together' is to sell as many excursions and other company products as possible. The 'rep' may be working on a bonus or percentage, or may even suffer a penalty if, for example, a certain quota of excursions is not sold.

Thus the tour representative's first loyalty is to the company. If the representative originates from the local area, region or destination country, they may also feel a loyalty towards local hoteliers, traders and residents. This may place a sense of responsibility towards the tourists notionally in the representative's charge a relatively poor third.

The tour guide

Usually a tour guide is based in a particular place or region (such as a historic city like York, Florence or Cuzco), has detailed, often specialist local knowledge and is in possession of a professionally recognized qualification or training experience, such as the UK Blue Badge. As such, the tour guide may engage any group of tourists for a relatively short time.

As a person with valuable specific knowledge and experience, the tour guide may often be working independently on a freelance basis and/or for a locally based organization contracted by visiting tour companies and groups. While providing a professional, well-informed service that has the ability to greatly enhance or diminish visitors' experience, often simply through the guide's personality and communication skills, the individual concerned may often feel a prime loyalty to the local area, its residents and employees. This attachment to place can positively enhance the service provided in bringing alive the local cultural and natural environment. But, paradoxically, the guide may feel little attachment or commitment to the individual tourists who benefit, often briefly, from their guiding expertise.

The tour leader

Also variously referred to as a tour escort or tour manager, a tour leader's roles are characterized by a finer balance of interests than those of either the tour 'rep' or the tour guide.

This is not least because this person travels with the group they are leading, and may be closely interacting with them for up to several weeks at a time. This reflects the fact that the tour leader will normally accompany a group for the whole journey/holiday, acting as an escort, guide, and source of information, assistance and reassurance for the tour group both collectively and individually. It is a role that combines the spontaneity of the tour 'rep's' role with some degree of the knowledge and experience held by tour guides, but often spread across a much wider geographical context (such as the routes of the Trans-Siberian railway or treks across major wildernesses).

The tour leader acts as an intermediary and liaison within and between several actors: the tour company and destination tourist organizations, the tour company and its clients on the tour, destination tourist organizations and tour guides and the tour group, and members of the tour group themselves (Fig. 7.1). Such an ambassadorial role can be important in terms of how the tour leader is seen to represent the tour company, the country of origin and the tourism industry, particularly in areas with little experience or history of visitors. This means trying to ensure that tour members follow the behaviour codes both of the society being visited and of the company, if it has them. This locates significant responsibility on the shoulders of the tour leader, who needs to discharge it with tact and diplomacy. An often-vulnerable position of responsibility coupled to a limited degree of authority is well exemplified in a range of facilitating roles that may be required. These include:

- *travel arrangements*: checking, collecting and processing tickets; liaising with local transport operatives (e.g. coach drivers), or perhaps driving;
- *accommodation arrangements*: checking in, relaying the group's individual and collective needs, overseeing the allocation of rooms (and room types), checking facilities and food requirements (see Box 7.3);
- *border crossing arrangements*: collecting passports, pre-checking visas, liaising

Fig. 7.1. Albania: tour group, Albturist bus and, in the left foreground, the local guide, an English teacher. At the time he was suffering from a bad headache and the tour leader's role included providing him with a steady supply of aspirin.

Box 7.3. The tour guide: balancing welfare and responsibility.

One of the authors, working as a tour guide with a group travelling on the southern arm of the Trans-Siberian express departing from Ulan Bator in Mongolia en route to China, was party to a 90-min, often heated discussion between seven tour leaders of six different nationalities. We were negotiating the allocation of times and logistics for meal sittings for a total of 150 tourists from our seven groups over the next 24 h, in a Chinese restaurant car which could only seat 32 people at a time (Fig. 7.2), with relatively slow meal service, other train passengers to consider and a managerial staff whose common language with the tour leaders was severely limited.

with border authorities, acting as intermediary in disputes, overseeing currency exchange arrangements, which may often take place in the middle of the night.

That tourism and travel are dependent upon so many and diverse individuals in a range of working contexts and holiday environments is both an inherent strength

Fig. 7.2. Chinese restaurant car and tour group on the Trans-Siberian (Mongolian) express.

and weakness of the sector, and it underpins much of what follows in this chapter. Personal contact and individual responsibility help to mediate and ameliorate corporate diktat; they can bring vitality and empathy to visitor experience, but can also, often for positive and altruistic, and sometimes necessary, reasons, transgress mission statements and codes of practice.

Ethical Codes

In response to the criticisms of tourist and tourism company behaviour, from the late 1970s, and encouraged by external pressure groups, the tourism industry began establishing minimum standards of behaviour and practice. As noted in Chapter 1, it became fashionable for firms to create codes of conduct or ethics codes, comprising lists of what they believed to be ethical behaviour (Table 7.4). The three key guiding principles for codes of conduct and behaviour for tourists have been stated frequently as: understanding the culture visited, respecting

and being sensitive to the host population and treading softly on the host environment. Several popular works have aimed to reinforce this message by encouraging 'responsibility' amongst tourists and travellers (e.g. Community Aid Abroad, 1990; Anscombe, 1991; Graham, 1991; Wood and House, 1991; Elkington and Hailes, 1992; Burbank, 1994).

Yet we also noted in Chapter 1 that Malloy and Fennell (1998b), who analysed 414 individual ethical statements from 40 tourism codes of ethics, found that 77% of these merely provided injunctions. These codes did not inform stakeholders of the reasons why they should abide by certain guidelines, thereby failing to locate and explain the nature of stakeholder responsibility. Indeed, while key factors have included the monitoring, take-up and effectiveness of such codes, a wide range of critical issues has emerged over the past decade and a half (Table 7.5).

Codes can provide tour operators with an opportunity to highlight best practice as

Table 7.4. Examples of codes of conduct (from Weeden, 2005: 239–240).

Organization	Title of code
ABTA	Traveller's Code
ECTWT	Code of Ethics for Tourism
responsibletravel.com	Tips for Responsible Travellers
RSPB	Code of Conduct for Birdwatchers
RSPCA	Fun in the Sun – or is it?
Survival for Tribal Peoples	Danger Tourists
Tearfund	Suggested Actions for Tourists
Tourism Concern	Goingtravelling
	The Himalayan Tourist Code
UNEP	Environmental Codes of Conduct for Tourism
VSO	Every Holiday has Hidden Extras Below the Surface
WTO	Global Code of Ethics for Tourism
	Tourism Bill of Rights
WTTC	The WTTC's Environmental Guidelines
WWF	Code of Conduct for Mediterranean Tourists
	Ten Principles for Arctic Tourism
	Code of Conduct for Tour Operators in the Arctic
	Code of Conduct for Tourists in the Arctic

RSPB, Royal Society for the Protection of Birds; RSPCA, Royal Society for the Prevention of Cruelty to Animals; UNEP, United Nations Environment Programme; VSO, Voluntary Service Overseas; WWF, Worldwide Fund for Nature.

Table 7.5. Critical issues for tourism ethical codes (from D'Amore, 1993; Wheeller, 1994b: 651; Mason and Mowforth, 1996; Payne and Dimanche, 1996; Mowforth and Munt, 1998: 216–217; Fennell, 1999, 2000; Farrell *et al.*, 2002a; Stark, 2002; Weeden, 2005: 234).

1.   They have emanated in such numbers from such a wide range of sources (Table 7.4) that their intrinsic worth has been devalued. Unless there is better coordination of and consistency between codes, there is the danger of confusing and conflicting messages continuing to be communicated. A dilution of their power through the ubiquity of their application can render such codes counterproductive.

2.   The production of codes within the tourism industry has often taken place as a result of external pressure rather than from spontaneous self-regulation. This move has been as a 'palliative to the pressure exerted by the environmental lobby and in anticipation of potential criticism' (Mowforth and Munt, 1998: 216), or even in response to actual negative publicity, in order to protect the name of the business.

3.   Despite their availability for a decade and a half, evidence of their take-up and impact appears limited, and there are virtually no data available on the effectiveness of codes of ethics in tourism. Indeed, an absence of enquiry holds true with respect to applied ethics generally.

4.   Once established, the ethical purpose of a code may be subordinated to the role of a marketing rather than a monitoring tool, serving as an attractor to self-perceived discerning and critical customers seeking an ethically comforting holiday experience by adding apparent quality and appeal to the product.

5.   Few codes offer measurable criteria or conform to a widely accepted set of standards.

6.   The existence of a code is, of course, no guarantee of ethical behaviour on the part of the company. It may act merely to state a company's legal responsibilities and the conduct it expects from its employees, rather than enumerating any ethical principles and aspirations that its management holds or aspires to. An analysis of a range of codes for ecotourism found that their real-life applications were limited by an overemphasis on the notion of 'rational trust'.

well as educating the consumer with regard to their expected behaviour. This was one of the reasons that the World Travel and Tourism Council (WTTC) established a database of codes of conduct for the travel and tourism industry. Yet what is really needed is an appropriate reference system that can help improve industry credibility (Mowforth and Munt, 1998: 217). At present, intending travellers and analysts are left posing a series of almost rhetorical questions: how have such codes been established? By which agency and in whose interests? For what purpose and for whom (Box 7.4)? Are such guidelines designed to be universal, or specific to a given region (Miller, 2001) or activity? Who, if anyone, monitors them? For example, Garrod and Fennell (2004) evaluated 58 whale-watching codes and found considerable variation among them. This was not considered to be propitious for the sustainable development of this activity, particularly in view of both how little is known about the nature of human–cetacean interactions and the complex and fragmentary regulatory context in which it takes place.

Within the tourism industry, therefore, one can perhaps argue with some justification that codes of practice and conduct often appear to have been employed to deflect responsibility from company management either to employees or, more especially, to tourists. That is not to argue that tourists should be absolved of responsibility for their behaviour in destination environments. But it suggests that codes of behaviour drawn up for tourists (although often not by tourists or with such 'stakeholder' representation) may reflect an element of lateral displacement of responsibility both from tourism companies and from host destination authorities.

D'Sa (1999) has argued, largely in relation to the impact of tourism on poorer countries (Chapter 5), that a global code of ethics, as evolved by the World Tourism Organization (Box 7.5 and Table 7.6), will only tinker with the imperialistic nature of tourism, the roots of which lie in a profit-driven, global economic system that disregards social costs and is, of course, much larger than the tourism industry.

Box 7.4. Cracking codes?

Intuitively, at least in some parts of the world, the whale-watching industry has developed a select number of guidelines to control the effects of its operations (e.g. keep at least 100 m away from whales; and when leaving the whales move 300 m away before increasing speed). No doubt these recommendations ease tensions that exist between man and beast. But are they established on the basis of hard empirical data? What are the effects, for example, of being 90 m away from whales?

Such codes are normatively accepted by the industry for the purpose of helping to bring further credibility to this form of tourism. But are the guidelines for the benefit of the whales, for the consciences of the tourists or for the legitimacy – or the perceived legitimacy – of the tourism industry?

Obee (1998) reports from British Columbia that witnesses have spotted over 100 tourist boats around a pod of 21 killer whales. The human response to this might be that such behaviour represents gross misconduct by tour operators. Yet, employing data supported by animal behaviourists, Obee contends that such traffic and the noise generated do not seem to affect whales, thereby explaining why at times they will approach research vessels with apparent curiosity. Some experts conclude that because whales continue to frequent the same locales, in spite of operators' boats and local people, who often steer their boats among whales, they appear not to be disturbed sufficiently to interrupt their feeding or migratory patterns. The issue with the whales may have become not one of animal harassment, but rather one of visitor perception.

Box 7.5. Antecedent frameworks for the WTO Global Code of Ethics.

1. Universal Declaration of Human Rights, 1948
2. International Covenant on Economic, Social and Cultural Rights, 1996
3. International Covenant on Civil and Political Rights, 1996
4. Warsaw Convention on Air Transport, 1929
5. Chicago Convention on International Civil Aviation, 1944, and the Tokyo, The Hague and Montreal Conventions in relation thereto
6. Convention on Customs Facilities for Tourism, 1954, and related Protocol
7. Convention concerning the Protection of the World Cultural and Natural Heritage, 1972
8. Manila Declaration on World Tourism, 1980
9. Resolution of the Sixth General Assembly of WTO (Sofia) adopting the Tourism Bill of Rights and Tourist Code, 1985
10. Convention on the Rights of the Child, 1989
11. Resolution of the Ninth General Assembly of WTO (Buenos Aires) concerning in particular travel facilitation and the safety and security of tourists, 1991
12. Rio Declaration on the Environment and Development, 1992
13. General Agreement on Trade in Services, 1994
14. Convention on Biodiversity, 1995
15. Resolution of the Eleventh General Assembly of WTO (Cairo) on the prevention of organized sex tourism, 1995
16. Stockholm Declaration Against the Commercial Sexual Exploitation of Children, 1996
17. Manila Declaration on the Social Impact of Tourism, 1997
18. Conventions and recommendations adopted by the International Labour Organization in the area of collective conventions, prohibition of forced labour and child labour, defence of the rights of indigenous peoples and equal treatment and non-discrimination in the workplace.

Source: WTO, 2001.

According to Weeden (2005: 235), the WTO Global Code can be interpreted as a frame of reference for the responsible and sustainable development of world tourism. But the Code stops short of advocating 'ethical tourism' and instead uses the term 'responsible tourism'. We would argue that ethics and responsibility complement each other. Ryan (2002: 17) suggests this is because, although tour operators might agree with principles underlying demands for an ethical approach to tourism development, it will be difficult to implement them because of the 'complex and pragmatic issues of management'.

Others have questioned the appropriateness of a code of ethics for tourism, arguing that the sector is based on service rather than a physical good, which does

Table 7.6. Summary of the WTO Global Code of Ethics (from WTO, 2001).

Article	Number of Paragraphs	Themes
1.	6	Tourism's contribution to mutual understanding and respect between peoples and societies: understanding and promotion of 'the ethical values common to humanity'; tourism should be conducted in harmony with destination attributes and traditions; the industry and destinations should be acquainted with and respect their tourists, for whom public authorities should provide protection; for their part, visitors should respect the law and have the responsibility to acquaint themselves with destination characteristics before their visit.
2.	5	Tourism as a vehicle for individual and collective fulfilment: it should be planned and practised as a privileged means of individual and collective fulfilment; activities 'should respect the equality of men and women', promote human rights and especially the individual rights of vulnerable groups; exploitation is the negation of tourism; the benefits of tourism should be included in education curricula.
3.	5	Tourism is a factor of sustainable development: all stakeholders should safeguard the natural environment; priority should be given to conserving 'rare and precious resources'; tourist flows should be staggered in time and space; tourism infrastructure and activities should be designed to protect the natural heritage; 'nature tourism and ecotourism are recognised as being particularly conducive to enriching and enhancing the standing of tourism'.
4.	4	Tourism, a user of the cultural heritage of mankind and a contributor to its enhancement: 'tourism resources belong to the common heritage of mankind [but] the communities in whose territories they are situated have particular rights and obligations to them'; tourism should respect and protect cultural sites, and should encourage traditional cultural products.
5.	4	Tourism as a beneficial activity for host countries and communities: 'local populations should be associated with tourism activities and share equitably in the economic, social and cultural benefits'; tourism should raise destinations' standard of living, with special attention to vulnerable and peripheral regions; tourism impact studies and information should precede development.
6.	6	Obligations of stakeholders in tourism development: responsibilities of the tourism industry in providing information and protection, public authorities for assistance in difficult circumstances, government to protect and warn of dangers, and the media to provide balanced information, and not promote sex tourism.
7.	4	Right to tourism: a universal right equally open to all, requiring a 'reasonable limitation of working hours and periodic holidays with pay'; social tourism should be developed.
8.	5	Liberty of tourist movements: there should be geographical, monetary and informational access, subject to international and national law.
9.	6	Rights of the workers and entrepreneurs in the tourism industry: guaranteed fundamental rights, including training, social protection, 'limited job insecurity', a 'specific status' for seasonal workers; 'multinational enterprises of the tourism industry should not exploit the dominant positions they sometimes occupy . . . they should involve themselves in local development'.
10.	3	Implementation of the principles of the Global Code of Ethics for Tourism: public and private stakeholders should cooperate, 'the stakeholders in tourism development should recognise the role of international institutions, among which the World Tourism Organisation ranks first', and NGOs; disputes should be referred to ('an impartial third body') the World Committee on Tourism Ethics.

Box 7.6. Welfare, ethics and outsourcing.

To reduce costs, British Airways (BA) contracted out a number of its ancillary services in the 1990s, including its in-flight catering arm, which it sold to Swissair in 1997. BA has continued to pursue cost reductions, squeezing its suppliers and forcing down contracted prices. Contract suppliers in their turn have faced some difficult decisions. In the case of Gate Gourmet, BA's prime in-flight catering supplies contractor for its Heathrow services, the company sacked 670 (mainly local Punjabi women) workers in August 2005, replacing them with lower-paid agency recruits from Eastern Europe and Somalia.

Many of the BA Heathrow baggage handlers and drivers who took part in an illegal 36-h walk-out in sympathy with the sacked women were their husbands and sons. Until BA contracted out its catering they all worked together. BA services were severely disrupted for a third successive August, with some 70,000 passengers stranded.

'BA's loss of £40m (and probably a lot more in future custom) should become a business-school exemplar on how the subcontracting culture can bring down a company' (Toynbee, 2005).

Gate Gourmet, which employs 22,000 people worldwide, was already in financial trouble, although controlled by the venture-capital giant Texas Pacific Group (owner of Burger King), who took it over when Swissair collapsed.

From BA's perspective, such outsourcing, through focusing on 'core competences', increases reported return on assets by reducing assets on the balance sheet, and raises revenues per employee by reducing the direct workforce. Thus share value is assisted while costs are driven down. But suppliers' margins cannot be squeezed indefinitely, and the welfare consequences of this example of a major global travel company passing on apparent responsibility saw the loss of employment for 670 women.

Sources: Caulkin, 2005; Milmo and Stevenson 2005; Toynbee, 2005.

not lend itself to standardization or control (Fleckenstein and Huebsch, 1999). Additionally, the holiday product is problematic because of its complexity. The length of the supply chain and the difficulty of trying to persuade subcontractors to adopt common ethical standards represent major logistical and ideological problems for operators who wish to pursue an ethical policy.

Ethical underpinning represents a systematic, if not systemic, approach, rather than a niche, and the term 'ethical' may be too fundamental and too personal for many businesses to apply it publicly to their activities (Weeden, 2005: 241). None the less, there is growing evidence that some mass market operators, such as First Choice and British Airways, are adopting 'sustainable' policies within their corporate objectives (Mintel, 2001) (but see Box 7.6).

There exist some good models of responsible industry behaviour. Details are shown in Box 7.7.

Holistic Responsibility?

A holistic approach to tourism welfare means that a responsible, ethically based approach taken by one set of stakeholders can only be effective if matched by an equally responsible approach pursued by the others (Box 7.8).

As noted in Chapter 3, the issue of health and safety advice to tourists is complicated by a range of factors. These include the age and health status of each individual, the destination, duration of stay, season, type of activities undertaken, shifts in current preventive and prophylactic prescriptions, and a range of local conditions that have a significant influence on the level of risk. As such, responsibility for such advice and its adoption is shared by a range of actors. There is an obvious conflict between the need for travel companies to remain competitive in pricing and to uphold their responsibility to protect the health and safety of their clients. Hunter-Jones (2000) found weaknesses and confusion among the various parties involved in the provision and taking of a holiday concerning the extent of their particular responsibilities. Walker and Page (2003) call for visitor well-being management at destinations to be better appreciated within the industry. They advocate the development of partnerships for this, particularly between tour operators and destination managers.

Box 7.7. The Responsible Tourism Awards.

The Responsible Tourism Awards, initiated in 2004, recognize companies and organizations in the travel industry that are deemed to be making a significant commitment to responsible tourism – that is, 'projects which make a positive contribution to conservation and the economies of local communities while minimizing the negative impacts that tourism can have' (Holliday, 2004).

Awards are made in ten categories organized by the online travel agent responsibletravel.com, in association with *The Times* (London) newspaper, World Travel Market (the annual UK tourism and travel promotion fair organized by Reed Elsevier) and *Geographical Magazine* (published by Campion Inter-active Publishing on behalf of the Royal Geographical Society with the Institute of British Geographers).

For the 2004 awards, the winners were chosen from more than 700 nominations sent in by readers of *Geographical Magazine* and *The Times* and visitors to responsibletravel.com's website, who were asked to identify holidays and tourism organizations that provided an enjoyable and responsible travel experience.

According to Justin Francis, managing director of responsibletravel.com, the awards 'reflect the changing agenda in responsible travel, away from focusing solely on the environment. "The judges were looking for travel companies that are not only eco-friendly, but also make a positive contribution to the economies of local communities"' (Hammond, 2005: 98).

Calabash Lodge and Tours of Port Elizabeth, South Africa, was chosen as joint overall winner because of its contribution to the township community. It had recently qualified for a Fair Trade in Tourism South Africa trademark (FITSA), a movement that encourages 'socially conscious' tourism in that country by recognizing tourism companies that use 'fair and responsible practices'. The key principles of FITSA are that companies ensure fair wages and working conditions for their staff, ethical business practice, and respect for human rights, culture and the environment.

Three other companies were highly commended in the 'Best for Poverty Reduction' category for their 'commitment to ensuring local communities benefit from tourism':

- Kahawa Shamba Kilimanjaro Native Cooperative Union, which offers coffee growers an alternative income through the organization and operation of tours in the Kilimanjaro area;
- Santa Lucia Eco-lodge in Ecuador, which has provided income to the local community by managing ecotourism; and
- Makasutu Cultural Forest in The Gambia, which has provided 150 jobs for local people in an area of high unemployment.

The second joint overall winner was Exodus Travel, which also won the 'Best Operator' award. The company has developed over 30 years to organize small-group holidays in 80 countries, including cycling and walking tours, overland, cultural and extreme sports trips. The company was singled out 'for integrating responsible tourism throughout its business . . . Where possible the company buys local produce and uses local services' (Hammond, 2005: 101).

The winner of the 'Best Accommodation' category was Casuarina Beach Club in Barbados, the largest employer of disabled people in Barbados. The club pays retired or unemployed people to repair elderly or disabled people's homes throughout Barbados. The chefs prepare and deliver food to 20 poor families every night. Guests also contribute to poverty alleviation in Barbados by purchasing voluntary organization bookmarks for $50 (<http://www.casuarina.com>).

In the UK, Hilton Hotels' environmental sustainability training programme was given highly commended status: launched in 2004, it involves the training of all 15,000 employees to raise awareness on how to reduce impact on the environment. The company publicly set a target to reduce utility consumption across properties in the UK and Ireland by 10% by 2006. All 78 UK and Ireland Hiltons have now created their own action plans, listing a total of 780 separate actions to be carried out.

Responsibletravel.com, one of the main sponsors of the awards, is backed by Body Shop, and sells holidays from around 200 travel firms, each of which needs to fulfil a series of criteria relating to codes of conduct, use of local suppliers, provision of advice on the social and political situation in each destination and advice to staff and customers on reducing the negative impacts they make (see also *The Observer* and Responsibletravel.com, 2005).

Perhaps the value of the awards is twofold:

- to act as a monitor of good (and bad) practice (there should also be an 'anti-award' or wooden spoon prize for poor performance); and
- to encourage long-term commitment within the industry of both large and small companies.

Sources: Clark, 2004: 344; Holliday, 2004; Hammond, 2005; with additions.

Box 7.8. Locating responsibility, responsibly?

In July 2005, as a series of walkouts among Italian air traffic controllers began, Ryanair, the largest carrier between Italy and the UK, called on its passengers to lobby the Italian authorities in protest at the disruption caused.

To coincide with the industrial action, Ryanair posted on its website a link to the site of ENAV, the Italian air navigation services agency. The budget airline's chief executive, Michael O'Leary, was characteristically direct in expressing his sense of responsibility. He was quoted as saying:

> They just go on strike routinely . . . So instead of passengers getting annoyed at us, we've said 'Here, contact the idiots who are supposed to run the service in Italy' and complain directly to them. These people live in ivory towers and don't hear often enough from the people they screw around all the time.

Source: Anon., 2005b.

Box 7.9. An example of private enterprise response to the need for training in travel health and welfare.

Adventure Lifesigns runs expedition care programmes both for adults joining the company's expeditions and for school groups. These teach the basics of first aid in a wilderness environment in 1-, 2- and 4-day courses. After successful completion, participants are awarded a (UK) Health and Safety Executive-approved certificate that is valid for 3 years. This is considered appropriate for anyone about to embark on a long overland trip, for gap-year students heading for jungles and deserts, and for those who simply want to keep safe on their travels.

Useful acronyms and mnemonics
Learning how to carry out an initial assessment of a casualty requires DRAB: assess for danger, check response, airway and breathing.
RICE reminds the trainee to treat soft tissue injuries with rest, ice, compression and elevation.

Practical advice to bear in mind
Falling coconuts are the biggest hazard on beaches (but not in Scotland).

You have more chance of someone coming to your aid in London if you shout 'fire!' rather than 'help!'

Coat mosquito nets with permethrin.
Suffocate a tick with Vaseline.
Apply vinegar or urine to a jellyfish sting.
If bitten by a poisonous beast, keep the bite lower than the line of the heart.

Sources: Noon, 2004; Adventure Lifesigns, 2005a, b, c.

Medical advice is probably best given by qualified personnel, and yet often no one source can address the diverse needs of the traveller (Cossar, 1996). Certainly Wilks *et al.* (2003) argue that travel agencies provide inconsistent health and safety information. They recommend that agencies should pursue appropriate continuing education and in-service training for their staff, both to keep pace with legal requirements and to add value to travel agencies' contributions.

Certainly, tourists have the right to receive information that is timely and sufficiently detailed to allow considered and informed travel decisions (Sharpley *et al.*, 1996; see also Chapter 3), an important ethical issue some observers place within the broader sustainable tourism debate (Ahmed *et al.*, 1994). Hobson and Dietrich (1994) argued that, if the tourism industry was going to adopt a responsible attitude towards its customers, then it had to take the initiative in areas such as health advice, or standards might need to be imposed from outside.

Individual tourist responsibility is, of course, critical in two ways. First, it is important to seek out from as many sources as necessary the most appropriate information required, for example on anti-malaria prophylaxis. Second, as Cartwright (2000) highlights, tourists need to ensure that they do not expose themselves to unnecessary risks. For those planning more adventurous activities, a wide range of short courses on various aspects of travel health and survival are now available (e.g. Box 7.9).

In the case of sunburn, Carter (1997b) highlights the irony that protective strategies appear to be unproblematic and easily adopted by tourists. In practice, however, often they are not adopted because of the continuing (if declining) social and cultural desirability of a suntan and confusion about key elements of protection, such as use of suncreams. While reinforcing this, Peattie *et al.* (2005) point out that health promotion strategies to encourage sun-safe behaviour typically rely on either providing knowledge about risks and protective behaviour or instilling fear through graphic images of the consequences, and sometimes both.

The long-term health risks that sunburn poses for tourists are significant, and the tourism industry needs to respond appropriately. The Anti-Cancer Council of Victoria (ACCV, 2003) has predicted that the increasing willingness of people to litigate could result in a growth in legal actions linked to sunburn and skin cancer. It highlights, somewhat pessimistically, tourism as a sector whose values are at odds with the promotion of sun-safety: an industry essentially motivated by profit rather than health concerns (ACCV, 2003), such that it cannot be relied upon to maintain a sun protection focus.

Whether the tourism industry has helped to create a demand for suntans or whether it has simply acted to meet that demand is a subject likely to create an inconclusive debate (Peattie *et al.*, 2005). What is clear is that annually the industry moves millions of people from environments in which the risks posed by sunburn are relatively low into ones in which they are relatively high. Ryan and Robertson (1997) found that over half of their sample of young New Zealand student travellers had been burnt while vacationing. These were tourists coming from the society in which awareness about the need to practise sun-safety is probably greatest. The vulnerabilities of those coming from cultures where awareness is lower and where demand for sunshine holidays is likely to be highest are a major cause for concern. This has significant implications in terms of those travellers' health and safety and raises important questions about who is responsible for their welfare and what action should be taken.

It is perhaps tempting for those within tourism to rely upon the law for guidance as to their responsibilities in relation to protecting consumers from health and safety risks. For example, within the UK's Package Travel, Package Holidays and Package Tours Regulations (SI 1992/3288) (based on EU regulations), the contractual responsibilities of operators include a provision that the vendor must provide in writing information about health formalities required for the journey and the stay. This establishes the principle that operators should be responsible for alerting consumers to the health issues involved in tourism, but, because of its narrow focus on diseases and on health formalities, it can fall short of addressing the realities of health risks within particular destinations.

Progress towards making tourism more sun-safe is likely to be slow if it depends upon legal definitions and responsibilities. The time lag between sun exposure and long-term health impacts makes causality hard to prove. Operators can argue that the consumer has effectively consented to the risk by choosing to book a holiday to a sunny destination. But Peattie *et al.* (2005) point to possible parallels with the tobacco industry, as one based on an individual pleasure voluntarily consumed, which was subject to discoveries about long-term health impacts and particularly the increased risk of cancer. After first being forced by regulation to communicate the risks clearly and alter the nature of their marketing communications, tobacco companies have found themselves subject to a barrage of legal actions from previous customers and even 'passive smokers'. The demonstration effect of industrial health and safety law suits being brought against employers in a number of countries on the basis of a failure to adequately protect their employees against the risks of sun overexposure may encourage similar cases brought against tour operators by customers.

Responsible marketing

To circumvent this and to pursue a more appropriate path to improved sun-safety within tourism, tour operators need to take a more proactive, voluntary approach. Peattie *et al.* (2005: 406) pose the question as to what the response would be to:

> a holiday brochure promoting holidays for teenagers which was filled with images of teenagers drinking to excess, experimenting with drugs, riding motorbikes without helmets and rock-climbing without safety equipment. The ensuing uproar would focus on the irresponsibility of promoting images of tourism behaviours that are likely to lead to self-harm.

They argue that the same charge could be laid against tourism brochure images of people being overexposed to the sun. The only significant difference between this and the other forms of risk-taking behaviour is that the potential consequences of sun exposure will not be immediate. Like these other forms of risk, however, one single incidence of unsafe behaviour could be the one that leads to later fatality.

This issue poses an interesting ethical dilemma for tourism marketing. The marketing of 'summer sun' holidays is the mainstay of the tourism industry, but it is clear that this product does constitute a very real health threat to customers. Such a threat for the industry has, until recently, appeared to be a case of 'the consequence of which we dare not speak'. Part of the problem is perhaps the wide range of individuals and agencies with potential responsibilities in this area of welfare protection (Table 7.7). This fragmentation re-emphasizes the fact that such issues need to be tackled in partnership with public policymakers, health providers and health educators within both tourist source and destination areas. The challenge for tourism is 'to deal responsibly with a risk which is entwined in a very fundamental way with the values, products and marketing approaches of the industry' (Peattie *et al.*, 2005: 407).

As regulatory frameworks tighten, responsible tourism marketing (Hudson and Miller, 2005) is likely to be subjected to increasing media scrutiny. As noted in Chapter 4, in the case of both the Australian Gold Coast and seaside resorts of southwest England, certain marketing ploys may

(unwittingly) encourage antisocial behaviour and indirectly contribute to a negative image of the destination being promoted, to the detriment of local residents and workers as well as visitors.

Symbolic Power or Powerlessness?

Perhaps much of this raises the question of whether, overall, the tourism industry actually wields any power and can realistically be a force for global welfare enhancement through deliberate policies and explicit acts. Despite the oft-quoted obfuscating filters of industry fragmentation and overlap/interdependence with a range of other change processes, are we able to discern specific outcomes that can be directly attributed to the organization and objectives of global tourism?

Superficially, there appears to be something of a paradox here, which only serves to emphasize what some view as the colonial, imperial role of global tourism. On the one hand, we are often told that tourism does not have a loud voice or representation in government in the tourism-generating, usually most developed, countries (e.g. McKercher, 1993b). This is perhaps reflected in the way in which 'tourism', if it is explicitly named at all, may be located within different state departments and ministries in different countries and may even be moved from one to another over time. This perhaps reflects three realities:

- that governments view the role of tourism in different ways and from different perspectives, reflecting tourism's multifaceted nature – encompassing employment, regional development, trade, foreign policy, social welfare, leisure, culture, transport, environment;
- that, as a corollary, tourism does not present a coherent image or functional role within government and, as a consequence, it is seen as ancillary or even marginal; and
- that as a consequence of such marginality and ephemerality, the politicians finding themselves in the roles of handling tourism within government tend to

Table 7.7. Sources of responsibility and potential action to promote sun-safety (from Segan *et al.*, 1999; Bränström *et al.*, 2003; Peattie *et al.*, 2005; with additions).

Sources of responsibility	Potential action
Travel agents	Highlight sun-safety information in brochures and elsewhere.
Holiday brochures	Include information on representative burn times alongside figures on average hours of sunshine for each destination.
Airlines	Include general warnings with the health and safety section, and place specific warnings tied to destination articles in in-flight magazines.
	Include warnings and information in audio-visual presentations on longer flights.
	Supplement children's entertainment packs with a sun-safe, 'legionnaire'-style cap (rather than a baseball cap) and a tube of suncream and include basic sun-safety educational material within the activity books, to provide an instant sun-safety kit.
Hotels and resorts	Post burn-time warnings and include sunscreen as part of the complimentary toiletries.
	Burn times and protection advice could be highlighted more as part of weather forecast information.
	Offer facilities and activities that provide shade, as well as opportunities for sun exposure, particularly during the middle of the day.
	Provide training to alert staff to risks and risk factors, particularly in relation to children, and to encourage them to intervene when they see people at risk.
Public policymakers	Communicate the message about the need to practise sun-safety when visiting sunny destinations.
	Provision of information leaflets at home and destination airports and other entry points, and on appropriate websites: e.g. the US State Department records 150,000 visits a day to its website for travellers <http://travel.state.gov>
Health professionals	Focus more on skin cancer prevention in patient advice in both tourist source and destination areas.
Pharmaceutical companies	Promote use of suncreams/sunscreens through sponsorship of events and activities at sunny destinations.
Tourists	Use personal UV exposure indicators where available.
	Employ common sense, particularly setting an example of safe behaviour if travelling with children.

be second-rate functionaries and at best low-level ministers, such that the voices of the tourism industry may not be best heard, interpreted and relayed through their offices.

To use a UK example, the neglect of rural tourism businesses in England and Wales by government in the aftermath of the 2001/2 foot-and-mouth disease outbreak is a prime and oft-cited example of a consequence of this positioning (e.g. Sharpley and Craven, 2001; Sharpley, 2003; Butler and Airey, 2005).

Indeed, even within the European Commission, while tourism is lauded as one of the most significant and vibrant of economic activities as well as bringing social, cultural and environmental benefits, there exists no separate commissioner for tourism. Instead, tourism forms one unit within the Enterprise Directorate-General, where it competes for resources with such sectors as aerospace and automotives, defence, pharmaceuticals and textiles (Coles and Hall, 2005).

On the other hand, in less developed countries, where tourism may play a much more significant role in a region's or country's economy, the power and influence of tourism, derived externally and/or from within, may be great. In the context of Barbados, for example, Pugh (2003) invokes the concept of symbolic power to illustrate this reality, drawing on a relatively local example. Symbolic power is:

> a legitimating form of power which involves the consent or active complicity of both dominant and dominated actors. Dominated actors are not passive bodies to whom power is applied, but rather people who believe in both the legitimacy of the power and the legitimacy of those who wield it. Bourdieu (1977) regards symbolic power as 'worldmaking power' due to its capacity to impose a legitimised vision of the social world.
>
> (Hillier and Rooksby, 2002: 8)

In Barbados, there appears to have been a 'democratic' consensual approach to the work of the National Commission for Sustainable Development (NCSD). Yet a draft sustainable development policy prepared by the NCSD in 1998, notionally the product of participatory procedures, did not include measures to control the direct environmental impacts of tourism because of the underlying role of its symbolic power. It was 'agreed' that tourism should not be questioned, despite the fact that all interest groups on the NCSD were supposed to discuss the environmental effects of each other's activities (Pugh, 2003: 128).

Further, the symbolic power of tourism was so strong that many members of the tourism sector did not feel the need to attend meetings of the NCSD, knowing that their actions would not be seriously questioned or checked by the Commission. Pugh (2003: 128) quotes one member of the Barbados Hotel and Tourism Association as saying 'we've got the money, contacts and public support to pretty much do what we want . . . why would we bother with such a small committee?' While one member of the NCSD said in an interview: 'this is Barbados . . . tourism gets special treatment, and I believe that it should . . . tourism is our bread and butter'. For Pugh (2003: 129),

the effects of the symbolic power of tourist interest groups therefore mean that stable power relations are far more common than outright conflict on the NCSD. This creates the impression of rational consensus, where in fact the embodied and unconscious effects of symbolic power are really at work below the surface. Thus, the effects of symbolic power are important in giving the impression that participatory planning is successful in producing rational results.

Such an ambivalent role enables tourism industry associations to play Janus-faced within the still stark structural dichotomy of developed generating countries and less developed destination regions. The cruise industry offers a specific instance of this. The International Council of Cruise Lines (ICCL: see also Chapter 4), which represents most major North American cruise lines, pursues a policy, according to its website, whereby it 'educates Washington leaders on the important economic contribution that the cruise industry makes in the US'. This is despite the fact that, through incorporating companies offshore and flying foreign flags, ICCL member companies pay virtually no taxes in the USA (War on Want and ITF, 2002: 24). Cruise companies are also influential over other national and local governments and port authorities. In Panama, a country notoriously sympathetic to shipping companies to encourage them to register their vessels there, Carnival Line reportedly secured a change in the law so that the compulsory day off per week for crew was placed at the discretion of the employer (Klein, 2002).

The ICCL is also active in the International Maritime Organization (IMO), lobbying on behalf of its members on questions of safety, the environment and pollution. For example, the ICCL won against an IMO recommendation that all new passenger ships should have a helicopter landing pad, which would have aided search and rescue at sea and, presumably, the airlifting of passengers or crew needing urgent medical attention. As noted in Chapter 4, the welfare of crews (particularly from poorer countries) on cruise ships often leaves a great deal to be desired (War on Want and

ITF, 2002: 1–2). Notably, the 'Shipboard Workplace Code of Conduct' issued by the ICCL in 1999 did not incorporate workers' rights to freedom of association. It was promoted as a measure of its members' 'commitment to providing passengers and employees alike with the optimal levels of safety and security while cruising'. The code is entirely voluntary and no monitoring or verification procedures were put in place. But, although a far weaker instrument than negotiated union agreements, the code can provide an extra tool for exerting pressure on companies, especially the non-unionized lines such as Carnival and Disney (War on Want and ITF, 2002: 25).

Conclusions

In this chapter we have looked at the way in which the tourism and travel industry has reacted to perceived requirements for better ethical underpinning and a sense of responsibility for the welfare of the industry's stakeholders. The sector, or at least various elements of it, has adopted notions of corporate social responsibility, ethical codes of behaviour and conduct, and an explicit emphasis on awarding and publicizing 'responsible' approaches to business. Yet there remain many shortcomings and inconsistencies, which can have a negative effect on the welfare of tourists, tourism workers and destination residents and environments. These raise question marks over the industry's ability to sustain stakeholder well-being. In particular, they may cast doubt over the claims that tourism can be an important element in poverty-reducing development policies (Chapter 5).

In the following, concluding chapter, a summary of the preceding chapters acts as the context for offering a global perspective on the welfare implications of tourism.

8

Summary and Conclusions: Beyond Tourism

On pouvait difficilement voir dans le développement du tourisme mondiale l'équivalent d'une cause noble.

(Houellebecq, 2001: 296)

Box 8.1. Chapter aims and summary.

This chapter seeks to: summarize and conclude, highlighting the key themes and significance of the previous chapters.
It does this by: summarizing the key points of the previous chapters and offering conclusions relating to the aims and objectives established in Chapter 1. In placing a welfare-centred approach within a global context, it addresses interrelated issues of travel, climate change and global welfare and the future of tourism.
Its key concepts are: welfare, ethics, responsibility, sustainability, development, global futures.
It concludes that: global environmental welfare considerations now overshadow the future of tourism and travel: the industry and the wider global community need to act now.

This final chapter first summarizes the key points of the previous chapters before offering some conclusions relating to the aims and objectives established in Chapter 1. Throughout the book we have made the point that tourism is only one facet of much wider processes. Similarly, in any discussion of sustainability, however framed, a

holistic perspective is required. We therefore conclude by addressing the global welfare context of tourism through an examination of the damaging (and largely unacknowledged) effects of tourism-driven transport and travel, arguing that some difficult, unpalatable and urgent decisions need to be made. Such decisions, thus far, most politicians have been unwilling to address. Indeed, the tourism and travel industries barely acknowledge that there might be global questions that require responsible responses, but rather prefer to perpetuate marketing ploys and conscience-soothing palliatives. While acknowledging that the operation of our global economic system makes it difficult for this to be otherwise, we make recommendations that could help improve the welfare of tourism's various stakeholders.

Summary

We have aimed both to emphasize the welfare dimensions of tourism processes and to suggest ways in which the conceptual debate surrounding the nature and role of tourism development can be advanced by employing a welfare lens for analysis. We argued that considering the welfare of actors and environments can assist an identification and understanding of the relationships between the stakeholders and other actors in tourism processes.

In particular, we have tried to emphasize and exemplify how our conception of 'welfare' and a welfare-centred approach can offer an appropriate framework for a post-sustainability paradigm for tourism development. In Chapter 1 we argued that 'welfare' as a concept and concern is applicable to both mass and 'alternative' forms of tourism and their implications. In this sense it is 'mode-blind' and as such helps to draw us away from the divisive debates on the nature, applicability and value of 'sustainable' forms of tourism. We argued that there is a need to focus the debate on the impacts, (dis)benefits and implications of tourism development more firmly upon ethical dilemmas, the nature and location of responsibility and the welfare trade-offs and outcomes of these.

This led us to argue that, within this role, conceptions of welfare, to be meaningful, need to be underpinned by a set of clear ethical principles. These in their turn can highlight the fact that tourism development, or rather those involved in decision-taking processes within it, often confronts ethical dilemmas. Such an underpinning and the dilemmas that may arise demand from all tourism development stakeholders a recognition and acknowledgement of their responsibilities. Although responsible tourism has become yet another marketing cliché, the location of responsibility and accountability is critical in assisting the emergence of a more ethically based tourism, which can take a greater account, a more holistic view, of the welfare implications of its development processes.

Further, we argued that a welfare focus enables us to extend our frame of reference beyond that of human participants, to draw into our debate both non-human animals involved in providing tourism experiences for humans and the ecological contexts of those experiences.

Finally, Chapter 1 highlighted the way in which tourism has embraced health, wellness and well-being. Although such a trend may simply reflect good business and the adoption of fashionable terms to promote further niche products, it does exemplify a conscious attempt to relate tourism, in this case if only for tourists, to explicit notions of enhanced welfare.

A welfare-centred approach places tourism within its wider social and global context. If tourism participation is currently viewed as (potentially) enhancing quality of life, then such a welfare component should be accessible to all who need it. Chapter 2 therefore evaluated access to and participation in tourism and the barriers that may inhibit or prevent certain groups in society – and indeed certain societies – from participating. It concluded that:

- wider global inequalities are reflected in the balance of tourism participation being dominated by generation from developed countries and regions, with little or no participation taking place from the poorer countries;
- if wider participation in (international) tourism is a likely outcome of improving living standards in less developed countries, embracing the hundreds of millions of people living in Africa, Asia and Latin America, this is likely to place an (even more) unsustainable burden on the planet; and
- inequalities in access in generating countries, a theme that tends to dominate the emerging literature in this area, emphasize poverty and disability as major factors inhibiting participation, but often fail to bring the two together or to consider the ripple of impacts that the pressures of poverty and disability, separately or together, exert on a wide range of kin, carers and friends.

Thus, as academics, teachers, practitioners, tourists and commentators already drawn into tourism processes, we face a potential personal sense of hypocrisy:

- we feel it is appropriate to want to see tourism participation increased and access improved for those currently constrained from taking part;
- but, in contrast, we hesitate to contemplate the broadening of tourism participation (globally): (i) because of the

ethical dilemma it poses for the already threatened global environment; and (ii) because it also threatens our own (already unsustainable, over-consuming) privileges in access to and participation in tourism and travel activity.

In Chapter 3 we focused on tourists through the framework of a tourist welfare cycle. This represented a simple modification to the characterization of the stages tourists pass through, from contemplating and preparing for a holiday to the 'residuals' when having returned home. The chapter highlighted perceived shortcomings in information that reduce the potential welfare of travellers, particularly in terms of preventive measures to protect health. But the chapter also emphasized the personal responsibility all tourists have, both for their own welfare and for those with whom they come into contact, a theme taken up in subsequent chapters.

However, a perpetual theme of the book is the question of blurred or overlapping responsibilities and the fact that the relative weight of responsibilities falling on the shoulders of stakeholders varies according to the nature of the issue, the time and the place. In articulating this, the chapter highlighted the difficult question of skin cancer resulting from excessive sun exposure. The latter is a core activity for many tourists and thus a *raison d'être* for much of the industry, while the former, a condition that may not be detected for up to 30 years, is thus almost impossible to relate back to potential causal factors.

Chapter 4 focused on welfare aspects of living and working in tourism destinations. One of the much-touted mantras of sustainable tourism, that it needs to be predicated on the participation of the local 'community', fails to acknowledge the often inadequate conceptualization and practicality of the latter term. In any destination, the role and significance of tourism will vary greatly, and such a role will interact differently with other aspects of the destination's development sectors in different ways. Notions of 'community' tied to 'tourism sustainability' may not reflect such a situation adequately.

A focus was placed upon the ethical nature of interactions between the major tourism actors within the destination, with trade-offs, and competitive and complementary roles being examined. Second homes, crime and health were addressed in this context. A number of aspects of and contexts for tourism employee welfare were then evaluated, including the complex issues surrounding labour migration.

This acted as a context for the following chapter (5), which focused on the nature and efficacy of pro-poor tourism (PPT) as an ethically based, tourism-employment-led development policy. Is tourism employment an appropriate mechanism for levering citizens of some of the most impoverished countries in the world out of poverty? Certainly, there are examples that show it can be. But tourism can only be one of a range of mechanisms involved in 'poverty reduction'. Moreover, by arguing that poverty can be relieved through greater participation in tourism employment, there is an implicit understanding that tourism should therefore be expanding in the poorest countries and regions. This contested notion confronts the ethical trade-off between (essential?) employment provision and (scarce?) resource consumption. As it is promoted by Western development NGOs and government departments, there is the further danger that PPT simply offers another route for the economic hegemony of the richest countries/companies over the poorest countries and peoples of the world.

Chapter 6 turned attention to a welfare-centred approach to the non-human animals involved in tourism and their wider captive and 'natural' environments. The human–animal relationship and the management of that relationship and its ethical context were explored. The expression of responsibility through codes of conduct and behaviour was related to the ever-broadening scope of the concept of 'ecotourism'. Social constructions of animals and their environments, and the perception of animals' relative merit and value, not least as 'edutainment', appear to be strongly culturally determined. This has important implications for their welfare and for the quality of human interactions with them in a recreational context.

The penultimate chapter (7), explored the nature of tourism industry responses to the growth of ethical concern through an explicit embrace of notions of corporate social responsibility. Given that CSR is articulated in such contested concepts as pro-poor tourism and ecotourism, we questioned whether such a trajectory within the tourism industry will actually enhance the welfare of stakeholders through such dimensions as those reflected in the book's previous chapters.

Tourism, Transport, Ethics and Global Welfare

> Global warming is a train wreck about to hit the world tourism business, and I think we've all been asleep at the switch.
> (Jerry Mallett, President of the US-based International Adventure Travel Society, cited in Siegle, 2005b)

We have raised a number of welfare-related issues that can be addressed, ameliorated or even resolved at a relatively local level, be it within the tourism-generating localities, in the destination regions or in the boardrooms and policy-planning offices of key industry participants. But this text has also been shaped by contemporary global events unfolding during its conception and writing. These have included:

- the role of perceived and actual 'global terrorism';
- the devastating Indian Ocean tsunami of December 2004;
- publication of a United Nations 10-year plan for combating global poverty, and subsequent G8 and popular media responses;
- the unveiling of Airbus Industrie's 'super-jumbo' A380; and
- increasingly alarming and urgent reports on global climate change.

Such factors emphasize that tourism needs to be viewed within a wider multidisciplinary and global context in order for us to begin to understand its (welfare) significance and role. Jones (1990: 283) argued that a major priority for social welfare in developing countries is the elimination of dependent underdevelopment. If this is so, then the tourism industry and the agencies supporting its diffusion in LDCs need to reflect on the longer-term social and political outcomes of tourism's economically driven embrace and their ethical implications. If the outcomes of tourism development are to be made more 'just' (Hultsman, 1995; D'Sa, 1999), it is likely that, failing radical change in the contemporary global, largely capitalist system, regulation will be required to ensure greater acknowledgement of the social, environmental and political consequences of tourists' and tourism promoters' pursuits. This must surely be the case where the global environment is concerned.

There are a number of ways in which this book could have been structured to address the welfare implications of tourism. Choosing specifically to focus on particular groups of 'actors' or stakeholders raises the danger of missing the bigger picture. In this penultimate section of our final chapter we wish to focus on a critical issue that has implications for the welfare of the planet and transcends the nature of the book's structure, cutting across the chapters that have preceded it. This is the nature and global welfare consequences of the inexorable demand for travel and transport – particularly motor vehicles and aircraft – created by increasing (domestic and) international tourism-related activities.

Many would consider access to a motor car and to air travel to be two of the most liberating aspects of their lives. Yet the negative welfare externalities of these activities affect not merely tourism destinations, but all global environments in an inextricably interlinked way. Gössling (2002b) points to the fact that the spatial globalization of the industry may be approaching its climax: that tourism has penetrated most 'corners' of the globe. In contrast, what he calls the 'societal internationalization' of tourism – whereby people from all countries participate on an equal footing – is still far off (see Chapter 2).

The sustainable tourism literature and sustainable transport literature have remained largely separate, partly because, as noted in Chapter 1, the tourism industry, in its promotion of the (claimed, potential) 'sustainability' of tourism, focuses on destination activity and largely chooses to ignore the means by which tourists actually travel to the destination from their home (see Gössling et al., 2002). Thus 'tourism', within the industry's interpretation and definition of its 'sustainability', appears to be a process and activity that applies almost exclusively to destinations, abstracted from the wider spatial context of travel and mobility.

This approach is clearly flawed in at least two ways:

- it dishonestly fails to identify the wider sustainability implications of tourism activity, and notably the externalities of motor car and air travel; and
- it thus defeats the notion and purpose of sustainability being a holistic concept by merely – and conveniently – focusing on one spatially expressed element of tourism activity.

With the potential prospect of unfettered tourism surpassing a total of 1 billion international arrivals by 2010 (WTO, 1997), Gössling warns that (post?)modernity has introduced a number of cycles into industrialized countries that heighten interest in tourism. These increase the intensity of its 'spatial globalization' and encourage its 'societal globalization' (Gössling, 2002b: 553) in a number of ways:

- lifestyle enhancement in modern societies demands seeking new impressions, seeing new environments and cultures, experiencing and learning, escaping the monotony of life, being free (e.g. Alderhold and Lohmann, 1995). The very experience of other countries and environments stimulates the wish to see more places;
- tourism leads to the decontextualization of the relationships individuals have with their local society and nature. The environment increasingly comes to

be understood as something global, and local identity is lost to the 'cosmopolitization' of the self through tourism, which in its turn leads to a heightened interest in travel;
- this spatial globalization has also led to the values of tourists from Western societies being absorbed and rapidly adopted in developing countries, such that the attachment of local residents to place might dissolve. Simultaneously, the interaction of tourists and residents results in an increased wish to travel; and
- long-distance tourism is based on the availability of financial resources to pay for it. But the generation of these financial resources is largely based on the use of (finite) natural resources (such as oil). Thus, both the generation of the financial resources for tourism and the process of travelling itself contribute to the depletion of natural resources. At the same time, the tourism industry generates new financial resources, which, in turn, enable others to participate in tourism.

These processes should be observed critically, Gössling argues, because the growth of tourism and the changes in human–environmental relations develop in parallel with the consumption and depletion of natural resources, both directly and indirectly, locally and globally, through transport use. Transport, and especially air transport, is responsible for the majority of environmental impacts associated with long-distance tourism (Gössling, 2000). Per unit of energy used, air travel has the greatest impact on climate change. Even though it accounts for only 15% of the leisure-related distances travelled globally, it is responsible for about 18% of the energy used and 37% of the contribution of leisure travel to global warming (Gössling, 2002a: 298). This is particularly problematic, because the United Nations Framework Convention on Climate Change (UN-FCCC) does not cover emissions from bunker fuels, such as aviation fuel sold at airports. As a result, emissions from international aviation are not under international policy control (Olsthoorn, 2001).

Most importantly, Gössling (2002b: 554) argues that

> a cosmopolitan configuration of the self through tourism might off-set the individual perception of being responsible for unsustainable environmental change. Sustainable tourism – the notion that its development can be managed in an environmentally neutral way – might thus be a contradiction in terms.

The use of motor vehicles has (indirect) impacts on the human rights and well-being of millions of people (e.g. Greene *et al.*, 1997; Newbery, 1998). Stacked up against perceived benefits for economic welfare and accessibility, negative externalities of motor car use include energy resource depletion, carbon dioxide emissions, emissions of toxic and harmful substances, land-use disruption, fragmentation of natural areas, waste and congestion, road accidents and noise pollution (Steg and Gifford, 2005).

Motor vehicles are a major source of greenhouse gases, contributing to climate change: in the UK, for example, they contribute approximately 20% of all greenhouse gases, with transport as a whole producing 35% (Hillman and Fawcett, 2004). On average, each car produces its own weight in carbon dioxide for every 6000 miles driven. Noxious fumes emitted by motor vehicles cause airborne pollution, estimated to contribute to some 25,000 premature deaths annually in the UK alone. Traffic accidents kill and seriously injure road users and pedestrians, especially children, indiscriminately. New road development consumes land and other resources, both in construction and, of course, in subsequent use. Multinational oil corporations and some oppressive governments benefit from oil revenues. Oil-dependent poor countries have an unusually high incidence of poverty, corruption, war and unrepresentative government (Clark, 2004: 316–317).

Petroleum use is the biggest contributor to climate change. Further, of course, it is the source of spills and consequent marine and land pollution, and the cause of deforestation and land degradation to make way for drilling and exploitation, often resulting in additional water, atmospheric and soil pollution. Negative impacts are also experienced from its by-products, in the form of agrochemicals and international conflict.

For some time, a 'StopEsso' boycott campaign has been supported by the environmental pressure groups Greenpeace and Friends of the Earth in response to Exxon Corporation's influence on the Bush administration's 2001 abandonment of the 1992 Kyoto Protocol on reducing emissions of the main greenhouse gases. The automotive corporations Ford, General Motors and DaimlerChrysler have all been leading supporters of George W. Bush and, as such, have sought to undermine evidence on human-induced climate change, for example through funding the Coalition for Vehicle Choice, an anti-Kyoto pressure group claiming to represent the American people (Clark, 2004: 324).

Both the petrochemical industry and motor manufacturers have been slow to promote environmentally acceptable fuel alternatives for motor vehicles. Such alternatives include:

- liquefied petroleum gas (LPG – propane): most petrol cars can be converted to sole or dual fuel;
- petrol–electric hybrids: these are currently expensive but becoming popular, not least for four-wheel-drive vehicles in the USA. Petrol is used to fire up the engine and charge up the battery, which can take over on downhill stretches or at lower speeds. At best, this is a compromise vehicle, in terms of both fuel and performance, and yet one currently favoured by US and Japanese manufacturers;
- electric cars: these have a range of no more than 240 km. Given current technology, an intensive infrastructure of recharging stations would be necessary if such vehicles were taken up in significant numbers;
- biodiesel: this is vegetable oil treated with ethanol and reduces greenhouse

emissions by about half compared with diesel, but is not 'carbon-neutral' as energy is required to prepare and distribute it. Although manufactured in about 35 plants across the USA, it is not viewed as a large-scale, long-term substitute for oil, since it would encourage more mono-crop industrial farming and compete for land with food production. Its use can be encouraged by suitable tax regimes, and it is currently tax-free in most of Europe (but not in the UK) and Texas (Clark, 2004: 322);

- hydrogen fuel cells: probably not available for large-scale use until around 2015. The city of Los Angeles possesses a few hydrogen fuel-cell-vehicles and operates a pilot high-pressure hydrogen fuel filling station. One or two hydrogen buses are being tested in the UK.

Steg and Gifford (2005: 59–60) offer two notes of caution. First, the mitigating effects of new technologies tend to be overshadowed by the continuing growth of car use. And, second, drivers may be tempted to use energy-efficient cars more often because of their supposed environmental friendliness and lower running costs: this has been referred to as the rebound effect or the Jevons principle.

Social measures to reduce overall car use, such as car sharing and car clubs/pools, appear less realistic for tourism purposes, although cars being used for recreational journeys are more likely to have a higher occupancy rate than vehicles used for commuting and other regular trips.

Although there is no wide agreement on a definition of 'sustainable transport', the term can be understood as referring to a transport system that in itself is structurally viable in an economic, environmental and social sense, and which does not impede the achievement of the overall sustainability of society (Greene et al., 1997; Donaghy et al., 2005; Richardson, 2005). This last phrase appears to be something that is often glaringly absent in discussions of 'sustainable tourism', but is pivotal in any critique of the sustainability of tourism, particularly that requiring long-haul travel.

This is because international and domestic air travel is highly energy-intensive and its speed enables and encourages people to travel long distances and frequently. Air transport use is increasing rapidly and, while most contemporary passenger aircraft generate around 25% more carbon dioxide than motor cars per person per kilometre, the real impact on climate change is about three times greater than such comparisons would suggest, because aircraft also emit water vapour and oxides of nitrogen and sulphur. These compound the greenhouse effect in the troposphere and lower stratosphere, where aircraft fly, and also damage the ozone layer.

Commercial aircraft account for 3–4% of total human impact on climate, equivalent to the impact of all terrestrial activity in the whole of Africa, and this impact is increasing. Although aircraft are gradually becoming more fuel-efficient, this marginal improvement is offset by increasing numbers of flights (not least stimulated by the proliferation of 'budget' airlines) and the long lead time before aircraft are replaced. The impact of air travel can only be reduced by diminishing passenger numbers, and thus frequency of flights. This can only be done by making the price of tickets reflect the true environmental costs of air travel (Himanen et al., 2005). Requiring airlines to pay tax on aviation fuel – which is currently duty-free – would be a necessary first step in positively acknowledging such external costs (Clark, 2004: 328–330). Of course, this would restrict particularly poorer people's access to certain types of tourism, and would need to be one of a raft of measures necessary to combat current rates of climate change (Fig. 8.1).

Apart from unsustainable practices that affect the welfare of current generations, transport also has a growing share in the exhaustion of natural resources and services (including, of course, the climate system). The impacts of exhaustion typically threaten to reduce the welfare of future generations, and raise serious questions concerning the appropriateness and effectiveness of current regulation.

Safety and health issues are still largely approached in a way that detaches them from other societal issues and policy arenas. Optimization tends to be viewed at the individual level, instead of taking a more holistic approach to social welfare: for example, including the health, welfare and financial consequences of a collective lack of physical exercise resulting from a car-dependent society (Greene, 2003). Further, the ageing of populations in many Organization for Economic Cooperation and Development (OECD) countries is a major driving force of lifestyle changes. As noted in Chapter 2, the soon-to-be retired, post-Second World War baby boomers will be more active and mobile than previous

cohorts of the 'elderly'. In North America, where there is much higher reliance on the automobile (Wachs, 2003) and much higher car fuel use per capita compared with the European Union (EU) (Table 8.1), this will also entail increased car use by the high proportion of retired persons who are expected to continue living in areas where public transport service is meagre or absent.

Transport problems and identified measures tend to be framed by policymakers as technical–economic problems or challenges. This is perhaps one reason why this area of policy does not relate well to tourism practice. Behavioural responses

Fig. 8.1. Freedom to travel more and 'cheaply': at what price?

Table 8.1. Comparative characteristics of vehicle use, fuel price and fuel intensity (from Fulton, 2004; Himanen *et al.*, 2005).

Countries	Weighted real fuel price, including taxes (US$/litre)	Vehicle-km per capita (×1000)	Average vehicle fuel intensity (litres/100 vehicle-km)	Car fuel use per capita (GJ/capita)
USA	0.26	13.0	12.0	52
Canada	0.44	8.2	11.8	33
Australia	0.51	8.2	11.3	32
Japan	0.55	3.9	11.3	14
EU[a]	0.70–1.00	6.0–7.5	7.2–9.2	16–20

[a]The EU figures (1998) represent minimum and maximum group values per item from the country group Denmark, Germany, Finland, France, Italy, The Netherlands and the UK.

tend to be presented in terms of obstacles and deviations from an 'ideal' pattern, which is usually defined in a predominantly rational and uniformly informed world instead of in a world of irrationality and distortion. Further, when policies are developed to mitigate negative impacts of transport in one domain, they may involve different institutional actors from those taking decisions in another domain, and conflicting policies may result.

Efforts to overcome this in the domains of safety and environment have been discussed by the OECD (1997). More comprehensive sustainability policies easily become entangled in the dominating views that exist in trade policy circles, reflecting the complicated policy mix that tourism represents – embracing the overlapping and often competing policy arenas of transport, trade, regional development, and human welfare and behaviour. One way to engage in more constructive discourse with other policy circles is to create better data sets, which enable overviews of the contribution of transport to the tourism sector and to the national economy, such as through the creation of transport satellite accounts (Link, 2005).

Where are We Going?

In their mapping of quality of life (QoL) indicators related to human well-being, Steg and Gifford (2005) argue that sustainable transport plans tend to be strongly opposed when users believe the plans will significantly reduce their well-being. They also note that, in everyday life, changes are normally met with initial resistance because people are not sure of positive consequences. After implementation, people soon adapt their behaviour and thus support for sustainability plans may be higher after they have been implemented.

Employing methodologies to calculate a quantitative measure of the environmental impact of travel and tourism through ecological footprint analysis (EFA), Gössling et al. (2002) found, for example, that, for international tourists flying to the Seychelles, more than 97% of their energy footprint was the result of air travel. This suggested that efforts to make tourist destinations more sustainable, such as through energy-saving devices or with the use of renewable energy sources, could only contribute marginal savings: 'Any strategy towards sustainable tourism must thus seek to reduce transport distances, and, vice versa, any tourism based air traffic needs per se to be seen as unsustainable' (Gössling et al., 2002: 208). However, as the footprint occurring within a destination was found to be small, Gössling et al. (2002) argue that regional tourism involving only short transport journeys may often be 'sustainable', at least from an ecological point of view.

But there currently appears to be a conspiracy of procrastination and denial that urgent action is needed to reduce global environmental impacts of transport and travel. For politicians, the perception of likely hostile short-term responses to necessary longer-term policies appears to induce sclerosis. Thus the UK government (like most Western administrations, including the EU) is Janus-faced. In its 2003 White Paper on energy, it committed itself to tackling climate change and announced a target for cutting 60% of carbon dioxide emissions by 2050. But, in the aviation White Paper later that same year, the government promised to facilitate an expected mass increase in air passenger traffic, if necessary by providing several new runways to cope with increased demand. There is no sign of the two positions being reconciled (McCarthy et al., 2005).

Most environmental pressure groups appear to be playing along with campaigns clearly designed to avoid alarming the public too much for fear of being counterproductive (Hillman, 2005). Thus carbon offsetting has become a fashionable way of atoning for having taken (long-distance) flights. 'But this is a bit like having your carbon cake and eating it' (Siegle, 2005a). Future Forests (<http://www.futureforests.com>) is the UK's leading carbon-neutral company, and its argument is a theme that has been adopted by some tour operators.

Crystal Holidays, for example, invites contributions from customers, which are then invested in an energy-saving project in the UK, and a sapling will be planted in a UK forest for each passenger who participates.

There are three concerns with such approaches. First, the latest research suggests that the carbon-sink function of trees could be much less effective than originally thought. Second, here is yet another example of unconscious global inequity: why should the tree be planted in the source country rather than in a poorer, possibly destination country, which is likely to suffer proportionately more from the deleterious effects of climate change exacerbated by profligate air travel? Third, what happens if the trees die prematurely or are burned in a forest fire?

Carbon offsetting of this kind would appear simply to legitimize unsustainable behaviour by salving the consciences of those who can afford to delegate (abnegate?) their individual responsibilities. For example, 'Thomas Cook takes environmental issues seriously,' asserts a company spokesman. 'But with mixed reports on the potential implications of climate change no formal plans are in place at the moment. It is currently too early to assess the likely business impact' (Siegle, 2005b).

Berkeley (2005) argues that emission trading schemes (ETSs) are untested and unproven on the scale currently envisaged across Europe. Including aviation in the embryonic European ETS would lead to massive fluctuations in supply and demand. ETSs began life in the USA as Kyoto compliance avoidance schemes, as part of a manoeuvre to replace regulation with schemes that pose as 'market' solutions. 'These schemes are simply gambling with our climate' (Berkeley, 2005: 10), and a debate continues on their equity and efficiency (e.g. Manne and Stephen, 2005).

Hillman (2005) contends that the only policy that can prevent the relatively 'safe' concentration of carbon emissions accumulating in the atmosphere from being exceeded is the Contraction and Convergence programme. This is proposed by the Global Commons Institute, which aims to lessen emissions at the same time as working towards an equal per capita ration for the world's population. Such rationing would have to be mandatory – reduction of carbon dioxide emissions on this scale could not realistically be achieved on a voluntary basis.

The early introduction of carbon rationing would provide a framework for delivering the essential reduction needed – and in an equitable way. There is, too, the issue of social justice with regard to developing countries, and Africa in particular, as transfer payments are made to their carbon-emission-thrifty population: the process should create an ecologically virtuous circle.

Reality suggests otherwise. Just as most international tourism activity is run by and for people from the world's most advanced economies, so its direct and indirect negative welfare externalities are borne by the poor, at global, national and regional levels. Even within the world's richest country, this became manifest in the wake of hurricane Katrina along the devastated US Gulf coast, causing a number of commentators to concur with the sentiment that 'it is the poor and weak who are invariably swept away first by climate change' (Hari, 2005: 37).

Politicians' attraction to 'carbon abatement technology' appears to be an attempted technological fix to please big business and meet short-term political needs. Such technology could involve, for example, stripping out carbon dioxide from power station emissions and burying it by pumping it under pressure into exhausted North Sea oilfields (e.g. Morgan, 2005). But, with unforeseen longer-term consequences, this may yet prove to be largely impractical.

There is, therefore, in the short term, a need for a menu of policies, such as shifting short-haul air travel to rail, raising fuel efficiency and fiscally regulating motor vehicle and air travel. Total external costs of air transport are currently estimated at c. €55 per 1000 passengers/km. Turning these external costs into a congestion charge for the skies by adding them to ticket prices would result in €5.5 per passenger/100 km. Such taxation could assist in paying for public services such as health, education and pensions.

> It is difficult to understand why the air transport industry continually seeks to deprive society of these benefits by refusing to face up to its responsibilities and pay tax on its fuel, VAT [value-added tax] on its tickets and the cost of its environmental impacts.
>
> (Berkeley, 2005: 10)

In the USA such a scheme has been rejected on the grounds of exerting 'unfair pressure on a struggling sector' (Skuse, 2005: 45), but the EU has reaffirmed the need for airline climate taxes as a necessary part of a climate policy drive to reduce emissions.

The underlying ethos of this book has been the need to connect the (welfare) outcomes of tourism processes to stakeholder recognition of the wider (global environmental) context within which the ethics underlying, and the responsibility for, such outcomes are placed. Reflecting elements of this, Holden (2003) argues that, although an ethical shift has taken place within tourism in recent years, this has been within an anthropocentric framework. What we have attempted to do in Chapter 6 in particular is to extend the welfare framework of tourism impacts beyond human participants to firmly incorporate non-human animals. Holden argues that such a non-anthropocentric ethic – which he refers to as the ethic of eco-holism – is essential, if not yet recognized, to underpin any attempt at rendering tourism a sustainable activity within natural environments. With clear wider environmental implications, he concludes, pessimistically, that the employment of such a 'radical' ethic would 'require a conceptual leap which would challenge the perceived interests of most tourism stakeholders who presently show little desire to take such a leap' (Holden, 2003: 106).

This re-emphasizes the apparent narrow view of tourism–environment relationships held by much of the tourism industry, as further reflected in the promotion of eco- and sustainable tourism that ignores the transport externalities involved in reaching the destination. Relating this back to climate change, Becken (2004) found that half of all tourists surveyed in Australia and New Zealand questioned any link between tourism and climate change. While 'tourism experts' interviewed saw a changing climate as a potential threat to tourism, they could not necessarily see tourism's fossil fuel consumption and carbon dioxide emissions as contributing to climate change.

Such apparent attitudes have encouraged Farrell and Twining-Ward (2004, 2005) to argue that most tourism researchers, and implicitly practitioners, have been schooled in a tradition of linear, specialized, predictable and deterministic cause-and-effect science. As such, they (we?) have not been conceptually equipped to appreciate that 'all natural and social systems are interdependent, nonlinear, complex adaptive systems', which are 'generally unpredictable, qualitative and characterized by causes giving rise to multiple outcomes' (Farrell and Twining-Ward, 2004: 277). There is a need, they contend, for new collective thinking – an 'epistemic community' (Haas, 1992; Cinquegrani, 2002) – to respond to global challenges. While the application of chaos approaches (e.g. Faulkner and Russell, 1997; McKercher, 1999; Faulkner, 2001) may be a step in the right direction, a re-conceptualization of the structure of tourism study is required in order to confront the challenges of what Farrell and Twining-Ward refer to as the 'sustainability transition'.

Will We Get There?

Geopolitical issues of access to travel and recreation resources will become an important focus of tension and potential conflict in the face of rapidly increasing global pressures. Although at a global level there remain obvious constraints on certain types of activities and restrictions on access in certain areas, generally there is relative freedom of movement and access around the globe, subject only to the ability to pay. But such freedoms are available largely because they are restricted to a privileged minority of the world's inhabitants. Although current carbon rationing schemes for mitigating environmental impacts seek an equitable outcome, what will be the result when, later this century, living standards have risen sufficiently in the currently very populous LDCs of Asia, Latin America and Africa for their citizens, justifiably, to want to join those of us who have long enjoyed the privileges of travel and become fellow global tourists?

Probable technology-induced mechanisms for relieving the pressures of terrestrial global tourism (Box 8.2) would be accessible to relatively small numbers and offer little in terms of alternative modes or environments for global tourism.

Will travel and recreation continue unabated, therefore, partly 'democratized' by web-based yield management air fare pricing mechanisms (e.g. Klein and Loebbecke, 2003), until there is 'global gridlock' and conflict over access to international travel and recreational resources becomes inevitable? Or will some unforeseen Malthusian break, even global terrorism, intervene irrevocably (D. Hall, 2004b: 4–5)?

Our emphasis in preceding chapters on the welfare-negative consequences of much tourism notwithstanding, the ability to travel, to be able to reflect on your own life and culture in relation to the first-hand experience of others, is a major and significant welfare consequence of our privilege to be able to travel across the globe. Perceptions of tourism as a force for good, intercultural understanding and world peace have viewed it, ethnocentrically, largely from that position of privilege and dominance. Volunteer tourism, for example (Chapters 1 and 5), although currently compromised by its semi-colonial 'charity' appeal, its gap-year curriculum vitae (CV) self-enhancement focus and its reinforcement of circuits of financial support back to donor countries, does have the potential to make a difference. But we are not convinced by Jaakson (2004b: 180) when he argues that 'There is a huge reservoir of untapped political power in an activist tourism, waiting to be implemented for the betterment of the world.' Indeed, Butcher's (2003) central thesis is that there is too

---

Box 8.2. Alternatives to terrestrial tourism?

Virtual-reality travel and tourism (VRTT)
Despite improving technology (e.g. Buchroithner, 2002), particularly the ability for two or more people to share virtual experiences (e.g. Liebman Parrinello, 2001), research and conventional wisdom suggest that the experience of VRTT and the use of real-time webcams merely whets appetites to undertake actual travel and tourism rather than offering a serious alternative to them (Cheong, 1995; Williams and Hobson, 1995).

Submarine travel and tourism
Although two-thirds of the earth's surface is water, it is mostly unexplored due to the limits on our ability to develop technology sufficient to withstand the physical pressure – both on material and on human bodies – at depth. Improvements in technology to reduce pressure on scarce land resources and to divert recreation and other activities to submarine environments do not appear to be imminent (e.g. Glowka, 2003). With possible small incremental technological improvements being more likely, the ocean depths will continue to act as a temporary escape for those few who can afford to get away from land-based mass recreation and the excesses of climate change. However, the perturbations of global warming may render submarine endeavours more difficult than they are at present.

Space travel and tourism
The precedents of three individual space tourists and the fact that a number of companies have accepted reservations for suborbital trips might suggest the potential for large numbers of people to travel outside the earth's atmosphere. However, even if issues of space sickness and passenger safety (radiation and collision with space debris are both serious threats) can be overcome in an acceptable manner, the cost of technology – particularly reusable launch vehicles – and the relative hostility of space authorities towards the use of space for recreational purposes remain obstacles to anything more than occasional individual and very brief space tourism activity by the extremely wealthy (Brown, 2004).

much moralizing in and about tourism, and this gets in the way of its primary hedonistic purpose.

Pro-poor tourism policies, offering the provision of (enhanced) employment in poor societies as one of a range of livelihood opportunities, do render tourism an important economic and social tool under appropriate circumstances. But tourism should not be a dominant mechanism that induces dependence. The International Labour Office (ILO) of the United Nations estimated that the events of '9/11' and reactions to them contributed to the loss of some 6.5 million jobs in travel and tourism, mostly in poor countries, as a result of a reduction in international (particularly air) travel (Clark, 2004: 344). Striking some 3 years later, the December 2004 Indian Ocean tsunami devastated a number of coastal tourism areas and, as well as the death and destruction wrought, rendered further thousands at least temporarily unemployed. As an immediate result, motivated variously by questions of personal safety, uncertainty and respect for the bereaved, many people cancelled holidays booked in the countries concerned.

But spokespersons for the beleaguered countries encouraged tourists to return in order that tourism employment in those regions not wholly devastated by the immediate impacts of the tidal wave could be maintained (Dyer, 2005; McGirk, 2005). Indeed, Sri Lanka, which lost some 130,000 people in the disaster, initiated a post-tsunami tourism programme 'Bounce Back Sri Lanka' (Sri Lanka Tourism, 2005), aimed particularly at repeat visitors, alongside a local community rebuilding and rehabilitation programme (adoptsrilanka.com, 2005).

The particular argument used to justify resuscitating tourism so soon after the disaster was that many tourism employees had lost their homes and belongings and therefore needed employment to help rebuild their lives as quickly as possible. But, aside from the dependency issues raised, this posed an ethical question for many intending tourists concerning the most appropriate time to return, if at all. As illustrated in Chapter 3, the ability to take such a sensitive decision rests largely on the provision

and dissemination of appropriate information: not necessarily an easy task in the aftermath of a natural disaster (BBC, 2005).

But, in the not so longer term, we are confronted here with the biggest trade-off of all, about which decisions to be made will need to be based upon realistic notions of global sustainability and not those often perpetrated by the tourism industry.

> the large amount of fossil fuels used for travel contributes significantly to climate change and has received increasing attention in the recent debate on leisure mobility and sustainability . . . Carlsson-Kanyama and Lindén (1999) estimate that the sustainable level of per capita energy consumption for travel was 11,000 MJ in 1996, a value that will decrease to 8,400 MJ in 2020 with a rising global population. This can be compared to the energy needed for a journey by aircraft, which will, for the flight alone, entail an energy use of about 4,500 MJ per capita.
> (Gössling and Mattsson, 2002: 26; see also Fig. 8.2)

In this sense, tourism and travel are fundamental to global welfare. The tourism industry is always ready to declare how the object of its efforts is now the most important economic activity across the globe and how it embraces a thousand million people or more. Whether true or not, the fact that the industry claims, and no doubt to some extent believes, this places an enormous responsibility upon its shoulders. Thus far, it appears to have done little to assume such responsibility or to deploy it for the benefit of global welfare. Yet

> if actors could make ethically sound decisions, then the industry would have more of a chance of being a vehicle of good will. The task we have at hand is to develop mechanisms to aid in making this a reality.
> (Fennell and Przeclawski, 2003: 149)

With this in mind, we offer the following recommendations in conclusion:

1. Much more work is necessary on an integrated approach to stakeholder welfare. In particular, the focus of tourism studies

Fig. 8.2. A strangely symbolic artefact for our future global (tourism) welfare? A nuclear flask raised on a plinth in front of the visitor centre, Sellafield nuclear reprocessing plant, Cumbria, north-west England.

needs to shift away from the dominance of tourists to the experiences of destination residents and tourism workers, about whom there is still a relatively limited literature, which tends to be regurgitated.

2.   There is a need for better conceptualization and holistic theorizing for tourism development studies, not least in drawing together the disparate (domestic tourism) experiences of richer and poorer societies.

3.   There is an emerging literature on ethics in tourism, but this needs to be more readily applicable to the tensions and trade-offs of everyday experience and better integrated with the business ethics literature. In short, it needs to be seen to be relevant and important for the industry's practitioners.

4.   This in turn requires more coherent relationships, with notions of 'corporate social responsibility' and better conceptualizations of responsibility and accountability within tourism, linked to critiques of 'responsible tourism' and 'green' marketing.

5.   There is a need for a better integration of animal welfare concepts into the literature, and non-anthropocentric conceptualizations of 'wildlife tourism', its interpretation and experiences.

6.   Outside the work of Stefan Gössling and his associates, there seems to be almost a denial of the relationships between tourism and travel's contribution to climate change and its implications, particularly for global equity in relation to access to and the scale of future tourism, travel and recreational resources. There is an urgent need for better integration of social science and natural science thinking in order to confront policymakers with verifiable facts.

7.   Not least in relation to the previous point, although not a new argument, there is an urgent need for the securing of alternative conceptualizations to the sustainability paradigm within tourism, and of tourism in relation to wider global sustainability issues.

8.   The tourism and travel industry's global body, the WTO, needs to take a far stronger lead in addressing urgent global issues directly related to travel activities: tourism ethics charters (Chapter 7) and pro-poor tourism programmes (Chapter 5) offer little more than embroidering the edges of a rapidly changing global landscape. There are many precedents for outside intervention to regulate the industry when internal action has proved insufficient. Current warnings

of the rate of climate change are unprecedented and require intervention.

Perhaps the most fundamental problem
for the tourism industry is that – whether it
likes it or not – it is firmly embedded in a
global economic system which, in its current mode of operation, is incorrigibly ineq-
uitable (and thus unethical). Thus, even
those in the industry who are genuinely
trying to pursue and promote ethical practices, to be self-consciously sustainable and
welfare-positive, are constrained ultimately
by the need to generate profits if they are to
continue in business at all.

Our final words were going to be: 'it
could be that only an environmental catastro-
phe in the developed world – say, the inun-
dation of New York or London – will be
sufficient to effect any lasting change'. As this
manuscript was about to be submitted for
publication, the social and environmental
consequences for the US Gulf coast of hurricane Katrina were beginning to become
apparent. Is it too much to hope that subsequent political reactions to these events
and their implications for global welfare
might prove our conclusions to be unduly
pessimistic?

References

Abel-Smith, B. and Titmuss, K. (eds) (1987) *The Philosophy of Welfare: Selected Writings of Richard M. Titmuss*. Allen & Unwin, London.

Abeyratne, R.I.R. (1995) Proposals and guidelines for the carriage of elderly and disabled persons by air. *Journal of Travel Research* 33(3), 52–59.

ACCV (2003) *Review of SunSmart Campaign 2000–2003*. Anti-Cancer Council of Victoria, Victoria, Australia.

Adams, D. (1979) *The Hitchhiker's Guide to the Galaxy*. BBC and William Heinemann, London.

Adams, H.R., Sleeman, J.M., Rwego, I. and New, J.C. (2001) Self-reported medical history survey of humans as a measure of health risk to the chimpanzees (*Pan troglodytes schweinfurthii*) of Kibale National Park, Uganda. *Oryx* 35(4), 308–312.

adoptsrilanka.com (2005) *adoptsrilanka.com*. adoptsrilanka.com, Galle <http://www.adoptsrilanka.com> (last accessed 24 May 2005).

Adventure Lifesigns (2005a) *Adventure Lifesigns*. Adventure Lifesigns, Aldershot, UK <http://www.adventurelifesigns.co.uk/> (accessed 5 April 2005).

Adventure Lifesigns (2005b) *Adventure Lifesigns: Adult Expeditions*. Adventure Lifesigns, Aldershot, UK <http://www.lifesignsgroup.co.uk/adventure/adult.php> (accessed 5 April 2005).

Adventure Lifesigns (2005c) *Adventure Lifesigns Health Advice*. Adventure Lifesigns Aldershot, UK <http://www.lifesignsgroup.co.uk/adventure/advice.php> (accessed 5 April 2005).

AHLA (American Hotel and Lodging Association) (2000) *Summary Report of the Survey of Usage of Accessible Hotel Guestrooms by Travelers with Disabilities*. American Hotel and Lodging Association, Washington, DC.

Ahmed, Z., Krohn, F. and Heller, V. (1994) International tourism ethics as a way to world understanding. *Journal of Tourism Studies* 5(2), 36–44.

Airey, D. (1994) Education for tourism in Poland: the PHARE Programme. *Tourism Management* 15(6), 467–470.

Airey, D. and Shackley, M. (1997) Tourism development in Uzbekistan. *Tourism Management* 18(4), 199–208.

Aitchison, C. (2000) Young disabled people, leisure and everyday life: reviewing conventional definitions for leisure studies. *Annals of Leisure Research* 3(1), 1–20.

Aitken, C. and Hall, C.M. (2000) Migrant and foreign skills and their relevance to the tourism industry. *Tourism Geographies* 2(1), 66–86.

Akama, J.S. (2004) Neocolonialism, dependency and external control of Africa's tourism industry: a case study of wildlife safari tourism in Kenya. In: Hall, C.M. and Tucker, H. (eds) *Tourism and Postcolonialism: Contested Discourses, Identities and Representations*. Routledge, London, pp. 140–152.

Akbar, A. (2004) Local beaches for local folk: surf guerrillas fight the out-of-towners. *The Independent*
    20 November, p. 19 <http://news.independent.co.uk/low_res/story.jsp?story=584787&host=3&dir=65>
    (last accessed 20 November 2004).
Alderhold, P. and Lohmann, M. (1995) *Urlaub und Reisen 94*. Forschungsgemeinschaft Urlaub und Reisen,
    Hamburg, Germany.
Allen, P. (1994) Brits in hol hell trap. *The Star* 14 April.
Amin, A. and Thrift, N. (1995) Globalisation, institutional thickness and the local economy. In: Healy, P.,
    Cameron, S., Davoudi, S., Graham, S. and Madani-Pour, A. (eds) *Managing Cities: the New Urban
    Context*. John Wiley & Sons, Chichester, UK, and New York, pp. 92–108.
Amoa, B.D. (1985) *Tourism in Africa*. All Africa Conference of Churches, Nairobi.
Anderson, R.A. (1987) *Wellness Medicine*. American Health Press, Lynnwood, Washington State.
Andrade, J. (2002) *Tourism Codes of Conduct and Poverty Issues*. Overseas Development Institute, London.
Andronicou, A. (1979) Tourism in Cyprus. In: de Kadt, E. (ed.) *Tourism: Passport to Development?* Oxford
    University Press, New York, pp. 237–264.
Ankomah, P.K. (1991) Tourism skilled labour. *Annals of Tourism Research* 18, 433–442.
Ankomah, P.K. and Crompton, J.L. (1990) Unrealized tourism potential: the case of sub-Saharan Africa.
    Tourism Management 11(3), 11–27.
Anon. (1992) British tourist killed by bear. *The Guardian* 18 September.
Anon. (1993) Public opinion survey on the life of the nation. *News from Japan* 42, 4–6.
Anon. (1995) Ecumenical Coalition on Third World Tourism. *Contours* 7, 1.
Anon. (1996) Japaner werkt zich somes letterlijk dood. *De Volkskrant* 30 March, p. 4.
Anon. (2005a) Raffarin defends loss of holiday. *The Independent* 3 May, p. 19.
Anon. (2005b) A chance for passengers to strike back? *The Independent* 9 July, Traveller p. 11.
Anon. (2005c) Ebookers drops Cuba. *The Observer* 8 May, Escape section p. 6 <http://observer.guardian.
    co.uk/print/0,3858,5188675-102284,00.html> (accessed 8 May 2005).
Anscombe, J. (1991) The gentle traveller. *New Woman* June, 51–53.
Antonak, R. and Livneh, H. (1988) *The Measurement of Attitudes Toward People with Disabilities*. Charles
    C. Thomas, Springfield, Illinois.
Ap, J. (1992) Residents' perceptions of tourism impacts. *Annals of Tourism Research* 19(4), 665–690.
Aramberri, J. (2001) The host should get lost: paradigms in the tourism theory. *Annals of Tourism Research*
    28(3), 738–761.
Archer, B. and Cooper, C. (1994) The positive and negative impacts of tourism. In: Theobald, W.F. (ed.)
    Global Tourism: the Next Decade. Butterworth-Heinemann, Oxford, UK, pp. 73–91.
Arthur, C. (2002a) Fear of flying may raise risk of fatal blood clot. *The Independent* 24 January.
Arthur, C. (2002b) First-class air passenger killed by blood clots. *The Independent* 22 March.
Ascher, B. (1984) Obstacles to international travel and tourism. *Journal of Travel Research* 22(3), 2–16.
Ascher, B. and Edgell, D. (1986) Barriers to international travel. *Travel and Tourism Analyst* October, 3–13.
Ashley, C. (2000) *The Impacts of Tourism on Rural Livelihoods: Experience in Namibia*. ODI Working Paper
    128, Overseas Development Institute, London.
Ashley, C. and Haysom, G. (2005) *From Philanthropy to a Different Way of Doing Business: Strategies and
    Challenges in Integrating Pro-Poor Approaches into Tourism Business*. ATLAS Africa, Pretoria <http://
    www.propoortourism.org.uk/Publications%20by%20partnership/propoor_business_ATLASpaper.pdf>
    (last accessed 9 July 2005).
Ashley, C. and Roe, D. (1998) *Enhancing Community Involvement in Wildlife Tourism: Issues and Challenge*.
    IIED Wildlife and Development Series No. 11, International Institute for Environment and Development,
    London.
Ashley, C., Boyd, C. and Goodwin, H. (2000) *Pro-Poor Tourism: Putting Poverty at the Heart of the Tourism
    Agenda*. Overseas Development Institute, London.
Ashley, C., Boyd, C. and Goodwin, H. (2001) *Pro-Poor Tourism Strategies: Making Tourism Work for the Poor*.
    Overseas Development Institute, London.
Ashworth, G. and Goodall, B. (1990) *Marketing Tourism Places*. Routledge, London.
Ateljevic, I. (2000) Circuits of tourism: stepping beyond the 'production–consumption' dichotomy. *Tourism
    Geographies* 2(4), 369–388.
ATIA (Australian Tourism Industry Association) (1990) *Environmental Guidelines for Tourist Developments*.
    ATIA, Sydney.
Ausenda, F. (ed.) (2003) *Green Volunteers. The World Guide to Voluntary Work in Nature Conservation*.
    Vacation Work, Oxford, UK.

Ayala, H. (1996) Resort ecotourism: a paradigm for the 21st century. *Cornell Hotel and Restaurant Administration Quarterly* 37, 46–53.

Aziz, H. (1995) Understanding attacks on tourists in Egypt. *Tourism Management* 16(2), 91–95.

Bachvarov, M. (2006) Tourism in Bulgaria. In: Hall, D., Smith, M. and Marciszewska, B. (eds) *Tourism in the New Europe: the Challenges and Opportunities of EU Enlargement*. CAB International, Wallingford, UK.

Bagguley, I. (1990) Gender and labour flexibility in hotel and catering. *Services Industry Journal* 10, 737–747.

Baldacchino, G. (1997) *Global Tourism and Informal Labour Relations: the Small-scale Syndrome at Work*. Mansell, London.

Ballantyne, R., Packer, J. and Beckman, E. (1998) Targeted interpretation: exploring relationships among visitors' motivations, activities, attitudes, information needs and preferences. *Journal of Tourism Studies* 9(2), 14–25.

Baloglu, S. and Mangaloglu, M. (2001) Tourism destination images of Turkey, Egypt, Greece and Italy as perceived by US-based tour operators and travel agents. *Tourism Management* 22(1), 1–9.

Bambra, C. (2004) The worlds of welfare: illusory and gender-blind? *Social Policy and Society* 3(3), 201–211.

Bambra, C. (2005) Cash versus services: 'worlds of welfare' and the decommodification of cash benefits and health cash services. *Journal of Social Policy* 34(2), 195–213.

Barbieri, A.F. and Carr, D.L. (2005) Gender-specific out-migration, deforestation and urbanization in the Ecuadorian Amazon. *Global and Planetary Change* 47(2–4), 99–110.

Barnes, J.I., Macgregor, J. and Weaver, L.C. (2002) Economic efficiency and incentives for change within Namibia's community wildlife use initiatives. *World Development* 30(4), 667–681.

Barrett, J. (1991) Global warming: economics of a carbon tax. In: Pearce, D., Barrett, S., Markandya, A., Barbier, E., Kerry, R., Turner, F. and Swanson, T. (eds) *BluePrint 2*. EarthScan, London, pp. 31–52.

Barrett-Brown, M. (1993) *Fair Trade*. Zed Books, London.

Barron, P. and Prideaux, B. (1998) Hospitality education in Tanzania: is there a need to develop environmental awareness? *Journal of Sustainable Tourism* 6(3), 224–237.

Barry, N. (1990) *Welfare*. Open University Press, Milton Keynes, UK.

Basala, S. and Klenosky, D. (2001) Travel style preferences for visiting a novel destination: a conjoint investigation across the novelty-familiarity continuum. *Journal of Travel Research* 40, 172–183.

Baum, T. and Mudambi, R. (1994) A Ricardian analysis of the fully inclusive tour industry. *Service Industries Journal* 14(1), 85–93.

BBC (2005) *Excess Baggage: Tourism after the Tsunami*. BBC Radio 4, 5 February, London <http://www.bbc.co.uk/radio4/excessbaggage/index_20050205.shtml> (last accessed 24 May 2005).

BBC News (2000a) 'Beach envy' fuels plastic surgery rush. *BBC News Online UK: Scotland* 20 August <http://news.bbc.co.uk/1/low/scotland/888578.stm> (last accessed 16 March 2005).

BBC News (2000b) Beating post-holiday blues. *BBC News Online UK* 29 August <http://news.bbc.co.uk/1/low/uk/901053.stm> (last accessed 16 March 2005).

Beard, J. and Ragheb, M.G. (1983) Measuring leisure motivation. *Journal of Leisure Research* 15(3), 219–228.

Beardsworth, A. and Bytman, A. (2001) The wild animal in late modernity: the case of the Disneyization of zoos. *Tourist Studies* 1(1), 83–104.

Becken, S. (2004) How tourists and tourism experts perceive climate change and carbon-offsetting schemes. *Journal of Sustainable Tourism* 12(4), 332–345.

Beckerleg, S. and Hundt, G.L. (2004) Structural violence in a tourist 'paradise'. *Development* 47(1), 109–114.

Beckwith, J. and Matthews, J. (1995) Measurement of attitudes of trainee professionals to people with disabilities. *Journal of Intellectual Disability Research* 39(4), 255–262.

Bedding, J. (2004) Saving the world – or scoring a free holiday? *The Observer* 14 November, pp. 2, 4 <http://observer.guardian.co.uk/print/0,3858,5062587-102284,00.html> (last accessed 14 November 2004).

Bedini, A. (2000) 'Just sit down so we can talk'. Perceived stigma and community recreation pursuits of people with disabilities. *Therapeutic Recreation Journal* 34(1), 55–68.

Beech, C. (2004) *The Fearless Traveller*. MQ Publications, London.

Behrens, R., Steffen, R. and Lock, D. (1994) Travel medicine: before departure. *Medical Journal of Australia* 160(7), 143–147.

Beirman, D. (2003) *Restoring Tourism Destinations in Crisis. A Strategic Marketing Approach*. CAB International, Wallingford, UK.

Beneria, L. (1999) The enduring debate over unpaid labour. *International Labour Review* 138(3), 287–309.

Bennett, M., King, B. and Milner, L. (2004) The health resort sector in Australia: a positioning study. *Journal of Vacation Marketing* 10(2), 122–137.

Bennett, R.J. and McCoshan, A. (1993) *Enterprise and Human Resource Development – Local Capacity Building*. Paul Chapman, London.

Bentham, J. (1982) *An Introduction to the Principles of Morals and Legislation*. Athlone Press, London.

Berkeley, T. (2005) A congestion charge for the skies is critical. *The Observer* 17 July, Business p. 10.

Berry, S. and Ladkin, A. (1997) Sustainable tourism: a regional perspective. *Tourism Management* 18(7), 433–440.

Bewes, P. (1993) Traumas and accidents. In: Behrens, R. and McAdam, K. (eds) *Travel Medicine*. Churchill Livingstone, London, pp. 454–464.

Birke, L. (2002) Effects of browse, human visitors and noise on the behaviour of captive orang utans. *Animal Welfare* 11(2), 189–202.

Bitgood, S., Patterson, D. and Benefield, A. (1988) Exhibit design and visitor behaviour: empirical relationships. *Environment and Behaviour* 20(4), 474–491.

BITS (Bureau International du Tourisme Social) (1992) A charter on the ethics of tourism and the environment. *BITS Information* 110, 12–13.

Björk, P. (2001) Sustainable tourism development, fact or fiction in small tourism companies? *Finnish Journal of Business Economics* 50(3), 271–289.

Black, P., Clark, N. and Clift, S. (1994) *Travel, Tourism and Sexual Health Risks: a Review of Research*. Travel, Lifestyles and Health Working Paper No. 5, Christ Church College, Canterbury, UK.

Blamey, R. (2001) Principles of ecotourism. In: Weaver, D. (ed.) *The Encyclopedia of Ecotourism*. CAB International, Wallingford, UK, pp. 5–22.

Blazey, M.A. (1992) Travel and retirement status. *Annals of Tourism Research* 19, 771–783.

Block, R. (1991) Conservation education in zoos. *Journal of Museum Education* 16(1), 6–7.

Bloom, J. (1996) A South African perpsective of the effects of crime and violence on the tourism industry. In: Pizam, A. and Mansfeld, Y. (eds) *Tourism, Crime and International Security Issues*. John Wiley & Sons, Chichester, UK, and New York, pp. 91–102.

Blowers, A. (1997) Environmental planning for sustainable development: the international context. In: Blowers, A. and Evans, B. (eds) *Town Planning into the 21st Century*. Routledge, London and New York, pp. 34–53.

Bob, U. and Musyoki, A. (2002) Gender geography in South Africa: facing challenges and exploring opportunities. *South African Geographical Journal* 84(1), 98–106.

Boissevain, J. (1977) Tourism and development in Malta. *Development and Change* 8, 523–538.

Boissevain, J. and Inglott, I.S. (1979) Tourism in Malta. In: de Kadt, E. (ed.) *Tourism: Passport to Development?* Oxford University Press, Oxford, UK, pp. 265–284.

Boles, J.S. and Babin, B.J. (1996) On the front lines: stress, conflict, and the customer service provider. *Journal of Business Research* 37(1), 41–50.

Bond, P. (2003) Norwalk virus is easy stowaway on cruise ships. *The Atlanta Journal – Constitution* 23 February, p. C8.

Boorstin, D. (1964) *The Image: a Guide to Pseudo-Events in America*. Harper & Row, New York.

Boorstin, J. (2003) Cruising for a bruising? *Fortune* 9 June, pp. 143–150.

Bor, R. (2003) Trends in disruptive passenger behaviour on board UK registered aircraft: 1999–2003. *Travel Medicine and Infectious Disease* 1(3), 153–157.

Borge, L., Nelson, W.C., Leitch, J.A. and Leistritz, F.L. (1991) *Economic Impact of Wildlife-based Tourism in Northern Botswana*. Agricultural Economics Report No. 262, Agriculture Experiment Station, North Dakota University, Fargo, North Dakota.

Borgström-Hansson, C. and Wackernagel, M. (1999) Rediscovering place and accounting space: how to re-embed the human economy. *Ecological Economics* 29(5), 203–213.

Born Free Foundation (2005) *Travellers' Alert*. Born Free Foundation, Horsham, UK <http://www.bornfree.org.uk/travellers.alert/> (last accessed 18 March 2005).

Boseley, S. (1995) Animal protester in hospital after fiesta bull attack. *The Guardian* 27 June.

Boserup, E. (1970) *Women's Role in Economic Development*. St Martin's Press, New York.

Bostock, S. (1987) Conservation as a moral justification for zoos. *Applied Animal Behaviour Science* 18(3–4), 387.

Bostock, S. (1993) *Zoos and Animal Rights – the Ethics of Keeping Animals in Captivity*. Routledge, London.

Botterill, T.D. (1991) A new social movement: Tourism Concern: the first two years. *Leisure Studies* 10, 203–217.

Boulstridge, E. and Carrigan, M. (2000) Do consumers really care about corporate responsibility? Highlighting the attitude–behaviour gap. *Journal of Communication Management* 4(4), 355–368.

Bourdieu, P. (1977) *An Outline of a Theory of Practice*. Cambridge University Press, Cambridge, UK.

Bow, S. (2002) *Working on Cruise Ships,* 3rd edn. Vacation Work, Oxford, UK.

Bowcott, O. (2005) Tourist fears after Turkish bus bombing. *The Guardian* 18 July, p. 6.

Boyd, S. and Hall, C.M. (2005) Nature-based tourism in peripheral areas: making peripheral destinations competitive. In: Boyd, S. and Hall, C.M. (eds) *Nature-based Tourism in Peripheral Areas.* Channel View, Clevedon, UK, pp. 273–280.

Boyd, S.W. and Singh, S. (2003) Destination communities: structures, resources and types. In: Singh, S., Timothy, D.J. and Dowling, R.K. (eds) *Tourism in Destination Communities.* CAB International, Wallingford, UK, pp. 19–33.

Boyne, S. and Hall, D. (2004) Place promotion through food and tourism: rural branding and the role of websites. *Place Branding* 1(1), 80–92.

Boyne, S., Carswell, F. and Hall, D. (2002) Reconceptualising VFR tourism: friends, relatives and migration in a domestic context. In: Hall, C.M. and Williams, A.M. (eds) *Tourism and Migration: New Relationships Between Production and Consumption.* Kluwer, Dordrecht, The Netherlands, pp. 241–256.

Bramwell, B. (1994) Rural tourism and sustainable rural tourism. *Journal of Sustainable Tourism* 2(1–2), 1–6.

Bramwell, B. and Lane, B. (1993) Sustainable tourism: an evolving global approach. *Journal of Sustainable Tourism* 1(1), 6–16.

Bramwell, B., Henry, I., Jackson, G., Goytia Prat, A., Richards, G. and van der Straaten, J. (eds) (1996) *Sustainable Tourism Management: Principles and Practice.* Tilburg University Press, Tilburg, the Netherlands.

Bränström, R., Ullén, H. and Brandberg, Y. (2003) A randomised population-based intervention to examine the effects of the ultraviolet index on tanning behaviour. *European Journal of Cancer* 39(7), 968–974.

Breech, J. (2000) The enigma of Holocaust sites as tourist attractions – the case of Buchenwald. *Managing Leisure* 5(1), 29–41.

Briedenham, J. (2004) Corporate social responsibility in tourism – a tokenistic agenda? *In Focus* 52, 11.

Bristow, M. (1994) The back of beyond. *BBC Wildlife* 12(7), 45–47.

Britton, S. (1982) The political economy of tourism in the Third World. *Annals of Tourism Research* 9(3), 331–358.

Brohman, J. (1996) New directions in tourism for Third World development. *Annals of Tourism Research* 23, 48–70.

Broom, D.M. (1992) Welfare and conservation. In: Ryder, R.D. (ed.) *Animal Welfare and the Environment.* Duckworth, London, pp. 90–101.

Brown, D.O. (1998) Debt-funded environmental swaps in Africa: vehicles for tourism development? *Journal of Sustainable Tourism* 6(1), 69–79.

Brown, F. (1998) *Tourism Reassessed: Blight or Blessing?* Butterworth-Heinemann, Oxford, UK.

Brown, F. (2004) The final frontier? Tourism in space. *Tourism Recreation Research* 29(1), 37–43.

Brunt, P. and Agarwal, S. (2004) Crime in English seaside resorts. In: McLellan, R. (ed.) *Tourism State of the Art II.* CD-ROM, The Scottish Hotel School, University of Strathclyde, Glasgow, UK.

Brunt, P., Mawby, R. and Hambly, Z. (2000) Tourist victimization and the fear of crime on holiday. *Tourism Management* 21(4), 417–424.

BTA/ETB (British Tourism Authority/English Tourist Board) (1998) *Sightseeing in the UK in 1997.* BTA/ETB Research Services, London.

Buchroithner, M. (2002) Creating the virtual Eiger North Face. *Journal of Photogrammetry and Remote Sensing* 57(1), 114–125.

Buckley, M. (ed.) (1997) *Post-Soviet Women: From the Baltic to Central Asia.* Cambridge University Press, Cambridge, UK.

Buckley, R. (1994) A framework for ecotourism. *Annals of Tourism Research* 21, 661–665.

Budeanu, A. (2005) Impacts and responsibilities for sustainable tourism: a tour operator's perspective. *Journal of Cleaner Production* 13(2), 89–97.

Budiansky, S. (1992) *The Covenant of the Wild: Why Animals Chose Domestication.* William Morrow, New York.

Budiansky, S. (1997) *The Nature of Horses: their Evolution, Intelligence and Behaviour.* Weidenfeld & Nicolson, London.

Bull, A.O. (1996) The economics of cruising: an application to the short ocean cruise market. *Journal of Tourism Studies* 7(2), 28–35.

BUPA (2004) *Post-holiday Blues.* BUPA, London <http://www.bupa.co.uk/health_information/asp/healthy_living/lifestyle/under_pressure/work/> (last accessed 16 March 2005).

Burbank, J. (1994) *Culture Shock: Nepal. A Guide to Customs and Etiquette.* Kuperard, London.

Burger, J. and Gochfield, M. (1993) Tourism and short term behavioural responses of nesting masked red-footed and blue-footed boobies in the Galapagos. *Environmental Conservation* 20(3), 255–259.

Burgess, J. (2003) Sustainable consumption: is it really achievable? *Consumer Policy Review* 13(3), 78–84.

Burnett, J.J. and Bender-Baker, H.B. (2001) Assessing the travel-related behaviors of the mobility-disabled consumer. *Journal of Travel Research* 40(1), 4–11.

Burnie, D. (1994) Ecotourists to paradise. *New Scientist* 16 April, pp. 24–27.

Butcher, J. (2003) *The Moralisation of Tourism: Sun, Sand . . . and Saving the World?* Routledge, London.

Butler, R.W. (1990) Alternative tourism: pious hope or Trojan horse? *Journal of Travel Research* 28(3), 40–45.

Butler, R.W. (1991) Tourism, environment and sustainable development. *Environmental Conservation* 18(3), 201–209.

Butler, R. and Airey, D. (2005) The foot-and-mouth outbreak of 2001: impacts on and implications for tourism in the United Kingdom. In: Aramberri, J. and Butler, R. (eds) *Tourism Development: Issues for a Vulnerable Industry*. Channel View Publications, Clevedon, UK, pp. 215–238.

Butler, R.W. and Hall, C.M. (1998) Conclusion: the sustainability of tourism and recreation in rural areas. In: Butler, R.W., Hall, C.M. and Jenkins, J. (eds) *Tourism and Recreation in Rural Areas*. John Wiley & Sons, Chichester, UK, and New York, pp. 249–258.

CAA (Civil Aviation Authority) (2001) *Travelling Safely*. CAA, London.

Calder, S. (2001) Airline buys half a million Airogym-devices to stop blood-clot deaths. *The Independent* 19 April.

Calder, S. (2005) A time to celebrate victory, not defeat. *The Independent* 9 July, Traveller p. 3.

Callanan, M. and Thomas, S. (2005) Volunteer tourism. In: Novelli, M. (ed.) *Niche Tourism: Contemporary Issues, Trends and Cases*. Elsevier, Amsterdam, pp. 183–200.

Campbell, L. (1999) Ecotourism in rural developing communities. *Annals of Tourism Research* 26(3), 534–553.

Canadian Centre for Ethics and Corporate Policy (1999) *Ethics Centre CA*. Canadian Centre for Ethics and Corporate Policy, Toronto <http://www.ethicscentre.com> (last accessed 8 April 2005).

Card, J.A. (2003) Aging and disability population trends: their impact on tourism in the future. *e-Review of Tourism Research* 1(1), 1–4 <http://ertr.tamu.edu>.

Carlsson-Kanyama, A. and Lindén, A.-L. (1999) Travel patterns and environmental effects now and in the future: implications of differences in energy consumption among socio-economic groups. *Ecological Economics* 30, 405–417.

Carney, D. (ed.) (1998) *Sustainable Rural Livelihoods: What Contribution Can We Make?* Department for International Development, London.

Carrigan, M. and Attalla, A. (2001) The myth of the ethical consumer – do ethics matter in purchase behavior? *Journal of Consumer Marketing* 18(7), 560–578.

Carroll, A.B. (1989) *Business and Society: Ethics and Stakeholder Management*. William Morrow, New York.

Carter, F.W. and Turnock, D. (2002) *Environmental Problems of East Central Europe,* 2nd edn. Routledge, London and New York.

Carter, R.W., Whiley, D. and Knight, C. (2004) Improving environmental performance in the tourism accommodation sector. *Journal of Ecotourism* 3(1), 46–68.

Carter, S. (1997a) The sexual behaviour of international travellers at two Glasgow GUM clinics. *International Journal of STD and AIDS* 8, 336–338.

Carter, S. (1997b) Who wants to be a 'peelie wally'? Glaswegian tourists' attitudes to sun tans and sun exposure. In: Clift, S. and Grawboski, P. (eds) *Tourism and Health: Risks, Research and Responses*. Mansell, London, pp. 139–150.

Carter, S. (1998) Tourists' and travellers' social construction of Africa and Asia as risky locations. *Tourism Management* 19(4), 349–358.

Cartwright, R. (2000) Reducing the health risks associated with travel. *Tourism Economics* 6(2), 159–167.

Cartwright, R.Y. (1992) The epidemiology of travellers' diarrhoea in British package holiday tourists. *PHLS Microbiology Digest* 9(3), 121–124.

Case, J. and Useem, J. (1996) Six characteristics in search of a strategy. *Inc.* 18(3), 46–55.

Castle, S. (2005) UK fury over MEP vote to end working time opt-out. *The Independent* 12 May, p. 67.

Cater, E.A. (1987) Tourism in the least developed countries. *Annals of Tourism Research* 14, 202–226.

Cater, E. (1994) Introduction. In: Cater, E. and Lowman, G. (eds) *Tourism: a Sustainable Option?* John Wiley & Sons, Chichester, UK, and New York, pp. 3–17.

Cater, E. and Lowman, G. (eds) (1994) *Tourism: a Sustainable Option?* John Wiley & Sons, Chichester, UK, and New York

Cattarinich, X. (2001) *Pro-poor Tourism Initiatives in Developing Countries: Analysis of Secondary Case Studies*. PPT Working Paper No. 8, Centre for Responsible Tourism, International Institute for Environment and Development and Overseas Development Institute, London.

Caulkin, S. (2005) Outsourcing and out of control. *The Observer* 28 August, Business p. 3.

Cavinato, J.L. and Cuckovich, M.L. (1992) Transportation and tourism for the disabled: an assessment. *Transportation Journal* 31(3), 46–53.

Ceballos-Lascurain, H. (1996) *Tourism, Ecotourism and Protected Areas: the State of Nature-based Tourism Around the World and Guidelines for its Development*. IUCN – World Conservation Union, Gland, Switzerland, and Cambridge, UK.

Chalker, B. (1994) Ecotourism: on the trail of destruction or sustainability? A minister's view. In: Cater, E. and Lowman, G. (eds) *Tourism: a Sustainable Option?* John Wiley & Sons, Chichester, UK, and New York, pp. 86–99.

Chamberlain, M. (1998) Changing attitudes to disability in hospitals. *The Lancet* 351, 771–772.

Chambers, C.M., Chambers, P.E. and Whitehead, J.C. (1994) Conservation organizations and the option value to preserve: an application of debt-for-nature swaps. *Ecological Economics* 9(2), 135–143.

Chaplin, D. (1999) Consuming work/productive leisure: the consumption patterns of second home environments. *Leisure Studies* 18, 41–55.

Chapple, C.K. (1993) *Non-violence to Animals, Earth, and Self in Asian Traditions*. State University of New York Press, Albany, New York.

Charatan, F. (2002) Viral gastroenteritis affects hundreds on cruise ships. *British Medical Journal* 325, 1192.

Chen, J.S., Chu, K.H.-L. and Wu, W.-C. (2000) Tourism students' perceptions of work values: a case of Taiwanese universities. *International Journal of Contemporary Hospitality Management* 12(6), 360–365.

Cheong, R. (1995) The virtual threat to travel and tourism. *Tourism Management* 16(6), 417–422.

Chesney-Lind, M. and Lind, I.Y. (1986) Visitors as victims: crimes against tourists in Hawaii. *Annals of Tourism Research* 13(2), 167–191.

Christenson, B., Lidin-Janson, I. and Kallings, I. (1987) Outbreak of respiratory illness on board a ship cruising to ports in Southern Europe and Northern Africa. *Journal of Infection* 14, 247–254.

Cinquegrani, R. (2002) Futuristic networks: cases of epistemic community? *Futures* 34(8), 779–783.

Cirules, E. (2004) *The Mafia in Havana: a Caribbean Mob Story*. Ocean Press, Melbourne, Australia.

Clark, D.A. (2002) Development ethics: a research agenda. *International Journal of Social Economics* 29(11), 830–848.

Clark, D. (2004) *The Rough Guide to Ethical Shopping*. Penguin, London.

Clark, I.D. and Cahir, D.A. (2003) Aboriginal people, gold, and tourism: the benefits of inclusiveness for goldfields tourism in regional Victoria. *Tourism, Culture and Communication* 4(3), 123–136.

Clark, K. (1977) *Animals and Men*. Thames & Hudson, London.

Clark, N. and Clift, S. (1994a) *A Survey of Student Health and Risk Behaviour on Holidays Abroad*. Travel, Lifestyles and Health Working Paper No. 3, Christ Church College, Canterbury, UK.

Clark, N. and Clift, S. (1994b) *A Quantitative and Qualitative Study of Students' Holiday Experiences with Particular Reference to Health and Risk Behaviour*. Travel, Lifestyles and Health Working Paper No. 6, Christ Church College, Canterbury, UK.

Clarke, H.R. and Ng, Y.-K. (1993) Tourism, economic welfare and efficient planning. *Annals of Tourism Research* 20(4), 613–632.

Clarke, P. and Linzey, A. (1990) *Political Theory and Animal Rights*. Pluto Press, London and Winchester, Massachusetts.

Cleverdon, R. and Kalisch, A. (2000) Fair trade in tourism. *International Journal of Tourism Research* 2, 171–187.

Clift, S. and Grabowski, P. (eds) (1997) *Tourism and Health*. Pinter, London.

Clift, S. and Page, S.J. (1994) Travel, lifestyles and health. *Tourism Management* 15(1), 69–70.

Clift, S. and Page, S.J. (eds) (1996) *Health and the International Tourist*. Routledge, London.

Cloke, P. and Little, J. (eds) (1997) *Contested Countryside Cultures: Otherness, Marginalisation and Rurality*. Routledge, London.

Clough, C. and Kew, B. (1993) *The Animal Welfare Handbook*. Fourth Estate, London.

Coalter, F. (1998) Leisure studies, leisure policy and social citizenship: the failure of welfare or the limits of welfare? *Leisure Studies* 17(1), 21–36.

Coast, E. (2002) Maasai socioeconomic conditions: a cross-border comparison. *Human Ecology* 30(1), 79–105.

Coccossis, H. (1996) Tourism and sustainability: perspectives and implications. In: Priestley, G.K., Edwards, J.A. and Coccossis, H. (eds) *Sustainable Tourism? European Experiences*. CAB International, Wallingford, UK, pp. 1–21.

Coccossis, H. and Nijkamp, P. (eds) (1995) *Sustainable Tourism Development*. Avebury, Aldershot, UK.

Cohen, B. (1963) *The Press and Foreign Policy*. Princeton University Press, Princeton, New Jersey.

Cohen, E. (1979) A phenomenology of tourist experiences. *Sociology* 13, 179–202.

Cohen, E. (1988) Authenticity and commoditization. *Annals of Tourism Research* 15, 371–386.

Cohen, E. (1996) A phenomenology of tourist experiences. In: Apostopoulos, Y., Leivadi, S. and Yiannakis, A. (eds) *The Sociology of Tourism: Theoretical and Empirical Investigations*. Routledge, London and New York, pp. 90–111.

Coles, T. and Hall, D. (2005) Tourism and EU enlargement. Plus ça change? *International Journal of Tourism Research* 7(2), 51–61.

Community Aid Abroad (1990) *Travel Wise and Be Welcome: a Guide to Responsible Travel in the 90s*. Community Aid Abroad, Melbourne, Australia.

Conill, A. (1998) Living with disability: a proposal for medical education. *Journal of the American Medical Association* 279(1), 83.

Conlin, M.V. (1996) Revitalizing Bermuda: tourism policy planning in a mature island destination. In: Harrison, L.C. and Husbands, W. (eds) *Practicing Responsible Tourism*. John Wiley & Sons, Chichester, UK, and New York, pp. 80–102.

Conway, S., Gilles, P. and Slack, R. (1990) *The Health of Travellers. A Report of the Study of People in Nottingham Concentrating upon Sexual Behaviour whilst Travelling Abroad and Risk Taking in the Context of STD and HIV Transmission*. Department of Public Medicine and Epidemiology, University of Nottingham and Nottingham Health Authority, Nottingham, UK.

Cook, S. and Hosey, G.R. (1995) Interaction sequences between chimpanzees and human visitors at the zoo. *Zoo Biology* 14(5), 431–440.

Coppock, V., Haydon, D. and Richter, I. (1995) *The Illusions of 'Post-Feminism': New Women, Old Myths*. Taylor & Francis, London.

Cornelissen, S. (2004) Sport mega-events in Africa: processes, impacts and prospects. *Tourism and Hospitality: Planning and Development* 1(1), 39–55.

Cossar, J. (1996) Travellers' health: a medical perspective. In: Clift, S. and Page, S. (eds) *Health and the International Tourist*. Routledge, London, pp. 23–43.

Cossar, J., Reid, D., Fallon, R., Bell, E., Riding, M., Follett, E., Dow, B., Mitchell, S. and Grist, N. (1994) A cumulative review of studies of travellers, their experience of illness and the implication of their findings. *Journal of Infection* 21(1), 27–42.

Cossens, J. and Gin, S. (1994) Tourism and AIDS: the perceived risk of HIV infection on destination choice. *Journal of Travel and Tourism Marketing* 3(4), 1–20.

Costa, J. (2004) The Portuguese tourism sector: key challenges for human resources management. *International Journal of Contemporary Hospitality Management* 16(7), 402–407.

Cousins, D. (1978) Man's exploitation of the gorilla. *Biological Conservation* 13(4), 287–297.

Craib, I. (1984) *Modern Social Theory*. Harvester, Brighton, UK.

Crane, L.A., Marcus, A.C. and Pike, D.K. (1993) Skin cancer prevention in preschools and daycare centers. *Journal of School Health* 63(5), 232–234.

Crawford, D.W. and Godbey, G. (1987) Reconceptualizing barriers to family leisure. *Leisure Sciences* 9(2), 119–128.

Crawford, D.W., Jackson, E.L. and Godbey, G. (1991) A hierarchical model of leisure constraints. *Leisure Sciences* 13, 309–320.

Crooke, P. and Morgan, M. (1998) *The Associational Economy – Firms, Regions, and Innovation*. Oxford University Press, Oxford, UK.

CSD (1999) *Commission on Sustainable Development*. Seventh Session, 19–30 April, CSD, New York.

Csikszentimihalyi, M. (1975) *Beyond Boredom and Anxiety*. Jossey-Bass, San Francisco, California.

Cukier, J. and Wall, G. (1994) Informal tourism employment: vendors in Bali, Indonesia. *Tourism Management* 15(6), 464–467.

Cullingford, C. (1995) Children's attitudes to holidays overseas. *Tourism Management* 16(2): 121–127.

Culyer, A.J. (1973) *The Economics of Social Policy*. Martin Robertson, London.

Curry, N. (1992) Recreation, access, amenity and conservation in the United Kingdom: the failure of integration. In: Bowler, I.R., Bryant, C.R. and Nellis, M.D. (eds) *Contemporary Rural Systems in Transition*,
Vol. 2. CAB International, Wallingford, UK, pp. 141–154.

Curtin, S. and Busby, G. (1999) Sustainable destination development: the tour operator perspective. *International Journal of Tourism Research* 1, 135–147.

Curtis, S. (1997) Rejuvenating holiday resorts: a Spanish case study. *Travel and Tourism Analyst* 2,
77–93.

Cushman, G., Veal, A.J. and Zuzanek, J. (1996) *World Leisure Participation: Free Time in the Global Village.*
CAB International, Wallingford, UK.

D'Amore, L.J. (1992) Promoting sustainable tourism: the Canadian approach. *Tourism Management* 13(3),
258–262.

D'Amore, L.J. (1993) A code of ethics and guidelines for socially and environmentally responsible tourism.
Journal of Travel Research 31(3), 64–66.

Daniels, M.J., Drogin Rodgers, E.B. and Wiggins, B.P. (2005) 'Travel tales': an interpretive analysis of
constraints and negotiations to pleasure travel as experienced by persons with physical disabilities.
Tourism Management, 26(6), 919–930.

Dann, G.M.S. (1977) Anomie, ego-enhancement and tourism. *Annals of Tourism Research* 4(4), 184–194.

Dann, G.M.S. (1995) A socio-linguistic approach towards changing tourist imagery. In: Butler, R. and
Pearce, D. (eds) *Change in Tourism: People, Places, Processes*. Routledge, London, pp. 114–136.

Dann, G.M.S. (1996) *The Language of Tourism: a Sociolinguistic Perspective*. CAB International, Wallingford, UK.

Dann, G. (2001) Senior tourism. *Annals of Tourism Research* 28(1), 235–238.

Dann, G.M.S. and Jacobsen, J.K.S. (2002) Leading the tourist by the nose. In: Dann, G.M.S. (ed.) *The Tourist as
a Metaphor of the Social World*. CAB International, Wallingford, UK, pp. 209–236.

Dann, G.M.S. and Jacobsen, J.K.S. (2003) Tourism smellscapes. *Tourism Geographies* 5(1), 3–25.

Dannenberg, A., Yashuk, J. and Feldman, R. (1982) Gastro-intestinal illness on passenger cruise ships,
1975–1978. *American Journal of Public Health* 72(5), 484–488.

Darcy, S. (1998) *Anxiety to Access: Tourism Patterns and Experiences of Disabled New South Wales People
with a Physical Disability*. Tourism New South Wales, Sydney, Australia.

Darcy, S. (2002) Marginalised participation: physical disability, high support needs and tourism. *Journal of
Hospitality and Tourism Management* 9(1), 61–72.

Dattilo, J. and Smith, R.W. (1990) Communicating positive attitudes toward people with disabilities through
sensitive terminology. *Therapeutic Recreation Journal* 24(1), 8–17.

D'Aveni, R. (1998) Hypercompetition closes in. *Financial Times* 4 February.

Davey, C. (2004) *The Complete Guide to Buying Property in France,* 2nd edn. Kogan Page, London and
Sterling, Virginia.

Davidson, P. (1996) The holiday and work experiences of young women with children. *Leisure Studies* 15,
89–103.

Davies, E. (2004) Crime wave hits Rio tourist trade. *The Independent* 17 November, p. 27.

Davies, M. (1990) Wildlife as a tourism attraction. *Environments* 20(3), 74–77.

Davies, R. (2001) *Driving Abroad*. Haynes Publishing, Yeovil, UK.

Davis, D., Allen, J. and Cosenza, R.M. (1988) Segmenting local residents by their attitudes, interests and
opinions towards tourism. *Journal of Travel Research* 27(2), 2–8.

Dawood, R. (1989) Tourists' health – could the travel industry do more? *Tourism Management* 10(4),
285–287.

Dawood, R. (1992) *Travellers' Health: How to Stay Healthy Abroad,* 3rd edn. Oxford University Press,
Oxford, UK.

DBV (Deutscher Bäderverband e.V.) (1998) *Jahresbericht 1997*. REHA-Verlag, Bonn, Germany.

Deacon, R.T. and Murphy, P. (1997) The structure of an environmental transaction: the debt for nature swap.
Land Economics 73(1), 1–24.

de Albuquerque, K. (1981) *Tourism and crime in the Caribbean: some lessons from the United States Virgin
Islands*. Paper presented at the Third Annual Meeting of the Association of Caribbean Studies,
Port-au-Prince, Haiti.

de Albuquerque, K. and McElroy, J. (1999) Tourism and crime in the Caribbean. *Annals of Tourism Research*
26(4), 968–984.

de Botton, A. (2002) *The Art of Travel*. Penguin, London and New York.

de Botton, A. (2005) Don't ask where, ask why. *The Observer* 2 January, Escape p. 24.

de Courcy, C. (1995) *The Zoo Story*. Claremont, Melbourne, Australia.

Decrop, A. and Snelders, D. (2005) A grounded typology of vacation decision-making. *Tourism Management* 26, 121–132.

Deem, R. (1996) No time for a rest? An exploration of women's work, engendered leisure and holidays. *Time and Society* 5, 5–25.

de Grazia, V. (1992) Leisure and citizenship: historical perspectives. In: *Proceedings of the VIII ELRA Congress*. European Leisure and Recreation Association, Bilbao, pp. 25–38.

de Kadt, E. (1979) *Tourism: Passport to Development?* Oxford University Press, Oxford, UK.

Deloitte Touche (1993) *Profiting from Opportunities*. Deloitte Touche, London.

Dembeck, H. (1961) *Mit Tieren Leben*. Econ-Verlag, Düsseldorf and Vienna.

de Pauli, L. (ed.) (2000) *Women's Empowerment and Economic Justice: Reflecting on Experience in Latin America and the Caribbean*. UNIFEM, New York.

Devarajan, S., Miller, M. and Swanson, E.V. (2002) *Goals for Development: History, Prospects, and Costs*. Policy Research Working Paper 2819, World Bank, Washington, DC.

Devedzic, M. (2002) Ethnic heterogeneity and gender in the Yugoslav seaside tourist region. In: Swain, M.B. and Momsen, J.H. (eds) *Gender/Tourism/Fun(?)*. Cognizant Communication Corporation, New York, pp. 143–153.

Devine, M.A. and Dattilo, J. (2001) Social acceptance and leisure lifestyles of people with disabilities. *Therapeutic Recreation Journal* 34(4), 306–322.

de Vries, A. (2003) *Buying a House in France*. Vacation Work, Oxford, UK.

de Vries, A. (2004) *Starting a Business in France*. Vacation Work, Oxford, UK.

de Vries, J. (1996) Beyond health status: construction and validation of the Dutch WHO quality of life assessment instrument. Unpublished PhD thesis, Tilburg University, Tilburg, The Netherlands.

DfID (Department for International Development) (1999) *Sustainable Livelihoods Guidance Sheets*. DfID, London.

Dieke, P.U.C. (2003) Tourism in Africa's economic development: policy implications. *Management Decision* 41(3), 287–295.

Di Giovanna, T., Rosen, T., Forsett, R., Silverston, K. and Kelen, G. (1992) Shipboard medicine: a new niche for emergency medicine. *Annals of Emergency Medicine* 21(12), 1476–1479.

Dillon, J., Rickinson, M., Sanders, D., Tearney, K. and Benefield, P. (2003) *Improving the Understanding of Food, Farming and Land Management Amongst School-age Children: a Literature Review*. National Foundation for Educational Research and King's College, London.

Dimanche, F. and Lepetic, A. (1999) New Orleans tourism and crime: a case study. *Journal of Travel Research* 38(1), 19–23.

Dimanche, F., Havitz, M.E. and Howard, D.R. (1991) Testing the involvement profile (IP) scale in the context of selected recreational and touristic activities. *Journal of Leisure Research* 23(1), 51–66.

Dogan, H.Z. (1989) Forms of adjustment: socio-cultural impacts of tourism. *Annals of Tourism Research* 16(2), 216–236.

Donaghy, K., Poppelreuter, S. and Rudinger, G. (eds) (2005) *Social Dimensions of Sustainable Transport: Transatlantic Perspectives*. Ashgate, Aldershot, UK.

Downes, J.J. (1996) The package travel directive – implications for organisers and suppliers. *Economic Intelligence Unit Travel and Tourism Analyst* 1, 78–92.

Downs, A. (1972) Up and down with ecology – the issue attention cycle. *The Public Interest* 28, 38–50.

Doxey, G.V. (1975) A causation theory of visitor–resident irritants: methodology and research influence. In: *Proceedings of the Travel Research Association 6th Annual Conference*. Travel Research Associaton, San Diego, California, pp. 195–198.

Driedger, D. (1987) Disabled people and international air travel. *Journal of Leisurability* 14(1), 13–19.

Drover, G. and Kerans, P. (eds) (1993) *New Approaches to Welfare Theory*. Edward Elgar, Aldershot, UK.

D'Sa, E. (1998) *Global Code of Ethics – What of NGO and Community Involvement?* Web Forum – Ethical Tourism: The Debate <http://www.mcb.co.uk/services/conferen/webforum/mcb-eit-session1/index.html> (site no longer active).

D'Sa, E. (1999) Wanted: tourists with a social conscience. *International Journal of Contemporary Hospitality Management* 11(2–3), 64–68.

Dube, L. and Renaghan, L.M. (2000) Marketing your hotel to and through intermediaries. *Cornell HRA Quarterly* 41(1), 73–83.

Duckett, S. (2002) *The Spa Directory*. Carlton Books, London.

Duffus, D. and Dearden, P. (1990) Non-consumptive wildlife-oriented recreation: a conceptual framework. *Biological Conservation* 53, 213–231.

Dunn, H.L. (1961) *High Level Wellness*. R.W. Beaty, Arlington, Virginia.

Dunn Ross, E.L. and Iso-Ahola, S.E. (1991) Sightseeing tourists' motivation and satisfaction. *Annals of Tourism Research* 18, 226–237.

Dunscombe, J. (1992) The EC Directive of Package Travel, and the interface between the travel industry and medical profession. Paper presented at the Healthy Travel Seminar, 18 November, International Society of Travel Medicine, London.

Dwyer, L., Burnley, I., Forsyth, P. and Murphy, P. (1993) *Tourism–Immigration Interrelationships*. Australian Government Publishing Service, Canberra, Australia.

Dyer, G. (2005) Paradise lost? Not from where I'm standing. *The Observer* 30 January, Escape pp. 2–3.

Eadington, W.R. (1999) The spread of casinos and their role in tourism development. In: Pearce, D.G. and Butler, R.W. (eds) *Contemporary Issues in Tourism Development*. Routledge, London, pp. 127–142.

Eberhardt, K. and Mayberry, W. (1995) Factors influencing entry-level occupational therapists' attitudes towards persons with disabilities. *American Journal of Occupational Therapy* 49(7), 629–636.

Eco, U. (1983) *Travels in Hyperreality*. Harcourt Brace, San Diego, California.

Ecotourism Society Pakistan (2004) Tregedy [sic] of death of five porters at Skardu working with Italian team on K-2. Ecotourism Society Pakistan <eco.tourism@comsats.net.pk> email to <atlas-euro.org–list>, 29 June.

ECTWT (Ecumenical Coalition on Third World Tourism) (1986) *Third World People and Tourism*. ECTWT, Bangkok.

ECTWT (Ecumenical Coalition on Third World Tourism) (1988) *Tourism: an Ecumenical Concern*. ECTWT, Bangkok.

Eder, K. (1988) *Die Vergesellschaftung der Natur: Studien zur Sozialen Evolution der Praktischen Vernunft*. Suhrkamp Verlag, Frankfurt am Main, Germany.

Edgell, D. (1990) *International Tourism Policy*. Van Nostrand Reinhold, New York.

Edmunson, B. (1997) Tanned to death. *American Demographics* 19(3), 37.

Elkington, J. (1999) *Cannibals with Forks: the Triple Bottom Line of 21st Century Business*. Capstone Publishing, Oxford, UK.

Elkington, J. and Hailes, J. (1992) *Holidays That Don't Cost the Earth: the Guide to Greener Holidays*. Victor Gollancz, London.

Elliott, R. (2000) *AH&MA Takes Strong Position that No Increase in Accessible Rooms Requirements be Mandated*. American Hotel and Lodging Association, Washington, DC.

el Saadawi, N. (trans. Eber, S.) (1991) *My Travels Around the World*. Methuen, London.

Engel, C. (2002) *Wild Health: How Animals Keep Themselves Well and What We Can Learn from Them*. Weidenfeld & Nicolson, London.

ESPA (European Spa Association) (1995) *Spas and Health Resorts in Europe*. ESPA, Bonn and Brussels.

Espin-Andersen, G. (1990) *The Three Worlds of Welfare Capitalism*. Polity Press, Cambridge, UK.

Espin-Andersen, G. (1999) *Social Foundations of Post-industrial Economies*. Oxford University Press, Oxford, UK.

ETC (English Tourism Council) (2000) *People with Disabilities and Holiday Taking*. ETC, London.

ETC (English Tourism Council) (2001) *Time for Action*. ETC, London.

European Commission (2003) *Basic Orientations for the Sustainability of European Tourism*. Enterprise Directorate-General, European Commission, Brussels.

Evans, N.G. and Stabler, M.J. (1995) A future for the package tour operator in the 21st century? *Tourism Economics* 1(3), 245–263.

Everett, D. (1999) *Buying and Restoring Old Property in France*, 2nd edn. Robert Hale, London.

Eyre, R. (1979) *The Long Search*. BBC and Collins, London.

FAACE (Fight Against Animal Cruelty in Europe) (2005) *Fight Against Animal Cruelty in Europe*. FAACE, Southport, UK <http://www.faace.co.uk/> (last accessed 9 April 2005).

Faits et Opinions (1987) *Europæenes Feriemønster*. Faits et Opinions, Paris.

Farrell, B. and Twining-Ward, L. (2004) Reconceptualizing tourism. *Annals of Tourism Research* 31(2), 274–295.

Farrell, B. and Twining-Ward, L. (2005) Seven steps towards sustainability: tourism in the context of new knowledge. *Journal of Sustainable Tourism* 13(2), 109–122.

Farrell, B.J., Cobbin, D.M. and Farrell, H.M. (2002a) Can codes of ethics really produce consistent behaviours? *Journal of Managerial Psychology* 17(6), 468–490.

Farrell, B.J., Cobbin, D.M. and Farrell, H.M. (2002b) Codes of ethics: their evolution, development and other controversies. *Journal of Management Development* 21(2), 152–163.

Faulkner, B. (2001) Towards a framework for tourism disaster management. *Tourism Management* 22, 135–147.

Faulkner, B. and Russell, R. (1997) Chaos and complexity in tourism: in search of a new perspective. *Pacific Tourism Review* 1, 93–102.

FCO (Foreign and Commonwealth Office) (2005) *Travel Advice by Country*. FCO, London <http://www.fco.gov.uk/servlet/Front?pagename=OpenMarket/Xcelerate/ShowPage&c> (last accesed 2 July 2005).

Fennell, D.A. (1999) *Ecotourism: an Introduction*. Routledge, London and New York.

Fennell, D.A. (2000) Tourism and applied ethics. *Tourism Recreation Research* 25(1), 59–69.

Fennell, D.A. and Malloy, D.C. (1995) Ethics and ecotourism: a comprehensive ethical model. *Journal of Applied Recreation Research* 20, 163–183.

Fennell, D.A. and Malloy, D.C. (1999) Measuring the ethical nature of tourism operators. *Annals of Tourism Research* 26, 928–943.

Fennell, D.A. and Przeclawski, K. (2003) Generating goodwill in tourism through ethical stakeholder interactions. In: Singh, S., Timothy, D.J. and Dowling, R.K. (eds) *Tourism in Destination Communities*. CAB International, Wallingford, UK, pp. 135–152.

Field, F. (2002) *Welfare Titans*. Civitas, London.

Filion, F., Foley, J. and Jacquemot, A. (1994) The economics of global tourism. In: Munasinghe, M. and McNeely, J. (eds) *Protected Area Economics and Policy: Linking Conservation and Sustainable Development*. World Bank, Washington, DC, pp. 234–254.

Financial Mail (2000) British hotels fear impact of proposed disability legislation. *Financial Mail* 10 September.

Finlay, T., James, L.R. and Maple, T.L. (1988) People's perception of animals: the influence of zoo environment. *Environment and Behavior* 20(4), 508–528.

Fisher, D. (1996) Sustainable tourism in southern Albania. *Albanian Life* 59, 27–29.

Fisher, D. (2004) The demonstration effect revisited. *Annals of Tourism Research* 31(2), 428–446.

Fisher, J. (2003) Surface and deep approaches to business ethics. *Leadership and Organization Development Journal* 24(2), 96–101.

Fitzgerald, R. (1986) Medical facilities and needs aboard a cruise ship: points to ponder before an ocean cruise. *Southern Medical Journal* 79, 1413–1415.

Fleckenstein, M.P. and Huebsch, P. (1999) Ethics in tourism – reality or hallucination? *Journal of Business Ethics* 19(1), 137–142.

Fleischer, A. and Pizam, A. (2002) Tourism constraints among Israeli seniors. *Annals of Tourism Research* 29, 106–123.

Fletcher, W. (2005) Scrooge's guide to corporate obligation. *The Times Higher* 29 April, p. 27.

Flognfeldt, T. (2002) Second-home ownership: a sustainable semi-migration. In: Hall, C.M. and Williams, A.M. (eds) *Tourism and Migration*. Kluwer, Dordrecht, The Netherlands, pp. 187–203.

Floro, M. and Schaeffer, K. (2001) Restructuring of labour markets in the Philippines and Zambia: the gender dimension. In: Beneria, L. and Bisnath, S. (eds) *Gender and Development: Theoretical, Empirical and Practical Approaches*, Vol. II. Elgar Publishing, London, pp. 393–418.

Fodness, D. (1992) The impact of family life cycle on the vacation decision-making process. *Journal of Travel Research* 2(2), 8–13.

Fong, Y.M. (1997) China wants Singapore to hire more of its seafarers. *InforMare* <http://www.informare.it/news/review/1997/st0009.htm> (last accessed 10 April 1998).

Font, X. and Harris, C. (2004) Rethinking standards from green to sustainable. *Annals of Tourism Research* 31(4), 986–1007.

Forsyth, T. (1995) Business attitudes to sustainable tourism. *Journal of Sustainable Tourism* 3(4), 210–231.

Forsyth, T. (1996) Bums on seats. *In Focus* Spring, 4–5.

Fost, D. (1998) The fun factor: marketing recreation to the disabled. *American Demographics* 20(2), 54–58.

Fountain, J. and Hall, C.M. (2002) The impact of lifestyle migration on rural communities: a case study of Akaroa, New Zealand. In: Hall, C.M. and Williams, A.M. (eds) *Tourism and Migration*. Kluwer, Dordrecht, The Netherlands, pp. 153–168.

Francken, D.A. and van Raaij, W.F. (1979) *Longitudinal Study of Vacationers' Information Acquisition Behavior*. Papers on Economic Psychology No. 2, Erasmus University, Rotterdam.

Francken, D.A. and van Raaij, W.F. (1981) Satisfaction with leisure time activities. *Journal of Leisure Research* 13, 337–352.

Franklin, A. (2003) The tourist syndrome: an interview with Zygmunt Bauman. *Tourist Studies* 3(2), 205–217.

Frantz, D. (1999) Gaps in sea laws shield pollution by cruise lines. *New York Times* 3 January.

Frary, M. (2005) Beat the queue blues. *Business Travel World* January, 20–21.

Fraser, K. (ed.) (1993) *Worst Journeys: the Picador Book of Travel*, 3rd edn. Picador, London.

Frean, A. (1992) Haven to end agony of the dancing bears. *The European* 18 June.

Fridgen, J.D. (1984) Environmental psychology and tourism. *Annals of Tourism Research* 11(1), 19–39.

Frohlick, S. (2004) 'Who is Lhakpa Sherpa?' Circulating subjectivities within the global/local terrain of Himalayan mountaineering. *Social and Cultural Geography* 5(2), 195–212.

Fujii, E.T. and Mak, J. (1980) Tourism and crime: implications for regional development policy. *Regional Studies* 14(1), 27–36.

Fulton, L. (2004) Current trends and sustainability scenarios in transport energy use. Paper presented in STELLA (Sustainable Transport in Europe and Links and Liaisons with the Americas) project (financed by EC DG TREN), 25–27 March, Brussels.

Fürsich, E. and Robins, M.B. (2004) Visiting Africa: constructions of nation and identity on travel websites. *Journal of Asian and African Studies* 39(1–2), 133–152.

Fussell, P. (1982) *Abroad: British Literary Travelling Between the Wars.* Oxford University Press, Oxford, UK.

Gallant, N., Mace, A. and Tewdwr-Jones, M. (2005) *Second Homes: European Perspectives and UK Policies.* Ashgate, Aldershot, UK.

Gandhi, M. (1959) *The Moral Basis of Vegetarianism.* Novajivan, Ahmedabad, India.

Gant, R. and Smith, J. (1992) Tourism and national development planning in Tunisia. *Tourism Management* 13(3), 331–336.

Garber, M., Hansesen, B. and Walkowitz, R.L. (2000) *The Turn to Ethics.* Routledge, London and New York.

Garfield, S. (2004) The burning issue. *The Observer Magazine* 18 July, pp. 24–32.

Garrod, B. and Fennell, D.A. (2004) Analysis of whalewatching codes of conduct. *Annals of Tourism Research* 31(2), 334–352.

Gately, I. (2004) *Planet Party: a World of Celebration.* Pocket Books, London.

Geldof, B. (2005) 'Our failure to tackle world poverty is now a joke'. *The Independent* 17 May, p. 28. <http://comment.independent.co.uk/low_res/story.jsp?story=638897&host=6&dir=142> (last accessed 17 May 2005).

George, R. (2003) Tourists' perceptions of safety and security while visiting Cape Town. *Tourism Management* 24(5), 575–585.

Ghimire, K.B. (2001) Regional tourism and South–South economic cooperation. *Geographical Journal* 167(2), 99–110.

Ghodsee, K. (2003) State support in the market: women and tourism employment in post-socialist Bulgaria. *International Journal of Politics, Culture and Society* 16(3), 465–482.

Gilbert, D. and Abdullah, J. (2002) A study of the impact of the expectation of a holiday on an individual's sense of well-being. *Journal of Vacation Marketing* 8(4), 352–361.

Gilbert, D. and Hudson, S. (2000) Tourism demand constraints: a skiing participation. *Annals of Tourism Research* 27(4), 906–925.

Gladwell, N.J. and Bedini, L.A. (2004) In search of lost leisure: the impact of caregiving on leisure travel. *Tourism Management* 25, 685–693.

Glowka, L. (2003) Putting marine scientific research on a sustainable footing at hydrothermal vents. *Marine Policy* 27(4), 303–312.

Glyptis, S. (1989) *Leisure and Unemployment.* Open University Press, Milton Keynes, UK.

Goa Foundation (1997) Green notes from Goa. *Tourism in Focus* 25, 16.

Goldsmith, M.F. (1998) Health woes grow in a shrinking world. *Journal of the American Medical Association* 279, 569–571.

Gompertz, L. (1824) *Moral Inquiries on the Situation of Man and Beast.* Westley & Parrish, London.

Gonsalves, P.S. (1991) Alternative tourism: a Third World perspective. *Lokayan Bulletin* 9(2), 23–28.

Gonzalez-Gaudiano, E. (2001) Complexity in environmental education. *Education Philosophy and Theory* 33(2), 153–166.

Goodin, R. (1988) *Reasons for Welfare: the Political Theory of the Welfare State.* Princeton University Press, Princeton, New Jersey.

Goodrich, J.N. and Goodrich, G.E. (1987) Health-care tourism – an exploratory study. *Tourism Management* 8(3), 217–222.

Goodwin, H. (2002) Pro-poor tourism: a new approach for poverty alleviation. In: World Tourism Organization (WTO) (ed.) *Tourism: a Catalyst for Sustainable Development in Africa.* WTO, Madrid, pp. 54–71.

Goodwin, H. (2005) *Pro-poor Tourism: Principles, Methodologies and Mainstreaming.* Keynote presented to International Conference on Pro-Poor Tourism Mechanisms and Mainstreaming, Universiti Teknologi Malaysia, 4–5 May, Melaka <http://www.propoortourism.org.uk/Publications%20by%20partnership/HG_Melaka_presentation.pdf> (last accessed 9 July 2005).

Goodwin, H. and Pender, L. (2005) Ethics in tourism management. In: Pender, L. and Sharpley, R. (eds) *The Management of Tourism*. Sage, London, pp. 288–304.

Gordon, G. and Townsend, C. (2001) *Tourism: Putting Ethics into Practice*. Tearfund, Teddington, UK.

Gössling, S. (2000) Sustainable tourism development in developing countries: some aspects of energy-use. *Journal of Sustainable Tourism* 8(5), 410–425.

Gössling, S. (2002a) Global environmental consequences of tourism. *Global Environmental Change* 12, 283–302.

Gössling, S. (2002b) Human–environmental relations with tourism. *Annals of Tourism Research* 29(2), 539–556.

Gössling, S. and Mattsson, S. (2002) Farm tourism in Sweden: structure, growth and characteristics. *Scandinavian Journal of Hospitality and Tourism* 2(1), 17–30.

Gössling, S., Borgström Hansson, C., Hörstmeier, O. and Saggel, S. (2002) Ecological footprint analysis as a tool to assess tourism sustainability. *Ecological Economics* 43, 199–211.

Gottlieb, A. (1982) Americans' vacations. *Annals of Tourism Research* 9(2), 165–187.

Goulet, D. (1973) *The Cruel Choice: a New Concept in the Theory of Development*. Atheneum, New York.

Goulet, D. (1997) Development ethics: a new discipline. *International Journal of Social Economics* 24(11), 1160–1171.

Gowdy, J. (2005) Toward a new welfare economics for sustainability. *Ecological Economics* 53, 211–222.

Grabowski, P. and Behrens, R.H. (1996) Provision of health information by British travel agents. *Tropical Medicine and International Health* 1(5), 730–732.

Grady, D. (2002) U.S. health officials call cruise ships safe, in spite of outbreaks. *New York Times* 28 November, p. A32.

Graham, S. (1991) *Handle with Care: a Guide to Responsible Travel in Developing Countries*. The Nobel Press, Chicago, Illinois.

Gratton, C. (1995) A cross-national/transnational approach to leisure research: the changing relationship between work and leisure in Europe. In: Richards, G. (ed.) *European Tourism and Leisure Education: Trends and Prospects*. Tilburg University Press, Tilburg, The Netherlands, pp. 215–232.

Grayson, E. and Marini, I. (1996) Simulated disability exercises and their impact on attitudes toward persons with disabilities. *International Journal of Rehabilitation Research* 19, 123–131.

Greeley, M. and Jenkins, R. (2001) *Mainstreaming the Poverty-reduction Agenda: an Analysis of Institutional Mechanisms to Support Pro-poor Policy Making and Implementation in Six African Countries*. Institute of Development Studies, University of Sussex, Brighton, UK.

Green, R. (2005) Community perceptions of environmental and social change and tourism development on the island of Koh Samui, Thailand. *Journal of Environmental Psychology* 25(1), 37–56.

Greene, D.L. (2003) Obstacles to policy implementation: fuel economy standards, the rebound effect and safety. Paper presented in STELLA (Sustainable Transport in Europe and Links and Liaisons with the Americas) project, 26–27 May, Quebec City.

Greene, D.L., Jones, D.W. and Delucci, M. (1997) *The Full Costs and Benefits of Transportation*. Springer, Berlin.

Grenfell, R. and Ross, N. (1994) How dangerous is that visit to the beach? A pilot study of beach injuries. *Australian Family Physician* 21, 1145–1148.

Griffin, J. (1986) *Well-being: Its Meaning, Measurement and Moral Importance*. Clarendon Press, Oxford, UK.

Griffith, M. and van Schaik, C.P. (1993) The impact of human traffic on the abundance and activity periods of Sumatran rain forest wildlife. *Conservation Biology* 7(3), 623–626.

Griffith, S. (2003) *Taking a Gap Year*, 3rd edn. Vacation Work, Oxford, UK.

Grover, S. (2004) *The Post-travelling Blues* <http://www.fazed.com/travel/post_holiday_blues.html> (last accessed 16 March 2005).

Guevara, E.C. (2003) *The Motorcycle Diaries. Notes on a Latin American Journey*. Ocean Press, Melbourne and New York.

Gunn, C. (1988) *Tourism Planning*. Taylor & Francis, London and New York.

Haas, P. (1992) Introduction: epistemic communities and international policy co-ordination. *International Organizations* 46(1), 1–35.

Habib, A.G. and Tambyah, P.A. (2004) Confusion in travellers. *Travel Medicine and Infectious Disease* 2(1), 23–25.

Habib, N. and Behrens, R. (2000) Travel health and infectious disease. In: Parsons, L. and Lister, G. (eds) *Global Health, a Local Issue*. The Nuffield Trust, London.

Hahnel, R. and Albert, M. (1990) *Quiet Revolution in Welfare Economics*. Princeton University Press, Princeton, New Jersey.

Haldrup, M. and Larsen, J. (2003) The family gaze. *Tourist Studies* 3(1), 23–46.

Hall, C.M. (1992) Sex tourism in South-east Asia. In: Harrison, D. (ed.) *Tourism and the Less Developed Countries*. Belhaven, London, pp. 64–74.

Hall, C.M. (1994a) Gender and economic interests in tourism prostitution: the nature, development and implications of sex tourism in South-east Asia. In: Kinnaird, V. and Hall, D. (eds) *Tourism: a Gender Analysis*. John Wiley & Sons, Chichester, UK, and New York, pp. 142–163.

Hall, C.M. (1994b) *Tourism and Politics: Policy, Power and Place*. John Wiley & Sons, Chichester, UK, and New York.

Hall, C.M. (2000) *Tourism Planning – Policies, Processes and Relationships*. Prentice-Hall, Harlow, UK.

Hall, C.M. (2002) Travel safety, terrorism and the media: the significance of the issue-attention cycle. *Current Issues in Tourism* 5(5), 458–466.

Hall, C.M. (2003a) Reflections on tourism policy and 'quality of life' issues. In: Swarbrooke, J., Smith, M. and Onderwater, L. (eds) *Quality of Life: ATLAS Reflections 2003*. ATLAS, Arnhem, pp. 29–31.

Hall, C.M. (2003b) Tourism issues, agenda-setting and the media. *e-Review of Tourism Research* 1(3), 42–45 <http://ertr.tamu.edu>.

Hall, C.M. and Müller, D.K. (2004) Introduction: second homes, curse or blessing? Revisited. In: Hall, C.M. and Müller, D.K. (eds) *Tourism, Mobility and Second Homes: Between Elite Landscape and Common Ground*. Channel View, Clevedon, UK, pp. 3–14.

Hall, C.M., Timothy, D.J. and Duval, D.T. (eds) (2004) *Safety and Security in Tourism: Relationships, Management and Marketing*. Haworth Press, Binghamton, New York.

Hall, D. (1984) Foreign tourism under socialism: the Albanian 'Stalinist' model. *Annals of Tourism Research* 11(4), 539–555.

Hall, D. (1990) Stalinism and tourism: a study of Albania and North Korea. *Annals of Tourism Research* 17(1), 36–54.

Hall, D. (1991a) Eastern Europe and the Soviet Union: overcoming tourism constraints. In: Hall, D. (ed.) *Tourism and Economic Development in Eastern Europe and the Soviet Union*. Belhaven, London, and Halsted, New York, pp. 49–78.

Hall, D. (1991b) Evolutionary pattern of tourism development in Eastern Europe and the Soviet Union. In: Hall, D. (ed.) *Tourism and Economic Development in Eastern Europe and the Soviet Union*. Belhaven, London, and Halsted, New York, pp. 79–115.

Hall, D. (1994) *Albania and the Albanians*. Frances Pinter, London.

Hall, D. (1995) Terrorising the terrorist. *Geographical* 67(2), 17.

Hall, D. (1999) Conceptualising tourism transport: inequality and externality issues. *Journal of Transport Geography* 7(4), 181–188.

Hall, D. (2000) Identity, community and sustainability: prospects for rural tourism in Albania. In: Richards, G. and Hall, D. (eds) *Tourism and Sustainable Community Development*. Routledge, London and New York, pp. 48–59.

Hall, D. (2001) Fear of flying? *Environmental Scientist* 10(2), 5–6.

Hall, D. (2004a) Branding and national identity: the case of Central and Eastern Europe. In: Morgan, N., Pritchard, A. and Pride, R. (eds) *Destination Branding: Creating the Unique Destination Proposition*, 2nd edn. Elsevier, Amsterdam, pp. 111–127.

Hall, D. (2004b) Introduction. In: Hall, D. (ed.) *Tourism and Transition: Governance, Transformation and Development*. CAB International, Wallingford, UK, pp. 1–24.

Hall, D. (2004c) Key themes and frameworks. In: Hall, D. (ed.) *Tourism and Transition: Governance, Transformation and Development*. CAB International, Wallingford, UK, pp. 25–51.

Hall, D. (2004d) Transport and tourism: equity and sustainability issues. In: Lumsdon, L. and Page, S.J. (eds) *Tourism and Transport: Issues and Agenda for the New Millennium*. Elsevier, Amsterdam, pp. 45–55.

Hall, D. and Brown, F. (1996) Towards a welfare focus for tourism. *Progress in Tourism and Hospitality Research* 2(1), 41–57.

Hall, D., Smith, M. and Marciszewska, B. (eds) (2006) *Tourism in the New Europe: the Challenges and Opportunities of EU Enlargement*. CAB International, Wallingford, UK.

Hall, D.R., Roberts, L.A., Wemelsfelder, F. and Farish, M. (2002) A critical evaluation of animal-related rural recreation and tourism attractions. In: Anon. (ed.) *Development, Community and Conservation: Conference Papers*, Vol. 1. Bhundelkand University, Jhansi, and Centre for Tourism Research and Development, Lucknow, pp. 150–164.

Halsall, D.A. (2001) Railway heritage and the tourist gaze: Stoomtram Hoorn-Medemblik. *Journal of Transport Geography* 9(2), 151–160.

Hammond, R. (2005) Reaping the rewards. *Geographical* 77(2), 97–103.

Hamnett, C. (1996) Social polarisation, economic restructuring and welfare state regimes. *Urban Studies* 33, 1407–1430.

Hampshire, D. (2002) *Retiring Abroad*. Survival Books, London.

Hampshire, D. (2003) *Buying a Home in France 2003–04*, 4th edn. Survival Books, London.

Hanna, N. and Wells, S. (1992) Sea sickness. *Focus* 5, 4–6.

Hannah, V. (2003) Long-haul flights can increase risk of strokes in passengers with heart defects, say scientists. *The Herald* (Glasgow) 24 June <http://www.theherald.co.uk/news/archive/24-6-19103-0-6-32.html> (accessed 24 June 2003).

Harada, M. (1996) Japan. In: Cushman, G., Veal, A.J. and Zuzanek, J. (eds) *World Leisure Participation: Free Time in the Global Village*. CAB International, Wallingford, UK, pp. 153–163.

Hari, J. (2005) New Orleans is a frightening glimpse of the future. *The Independent* 3 September, p. 37.

Harper, D.W. (2001) Comparing tourists' crime victimization. *Annals of Tourism Research* 28(4), 1053–1056.

Harris, C.B. and Welsby, P.D. (2000) Health advice and the traveller. *Scottish Medical Journal* 45(1), 14–16.

Harris, D.R. (1967) North Africa (excluding Egypt). In: Hodder, B.W. and Harris, D.R. (eds) *Africa in Transition*. Methuen, London, pp. 35–94.

Harrison, D. (1993) Bulgarian tourism: a state of uncertainty. *Annals of Tourism Research* 20(3), 519–534.

Harrison, D. (2001) Tourism and less developed countries: key issues. In: Harrison, D. (ed.) *Tourism in the Less Developed World: Issues and Case Studies*. CAB International, Wallingford, UK, pp. 23–46.

Hart, A. (2003) *Going to Live in France*, 2nd edn. How To Books, Oxford, UK.

Hartgarten, S. (1994) Injury prevention: a crucial aspect of travel medicine. *Journal of Travel Medicine* 1(1), 45–50.

Hartl, M. (2003) *Rural Women's Access to Land and Property in Selected Countries*. Sustainable Development Department, Food and Agriculture Organization of the United Nations, Rome.

Haukeland, J.V. (1990) Non-travellers: the flip-side of motivation. *Annals of Tourism Research* 17(2), 172–184.

Haulot, A. (1981) Social tourism: current dimensions and future developments. *Tourism Management* 2(3), 207–212.

Hautzinger, S. (2002) Will the real commodity please stand up? Skiing and 'touristsic' real estate in Eagle Valley, Colorado. *Research in Economic Anthropology* 21, 343–366.

Hawkes, S. (1994) Risk behaviour and HIV prevalence in international travellers. *AIDS* 8, 247–252.

Hawkins, B.P., Peng, J., Hsieh, C. and Eklund, S.J. (1999) Leisure constraints: a replication and extension of construct development. *Leisure Sciences* 21, 179–192.

Haywood, K. (1990) Revising and implementing the marketing concept as it applies to tourism. *Tourism Management* 11(3), 195–205.

Haywood, K.M. (1993) Sustainable development for tourism: a commentary with an organisational perspective. In: Butler, R., Nelson, J. and Wall, G. (eds) *Tourism and Sustainable Development: Monitoring, Planning and Managing*. Department of Geography Publication Series, University of Waterloo, Waterloo, Ontario, pp. 233–241.

Heckle, H. (2004) Locals turn tide in battle of beach-hogs. *The Guardian* 23 August <http://www.guardian.co.uk/print/0,3858,4999300–103681,00.html> (last accessed 18 March 2005).

Hendee, J. and Roggenbuck, J. (1984) Wilderness related education as a factor increasing demand for wilderness. Paper presented at the International Forest Congress Convention, 5 August, Quebec City.

Henderson, D. (2005) *The Role of Business in the Modern World*. Institute of Economic Affairs, London.

Henderson, D.K. (1994) Travel agent commissions. *Air Transport World* 31(10), 102–105.

Henderson, J.C. (2000) War as a tourist attraction: the case of Vietnam. *International Journal of Tourism Research* 2, 269–280.

Henderson, J.C. and Ng, A. (2004) Responding to crisis: severe acute respiratory syndrome (SARS) and hotels in Singapore. *International Journal of Tourism Research* 6(6), 411–419.

Henderson, K.A., Stalnaker, D. and Taylor, G. (1988) The relationship between barriers to recreation and gender-role personality traits for women. *Journal of Leisure Research* 20(1), 69–80.

Hendry, J. (2004) *Between Enterprise and Ethics. Business and Management in a Bimoral Society*. Oxford University Press, Oxford and New York.

Hertel, L. (2001) Wellness. In: Deutscher Heibäderverband e.V. (ed.) *Deutscher Bäderkalender*. Flöhmann-Verlag, Bonn and Gütersloh, Germany, pp. 164–172.

Hessels, A. (1973) *Vakantie en Vakantiebesteding sinds de Eeuwwisseling*. Gianotten, Tilburg, The Netherlands.

Hetherington, P. (2004) From Calais to Kent? All in a day's work. *The Guardian* 22 November, p. 26.

Hicks, D. and Bord, D. (2001) Learning about global issues: why most educators only make things worse. *Environmental Education Research* 7(4), 413–425.

Hill, D. and Dixon, H. (1999) Promoting sun protection in children: rationale and challenges. *Health Education and Behaviour* 26(3), 409–417.

Hillebrand, O. and Weintögl, G. (2001) *Handbuch für den Kurartz*. ÖÄK-Verlag, Vienna.

Hillier, J. and Rooksby, E. (eds) (2002) *Habitus: a Sense of Place*. Ashgate, Aldershot, UK.

Hillman, M. (2005) It's time to go on a low-carbon diet. *The Guardian* 8 July, p. 16.

Hillman, M. and Fawcett, T. (2004) *How We Can Save the Planet*. Penguin Books, London.

Hilton Hotels Corporation (1995) *Travel Time Report*. Hilton Hotels, Beverly Hills, California.

Himanen, V., Lee-Gosselin, M. and Perrels, A. (2005) Sustainability and the interactions between external effects of transport. *Journal of Transport Geography* 13(1), 23–28.

Hinch, T. (1998) Ecotourists and indigenous hosts: diverging views on their relationship with nature. *Current Issues in Tourism* 1(1), 120–124.

Hinch, T. (2001) Indigenous territories. In: Weaver, D.B. (ed.) *The Encyclopaedia of Ecotourism*. CAB International, Wallingford, UK, pp. 345–357.

Hinch, T. and Jackson, E. (2000) Leisure constraints research: its value as a framework for understanding tourism seasonality. *Current Issues in Tourism* 3, 87–106.

Hindle, C., Bindloss, J., Fletcher, M., Hole, A., Humphreys, A. and White, J. (2003) *The Gap Year Book*. Lonely Planet, Hawthorn, Australia.

Hobson, P. and Dietrich, V. (1994) Tourism health and quality of life: challenging the responsibility of using the traditional tenets of sun, sea, sand and sex in tourism marketing. *Journal of Travel and Tourism Marketing* 3(4), 21–38.

Hodder, B.W. and Harris, D.R. (eds) (1967) *Africa in Transition*. Methuen, London.

Hodson, M. (2004) *Passport to Safer Travel*, 3rd edn. Thomas Cook, Peterborough, UK.

Hogan, J.J. (1992) Turnover and what to do about it. *Cornell Hotel and Restaurant Administration Quarterly* 33(1), 40–45.

Holbrook, C. (2004) *Retiring to Spain. Everything You Need to Know*. Age Concern England, London.

Holden, A. (2003) In need of new environmental ethics for tourism? *Annals of Tourism Research* 30(1), 94–108.

Holden, P. (ed.) (1984) *Alternative Tourism*. Ecumenical Coalition on Third World Tourism (ECTWT), Bangkok.

Holiday Care (2005) *Holiday Care: the UK's Premier Holiday and Travel Information Service for Disabled and Older People*. Holiday Care, Croydon, UK <http://www.holidaycare.org.uk/> (last accessed 8 April 2005).

Holland, J. (2000) Consensus and conflict: the socioeconomic challenge facing sustainable tourism development in southern Albania. *Journal of Sustainable Tourism* 8(6), 510–524.

Holliday, G. (2004) theecotourist [*sic*]. *Sunday Herald Magazine* 26 December, p. 44.

Hollinshead, K. (1992) 'White' gaze, 'red' people – shadow visions: the disidentification of 'Indians' in cultural tourism. *Leisure Studies* 11, 43–64.

Honderich, T. (1995) *The Oxford Companion to Philosophy*. Oxford University Press, Oxford and New York.

Hornborg, A. (2000) From animal masters to ecosystem services: exchange, personhood, and ecological practice. In: Hornborg, A. and Pálsson, G. (eds) *Negotiating Nature: Culture, Power and Environmental Argument*. Lund University Press, Lund, Sweden, pp. 132–152.

Hosey, G.R. (2000) Zoo animals and their human audiences: what is the visitor effect? *Animal Welfare* 9(4), 343–357.

Hosey, G.R. and Druck, P.L. (1987) The influence of zoo visitors on the behaviour of captive primates. *Applied Animal Behaviour Science* 18(1), 19–29.

Hottala, P. (2002) Culture confusion: intercultural adaptation. *Annals of Tourism Research* 29(1), 31–52.

Houellebecq, M. (2001) *Plateforme*. Editions J'ai Lu, Paris.

Houghton, J.T., Ding, Y., Gripps, D.J., Noguer, M., van der Linden, P.J., Dai, X., Maskell, K. and Johnson, C.A. (eds) (2001) *Climate Change 2001: the Scientific Basis. Contribution of Working Group I to the Third Assessment Report of the Intergovernmental Panel on Climate Change*. Cambridge University Press, Cambridge and New York.

House of Commons (2002) *Response to the Report of the Policy Commission on the Future of Farming and Food by HM Government*. The Stationery Office, London.

House of Lords (1994) *Report From the Select Committee on Sustainable Development*, Vol. 1. HMSO, London.

Howard, D.R. and Madrigal, R. (1990) Who makes the decision: the parent or the child? The perceived influence of parents and children on the purchase of recreational services. *Journal of Leisure Research* 22(3), 244–258.

Howie, F. (2000) Establishing the common ground: tourism, ordinary places, grey areas and environmental quality in Edinburgh, Scotland. In: Richards, G. and Hall, D. (eds) *Tourism and Sustainable Community Development*. Routledge, London and New York, pp. 101–118.

Hrynik, H.J. (1990) Debt-for-nature swaps: effective but not enforceable. *Case Western Reserve Journal of International Law* 22(1), 141–163.

HSE (Health and Safety Executive) (2001) *E. coli 0157*. HSE Books, London.

HSE (Health and Safety Executive) (2002a) *Avoiding Ill Health at Open Farms – Advice to Farmers*. Agriculture Information Sheet No. 23 (revised), HSE Books, London.

HSE (Health and Safety Executive) (2002b) *Avoiding Ill Health at Open Farms – Advice to Teachers*. AIS23 Supplement (revised), HSE Books, London.

HSE (Health and Safety Executive) (2002c) *Common Zoonoses in Agriculture*. Agriculture Information Sheet No. 2 (revised), HSE Books, London.

Hsieh, S. and O'Leary, T. (1993) Communication channels to segment pleasure travellers. *Journal of Travel and Tourism Marketing* 2(2/3), 57–75.

Huang, R. (2004) Provincial government roles in Chinese tourism development: the case of Hunan. In: Hall, D. (ed.) *Tourism and Transition: Governance, Transformation and Development*. CAB International, Wallingford, UK, pp. 169–183.

Hudson, S. and Miller, G.A. (2005) The responsible marketing of tourism: the case of Canadian mountain holidays. *Tourism Managament* 26, 133–142.

Hudson, S., Snaith, T., Miller, G.A. and Hudson, P. (2001) Distribution channels in the travel industry: using mystery shoppers to understand the influence of travel agency recommendations. *Journal of Travel Research* 40(2), 145–148.

Hughes, H. (1984) Government support for tourism in the UK: a different perspective. *Tourism Management* 5(1), 13–19.

Hughes, H. (1991) Holidays and the economically disadvantaged. *Tourism Management* 12(3), 193–196.

Hugill, P.J. (1975) Social contact on the Golden Mile. *Annals of the Association of American Geographers* 65(2), 214–228.

Hulme, D. and Shepherd, A. (2003) Conceptualizing chronic poverty. *World Development* 31, 403–423.

Hultsman, J. (1995) Just tourism: an ethical framework. *Annals of Tourism Research* 22(3), 553–567.

Hummel, J. (2002) *Re-inventing Sustainable Tourism: Correcting the Existing? The Role of SNV Netherlands Development Organisation in Development of Pro-poor Sustainable Tourism*. SNV Nepal, Kathmandu.

Hunt, D. (2003) *Starting and Running a B&B in France*. How To Books, Oxford, UK.

Hunt, J. (2004) Gender and development. In: Kingsbury, D., Remenyi, J., McKay, J. and Hunt, J. (eds) *Key Issues in Development*. Palgrave Macmillan, Basingstoke, UK, pp. 243–265.

Hunter, C. (1995) On the need to re-conceptualise sustainable tourism development. *Journal of Sustainable Tourism* 3(3), 155–165.

Hunter, C. (1997) Sustainable tourism as an adaptive paradigm. *Annals of Tourism Research* 24(4), 850–867.

Hunter, T. (1991) 5pc of foreign travellers 'end up in hospital'. *The Guardian* 2 July.

Hunter-Jones, J. (2000) Identifying the responsibility for risk at tourism destinations: the UK experience. *Tourism Economics* 6(2), 187–198.

Hunter-Jones, P. (2004) Young people, holiday-taking and cancer – an exploratory analysis. *Tourism Management* 25, 249–258.

Hunter-Jones, P. and Hayward, C. (1998) Leisure consumption and the United Kingdom (UK) zoo. In: Ravenscroft, N., Philips, D. and Bennett, M. (eds) *Tourism and Visitor Attractions. Leisure, Culture and Commerce*. Leisure Studies Association, Eastbourne, UK, pp. 97–107.

Husband, S. (2005) Fasten your seatbelts, we are in for a bumpy ride. *The Independent* 5 February, pp. 16–17.

Igoe, M. and Howell, J. (2002) *Buying a Property in France*. Cadogan, London.

ILAM (Institute of Leisure and Amenity Management) (2000) *Performance Indicators for Leisure and Cultural Services 2000/2001*. ILAM, Reading, UK.

Imrie, R. (1997) Rethinking the relationships between disability rehabilitation, and society. *Disability and Rehabilitation* 19(7), 263–271.

Imrie, R. (2000) Disabling environments and the geography of access policies. *Disability and Society* 15(1), 5–24.

Ingold, P., Huber, B., Neuhaus, P., Mainini, B., Marbacher, H., Schinidrig-Petrig, R. and Zeller, R. (1993) Tourism and sports in the alps – a serious problem for wildlife? *Revue Suisse de Zoologie* 100(3), 529–545.

Ioannides, D. (1995) A flawed implementation of sustainable tourism: the experience of Akamas, Cyprus. *Tourism Management* 16(8), 583–592.

IPE (International Petroleum Exchange) (1998) *A Proposal to Reduce CO$_2$ Emissions in the European Union through the Introduction of an Emissions Trading Program.* IPE, London.

Iredale, R. (2005) Gender, immigration policies and accreditation: valuing skills of professional women migrants. *Geoforum* 36(2), 155–166.

Ireland, M. (1993) Gender and class relations in tourism employment. *Annals of Tourism Research* 20(4), 666–684.

Iso-Ahola, S.E. (1980) *The Social Psychology of Leisure and Recreation.* William C. Brown, Dubuque, Iowa.

Iso-Ahola, S.E. and Mannell, R.C. (1985) Social and psychological constraints on leisure. In: Wade, M.G. (ed.) *Constraints on Leisure.* Charles C. Thomas, Springfield, Illinois, pp. 35–82.

IUCN (World Conservation Union) (1980) *World Conservation Strategy.* IUCN, Morges, Switzerland.

IUCN (World Conservation Union) (1991) *Caring for the Earth: a Strategy for Sustainable Living.* IUCN, Gland, Switzerland.

IUDZG (The World Zoo Organization, with the Captive Breeding Specialist Group of IUCN/SSC) (1993) *The World Zoo Conservation Strategy.* The Chicago Zoological Society, Brookfield, Illinois.

Iyengar, S. and Kinder, D.K. (1987) *News that Matters: Television and American Opinion.* Chicago University Press, Chicago, Illinois.

Iyer, P. (2004) Welcome to a world without clocks, maps or guidebooks. *The Observer* 19 December, Escape pp. 2–3.

Jaakson, R. (2004a) Beyond the tourist bubble? Cruiseship passengers in port. *Annals of Tourism Research* 31(1), 44–60.

Jaakson, R. (2004b) Globalisation and neocolonialist tourism. In: Hall, C.M. and Tucker, H. (eds) *Tourism and Postcolonialism: Contested Discourses, Identities and Representations.* Routledge, London and New York, pp. 169–183.

Jackson, E.L. (1999) Comment on Hawkins *et al.*, 'Leisure constraints: a replication and extension of construct development'. *Leisure Sciences* 21, 195–199.

Jackson, E.L. and Scott, D. (1999) Constraints to leisure. In: Jackson, E.L. and Burton, T.L. (eds) *Leisure Studies: Prospects for the Twenty-first Century.* Venture Publishing, State College, Pennsylvania, pp. 299–321.

Jackson, G. and Morpeth, N. (1999) Local Agenda 21 and community participation in tourism policy and planning: future and fallacy. *Current Issues in Tourism* 2(1), 1–38.

Jackson, G. and Morpeth, N. (2000) Local Agenda 21: reclaiming community ownership in tourism or stalled process? In: Richards, G. and Hall, D. (eds) *Tourism and Sustainable Community Development.* Routledge, London and New York, pp. 119–134.

Jackson, W. (2003) A lifecycle approach to demographic change in Australia. Paper presented at the 4th International Research Conference on Social Security, 5–7 May, Antwerp <http://www.issa.int/pdf/anvers03/topic2/2jackson.pdf> (last accessed 9 April 2005).

Jacobsen, J.K.S. and Haukeland, J.V. (2002) A lunch with a view: motor tourists' choices and assessments of eating places. *Scandinavian Journal of Hospitality and Tourism* 2(1), 4–16.

Jafari, J. (1987) Tourism models: the sociocultural aspects. *Tourism Management* 8(2), 151–157.

Jafari, J. (1989) An English langauge literature review. In: Bystrzanowski, J. (ed.) *Tourism as a Factor of Change: a Socio-cultural Study.* Center for Research and Documentation in Sciences, Vienna, pp. 17–60.

Jamal, T.B. (2004) Virtue ethics and sustainable tourism pedagogy: phronesis, principles and practice. *Journal of Sustainable Tourism* 12(6), 530–545.

Jansen-Verbeke, M. and van Renkom, J. (1996) Scanning museum visitors: urban tourism marketing. *Annals of Tourism Research* 23, 364–375.

Jeffreys, S. (2003) Sex tourism: do women want it too? *Leisure Studies* 22(3), 223–238.

Jenkins, O.H. (2003) Photography and travel brochures: the circle of representation. *Tourism Geographies* 5(3), 305–328.

Johnson, J., Maertins, M., Shalit, M., Bierbaum, T., Goldman, D. and Lowe, R. (1991) Wilderness emergency medical services: the experiences at Sequoia and Kings Canyon national parks. *American Journal of Emergency Medicine* 9(3), 211–216.

Johnston, J. (2004) Holiday blues? You need a day off. *Sunday Herald* (Glasgow) 29 August <http://www.sundayherald.com/print44430> (last accessed 16 March 2005).

Johnston, R. and Mehra, S. (2002) Best-practice complaint management. *Academy of Management Executive* 16(4), 145–154.

Jones, C., Parker, M. and ten Bos, R. (2005) *Ethics for Business: a Critical Text.* Routledge, London.

Jones, H. (1990) *Social Welfare in Development.* Macmillan, London.

Jones, N. (2001) *The Rough Guide to Travel Health*. Rough Guides, London.

Jud, D.G. (1975) Tourism and crime in Mexico. *Social Science Quarterly* 56(2), 324–330.

Kabeer, N. (2003) *Gender Mainstreaming in Poverty Eradication and the Millennium Development Goals. A Handbook for Policy-makers and Other Stakeholders*. Commonwealth Secretariat/International Development Research Centre/Canadian International Development Agency, Ottawa.

Kagan, S. (1989) *The Limits of Morality*. Oxford University Press, Toronto, Ontario.

Kahn, J. (2000) Creating an online community – and a market – for the disabled. *Fortune* 7 February, p. 188.

Kalisch, A. (2000) Corporate social responsibility in the tourism industry. *Fair Trade in Tourism Bulletin* 2, 1–4.

Kalisch, A. (2002) *Corporate Futures: Social Responsibility in the Tourism Industry*. Tourism Concern, London.

Kamsma, T. and Bras, K. (2000) Gili Trawangan – from desert island to 'marginal' paradise: local participation, small-scale entrepreneurs and outside investors in an Indonesian tourist destination. In: Richards, G. and Hall, D. (eds) *Tourism and Sustainable Community Development*. Routledge, London and New York, pp. 170–184.

Karatepe, O.M. and Sokmen, A. (2006) The effects of work role and family role variables on psychological and behavioral outcomes of frontline employees. *Tourism Management*, 27(2), 255–268.

Karwacki, J. and Boyd, C. (1995) Ethics and ecotourism. *Business Ethics* 4, 225–232.

Kasza, G. (2002) The illusion of welfare regimes. *Journal of Social Policy* 31(2), 271–287.

Katcher, A.H. and Beck, A.M. (1988) Health and caring for living things. In: Rowan, A. (ed.) *Animals and People Sharing the World*. University Press of New England, Hanover, New Hampshire, pp. 53–73.

Keller, R.T. (1983) Predicting absenteeism from prior absenteeism, attitudinal factors, and nonattitudinal factors. *Journal of Applied Psychology* 68, 536–540.

Kenna, M.E. (1993) Return migrants and tourism development: an example from the Cyclades. *Journal of Modern Greek Studies* 11(1), 75–95.

Kenyon, J. (1996) *No Problem! Worldwise Travel Tips for Mature Adventurers*. Orca , Vancouver.

Kester, J. (2003) Cruise tourism. *Tourism Economics* 9(3), 337–350.

Kidd, A.H., Kidd, R.M. and Zasloff, R.L. (1995) Developmental factors in positive attitudes toward zoo animals. *Psychological Reports* 76(1), 71–81.

Kids Out (2005) *Kids Out*. Kids Out, Leighton Buzzard, UK <http://www.kidsout.org.uk> (last accessed 27 May 2005).

Kilby, P. (2001) Women's empowerment in India – the voices of women. Paper presented at Gender and Globalisation in the Asia–Pacific conference, November, Canberra.

Kiley-Worthington, M. (1990) *Animals in Circuses and Zoos – Children's World*. Little Eco-Farms Publishing, Basildon, UK.

Kimmel, J.R. (1999) Ecotourism as environmental learning. *Journal of Environmental Education* 30(2), 40–45.

Kimura, S.P., Mikolashek, P.L. and Kirk, S.A. (1975) Madness in paradise: psychiatric crises among newcomers in Honolulu. *Hawaii Medical Journal* 34(8), 275–278.

King, R. (ed.) (1986) *Return Migration and Regional Economic Problems*. Croom Helm, London.

King, R. (1995) Tourism, labour and international migration. In: Montanari, A. and Williams, A.M. (eds) *European Tourism: Regions, Spaces and Restructuring*. John Wiley & Sons, Chichester, UK, and New York, pp. 177–190.

King, R., Warnes, A.M. and Williams, A.M. (2000) *Sunset Lives: British Retirement Migration to the Mediterranean*. Berg, London.

Kinnaird, V. and Hall, D. (eds) (1994) *Tourism: a Gender Analysis*. John Wiley & Sons, Chichester, UK, and New York.

Kinnaird, V. and Hall, D. (1996) Understanding tourism processes: a gender-aware framework. *Tourism Management* 17(2), 95–102.

Kinnaird, V. and Hall, D. (2000) Theorizing gender in tourism research. *Tourism Recreation Research* 25(1), 71–84.

Kitzinger, J. and Miller, D. (1992) African AIDS: the media and audience beliefs. In: Aggelton, P., Davies, P. and Hart, G. (eds) *AIDS, Rights, Risk and Reason*. Falmer Press, London.

Klein, R. (2002) *Cruise Ship Blues: the Underside of the Cruise Industry*. New Society Publishers, Gabriola Island, Gabriola BC.

Klein, S. and Loebbecke, C. (2003) Emerging pricing strategies on the web: lessons from the airline industry. *Electronic Markets* 13(1), 46–58.

Klemm, M. (1992) Sustainable tourism development: Languedoc-Roussillion thirty years on. *Tourism Management* 13, 169–180.

Klenosky, D.B. and Gitelson, R.E. (1998) Travel agents' destination recommendations. *Annals of Tourism Research* 25(3), 661–674.

Kline, J.M. (2005) *Ethics for International Business. Decision-making in a Global Political Economy*. Routledge, London.

Koch, E., de Beer, G. and Elliffe, S. (eds) (1998) SDIs, tourism-led growth and the empowerment of local communities in South Africa. *Development Southern Africa* 15(5), Special Issue.

Kohn, T. (1997) Island involvement and the evolving tourist. In: Abram, S., Waldren, J. and Macleod, D.V.L. (eds) *Tourists and Tourism: Identifying with People and Places*. Berg, Oxford, pp. 13–28.

KPMG (KPMG Peat Marwick Management Consultants) (1991) *The Tourism Labour Market: Constraints and Attitudes*. KPMG, Sydney.

Kraus, L.E., Stoddard, S. and Gilmartin, D. (1996) *Chartbook on Disabilities in the United States*. InfoUse, Berkeley, California.

Krippendorf, J. (1989) *The Holiday-makers: Understanding the Impact of Travel and Tourism*. Butterworth-Heinemann, Oxford, UK.

Kristen, C. (2003) *Buy to Let in France*. How To Books, Oxford, UK.

Kuentzel, W.F. and Ramaswamy, V.M. (2005) Tourism and amenity migration: a longitudinal analysis. *Annals of Tourism Research* 32(2), 419–438.

Kulcsar, L. and Verbole, A. (1997) *National Action Plans for the Integration of Rural Women in Development: Case Studies in Hungary and Slovenia*. Food and Agriculture Organization of the United Nations, Rome.

Kulindwa, K. (2002) Economic reforms and the prospect for sustainable development in Tanzania. *Development Southern Africa* 19(3), 389–403.

Kumate, J. (1997) Infectious diseases in the 21st century. *Archives of Medical Research* 28(2), 155–161.

Laing, S. (2004) *Consuming for Good? The Role of Consumers in Driving Responsible Business*. AGENDA and the Scottish Consumer Council, Edinburgh, UK. <http://www.agenda-scotland.org/home.shtml> (last accessed 17 March 2005).

Lam, T., Zhang, H. and Baum, T. (2001) An investigation of employees' job satisfaction: the case of hotels in Hong Kong. *Tourism Management* 22(2), 157–165.

Lamb, B. and Davidson, S. (1996) Tourism and transportation in Ontario, Canada. In: Harrison, L. and Husbands, W. (eds) *Practising Responsible Tourism*. John Wiley & Sons, Chichester, UK, and New York, pp. 261–276.

Lane, B. (1994) Sustainable rural tourism strategies: a tool for development and conservation. *Journal of Sustainable Tourism* 2(1–2), 102–111.

Langer, E.J. and Piper, A.T. (1987) The prevention of mindlessness. *Journal of Personality and Social Psychology* 52, 269–278.

Langley James (2003) Post holiday blues. *Langley James Consultancy Newsletter* September <http://ljnews.co.uk/pfNewsDetail51.htm> (last accessed 15 March 2005).

Lankford, S.V. and Howard, D.R. (1994) Developing a tourism impact scale. *Annals of Tourism Research* 21(1), 121–139.

Lanz Kaufmann, E. (1999) *Wellness-Tourismus: Marktanalyse und Qualitätsanforderungen für die Hotellerie-Schnittstellen zur Gesundheitsförderung*. Forschungsinstitut für Freizeit und Tourismus der Universität Bern, Berne, Switzerland.

LaPlante, M.P. (1991) The demographics of disability. *The Millbank Quarterly* 2, 55–77.

Laredo, J. (2003) *The Best Places to Buy a Home in France*. Survival Books, London.

Laredo, J. (2004) *Renovating and Maintaining Your French Home*, 2nd edn. Survival Books, London.

Lash, C. and Urry, J. (1994) *Economies of Signs and Space*. Sage, London.

Laurance, J. (2000) Peers warn of fatal blood clots on long journeys. *The Independent* 23 November.

Lavine, M. and Kraus, S. (2001) *A Farmers' Guide for Hosting Farm Visits for Children*. Sustainable Agriculture Research and Education Program, University of California, Davis, California.

Law, J., Pearce, P.L. and Woods, B.A. (1995) Stress and coping in tourist attraction employees. *Tourism Management* 16(4), 277–284.

Lawlor, D.A., Burke, J., Bouskill, E., Conn, G., Edwards, P. and Gillespie, D. (2000) Do British travel agents provide adequate health advice for travellers? *The British Journal of General Practice: the Journal of the Royal College of General Practitioners* 50(456), 567–568.

Lawson, V. and Kinsella, K. (1996) *Aging in the United States: Past, Present and Future*. International Programs Center, Population Division, US Bureau of the Census, Washington, DC.

Lawton, G. and Page, S. (1997) Evaluating travel agents' provision of health advice to travellers. *Tourism Management* 18(2), 89–104.

Laxson, J.D. (1991) How 'we' see 'them': tourism and Native Americans. *Annals of Tourism Research* 18(3), 365–391.

Lea, J.P. (1993) Tourism development ethics in the Third World. *Annals of Tourism Research* 20(4), 701–715.

Leggat, P.A. (2000) Sources of health advice given to travellers. *Journal of Travel Medicine* 7(2), 85–88.

Leggat, P.A. and Goldsmid, J.M. (2004) Travellers' diarrhoea: health advice for travellers. *Travel Medicine and Infectious Disease* 2(1), 17–22.

Leggat, P.A., Griffiths, R. and Leggatt, F.W. (2005) Emergency assistance provided abroad to insured travellers from Australia. *Travel Medicine and Infectious Disease* 3(1), 9–17.

Leiper, N. (1995) *Tourism Management*. TAFE Publications, Collingwood, Australia.

Lennon, J. and Foley, M. (1999) Interpretation of the unimaginable: the U.S. Holocaust Memorial Museum, Washington D.C. and 'dark tourism'. *Journal of Travel Research* 38(1), 46–50.

Lennon, J. and Foley, M. (2002) *Dark Tourism: the Attraction of Death and Disaster*. Continuum, London.

Leopold, A. (1949/1968) *A Sand County Almanac and Sketches Here and There*. Oxford University Press, New York.

Lepp, A. and Gibson, H. (2003) Tourist roles, perceived risk and international tourism. *Annals of Tourism Research* 30(3), 606–624.

Leslie, D. (2005) Rural tourism businesses and environmental management systems. In: Hall, D., Kirkpatrick, I. and Mitchell, M. (eds) *Rural Tourism and Sustainable Business*. Channel View, Clevedon, UK, pp. 249–267.

Leslie, D. and Hughes, G. (1997) Local authorities and tourism in the UK. *International Journal of Managing Leisure* 2(3), 143–154.

L'Etang, J. (1992) A Kantian approach to codes of ethics. *Journal of Business Ethics* 11, 737–744.

Letic, L. and Rumbak, R. (eds) (2004) *Slovenia's Health Resorts*. Slovenian Tourist Board, Ljubljana.

Lever, A. (1987) Spanish tourism migrants: the case of Lloret de Mar. *Annals of Tourism Research* 14(4), 449–470.

Levy, D. and Lerch, P. (1991) Tourism as a factor in development: implications for gender and work in Barbados. *Gender and Society* 5, 67–85.

Liebman Parrinello, G. (2001) The technological body in tourism research and praxis. *International Sociology* 16(2), 205–219.

Lindberg, K. and Johnson, R.L. (1997) Modeling resident attitudes toward tourism. *Annals of Tourism Research* 24(2), 402–424.

Lindberg, K., Furze, B., Staff, M. and Black, R. (1997) *Ecotourism in the Asia–Pacific Region: Issues and Outlook*. The International Ecotourism Society, Bennington.

Lindberg, K., Anderssson, T.D. and Dellaert, B.G.C. (2001) Tourism development: assessing social gains and losses. *Annals of Tourism Research* 28(4), 1010–1030.

Lindfelt, L.-L. (2004) Ethics codes in Finnish business. *Finnish Journal of Business Economics* 53(3), 242–259.

Lindgren, C. (1996) Chronic sorrow in persons with Parkinson's and their spouses. *Scholarly Inquiry for Nursing Practice* 10, 351–366.

Lindstrom, M. (2003) *Brandchild*. Kogan Page, London.

Link, H. (2005) Transport accounts – methodological concepts and empirical results. *Journal of Transport Geography* 13(1), 41–57.

Linzey, A. (1976) *Animal Rights: a Christian Assessment*. SCM Press, London.

Linzey, A. (1987) *Christianity and the Rights of Animals*. SPCK, London, and Crossroad, New York.

Linzey, A. and Cohn-Sherbok, D. (1997) *After Noah: Animals and the Liberation of Theology*. Mowbray, London.

Linzey, A. and Regan, T. (1989) *Animals and Christianity: a Book of Readings*. SPCK, London.

Little, K. (1991) On safari: the visual politics of a tourist representation. In: Howes, D. (ed.) *The Varieties of Sensory Experience: a Sourcebook in the Anthropology of the Sense*. University of Toronto, Toronto, Ontario, pp. 149–163.

Littlejohn, D. and Watson, S. (2004) Developing graduate managers for hospitality and tourism. *International Journal of Contemporary Hospitality Management* 16(7), 408–414.

Litvin, S. (1999) The minefield of the middle: real problems facing the mid-size travel agent. In: Moisey, R.N., Nickerson, N.N. and Klenosky, D.B. (eds) *Navigating the Global Waters, 30th Annual Conference Proceedings*. TTRA, Boise, Idaho, pp. 118–133.

Litvin, S.W., Xu, G. and Kang, S.K. (2004) Spousal vacation-buying decision making revisited across time and place. *Journal of Travel Research* 43(2), 193–198.

Livingston, J. (1981) *The Fallacy of Wildlife Conservation*. McLelland and Stewart, Toronto, Ontario.

Locke, E.A. (1976) The nature and consequences of job satisfaction. In: Dunnetter, M.D. (ed.) *Handbook of Industrial and Organizational Psychology*. Rand-McNally, Chicago, Illinois, pp. 1297–1349.

Locke, R. (2003) *Note on Corporate Citizenship in a Global Economy*. Sloan School of Management and Department of Political Science, Massachussetts Institute of Technology, Boston, Massachusetts.

Lordkipanidze, M., Brezet, H. and Backman, M. (2005) The entrepreneurship factor in sustainable tourism development. *Journal of Cleaner Production* 13(8), 787–798.

Loughland, T., Reid, A., Walker, K. and Petocz, P. (2003) Factors influencing young people's conceptions of environment. *Environmental Education Research* 9(1), 3–20.

Loundsbury, J.W. and Franz, C.P. (1990) Vacation discrepancy: a leisure motivation approach. *Psychological Reports* 66(2), 699–702.

Lumsdon, L. and Page, S.J. (2004) Progress in transport and tourism research: reformulating the transport–tourism interface and future research agendas. In: Lumsdon, L. and Page, S.J. (eds) *Tourism and Transport: Issues for the New Millennium*. Elsevier, Amsterdam, pp. 1–27.

MacCannell, D. (1973) Staged authenticity: arrangements of social space in tourist settings. *American Journal of Sociology* 79, 589–603.

MacCannell, D. (1976) *The Tourist: a New Theory of the Leisure Class*. Macmillan, London.

McCarthy, M., Wolf, M. and Harrison, M. (2005) Revealed: the real cost of air travel. *The Independent* 28 May, pp. 1–2.

McCool, S.F. and Moisey, R.N. (2001) *Tourism, Recreation and Sustainability: Linking Culture and the Environment*. CAB International, Wallingford, UK.

MacCormack, G. (1991) The price of affluence: the political economy of Japanese leisure. *New Left Review* 188, 21–35.

McEwan, J. (1987) UK travel agencies – future marketing strategies. *Tourism Management* 8(2), 171–173.

McGehee, N.G. and Norman, W.C. (2001) Alternative tourism as impetus for consciousness-raising. *Tourism Analysis* 6(3–4), 239–251.

McGirk, J. (2005) After the tsunami: Thais struggle to rebuild the hotels of Koh Phi Phi – and its reputation. *The Independent* 1 February, p. 26.

McGrath, J.E. (1970) *Social and Psychological Factors in Stress*. Holt, Rinehart & Winston, New York.

McGuire, F., Dottavio, D. and O'Leary, J. (1986) Constraints to participation in outdoor recreation across the life span: a nationwide study of limitors and prohibitors. *The Gerontologist* 26, 538–544.

McGuire, F., Uysal, M. and McDonald, G. (1988) Attracting the older traveller. *Tourism Management* 9(2), 161–163.

Machlis, G.E. and Burch, W.R. (1983) Relations between strangers: cycles of structure and meaning in tourist systems. *Sociological Review* 31(4), 666–692.

McIntosh, R.W. and Goeldner, C.R. (1990) *Tourism Principles, Practices, Philosophies*, 6th edn. John Wiley & Sons, New York.

MacKay, J. (2001) Global sex: sexuality and sexual practices around the world. *Sexual and Relationship Therapy* 16(1), 71–82.

McKercher, B. (1993a) Some fundamental truths about tourism: understanding tourism's social and environmental impacts. *Journal of Sustainable Tourism* 1(1), 6–16.

McKercher, B. (1993b) The unrecognized threat to tourism. Can tourism survive 'sustainability'? *Tourism Management* 14(2), 131–136.

McKercher, B. (1999) A chaos approach to tourism. *Tourism Management* 20, 425–434.

McKercher, B., Packer, T., Yau, M. and Lam, P. (2003) Travel agents: facilitators or inhibitors of travel for people with disabilities? *Tourism Management* 24(4), 465–474.

Mackie, V. (1988) Division of labour: multinational sex in Asia. In: McCormack, G. and Sugimoto, Y. (eds) *The Japanese Trajectory: Modernisation and Beyond*. Cambridge University Press, Cambridge, UK, pp. 218–232.

Macleod, D. (1999) Tourism and the globalization of a Canary Island. *Journal of the Royal Anthropological Institute* 5, 443–456.

Macleod, D. (2003) Ecotourism for rural development in the Canary Islands and the Caribbean. In: Hall, D., Roberts, L. and Mitchell, M. (eds) *New Directions in Rural Tourism*. Ashgate, Aldershot, UK, and Burlington, Vermont, pp. 194–204.

Macnaghten, P. and Urry, J. (1998) *Contested Natures*. Sage, London.

McPherson, A. and MacFarlane, A. (1992) *The Virgin Now Boarding: a Globetrotter's Guide to Health, Sex and Survival*. Arrow Books, London.

Madrigal, R. (1993) Parents' perceptions of family members' relative influence in vacation decision making. *Journal of Travel and Tourism Marketing* 2(4), 39–57.

Mahoney, R. (1992) Debt-for-nature swaps: who really benefits? *The Ecologist* 22(3), 97–103.

Mahony, K. and van Zyl, J. (2001) *Practical Strategies for Pro-poor Tourism. Case Studies of Makuleke and Manyeleti Tourism Initiatives.* Working Paper No. 2, CRT, IIED and ODI PPT, London <http://www.propoortourism.org.uk/safrica_cs2.pdf> (last accessed 6 July 2005).

Malloy, D.C. and Fennell, D.A. (1998a) Ecotourism and ethics: moral development and organizational cultures. *Journal of Travel Research* 36(2), 47–56.

Malloy, D.C. and Fennell, D.A. (1998b) Codes of ethics and tourism: an exploratory content analysis. *Tourism Management* 19(5), 453–461.

Manne, A.S. and Stephen, G. (2005) Global climate change and the equity–efficiency puzzle. *Energy* 30(14), 2525–2536.

Mannell, R., Zuzanek, J. and Larson, R. (1988) Leisure states and 'flow' experiences: testing perceived freedom and intrinsic motivation hypotheses. *Journal of Leisure Studies* 20(4), 289–304.

Mansfeld, Y. (1992) From motivation to actual travel. *Annals of Tourism Research* 19(3), 399–419.

Marini, I. (1996) Participant perceptions of disability sensitivity exercises: implications for practice. *SCI Psychosocial Process* 9(2/3), 75–77.

Marks, K. (2005) Crocodiles bring terror to Australian national park. *The Independent* 7 May, p. 31.

Marshall, P. (1992) *Nature's Web*. M.E. Sharpe, London.

Martin, A. (2004) Surfing: trouble in paradise. *The Independent* 4 December, pp. 70–71 <http://sport.independent.co.uk/low_res/story.jsp?story=589507&host=18&dir=106> (accessed 4 December 2004).

Martin, P., Martin, S. and Pastore, F. (2002) Best practice options: Albania. *International Migration* 40(3), 103–118.

Martin, W. and Mason, S. (1987) Social trends and tourism futures. *Tourism Management* 8(2), 112–114.

Maslow, A. (1970) *Motivation and Personality*, 2nd edn. Harper, New York.

Mason, P. (2003) *Tourism Impacts, Planning and Management*. Butterworth-Heinemann, Oxford, UK.

Mason, P. and Mowforth, M. (1996) Codes of conduct in tourism. *Progress in Tourism and Hospitality Research* 2, 151–167.

Mason, P., Grabowski, P. and Du, W. (2005) Severe acute respiratory syndrome, tourism and the media. *International Journal of Tourism Research* 7(1), 11–21.

MASTA (Medical Advisory Services for Travellers Abroad) (2003) *MASTA: Minding Your Health Abroad.* MASTA, London <http://www.masta.org> (last accessed 1 March 2005).

Masterton, A.M. (1992) Environmental ethics. *Island Destinations (a Supplement to Tour and Travel News)* November, 16–18.

Mathieson, A. and Wall, G. (1982) *Tourism: Economic, Physical and Social Impacts*. Longman, London.

Mawby, R.I., Brunt, P. and Hambly, Z. (2000) Fear of crime among British holidaymakers. *British Journal of Criminology* 40(3), 468–479.

Max-Neef, M. (1992) Development and human needs. In: Elkins, P. and Max-Neef, M. (eds) *Real-life Economics: Understanding Wealth Creation.* Routledge, London and New York, pp. 81–102.

Mayaka, M. and King, B. (2002) A quality assessment of education and for Kenya's tour-operating sector. *Current Issues in Tourism* 5(2), 112–133.

Mbaiwa, J.E. (2005a) Enclave tourism and its socio-economic impacts in the Okavango Delta, Botswana. *Tourism Management* 26, 157–172.

Mbaiwa, J.E. (2005b) The problems and prospects of sustainable tourism development in the Okavango Delta, Botswana. *Journal of Sustainable Tourism* 13(3), 203–227.

Mead, P.S., Slutsker, L. and Dietz, V. (1999) Food related illness and death in the United States. *Emergent Infectious Diseases* 5, 607–625.

Medvedev, K. (1998) A review of women's emancipation in Hungary: limited successes offer some hope. *Transition* 26 February.

Meikle, J. (2001) Rabbits blamed as *E. coli* infects 10 children. *The Guardian* 9 November.

Middleton, V. (1994) *Marketing Travel and Tourism,* 2nd edn. Butterworth-Heinemann, Oxford, UK.

Middleton, V.T.C. and Hawkins, R. (1998) *Sustainable Tourism: a Marketing Perspective.* Butterworth-Heinemann, Oxford, UK.

Mihalič, T. (1999) Equity in outgoing tourism through tourist certificates. *International Journal of Contemporary Hospitality Management* 11(2–3), 128–131.

Mihill, C. (1995) Skin cancer increases 10pc a year as public ignore warnings. *The Guardian* 16 May.

Milbourne, P. (ed.) (1997) *Revealing Rural 'Others': Representation, Power and Identity in the British Countryside.* Pinter, London.

Miller, G. (2001) Corporate responsibility in the UK tourism industry. *Tourism Management* 22(6), 589–598.

Miller, A.R. and Grazer, W.F. (2002) The North American cruise market and Australian tourism. *Journal of Vacation Marketing* 8(3), 221–234.

Miller, G.A. and Kirk, E. (2002) The Disability Discrimination Act: time for the stick? *Journal of Sustainable Tourism* 10(1), 82–88.

Milmo, C. and Arthur, C. (2000) Death after flight triggers calls for air travel enquiry. *The Independent* 24 October.

Milmo, C. and Stevenson, R. (2005) Gate Gourmet faces financial crisis over creditors' demands. *The Independent* 16 August, p. 8.

Ministry of Education (1958) *Schools and the Countryside*. HMSO, London.

Mintel (2001) *The Green and Ethical Consumer*. Mintel International Group, London.

Mintzberg, H. (1996) Managing government, governing management. *Harvard Business Review* 74 (May–June), 75–83.

Mitchell, H. and Hosey, G. (2005) *Zoo Research Guidelines: Studies of the Effects of Human Visitors on Zoo Animal Behaviour*. BIAZA (British and Irish Association of Zoos and Aquariums), London <http://www.zoofederation.org.uk/uploads/Zoo%20Research%20Guidelines%20-%20Visitor%20Effects.pdf> (last accessed 14 April 2005).

Moctezuma, P. (2001) Community-based organization and participatory planning in south-east Mexico City. *Environment and Urbanization* 13(2), 117–133.

Moennig, V. (1992) Veränderungen in der Dynamik von viralen Infektionkrankheiten. *Deutsche Tierärztliche Wochenschrift* 99(7), 290–292.

Mok, C. and Armstrong, R. (1995) Leisure travel destination choice criteria of Hong Kong residents. *Journal of Travel and Tourism Marketing* 14(1), 99–104.

Monk, J. and Alexander, C.S. (1986) Free port fallout: gender, employment and migration on Margarita Island. *Annals of Tourism Research* 13(3), 393–413.

Monkey World (2004) *Monkey World Ape Rescue Centre*. Monkey World, Wareham, UK.

Monkey World (2005) *Monkey World Ape Rescue Centre*. Monkey World, Wareham, UK <http://www.monkeyworld.co.uk/> (last accessed 4 April 2005).

Moore, H. (1994) *A Passion for Difference: Essays in Anthropology and Gender*. Indiana University Press, Bloomington, Indiana.

Moore, K. (1970) Modernization in a Canary island village: an indicator of social change in Spain. *Journal of the Royal Anthropological Society* 2, 19–34.

Moore, K., Cushman, G. and Simmons, D. (1995) Behavioral conceptualization of tourism and leisure. *Annals of Tourism Research* 22(1), 67–85.

Morgan, D., Brandth, B. and Kvande, E. (eds) (2005) *Gender, Bodies and Work*. Ashgate, Aldershot, UK.

Morgan, K. (1997) The learning region: institutions, innovation and regional renewal. *Regional Studies* 31(5), 491–503.

Morgan, N. and Pritchard, A. (1998) *Tourism, Promotion and Power: Creating Images, Creating Identities*. John Wiley & Sons, Chichester, UK, and New York.

Morgan, O. (2005) Bury CO_2 at sea, says DTI. *The Observer* 12 June, Business p. 4.

Moriarty, B.J. (2000) Australian circuses as cooperative communities. *International Journal of Educational Research* 33(3), 297–307.

Morris, D. (1964) The response of animals to a restricted environment. *Symposia of the Zoological Society of London* 13, 99–118.

Morrison, A.M. (1989) *Hospitality and Travel Marketing*. Delmar, Albany, New Jersey.

Moscardo, G. (1996) Mindful visitors, heritage and tourism. *Annals of Tourism Research* 23(2), 376–397.

Mottiar, Z. and Quinn, D. (2004) Couple dynamics in household tourism decision making: women as the gatekeepers? *Journal of Vacation Marketing* 10(2), 149–160.

Moulin, C. (1983) Social tourism: developments and prospects in Quebec. In: Murphy, P. (ed.) *Tourism in Canada: Selected Issues and Options*. University of Victoria, Victoria, British Columbia, pp. 122–145.

Mowforth, M. and Munt, I. (1998) *Tourism and Sustainability. New Tourism in the Third World*. Routledge, London.

Mowforth, M. and Munt, I. (2003) *Tourism and Sustainability. New Tourism in the Third World*, 2nd edn. Routledge, London.

Moynahan, B. (1983) *Fool's Paradise*. Pan Books, London.

Moynahan, B. (1985) *The Tourist Trap*. Pan Books, London.

Muir, F. (1993) Managing tourism to a sea-bird nesting island. *Tourism Management* 14(2), 99–105.

Müller, D. (2002) German second home development in Sweden. In: Hall, C.M. and Williams, A.M. (eds) *Tourism and Migration*. Kluwer, Dordrecht, The Netherlands, pp. 169–185.

Müller, D. (2005) Second home tourism in the Swedish mountain range. In: Hall, C.M. and Boyd, S. (eds) *Nature-based Tourism in Peripheral Areas: Development or Disaster?* Channel View, Clevedon, UK, pp. 133–148.

Müller, H. and Lanz, E. (1998) Wellnesstourismus in der Schweiz: Definition, Abrenzung und empirische Angebotsanalyse. *Tourismus Journal* 2(4), 477–494.

Muloin, S. (1992) Wilderness access for persons with a disability. In: Harper, G. and Weiler, B. (eds) *Ecotourism*. Bureau of Tourism Research, Canberra, pp. 20–25.

Mumma, C. (1986) Perceived losses following stroke. *Rehabilitation Nursing* 11(3), 19–24.

Murphy, P.E. (1985) *Tourism: a Community Approach*. Methuen, London.

Murphy, P.E. and Murphy, A.E. (2004) *Strategic Management for Tourism Communities: Bridging the Gaps*. Channel View, Clevedon, UK.

Murray, M. and Sproats, J. (1990) The disabled traveler: tourism and disability in Australia. *Journal of Tourism Studies* 1(1), 9–14.

Musa, G., Hall, C.M. and Higham, J.E.S. (2004) Tourism sustainability and health impacts in high altitude adventure, cultural and ecotourism destinations: a case study of Nepal's Sagarmatha National Park. *Journal of Sustainable Tourism* 12(4), 306–331.

Myers, O.E., Saunders, C.D. and Garrett, E. (2003) What do children think animals need? Aesthetic and psycho-social conceptions. *Environmental Education Research* 9(3): 305–325.

Nahrstedt, W. (2004) Wellness: a new perspective for leisure centers, health tourism, and spas in Europe on the global health market. In: Weiermair, K. and Mathies, C. (eds) *The Tourism and Leisure Industry: Shaping the Future*. The Haworth Hospitality Press, New York and London, pp. 181–198.

Naik, A. (2003) *Travel Calm: Secrets for Stress-free Travel*. Judy Piatkus, London.

Nalbantogly, G. (2005) Briton killed in Turkey terror blast. *The Sunday Herald* (Glasgow) 17 July, pp. 1–2.

Nash, R.F. (1989) *The Rights of Nature: a History of Environmental Ethics*. University of Wisconsin Press, Madison, Wisconsin.

Neiss, S., Joyal, S. and Triets, S. (1995) US repeat and VFR visitors to Canada: come again eh! *Journal of Travel Research* 6(1), 27–37.

Nel, E. and Binns, T. (2002) Place marketing, tourism promotion, and community-based local economic development in post-apartheid South Africa: the case of Still Bay – the 'bay of sleeping beauty'. *Urban Affairs Review* 38(2), 184–208.

Ness, A.R., Frankel, S.J., Gunnel, D.J. and Smith, G.D. (1999) Are we dying for a tan? *British Medical Journal* 319, 114–116.

Netemeyer, R.G., Brashear-Alejandro, T. and Boles, J.S. (2004) A cross-national model of job-related outcomes of work role and family role variable, a retail sales context. *Journal of the Academy of Marketing Science* 32(1), 49–60.

Neto, F. (2003) A new approach to sustainable tourism development: moving beyond environmental protection. *Natural Resources Forum* 27(3), 212–222.

Newbery, D.M. (1998) *Fair Payment from Road-users: a Review of the Evidence on Social and Environmental Costs*. Automobile Association (AA), Basingstoke, UK.

Nicholson, A.N., Cummin, A.R. and Giangrande, P.L.F. (2003) The airline passenger: current medical issues. *Travel Medicine and Infectious Disease* 1(2), 94–102.

Nicholson-Lord, D. (1995) Foreign holidays 'are becoming more dangerous'. *The Independent* 10 May.

Nickerson, N.P. and Jurowski, C. (2000) The influence of children on vacation travel patterns. *Journal of Vacation Marketing* 7(1), 19–30.

Nilsson, P.Å. (2001) Tourist destination development: the Åre Valley. *Scandinavian Journal of Hospitality and Tourism* 1(1), 54–67.

Nolan, S.D. (1976) Tourists' use and evaluation of travel information sources: summary and conclusions. *Journal of Travel Research* 14(1), 6–8.

Noon, A. (2004) Prepare for emergencies. *The Independent* 13 November, Travel Supplement p. 12.

Norfolk, D. (1994) Holidays in hell. *Business Traveller* 19(8), 19.

Norman, P., Boyle, P. and Rees, P. (2005) Selective migration, health and deprivation: a longitudinal analysis. *Social Science and Medicine* 60(12), 2755–2771.

Norton, A. (1996) Experiencing nature: the reproduction of environmental discourse through safari tourism in East Africa. *Geoforum* 27(3), 355–373.

Novelli, M. and Humavindu, M.N. (2005) Wildlife tourism. Wildlife use vs local gain: trophy hunting in Namibia. In: Novelli, M. (ed.) *Niche Tourism: Contemporary Issues, Trends and Cases*. Elsevier, Amsterdam, pp. 171–182.

Nozawa, H. (1992) A marketing analysis of Japanese outbound travel. *Tourism Management* 13(2), 226–233.

NTIC (National Tourist Information Centre) (2004) *Bulgaria: Mineral Waters and Spa Tourism*. NTIC, Sofia.

Nyaupane, G.P., Morais, D.B. and Graefe, A.R. (2004) Nature tourism constraints: a cross-activity comparison. *Annals of Tourism Research* 31(3), 540–555.

Nylander, M. (2001) National policy for 'rural tourism': the case of Finland. In: Roberts, L. and Hall, D. (eds) *Rural Tourism and Recreation: Principles to Practice*. CAB International, Wallingford, UK, pp. 77–81.

Nylander, M. and Hall, D. (2005) Rural tourism policy: European perspectives. In: Hall, D., Kirkpatrick, I. and Mitchell, M. (eds) *Rural Tourism and Sustainable Business*. Channel View, Clevedon, UK, pp. 17–40.

Obee, B. (1998) Eco-tourism boom – how much can wildlife take? *Beautiful British Columbia* 40, 7–17.

Odberg, F.O. (1992) Bullfighting and animal welfare. *Animal Welfare* 1(1), 3–12.

O'Donovan, D., Hindle, J.E., McKeown, S. and O'Donovan, S. (1993) Effect of visitors on the behaviour of female cheetahs *Acinonyx jubatus*. *International Zoo Yearbook* 32, 238–244.

OECD (Organization for Economic Cooperation and Development) (1997) *Integrated Environment/Safety Strategies – Expert Group Report*. Road Transport Research Programme, OECD, Paris.

OECD (Organization for Economic Cooperation and Development) EAP Task Force (2002) *Debt for Development and Environment Swap in Georgia. Institutional Options for Negotiations and Implementation of Bilateral Swap Agreements*. OECD, Paris.

OECD (Organization for Economic Cooperation and Development) Phare (1998) *Swapping Debt for the Environment*. OECD, Paris.

O'Grady, A. (1990) *The Challenge of Tourism: Learning Resources for Study and Action*. Ecumenical Coalition on Third World Tourism (ECTWT), Bangkok.

O'Grady, R. (1981) *Third World Stopover: the Tourism Debate*. World Council of Churches, Geneva.

O'Hare, G. and Barrett, H. (1999) Regional inequalities in the Peruvian tourist industry. *Geographical Journal* 165(1), 47–61.

Oliver, M. (1989) Disability and dependency: a creation of industrial societies? In: Barton, L. (ed.) *Disability and Dependency*. Fullmer, London, pp. 6–21.

Olsthoorn, X. (2001) Carbon dioxide emissions from international aviation: 1950–2050. *Journal of Air Transport Management* 7(2), 87–93.

Oppermann, M. (1992) International tourist flows in Malaysia. *Annals of Tourism Research* 19, 482–500.

Oppermann, M. (1999) Sex tourism. *Annals of Tourism Research* 26(2), 251–266.

Orams, M.B. (1995) Development and management of a wild dolphin feeding program at Tangalooma, Australia. *Aquatic Mammals* 21, 39–51.

Orams, M.B. (1996) A conceptual model of tourist–wildlife interaction: the case for education as a management strategy. *Australian Geographer* 27(1), 39–51.

Orams, M.B. (2002) Feeding wildlife as a tourist attraction: a review of issues and impacts. *Tourism Management* 23(3), 281–293.

Ormrod, S. (1994) Showboat as ark. *BBC Wildlife* 12(7), 40–44.

O'Rourke, P.J. (1989) *Holidays in Hell*. Pan Books, London.

Oxaal, Z. and Baden, S. (1997) *Gender and Empowerment: Definitions, Approaches and Implications for Policy*. BRIDGE Report No. 40, University of Sussex, Brighton, UK.

Page, S.J., Brunt, P., Busby, G. and Connell, J. (2001) *Tourism: a Modern Synthesis*. Thomson, London.

Page, S.J., Bentley, T. and Walker, L. (2005) Tourist safety in New Zealand and Scotland. *Annals of Tourism Research* 32(1), 150–166.

Pascale, R.T. and Athos, A.G. (1986) *The Art of Japanese Management*. Penguin, Harmondsworth, UK.

Pasumarty, K., Dolinsky, A., Stinerock, R. and Korol, T. (1996) Consumer behaviour and marketing strategy: a multinational study of children's involvement in the purchase of hospitality services. *Hospitality Research Journal* 19(4), 87–112.

Patterson, A. (1990) Debt-for-nature swaps and the need for alternatives. *Environment* 32(10), 5–12.

Payne, C.J.I. (2003) Vero cytoxin-producing *Escherichia coli* O157 gastroenteritis in farm visitors, North Wales. *Emerging Infectious Diseases* 9(5) <http://www.cdc.gov/ncidod/EID/vol9no5/02–0237.htm>.

Payne, D. and Dimanche, F. (1996) Towards a code of conduct for the tourism industry: an ethics model. *Journal of Business Ethics* 15(9), 997–1007.

Payne, E.F.J. (ed. and trans.) (1965) *Schopenhauer: On the Basis of Morality*. Bobbs-Merrill, New York.

PCFFF (Policy Commission on the Future of Food and Farming) (Curry Commission) (2002) *The Future of Food and Farming.* Stationery Office, London.

Peach, H.G. and Bath, N.E. (1999) Visitors without health and safety information in North Queensland: extent of the problem. *Journal of Tourism Studies* 10(2), 62–69.

Pearce, D.G. (1992) *Tourism Organizations.* Longman, Harlow, UK.

Pearce, P. (1982) *The Social Psychology of Tourist Behaviour.* Pergamon, Oxford, UK.

Pearce, P.L. (1988) *The Ulysses Factor: Evaluating Visitors in Tourist Settings.* Springer Verlag, New York.

Pearce, P.L. (1991) *Dreamworld. A Report on Public Reactions to Dreamworld and Proposed Developments at Dreamworld.* Department of Tourism, James Cook University, Townville, Australia.

Pearce, P., Moscardo, G. and Ross, G. (1996) *Tourism Community Relationships.* Pergamon, Oxford, UK.

Pearlman, M. (1990) Conflicts and constraints in Bulgaria's tourism sector. *Annals of Tourism Research* 17(1), 103–122.

Peat, M. (1997) Attitudes and access: advancing the rights of people with disabilities. *Canadian Medical Association Journal* 156(5), 657–659.

Peattie, S., Clarke, P. and Peattie, K. (2005) Risk and responsibility in tourism: promoting sun-safety. *Tourism Management* 26, 399–408.

Pechlaner, H. and Tshurtschenthaler, P. (2003) Tourism policy, tourism organizations and change management in Alpine regions and destinations: a European perspective. *Current Issues in Tourism* 6(6), 508–539.

Peet, R. (1991) *Global Capitalism – Theories of Social Development.* Routledge, London.

Pelton, R.Y. (1999) *Come Back Alive.* Broadway, New York.

Pelton, R.Y. and Aral, C. (eds) (1998) *Fielding's Hot Spots: Travel in Harm's Way.* Fielding Worldwide, Redondo Beach, California.

Pennington-Gray, L. and Kerstetter, D. (2002) Testing a constraints model within the context of nature-based tourism. *Journal of Travel Research* 40, 416–423.

Pernice, R. and Lys, K. (1996) Interventions for attitude change toward people with disabilities: how successful are they? *International Journal of Rehabilitation Research* 19, 171–174.

Petrick, J. (2003) Measuring cruise passengers' perceived value. *Tourism Analysis* 7 (3–4), 251–258.

Phillips, D.I. (2002) The Disability Discrimination Act revisited – implications of 2004 for tourism and hospitality. *Insights* A45–A55.

Phizacklea, A. (ed.) (1983) *One Way Ticket: Migration and Female Labour.* Routledge & Kegan Paul, London.

Pickersgill, S. (1996) Does the traditional zoo have a future in the UK? In: Robinson, M., Evans, N. and Callaghan, P. (eds) *Culture as the Tourist Product.* Business Education Publishers, Sunderland, UK, pp. 345–360.

Pine, B.J. and Gilmore, J.H. (1998) Welcome to the experience economy. *Harvard Business Review* July–August, 97–105.

Pinker, R. (1979) *The Idea of Welfare.* Heinemann, London.

Pi-Sunyer, O. (2004) Fear and fantasy: the elsewheres of post-9/11 tourism. *e-Review of Tourism Research* 2(4), 17–19 <http://ertr.tamu.edu>.

Pizam, A. (1982) Tourism and crime: is there a relationship? *Journal of Travel Research* 20(1), 7–10.

Pizam, A. and Mansfeld, Y. (eds) (1996) *Tourism, Crime and International Security Issues.* John Wiley & Sons, New York.

Pizam, A. and Telisman-Kosuta, N. (1989) Tourism as a factor of change: results and analysis. In: Bytstrzanowski, J. (ed.) *Tourism as a Factor of Change: a Socio-cultural Study.* Vienna Centre, Vienna, pp. 60–63.

Pizam, A., Tarlow, P. and Bloom, J. (1997) Making tourists feel safe: whose responsibility is it? *Journal of Travel Research* 3(3), 23–28.

Plant, R. (1991) *Modern Political Thought.* Basil Blackwell, Oxford, UK.

Plog, S.C. (1974) Why destination areas rise and fall in popularity. *Cornell Hotel and Restaurant Administration Quarterly* 14(3), 13–16.

Plog, S.C. (1990) A carpenter's tools: an answer to Stephen L.J. Smith's review of psychocentrism/allocentrism. *Journal of Travel Research* 28(4), 43–44.

Poirier, R.A. (1995) Tourism and development in Tunisia. *Annals of Tourism Research* 22(1), 157–171.

Pollock, N.C. (1968) *Africa.* University of London Press, London.

Pomeranz, F. (2004) Ethics: toward globalization. *Managerial Auditing Journal* 19(1), 8–14.

Poon, A. (1993) *Tourism, Technology and Competitive Strategies.* CAB International, Wallingford, UK.

Porritt, J. (1996) Hush hush, whisper who dares . . . the one word that defines green living is a conservation stopper. *Country Living* 127 (July), 27.

Postma, A. (2003) Conference presentation 'Quality of Life'. In: Swarbrooke, J., Smith, M. and Onderwater, L. (eds) *Quality of Life: ATLAS Reflections 2003*. ATLAS, Arnhem, The Netherlands, pp. 9–18.

Potier, M. (1991) Debt-for-nature swaps. *Land Use Policy* 8(3), 211–213.

Potts, F.C., Goodwin, H. and Walpole, M.J. (1996) People, wildlife and tourism in and around Hwange National Park, Zimbabwe. In: Price, M.F. (ed.) *People and Tourism in Fragile Environments*. John Wiley & Sons, Chichester, UK, and New York, pp. 199–220.

Poulsen, T.M. (1977) Migration on the Adriatic coast: some processes associated with the development of tourism. In: Kostanick, H.L. (ed.) *Population and Migration Trends in Eastern Europe*. Westview, Boulder, Colorado, pp. 197–215.

Pownall, K. (2004) *No Going Back – Buying Abroad*. Time Warner, London.

Prager, J.H. (1999) People with disabilities are next consumer niche. *Wall Street Journal* 15 December, pp. B1–B2.

Pratt, L. (2004) Why we got in the saddle for Africa. *The Observer* 14 November, p. 5 <http://observer.guardian.co.uk/print/0,3858,5062591-102284,00.html> (last accessed 14 November 2004).

Prentice, R. (1993) Community-driven tourism planning and residents' preferences. *Tourism Management* 14(3), 218–227.

Prentice, R.C., Witt, S.F. and Wydenbach, E.G. (1994) The endearment behaviour of tourists through their interaction with the host community. *Tourism Management* 15(2), 117–125.

Price, G.G. (2003) Ecotourism and the development of environmental literacy in Australia. *e-Review of Tourism Research* 1(1), 72–75 <http://ertr.tamu.edu>.

Prideaux, B. (1996) The tourism crime cycle. In: Pizam, A. and Mansfeld, Y. (eds) *Tourism, Crime and International Security Issues*. John Wiley & Sons, Chichester, UK, and New York, pp. 59–75.

Priest, S. and Bunting, C. (1993) Changes in perceived risk and competence during whitewater canoeing. *Journal of Applied Recreation Research* 18(4), 265–280.

Provost, S. and Soto, J.C. (2001) Predicators of pretravel consultation in tourists from Quebec (Canada). *Journal of Travel Medicine* 8(2), 66–67.

Przeclawski, K. (1994) *Tourism and the Contemporary World*. University of Warsaw, Warsaw.

Przeclawski, K. (1996) Deontology of tourism. *Progress in Tourism and Hospitality Research* 2(3), 239–245.

Pugh, J. (2003) A consideration of some of the sociological mechanisms shaping the adoption of participatory planning in Barbados. In: Pugh, J. and Potter, R.B. (eds) *Participatory Planning in the Caribbean: Lessons from Practice*. Ashgate, Aldershot, UK, pp. 118–137.

Pybus, E. (2002) *Live and Work in France*, 4th edn. Vacation Work, Oxford.

Pybus, V. (2003) *International Voluntary Work*, 8th edn. Vacation Work, Oxford.

Pyo, S. and Howell, R. (1988) Social tourism: the Korean case. *Tourist Review* 3, 16–19.

Quiroga, I. (1990) Characteristics of package tours in Europe. *Annals of Tourism Research* 17, 185–207.

Rathkey, P. (1990) *Time Innovations and the Deployment of Manpower*. Avebury, Aldershot, UK.

Rátz, T. and Púczko, L. (2002) *The Impacts of Tourism: an Introduction*. Häme Polytechnic, Hämeenlinna, Finland.

Ray, N.M. and Ryder, M.E. (2003) 'Ebilities' tourism: an exploratory discussion of the travel needs and motivations of the mobility-disabled. *Tourism Management* 24(1), 57–72.

Reade, L.S. and Waran, N.K. (1996) The modern zoo: how do people perceive zoo animals? *Applied Animal Behaviour Science* 47(1–2), 109–118.

Redclift, M. (1987) *Sustainable Development: Exploring the Contradictions*. Methuen, London.

Rees-Mogg, W. (1999) A culture of corruption. *The Times* 15 February, p. 18.

Regan, T. (1988) *The Case for Animal Rights*. Routledge, London and New York.

Regan, T. and Singer, P. (eds) (1989) *Animal Rights and Human Obligations*. Prentice-Hall International, New York.

Reilly, R.T. (1988) *Travel and Tourism Marketing Techniques*, 2nd edn. Delmar Publishing, Albany, New York.

Remenyi, J. (2004) Poverty and development: the struggle to empower the poor. In: Kingsbury, D., Remenyi, J., McKay, J. and Hunt, J. (eds) *Key Issues in Development*. Palgrave Macmillan, Basingstoke, UK, pp. 190–220.

Renard, Y. (2001) *Practical Strategies for Pro-poor Tourism: a Case Study of the St. Lucia Heritage Tourism Programme*. PPT Working Paper No. 7, Centre for Responsible Tourism, International Institute for Environment and Development and Overseas Development Institute, London.

Reynolds, P.C. and Braithwaite, D. (2001) Towards a conceptual framework for wildlife tourism. *Tourism Management* 22(1), 31–42.

Richards, G. (1996) Production and consumption of European cultural tourism. *Annals of Tourism Research* 23(2), 261–283.

Richards, G. (1999) Vacations and the quality of life: patterns and structures. *Journal of Business Research* 44, 189–198.

Richards, G. and Hall, D. (2000) The community: a sustainable concept in tourism development? In: Richards, G. and Hall, D. (eds) *Tourism and Sustainable Community Development*. Routledge, London and New York, pp. 1–13.

Richardson, B.C. (2005) Sustainable transport: analysis frameworks. *Journal of Transport Geography* 13(1), 29–39.

Richardson, J. (1996) *Marketing Australian Travel and Tourism*. Hospitality Press, Melbourne, Australia.

Richter, L. (1992) Political instability and tourism in the Third World. In: Harrison, D. (ed.) *Tourism and the Less Developed Countries*. Belhaven Press, London, pp. 35–46.

Richter, L.K. and Richter, W.L. (1999) Ethics challenges: health, safety and accessibility in international travel and tourism. *Public Personnel Management* 28(4), 595–615.

Richter, L. and Waugh, W. (1986) Terrorism and tourism as logical companions. *Tourism Management* 7(4), 230–238.

Ripley, J. (2003) Feeling blue? It's post-holiday stress. *The Scotsman* 3 September <http://www.leisure. scotsman.com/home/text_only.cfm?id=7789> (last accessed 16 March 2005).

Ritchie, B. (1992) New realities, new horizons – leisure, tourism and society in the third millennium. In: *The Annual Review of Travel*. American Express, New York, pp. 11–26.

Ritchie, B.W. (2003) *Managing Educational Tourism*. Channel View, Clevedon, UK.

Ritchie, J.R.B. (1975) Some critical aspects of measurement theory and practice in travel research. *Journal of Travel Research* 14(1), 1–10.

Ritvo, H. (1988) The emergence of modern pet keeping. In: Rowan, A.N. (ed.) *Animals and People Sharing the World*. University Press of New England, Hanover, New Hampshire, pp. 13–31.

Robbins, S.P. and Coulter, M. (1996) *Management*. Prentice-Hall, Upper Saddle River, New Jersey.

Roberts, L. and Hall, D. (2001) *Rural Tourism and Recreation: Principles to Practice*. CAB International, Wallingford, UK.

Robins, J. (2004) Holiday in ruins. If your away days were awful, why not bring home a payout? *The Observer* 29 August <http://observer.guardian.co.uk/print/0,3858,5003874-102272,00.html> (last accessed 18 March 2005).

Robins, P. (1990) *Sun Sense*. The Skin Cancer Foundation, New York.

Robinson, D.W. (1994) Strategies for alternative tourism: the case of tourism in Sagarmatha (Everest) National Park. In: Seaton, A.V. (ed.) *Tourism: the State of the Art*. John Wiley & Sons, Chichester, UK, and New York, pp. 691–702.

Robinson, M. (1989) The zoo that is not: education for conservation. *Conservation Biology* 13(3), 213–215.

Robson, E. (2002) A nation of lace workers and glassblowers? Gendering of the Maltese souvenir handicraft industry. In: Swain, M.B. and Momsen, J.H. (eds) *Gender/Tourism/Fun(?)*. Cognizant Communication Corporation, New York, pp. 109–117.

Robson, J. and Robson, I. (1996) From shareholders to stakeholders: critical issues for tourism marketers. *Tourism Management* 17(7), 533–540.

Roche, M. (1992) *Rethinking Citizenship: Welfare, Ideology and Change in Modern Society*. Polity Press, Cambridge, UK.

Rodger, J.J. (2003) Social solidarity, welfare and post-emotionalism. *Journal of Social Policy* 32(3), 403–421.

Rodriguez-Garcia, R. (2001) The health–development link: travel as a public health issue. *Journal of Community Health* 26(2), 93–112.

Roe, D. and Urquhart, P. (2001) *Pro-poor Tourism: Harnessing the World's Largest Industry for the World's Poor*. International Institute for Environment and Development, London.

Roedder John, D. (1999) Consumer socialization of children: a retrospective look at twenty-five years of research. *Journal of Consumer Research* 26(4), 183–216.

Rogerson, C.M. (2002) Tourism and local economic development: the case of the Highlands Meander. *Development Southern Africa* 19(1), 143–167.

Rojek, C. (1993a) After popular culture: hyperreality and leisure. *Leisure Studies* 12(4), 277–289.

Rojek, C. (1993b) *Ways of Escape: Modern Transformations in Leisure and Travel*. Macmillan, Basingstoke, UK.

Rojek, C. (1995) Veblen, leisure and human need. *Leisure Studies* 14, 73–86.

Romeril, M. (1989) Tourism and the environment – accord or discord? *Tourism Management* 10(3), 205–208.

Ronen, S. (1986) Equity perception in multiple comparison: a field study. *Human Relations* 39, 333–346.

Ross, G.F. (1993a) Help-seeking responses to work stress among rural and regional hospitality industry workers. *Regional Journal of Social Issues* 27, 92–98.

Ross, G.F. (1993b) Type, severity and incidence of work stressors among Australian hospitality industry employees. *Australian Journal of Leisure and Recreation* 3(4), 5–12.

Ross, G.F. (2003) Ethical ideals and expectations regarding visitor, staff, and management among potential tourist industry employees. *Tourism Analysis* 8(2), 211–215.

Roth, C.E. (1991) Towards shaping environmental literacy for a sustainable future. *ASTM Standardization News* April, 42–45.

Rowan, A.N. (ed.) (1988) *Animals and People Sharing the World.* University Press of New England, Hanover, New Hampshire.

Rowan, A.N. and Beck, A.M. (1994) The health benefits of human–animal interaction. *Anthrozoos* 7(2), 85–89.

Rowlands, J. (1995) A word of the times, but what does it mean? Empowerment in the discourse and practice of development. In: Afshav, H. (ed.) *Women and Empowerment: Illustrations from the Third World.* Macmillan, Basingstoke, UK, pp. 11–34.

Russell, C.L. and Ankenman, M.J. (1996) Orangutans as photographic collectibles: ecotourism and the commodification of nature. *Tourism Recreation Research* 21(1), 71–78.

Rust, R.T., Stewart, G.L., Miller, H. and Pielack, D. (1996) The satisfaction and retention of frontline employees, a customer satisfaction measurement approach. *International Journal of Service Industry Management* 75(5), 62–80.

Ryan, C. (1991) *Recreational Tourism: a Social Science Perspective.* Routledge, London.

Ryan, C. (1992) The child as a visitor. In: Ritchie, J.B. and Hawkside, D. (eds) *World Travel and Tourism Review – Indicators, Trends and Issues,* Vol. 2. CAB International, Wallingford, UK, pp. 135–139.

Ryan, C. (1993) Crime, violence, terrorism and tourism: an accidental or intrinsic relationship? *Tourism Management* 14, 173–183.

Ryan, C. (1994) Leisure and tourism – the application of leisure concepts to tourist behaviour – a proposed model. In: Seaton, A.V. (ed.) *Tourism: the State of the Art.* John Wiley & Sons, Chichester, UK, and New York, pp. 294–307.

Ryan, C. (1997) *The Tourist Experience: a New Introduction.* Cassell, London.

Ryan, C. (1998) Saltwater crocodiles as tourist attractions. *Journal of Sustainable Tourism* 6(4), 314–327.

Ryan, C. (2002) Equity, management, power sharing and sustainability – issues of the 'new tourism'. *Tourism Management* 23(1), 17–26.

Ryan, C. (2003) *Recreational Tourism: Demands and Impacts.* Channel View, Clevedon, UK.

Ryan, C. and Kinder, R. (1996) Sex, tourism and sex tourism: fulfilling similar needs? *Tourism Management* 17(7), 507–518.

Ryan, C. and Montgomery, D. (1994) The attitudes of Bakewell residents to tourism and numbers in community responsive tourism. *Tourism Management* 15(5), 358–369.

Ryan, C. and Robertson, E. (1997) The New Zealand student–tourist and risk behaviours. In: Clift, S. and Grabowski, P. (eds) *Tourism and Health: Risks, Research and Responses.* Mansell, London, pp. 119–139.

Ryan, C., Robertson, E. and Page, S. (1996) New Zealand students: risk behaviours while on holiday. *Tourism Management* 16(1), 64–69.

Ryder, R.D. (1975) *Victims of Science: the Use of Animals in Research.* Davis-Poynter, New York.

Ryder, R.D. (1989) *Animal Revolution: Changing Attitudes Towards Speciesism.* Blackwell, Oxford, UK.

Safier, M. (1994) Potential and prospects for tourism in the world today. In: Baskin, G. and Twite, R. (eds) *The Conversion of Dreams: Tourism in the Middle East.* Israel/Palestine Centre for Research and Information, Jerusalem, pp. 1–11.

Sager, D. (1993) Blood in the snow. *The Independent on Sunday* 24 January.

Sahn, D.E. and Stifel, D.C. (2003) Progress toward the Millennium Development Goals in Africa. *World Development* 31(1), 23–52.

Sainsbury, D. (1994) *Gender and Welfare State Regimes.* Oxford University Press, Oxford, UK.

Sainsbury, D. (ed.) (1999) *Gendering Welfare States.* Sage, London.

Salvà-Thomàs, P.A. (2002) Foreign immigration and tourism development in Spain's Balearic Islands. In: Hall, C.M. and Williams, A.M. (eds) *Tourism and Migration.* Kluwer, Dordrecht, The Netherlands, pp. 119–134.

Samarasuriya, S. (1982) *Who Needs Tourism? Employment for Women in the Holiday Industry of Sudugama, Sri Lanka.* Research Project Women and Development, Colombo and Leiden.

Samuel, N. (1986) Free time in France: a historical and sociological survey. *International Social Science Journal* 107, 47–63.

Samuel, N. (1993) Vacation time and the French family. *World Leisure and Recreation* 35, 15–16.

Sant, M. amd Simons, P. (1993) Counterurbanization and coastal development in New South Wales. *Geoforum* 24(3), 291–306.

Sapsford, W. (2004) *Fit to Fly*. New Holland Publishers, London.

Sarabahksh, M., Carson, D. and Lindgren, E. (1989) Hospitality managers' stress and quality of life: recommendations for change. *Hospitality Education and Research Journal* 13(3), 239–244.

Sarkar, A.U. and Ebbs, K.L. (1992) A possible solution to tropical troubles? Debt-for-nature swaps. *Futures* 24(7), 653–668.

Sassen, S. (1991) *The Global City: New York, London, Tokyo*. Princeton University Press, Princeton, New Jersey.

Schänzel, H.A. and McIntosh, A. (2000) An insight into the personal and emotive context of wildlife viewing at the Penguin Place, Otago Peninsula, New Zealand. *Journal of Sustainable Tourism* 8(1), 36–52.

Schaufeli, W.B., Maslach, C. and Marek, T. (1993) *Professional Burnout: Recent Developments in Theory and Research*. Taylor & Francis, Washington, DC.

Schobersberger, W., Greie, S. and Humpeler, E. (2004) Alpine health tourism: future prospects from a medical perspective. In: Weiermair, K. and Mathies, C. (eds) *The Tourism and Leisure Industry: Shaping the Future*. Haworth Hospitality Press, New York, pp. 199–208.

Scholl, R.W., Cooper, E.A. and McKenna, J.F. (1987) Referent selection in determining equity perception: differential effects on behavioral and attitudinal outcomes. *Personnel Psychology* 40, 113–127.

Schor, J. (1991) *The Overworked American: the Unexpected Decline of Leisure*. Basic Books, New York.

SCIEH (Scottish Centre for Infection and Environmental Health) (2005) *fitfortravel*. SCIEH and Health Protection Scotland, Glasgow <http://www.fitfortravel.scot.nhs.uk> (last accessed 25 May 2005).

Scott, D. (1991) The problematic nature of participation in contract bridge: a qualitative study of group-related constraints. *Leisure Sciences* 13, 321–336.

Scott, J. (1995) Sexual and national boundaries in tourism. *Annals of Tourism Research* 22(2), 385–403.

Scott, J. (1997) Chances and choices: women and tourism in northern Cyprus. In: Sinclair, M.T. (ed.) *Gender, Work and Tourism*. Routledge, London and New York, pp. 60–90.

Scott, K. (2004) Holiday Britons killed in Florida as car hits tanker. *The Guardian* 20 December.

Scott, K. (2005) Family: the cause of many a holiday snap. *The Guardian* 29 August, p. 4.

Scottish Seabird Centre (2005) *Get Close!* Scottish Seabird Centre, North Berwick, UK <http://www.seabird.org/> (last accessed 4 April 2005).

Seaton, A.V. (1992) Social stratification in tourism choice and experience since the war. *Tourism Management* 13(1), 106–111.

Seaton, A.V. (1996) Tourism and relative deprivation: the counter-revolutionary pressures of tourism in Cuba. In: Robinson, M., Evans, N. and Callaghan, P. (eds) *Tourism and Culture: Image, Identity and Marketing*. Business Education Publishers, Sunderland, UK, pp. 197–216.

Seaton, A.V. (1997) Demonstration effects or relative deprivation? The counter-revolutionary pressures of tourism in Cuba. *Progress in Tourism and Hospitality Research* 3(4), 307–320.

Seaton, A.V. (2002) Tourism as metempsychosis and metensomatosis: the personae of eternal recurrence. In: Dann, G.M.S. (ed.) *The Tourist as a Metaphor of the Social World*. CAB International, Wallingford, UK, pp. 135–168.

Seaton, A.V. and Tagg, S. (1995) The family vacation in Europe: paedonomic aspects of choices and satisfactions. *Journal of Travel and Tourism Marketing* 4(1), 1–21.

Sefton, J.M. and Burton, T.L. (1987) The measurement of leisure motivations and satisfaction: a replication and an extension. Paper presented at the Fifth Canadian Congress on Leisure Research, Dalhousie University, Halifax, Canada.

Segan, C.J., Borland, R. and Hill, D.J. (1999) Development and evaluation of a brochure on sun protection and sun exposure for tourists. *Health Education Journal* 58, 177–191.

Serpell, J. (1986) *In the Company of Animals: a Study of Human–Animal Relationships*. Basil Blackwell, Oxford, UK.

Serrell, B. (1981) The role of zoos, parks and aquariums in environmental education. *Journal of Environmental Education* 12(3), 41–42.

Shackley, M. (1996) *Wildlife Tourism*. International Thomson Business Press, London.

Shah, K. (2000) *Tourism, the Poor and Other Stakeholders: Asian Experience*. ODI Fair-Trade in Tourism Paper, Overseas Development Institute, London.

Sharpley, R. (2000) Tourism and sustainable development: exploring the theoretical divide. *Journal of Sustainable Tourism* 8(1), 1–19.

Sharpley, R. (2001) Sustainable rural tourism development: ideal or idyll? In: Roberts, L. and Hall, D. (eds) *Rural Tourism and Recreation: Principles to Practice.* CAB International, Wallingford, UK, pp. 57–58.

Sharpley, R. (2003) Rural tourism and sustainability – a critique. In: Hall, D., Roberts, L. and Mitchell, M. (eds) *New Directions in Rural Tourism.* Ashgate, Aldershot, UK, pp. 38–53.

Sharpley, R. and Craven, B. (2001) The 2001 foot and mouth crisis – rural economy and tourism policy implications: a comment. *Current Issues in Tourism* 4, 527–537.

Sharpley, R. and Sundaram, P. (2005) Tourism: a sacred journey? The case of ashram tourism, India. *International Journal of Tourism Research* 7(3), 161–171.

Sharpley, R., Sharpley, J. and Adams, J. (1996) Travel advice or trade embargo? The impacts and implications of official travel advice. *Tourism Management* 17(1), 1–7.

Sharrock, D. (1994) Joint drive for tourism. *The Guardian* 25 November.

Shaw, D.S. and Clarke, I. (1999) Belief formation in ethical consumer groups: an exploratory study. *Marketing Intelligence and Planning* 17(2), 109–119.

Shaw, G. and Coles, T. (2004) Disability, holiday making and the tourism industry in the UK: a preliminary survey. *Tourism Management* 25(3), 397–403.

Shaw, G. and Williams, A.M. (2002) *Critical Issues in Tourism,* 2nd edn. Blackwell, Oxford, UK.

Sheldon, P.J. and Fox, M. (1988) The role of foodservice in vacation choice and experience: a cross-cultural analysis. *Journal of Travel Research* 27(4), 9–15.

Sherlock, K. (2001) Revisiting the concept of hosts and guests. *Tourist Studies* 1(3), 271–295.

Shickle, D., Nolan-Farrell, M.Z. and Evans, M.R. (1998) Travel brochures need to carry better health advice. *Communicable Disease and Public Health* 1, 41–43.

Siegle, L. (2005a) Plane speaking. *The Observer Magazine* 29 May, p. 56.

Siegle, L. (2005b) Tourists keep heads in the sand. *The Observer* 26 June, Special Report on Climate Change p. 12.

Simons, T. and Enz, C.A. (1995) Motivating hotel employees. *Cornell Hotel and Restaurant Administration Quarterly* 36(1), 20–27.

Simpson, F. and Roberts, L. (2000) Help or hindrance? Sustainable approaches to tourism consultancy in Central and Eastern Europe. *Journal of Sustainable Tourism* 8(6), 491–509.

Sims, R.R. (1991) The institutionalization of organizational ethics. *Journal of Business Ethics* 10, 493–506.

Sinclair, T., Fryxell, J. and Caughley, G. (2005) *Wildlife Ecology, Management and Conservation,* 2nd· edn. Blackwell, Oxford, UK.

Singapore Zoo (2005) *Welcome to Singapore Night Safari.* Singapore Zoo, Singapore <http://www. nightsafari.com.sg/about/facts.htm> (last accessed 14 March 2005).

Singer, P. (ed.) (1985) *In Defence of Animals.* Basil Blackwell, Oxford, UK.

Singer, P. (1990) *Animal Liberation: a New Ethics for our Treatment of Animals,* 2nd edn. Jonathan Cape, London.

Singer, P. (1993) *Practical Ethics,* 2nd edn. Basil Blackwell, Oxford, UK.

Singh, S., Timothy, D.J. and Dowling, R.K. (2003) Tourism and destination communities. In: Singh, S., Timothy, D.J. and Dowling, R.K. (eds) *Tourism in Destination Communities.* CAB International, Wallingford, UK, pp. 1–17.

Sirakaya, E., Teye, V. and Sönmez, S.F. (2001) Examining the sources of differential support for tourism industry in two Ghanaian cities. *Tourism Analysis* 6(1), 29–40.

Sizer, S.R. (1999) The ethical challenges of managing pilgrimages to the Holy Land. *International Journal of Contemporary Hospitality Management* 11(2–3), 85–90.

Skuse, I. (2005) New airline ticket taxes – are airlines a soft touch? *Business Travel World* July, p. 45.

Small, J. (2003) The voices of older women tourists. *Tourism Recreation Research* 28(2), 31–39.

Smaoui, A. (1979) Tourism and employment in Tunisia. In: de Kadt, E. (ed.) *Tourism: Passport to Development?* Oxford University Press, Oxford, UK, pp. 101–110.

Smart, J. and Williams, B. (1973) *Utilitarianism: For and Against.* Cambridge University Press, Cambridge, UK.

Smith, G. (1999) Toward a United States policy on traveler safety and security: 1980–2000. *Journal of Travel Research* 38(1), 62–65.

Smith, M. and Duffy, R. (2003) *The Ethics of Tourism Development.* Routledge, London and New York.

Smith, M.K. (2003) Holistic holidays: tourism and the reconciliation of body, mind, spirit. *Tourism Recreation Research* 28(1), 103–108.

Smith, M.K. and Kelly, C. (2004) 'Stop the world – I want to get off!' Is holistic tourism becoming the ultimate route to escapism? In: MacLellan, R. (ed.) *Tourism: State of the Art II.* CD-ROM, University of Strathclyde, Glasgow, UK.

Smith, N.C. (1990) *Morality and the Market.* Routledge, London.

Smith, P.C., Kendall, L.M. and Hulin, C.L. (1996) *The Measurement of Satisfaction in Work and Retirement: a Strategy for the Study of Attitudes.* Rand McNally, Chicago, Illinois.

Smith, R.W. (1987) Leisure of disabled tourists: barriers to participation. *Annals of Tourism Research* 14(3), 376–389.

Smith, V.L. (1994) Boracay, Philippines: a case study in 'alternative' tourism. In: Smith, V.L. and Eadington, W.R. (eds) *Tourism Alternatives.* John Wiley & Sons, Chichester, UK, and New York, pp. 133–157.

Smith, V.L. (1998) War and tourism: an American ethnography. *Annals of Tourism Research* 25(1), 202–227.

Smith, V. and Hughes, H. (1999) Disadvantaged families and the meaning of holiday. *International Journal of Tourism Research* 1(2), 123–133.

Smyth, R. (1986) Public policy for tourism in Northern Ireland. *Tourism Management* 7, 120–126.

Social Tourism Study Group (1976) *Holidays: the Social Need.* ETB, London.

Soederberg, S. (2002) On the contradictions of the new international financial architecture: another procrustean bed for emerging markets? *Third World Quarterly* 23(4), 607–620.

SOEID (Scottish Office Education and Industry Department) (1996) *Visits to Farms/Health Tips for Teachers Leading School Visits to Farms.* Letter and Appendix to Directors of Education in Scotland, 16 December, SOEID, Edinburgh, UK.

Sofield, T.H.B. (2003) *Empowerment for Sustainable Tourism Development.* Elsevier, Amsterdam.

Sofield, T.H.B. and Li, F.M.S. (1998) Tourism development and cultural policies in China. *Annals of Tourism Research* 25(2), 362–392.

Sönmez, S. and Graefe, A. (1998a) Determining future travel behavior from past travel experience and perceptions of risk and safety. *Journal of Travel Research* 37(4), 171–177.

Sönmez, S. and Graefe, A. (1998b) Influence of terrorism risk on foreign tourism decisions. *Annals of Tourism Research* 25(1), 112–144.

Sorabji, R. (1993) *Animal Minds and Human Morals: the Origins of the Western Debate.* Duckworth, London.

Sørensen, A. (1997) Travel as attraction. Paper presented at International Tourism Research Conference: Peripheral Area Tourism, Research Centre of Bornholm, Nexø, Denmark.

Sørensen, A. and Nilsson, P.Å. (1999) Virtual rurality versus rural reality in rural tourism – contemplating the attraction of the rural. Paper presented at the Eighth Nordic Symposium in Hospitality and Tourism Research, 18–21 November, Alta, Norway.

Sorrell, R.D. (1988) *St Francis of Assisi and Nature: Tradition and Innovation in Western Christian Attitudes toward the Environment.* Oxford University Press, Oxford, UK.

Spa Golf Club (2004) *Golf and Spa Packages.* Spa Golf Club, Piešťany, Slovakia.

Spivack, S.E. (1994) Food protection and tourism. *Annals of Tourism Research* 21(1), 185–187.

Sprigge, T. (1987) *The Rational Foundations of Ethics.* Routledge & Kegan Paul, London.

Spurr, D. (1993) *The Rhetoric of Empire: Colonial Discourse in Journalism, Travel Writing, and Imperial Administration.* Duke University Press, London.

Sri Lanka Tourism (2005) Big guns drive tourism revival. *4Hoteliers: Hospitality & Travel News* 29 January <http://www.4hoteliers.com/4hots_nshw.php?mwi=1712> (last accessed 24 May 2005).

Stark, J.C. (2002) Ethics and ecotourism: connections and conflicts. *Philosophy and Geography* 5(1), 101–113.

Stears, D. (1996) Travel health promotion: advances and alliances. In: Clift, S. and Page, S. (eds) *Health and the International Tourist.* Routledge, London, pp. 215–234.

Steg, L. and Gifford, R. (2005) Sustainable transportation and quality of life. *Journal of Transport Geography* 13(1), 59–69.

Stewart, E.J., Hayward, B.M. and Devlin, P.J. (1998) The 'place' of interpretation: a new approach to the evaluation of interpretation. *Tourism Management* 19(3), 257–266.

Storper, M. (1995) The resurgence of regional economies. *European Urban and Regional Studies* 2, 191–219.

Streltzer, J. (1979) Psychiatric emergencies in travelers to Hawaii. *Comprehensive Psychiatry* 20(5), 463–468.

Sumner, L.W. (1992) Two theories of the good. *Social Philosophy and Policy* 9, 1–14.

Sunoo, B.P. (1996) Vacations: going once, going twice, sold. *Personnel Journal* August, 72–80.

Swain, M.B. (1990) Commoditizing ethnicity in Southwest China. *Cultural Survival Quarterly* 14(1), 26–30.

Swain, M.B. (1995) Gender in tourism. *Annals of Tourism Research* 22(2), 247–266.

Swan, S. and Laufer, P. (2004) *Safety and Security for Women Who Travel.* Travelers' Tales, San Francisco.

Swarbrooke, J. (1999) *Sustainable Tourism Management.* CAB International, Wallingford, UK.

Swarbrooke, J. (2003) Introduction. In: Swarbrooke, J., Smith, M. and Onderwater, L. (eds) *Quality of Life: ATLAS Reflections 2003.* ATLAS, Arnhem, pp. 5–7.

Swiac, C. (ed.) (2003) *Fodor's Healthy Escapes.* Fodor, New York.

Swinyard, W.R. and Sim, C.P. (1987) Perception of children's influence on family decision processes. *Journal of Consumer Marketing* 4(1), 25–38.

Szivas, E. and Riley, M. (2002) Labour mobility and tourism in the post 1989 transition in Hungary. In: Hall, C.M. and Williams, A.M. (eds) *Tourism and Migration*. Kluwer, Dordrecht, The Netherlands, pp. 53–72.

Tarlow, P. (2003) Tourism in a postenchanted world: new ideas, new strategies. *e-Review of Tourism Research* 1(2), 28–31 <http://ertr.tamu.edu>.

Tarlow, P.E. (2004a) The many aspects of tourism surety. *Tourism and Moore's Tourism Tidbits*, circulated online from <tourism@bihs.net> 1 February.

Tarlow, P.E. (2004b) The Anaheim study. *Tourism and Moore's Tourism Tidbits*, circulated online from <tourism@bihs.net> 28 February.

Tarlow, P.E. (2004c) Tourism and health. *Tourism and Moore's Tourism Tidbits*, circulated online from <tourism@bihs.net> 29 April.

Tarlow, P.E. (2005) Dark tourism – the appealing 'dark' side of tourism and more. In: Novelli, M. (ed.) *Niche Tourism: Contemporary Issues, Trends and Cases*. Elsevier, Amsterdam, pp. 47–58.

Tasker, A., Akinola, O. and Cohen, A.T. (2004) Review of venous thromboembolism associated with air travel. *Travel Medicine and Infectious Disease* 2(2), 75–79.

Tax, S.S. and Brown, S.W. (1998) Recovering and learning from service failure. *Sloan Management Review* 40, 75–88.

Taylor, J.S. (2001) Dollars are a girl's best friend? Female tourists' sexual behaviour in the Caribbean. *Sociology* 35(3), 749–764.

Taylor, V. (1999) *A Quick Guide to Mainstreaming in Development Planning*. Commonwealth Secretariat, London.

Tearfund (2000) *Tourism: an Ethical Issue*. Tearfund, London.

Teuscher, H. (1983) Social tourism for all – the Swiss Travel Saving Fund. *Tourism Management* 4(3), 216–219.

Teye, V.B. (1988) Prospects for regional tourism cooperation in Africa. *Tourism Management* 9(3), 221–234.

Teye, V. and Leclerc, D. (1998) Product and service delivery satisfaction among North American cruise passengers. *Tourism Management* 19(2), 153–160.

Teye, V., Sönmez, S.F. and Sirakaya, E. (2002) Residents' attitudes toward tourism development. *Annals of Tourism Research* 29(3), 668–688.

Thanh-Dam, T. (1990) *Sex, Money and Mobility: Prostitution and Tourism in South-east Asia*. Zed Books, London.

Thapa, S. and Thapa, B. (2002) Debt-for-nature swaps: potential applications in Nepal. *International Journal of Sustainable Development and World Ecology* 9, 239–255.

The Guardian (1995) Holiday firm bans bloodsports. *The Guardian* 22 June.

The Observer and Responsibletravel.com (2005) The better travel guide. *The Observer* 23 January, Special Supplement.

Theocharous, A. (2004) The impact of political instability on the tourism industries of selected Mediterranean destinations: a neural network approach. In: Hall, D. (ed.) *Tourism and Transition: Governance, Transformation and Development*. CAB International, Wallingford, UK, pp. 147–167.

Thomas, K. (1983) *Man and the Natural World: Changing Attitudes in England, 1500–1800*. Allan Lane, London.

Thompson, M. and Homewood, K. (2002) Entrepreneurs, elites, and exclusion in Maasailand: trends in wildlife conservation and pastoralist development. *Human Ecology* 30(1), 107–138.

Thornton, P.R., Shaw, G. and Williams, A.M. (1997) Tourist group holiday decision-making and behaviour: the influence of children. *Tourism Management* 18(5), 287–297.

TIAA (Travel Industry Association of America) (2002) *TravelScope*. Travel Industry Association of America <http://www.tia.org>.

Tibbs, H. (1993) *Industrial Ecology: an Environmental Agenda for Industry*. Global Business Network, Emeryville, California.

TIES (The International Ecotourism Society) (2003) *Ecotourism Statistical Fact Sheet*. The International Ecotourism Society <http://www.ecotourism.org> (last accessed 3 May 2005).

Timms, M., McHugh, S., O'Carrol, A. and James, T. (1997) Assessing impact of disability awareness training using the attitudes towards disabled persons scale (ATDP-Form). *International Journal of Rehabilitation Research* 20, 319–323.

Timothy, D.J. and Ioannides, D. (2002) Tour operator hegemony: dependency, oligopoly and sustainability in insular destinations. In: Apostolopoulos, Y. and Gayle, D.J. (eds) *Island Tourism and Sustainable Development: Caribbean, Pacific, and Mediterranean Experiences*. Praeger, Westport, Connecticut, pp. 181–198.

Titmuss, R.M. (1968) *Commitment to Welfare*. George Allen & Unwin, London.

Titmuss, R.M. (1976) *Commitment to Welfare*, 2nd edn. George Allen & Unwin, London.

Toh, R.S., Rivers, M.J. and Ling, T.W. (2005) Room occupancies: cruise lines out-do the hotels. *International Journal of Hospitality Management* 24(1), 121–135.

Tokarski, W. and Michels, H. (1996) Germany. In: Cushman, G., Veal, A.J. and Zuzanek, J. (eds) *World Leisure Participation: Free Time in the Global Village*. CAB International, Wallingford, UK, pp. 107–112.

Topham, G. (2005) At home, I am a tourist. *The Guardian* 7 March <http://www.guardian.co.uk/print/0,3858,5141873-103677,00.html> (last accessed 18 March 2005).

Tourism Concern (2001) *The International Network on Fair Trade in Tourism*. Tourism Concern, London <http://www.tourismconcern.org.uk/downloads/pdfs/fairtrade-introduction.pdf> (last accessed 5 May 2005).

Tourism Concern (2002) *Trekking Wrongs: Porters Rights*. Tourism Concern, London <http://www.tourismconcern.org.uk/campaigns/porters> (last accessed 23 August 2004).

Tourism Concern (2004) *Sun, Sand, Sea and Sweatshops*. Tourism Concern, London <http://www.tourismconcern.org.uk/campaigns/ssss> (last accessed 2 May 2005).

Tourism Concern and WWF (1992) *Beyond the Green Horizon. A Discussion Paper on Principles for Sustainable Tourism*. WWF UK, Godalming, UK.

Townsend, J.G. and Townsend, A.R. (2004) Accountability, motivation and practice: NGOs North and South. *Social and Cultural Geography* 5(2), 271–284.

Townsend, M. (2001) Airlines to be sued over DVT deaths. *The Observer* 29 July.

Toynbee, J.M.C. (1976) *Animals in Roman Life and Art*. Thames & Hudson, London.

Toynbee, P. (2005) Free-market buccaneers. *The Guardian* 19 August <http://www.guardian.co.uk/print/0,3858,5266196-111586,00.html> (last accessed 23 August 2005).

Trauer, B. and Ryan, C. (2005) Destination image, romance and place experience – an application of intimacy theory in tourism. *Tourism Management* 26, 481–491.

Travel Weekly (1998) Have you been ill on vacation? *Travel Weekly* 30 July, p. 18.

Tregakis, C. (2002) Social model theory: the story so far. *Disability and Society* 17(4), 457–470.

Troisgros, S. (1980) Social tourism. *Annals of Tourism Research* 7(3), 487–490.

Tseng, W., Lin, T. and Yeh, E. (1995) Chinese societies and mental health. In: Lin, T., Tseng, W. and Yeh, E. (eds) *Chinese Societies and Mental Health*. Oxford University Press, Hong Kong, pp. 3–18.

Tuan, Y.-F. (1984) *Dominance and Affection: the Making of Pets*. Yale University Press, New Haven and London.

TUC (Trades Union Congress) and ETB (English Tourist Board) (1980) *Holidays – the Social Need*. ETB, London.

Tudge, C. (1991) *Last Animals at the Zoo*. Hutchinson Radius, London.

Turco, D.M., Stumbo, N. and Garncarz, J. (1998) Tourism constraints for people with disabilities. *Parks and Recreation* 33(9), 78–84.

Turley, S.K. (1999) Exploring the future of the traditional UK zoo. *Journal of Vacation Marketing* 5(4), 340–355.

Turley, S.K. (2001) Children and the demand for recreational experiences: the case of zoos. *Leisure Studies* 20(1), 1–18.

Turner, R., Miller, G. and Gilbert, D. (2001) The role of UK charities and the tourism industry. *Tourism Management* 22, 463–472.

Twyman, C. (2000) Participatory conservation? Community-based natural resource management in Botswana. *Geographical Journal* 166(4), 323–335.

UCLH NHS Trust (2003) *Looking After the Health of British Travellers*. University College London Hospitals, London <http://www.uclh.org/news/pr_21-07-03_nathnac.shtml> (last accessed 25 May 2005).

UK Passport Service (nd) *Keep Your Passport Safe While You're Away*. UK Passport Service, London.

UNDP (United Nations Devlopment Programme) (2005) *Human Development Report 2004: Cultural Liberty in Today's Diverse World*. UNDP, New York.

UNEP (United National Environment Programme) (2003) *Tourism and Local Agenda 21 – the Role of Local Authorities in Sustainable Tourism*. UNEP, Paris.

United Nations (2002) *Report of the World Summit on Sustainable Development*. United Nations, New York.

United Nations (2005) *The Millennium Development Goals Report*. United Nations, New York.

Unwin, T. (1998) Ethical dimensions of rural tourism in Estonia. Paper presented at the Ethics in Tourism Virtual Conference. <http://www.mcb.co.uk/services/conferen/jan98/eit/3_unwin.html> (page no longer active).

Upchurch, R.S. and Ruhland, S.K. (1995) An analysis of ethical work climate and leadership relationship in lodging operations. *Journal of Travel Research* 34(2), 36–42.

Urry, J. (1990) *The Tourist Gaze: Leisure and Travel in Contemporary Societies*. Sage, London.

Urry, J. (1995) *Consuming Places*. Routledge, London and New York.

Urry, J. (2000) *Sociology Beyond Societies: Mobilities for the Twenty-first Century.* Routledge, London.

Vainopoulos, R. (2004) *Choisir et Réussir ses Vacances à l'Étranger.* Ballard, Paris.

van Gerwen, L.J., Diekstra, R.F.W., Arondeus, J.M. and Wolfger, R. (2004) Fear of flying treatment programs for passengers: an international update. *Travel Medicine and Infectious Disease* 2(1), 27–35.

van Linge, J. (1992) How to out zoo the zoo. *Tourism Management* 13(1), 115–117.

van Raaij, W.F. and Francken, D.A. (1984) Vacation decisions, activities and satisfactions. *Annals of Tourism Research* 11(1), 101–112.

Vardy, P. and Grosch, P. (1999) *The Puzzle of Ethics,* 2nd edn. Fount, London.

Veijola, S. and Jokinen, E. (1994) The body in tourism. *Theory, Culture and Society* 11, 125–151.

Verbole, A. (2003) Networking and partnership building for rural tourism development. In: Hall, D., Roberts, L. and Mitchell, M. (eds) *New Directions in Rural Tourism.* Ashgate, Aldershot, UK, and Burlington, Vermont, pp. 152–168.

Verbole, A. and Mele-Petric, M. (1996) *National Action Plan for Integration of Farm and Rural Women in Development: a Case Study of Slovenia.* FAO Workshop, Wageningen, The Netherlands.

Viskovic, N. (1993) Zootourism. *Turizam* 41(1–2), 23–25.

Vitaliev, V. (1993) Pat the dog – to keep the human spirit alive. *The European* 10 June.

Vollmer, H.M. and Kinney, J.A. (1955) Age, education and job satisfaction. *Personnel* 32, 38–44.

Wachs, M. (2003) Prices and charges as a strategy for sustainable transportation. Paper presented in STELLA (Sustainable Transport in Europe and Links and Liaisons with the Americas) project (financed by EC DG TREN), 26–27 May, Quebec City.

Walker, L. and Page, S.J. (2003) Risks, rights and responsibilities in tourist well-being: who should manage visitor well-being at the destination? In: Wilks, J. and Page, S.J. (eds) *Managing Tourist Health and Safety in the New Millennium.* Pergamon, Amsterdam, pp. 215–235.

Walker, S. (1983) A comparison of the attitudes of students and non-students towards the disabled in Ghana. *International Journal of Rehabilitation Research* 6(3), 313–320.

Walle, A.H. (1995) Business ethics and tourism: from micro to macro perspectives. *Tourism Management* 16(4), 263–268.

Walls, J. (2002) British tourist killed by performing elephant. *The Guardian* 26 April.

Wang, C. (1992) Culture, meaning and disability: injury prevention campaigns and the production of stigma. *Social Science and Medicine* 35(9), 1093–1102.

Wang, N. (1999) Rethinking authenticity in tourism experience. *Annals of Tourism Research* 26(2), 349–370.

War on Want and ITF (International Transport Workers Federation) (2002) *Sweatships.* War on Want and ITF, London and New York <http://www.waronwant.org/download.php?id=71> (last accessed 26 March 2005).

Warr, P. and Wall, T. (1984) *Work and Wellbeing.* Penguin, Harmondsworth, UK.

Watson, J. (1999) Safety fears as fliers feel the squeeze. *Scotland on Sunday* 27 June.

Wayman, R. (1995) Kurds sentence tourism to death. *The European* 9 June.

WCED (World Commission on Environment and Development) (1987) *Our Common Future.* Oxford University Press, Oxford, UK.

Weale, A. (1978) *Equity and Social Policy.* Routledge & Kegan Paul, London.

Wearing, S. (2001) *Volunteer Tourism: Experiences That Make a Difference.* CAB International, Wallingford, UK.

Weatherly, K.A. and Tansik, D.A. (1993) Tactics used by customer-contact workers, effects of role stress, boundary spanning and control. *International Journal of Service Industry Management* 4(3), 4–17.

Weaver, A. (2005) The McDonaldization thesis and cruise tourism. *Annals of Tourism Research* 32(2), 346–366.

Weaver, D.B. (2003) 'Volunteer Tourism: Experiences That Make a Difference' (book review). *Tourism Review International* 7(1), 58–60.

Webster, J. (2005) *Animal Welfare: Limping Towards Eden.* Blackwell, Oxford.

Weeden, C. (2005) Ethical tourism. In: Novelli, M. (ed.) *Niche Tourism: Contemporary Issues, Trends and Case Studies.* Elsevier, Amsterdam, pp. 233–245.

Weiner, E. (1997) Assessing the implications of political and economic reform in the post-socialist era: the case of Czech and Slovak women. *East European Quarterly* 31(3), 473–502.

Wemelsfelder, F. (1997) Investigating the animal's point of view: an inquiry into a subject-based method of measurement in the field of animal welfare. In: Dol, M., Kasanmoentalib, S., Lijmbach, S., Rivas, E. and van den Bos, R. (eds) *Animal Consciousness and Animal Ethics.* Van Gorcum, Assen, The Netherlands, pp. 73–89.

Wemelsfelder, F. (1999) The problem of animal consciousness and its consequences for the measurement of animal suffering. In: Dollins, F. (ed.) *Attitudes to Animals: Views in Animal Welfare.* Cambridge University Press, Cambridge, UK, pp. 37–53.

Werner, S., Hydgin, M., Morrison, F. and Chin, J. (1976) Gastro-enteritis on a cruise ship – a recurring problem. *Public Health Reports* 91, 433–436.

Westacott, E. (1962) *Spotlights on Performing Animals.* Daniel, Saffron Walden, UK.

Wheeler, M. (1992) Applying ethics to the tourism industry. *Business Ethics – a European Review* 1(4), 227–235.

Wheeler, M. (1993) Tourism marketers in local government. *Annals of Tourism Research* 20(2), 354–356.

Wheeler, M. (1994) The emergence of ethics in tourism and hospitality. *Progress in Tourism, Recreation and Hospitality Management* 6, 46–56.

Wheeler, M. (1995) Tourism marketing ethics: an introduction. *International Marketing Review* 12(4), 38–49.

Wheeller, B. (1991) Tourism's troubled times: responsible tourism is not the answer. *Tourism Management* 12(1), 91–96.

Wheeller, B. (1993) Sustaining the ego. *Journal of Sustainable Tourism* 1(2), 121–129.

Wheeller, B. (1994a) Ecotourism: a ruse by any other name. In: Cooper, C.P. and Lockwood, A. (eds) *Progress in Tourism, Recreation and Hospitality Management,* Vol. 6. John Wiley & Sons, Chichester, UK, pp. 3–11.

Wheeller, B. (1994b) Egotourism, sustainable tourism and the environment: a symbiotic or shambolic relationship? In: Seaton, A.V. (ed.) *Tourism: the State of the Art.* John Wiley & Sons, Chichester, UK, and New York, pp. 647–654.

Wheeller, B. (2005) Ecotourism/egotourism and development. In: Hall, C.M. and Boyd, S. (eds) *Nature-based Tourism in Peripheral Areas: Development or Disaster?* Channel View, Clevedon, UK, pp. 263–272.

White, L. (1967) The historical roots of our ecological crisis. *Science* 155, 1203–1207.

Whiting, R. (2004) *Buying and Renovating a Property in France.* How To Books, Oxford, UK.

Whitney, D.L. (1989) The ethical orientation of hotel managers and hospitality students: implications for industry, education and youthful careers. *Hospitality Education and Research Journal* 13(3), 187–192.

WHO (World Health Organization) (1998a) *Antimicrobial Resistance.* Fact Sheet No. 194, WHO, Geneva.

WHO (World Health Organization) (1998b) *Emerging and Re-emerging Infectious Diseases.* Fact Sheet No. 97 (revised), WHO, Geneva.

WHO (World Health Organization) (2000a) *Hepatitis C.* Fact Sheet No. 164, WHO, Geneva.

WHO (World Health Organization) (2000b) *El Niño and its Health Impacts.* Fact Sheet No. 192, WHO, Geneva.

Wight, P. (1993) Ecotourism: ethics or eco-sell? *Journal of Travel Research* 31(1), 3–9.

Wilks, J. and Oldenburg, B. (1995) Tourist health – the silent factor in customer service. *Australian Journal of Hospitality Management* 2(2), 13–23.

Wilks, J. and Page, S.J. (eds) (2003) *Managing Tourist Health and Safety in the New Millennium.* Pergamon, Amsterdam.

Wilks, J., Pendergast, D. and Holzheimer, L. (2003) Travel agents' health and safety advice. In: Wilks, J. and Page, S.J. (eds) *Managing Tourist Health and Safety in the New Millennium.* Pergamon, Amsterdam, pp. 117–126.

Williams, A.M. and Hall, C.M. (2002) Tourism, migration, circulation and mobility: the contingencies of time and place. In: Hall, C.M. and Williams, A.M. (eds) *Tourism and Migration.* Kluwer, Dordrecht, The Netherlands, pp. 1–52.

Williams, F. and Copus, A. (2005) Business development, rural tourism and the implications of 'milieu'. In: Hall, D., Kirkpatrick, I. and Mitchell, M. (eds) *Rural Tourism and Sustainable Business.* Channel View, Clevedon, UK, pp. 305–322.

Williams, J. and Lawson, R. (2001) Community issues and resident opinions of tourism. *Annals of Tourism Research* 28(2), 269–290.

Williams, J.M. (1999) Disabled people work their way up to TV ads. *Advertising Age* 16 August, p. 30.

Williams, P. and Hobson, J.S.P. (1995) Virtual reality and tourism: fact or fantasy. *Tourism Management* 16(6), 423–427.

Wilson-Howarth, J. (1995) *Bugs, Bites and Bowels.* Cadogan, London.

Winch, V. and Watson, R. (1992) *Responsibility in Business: Decisions, Issues and Ethics: a Case-study Approach.* Hodder & Stoughton, London.

Wood, K. and House, S. (1991) *The Good Tourist: a Worldwide Guide for the Green Traveller*. Mandarin, London.

Wood, R.E. (2000) Caribbean cruise tourism: globalization at sea. *Annals of Tourism Research* 27(2), 345–370.

Wood, R.E. (2004) Cruise ships: deterritorialized destinations. In: Lumsdon, L. and Page, S. (eds) *Tourism and Transport: Issues and Agenda for the New Millennium*. Elsevier, Amsterdam, pp. 133–145.

Woodhams, C. and Corby, S. (2003) Defining disability in theory and practice: a critique of the British Disability Discrimination Act 1995. *Journal of Social Policy* 32(2), 159–178.

Woods, R.H. (1992) *Managing Hospitality Human Resources*. Educational Institute of the American Hotel and Motel Association, East Lansing, Michigan.

Wright, M. (2003) *The Virgin Travel Health Handbook*. Virgin Books, London.

Wright, P.C., Szeto, W.F. and Lee, S.K. (2003) Ethical perceptions in China: the reality of business ethics in an international context. *Management Decision* 41(2), 180–189.

WTO (World Tourism Organization) (1985) *Tourism Bill of Rights*. WTO, Madrid.

WTO (World Tourism Organization) (1997) *Tourism 2020 Vision*. WTO, Madrid.

WTO (World Tourism Organization) (2001) *Global Code of Ethics for Tourism*. WTO, Madrid <http://www.world-tourism.org/code_ethics/pdf/lamguages/Codigo%20Etico%20Ing.pdf> (last accessed 24 June 2005).

WTO (World Tourism Organization) (2002) *Tourism Highlights 2002*. WTO, Madrid <http://www.world-tourism.org>.

WTO (World Tourism Organization) (2004) *ST-EP (Sustainable Tourism – Eliminating Poverty)*. WTO, Madrid <http://www.world-tourism.org/step/menu.html> (last accessed 18 March 2005).

WTO (World Tourism Organization) (2005) *World Tourism Barometer*, Vol. 3, No. 1. WTO, Madrid <http://www.world-tourism.org>.

WTTC (World Travel and Tourism Council) (2002) *Corporate Social Leadership in Travel and Tourism*. WTTC, London.

WTTC (World Travel and Tourism Council), WTO (World Tourism Organization) and Earth Council Report (1996) *Agenda 21 for the Travel and Tourism Industry: Towards Environmentally Sustainable Development*. WTTC, Madrid.

Yamamura, T. (2004) Authenticity, ethnicity and social transformation at World Heritage Sites: tourism, retailing and cultural change in Lijiang, China. In: Hall, D. (ed.) *Tourism and Transition: Governance, Transformation and Development*. CAB International, Wallingford, UK, pp. 185–200.

Yaman, H.R. (2003) Skinner's naturalism as a paradigm for teaching business ethics: a discussion from tourism. *Teaching Business Ethics* 7(2), 107–122.

Yarnal, C. (2004) Missing the boat? A playfully serious look at a group cruise tour experience. *Leisure Sciences* 26(4), 349–372.

Yau, M.K.-S., McKercher, B. and Packer, T.L. (2004) Traveling with a disability: more than an access issue. *Annals of Tourism Research* 31(4), 946–960.

Yeung, S.Y.-C., Wong, S.C.-K. and Chan, B.M.-L. (2002) Ethical beliefs of hospitality and tourism students towards their school life. *International Journal of Contemporary Hospitality Management* 14(4), 183–192.

Young, G. (1973) *Tourism: Blessing or Blight?* Penguin, Harmondsworth, UK.

Young, K. (1998) *Seal Watching in the UK and Republic of Ireland*. International Fund for Animal Welfare UK, London.

Zagor, K. (1995) The hidden cost of bargain breaks. *The Guardian* 17 June.

Zhang, H.Q., Chong, K. and Ap, J. (1999) An analysis of tourism policy development in modern China. *Tourism Management* 20(4), 471–485.

Zimmer, Z., Brayley, R.E. and Searle, S.E. (1995) Whether to go and where to go: identification of important influences on seniors' decisions to travel. *Journal of Travel Research* 34(1), 3–10.

Zuckerman, J.N. (2004) Travel medicine and malaria – a review of the current issues. *Travel Medicine and Infectious Disease* 2(3–4), 117.

Index